Yuval Ben-Bassat is Senior Lecturer in the Department of Middle Eastern History, University of Haifa, and holds a PhD in Near Eastern Languages and Civilizations from the University of Chicago. He is the co-editor of *Late Ottoman Palestine: The Period of Young Turk Rule* (I.B.Tauris, 2011).

PETITIONING THE SULTAN

Protests and Justice in Late Ottoman Palestine
1865–1908

Yuval Ben-Bassat

I.B. TAURIS
LONDON • NEW YORK • OXFORD • NEW DELHI • SYDNEY

BLOOMSBURY ACADEMIC
Bloomsbury Publishing Plc
50 Bedford Square, London, WC1B 3DP, UK
1385 Broadway, New York, NY 10018, USA
29 Earlsfort Terrace, Dublin 2, Ireland

BLOOMSBURY, BLOOMSBURY ACADEMIC and the Diana logo
are trademarks of Bloomsbury Publishing Plc

First published in 2013 by I. B. Tauris
This paperback edition published by Bloomsbury Academic 2021

A catalogue record for this book is available from the British Library.

A catalog record for this book is available from the Library of Congress.

ISBN: HB: 978-1-7807-6457-3
PB: 978-0-7556-4359-2

Typeset by Newgen Publishers, Chennai

To find out more about our authors and books visit
www.bloomsbury.com and sign up for our newsletters.

To my beloved parents, Yehuda and Nurith

CONTENTS

LISTS OF TABLES, DISPLAY MATERIAL AND APPENDICES

Maps

Tables

Documents

Illustrations

Appendices

NOTE ON
TRANSLITERATION

The use of both Ottoman Turkish and Arabic sources in this book complicates the issue of transliterations. In general, when referring to sources in Ottoman Turkish, I have transliterated into modern Turkish. When referring to terms and proper names in Arabic, a modified system of transliteration has been adopted that eliminates under-dots on consonants and macrons on vowels and uses a representation of the 'ayn and *hamza*. Well-known terms such as *mufti*, *shari'a* and *waqf* are used throughout this book in the popular way they are known in English. The author hopes that these measures will make the text easily accessible.

With regard to dates, Ottoman documents during the period covered here used several different calendars – such as the *hicri* calendar, the Ottoman administrative *mali* calendar and, in some petitions, even the international Gregorian calendar. When converting dates from the *hicri* and *mali* calendars to the Gregorian calendar, a difference of one day can sometimes occur. In general throughout this book, when referring to a specific document several times, the full details including the dates are only given when it is first mentioned.

ACKNOWLEDGMENTS

Many individuals and organizations contributed to this project, which has taken several years to complete. I am grateful to the German-Israeli Foundation for Scientific Research and Development (GIF) for its generous support, which made the whole process much easier and more effective. Funds for various sections of the project were also provided by the Dean of Humanities, the Research Authority, and the Rector of the University of Haifa, to whom I express my gratitude.

Special thanks go to my colleagues in the Department of Middle Eastern History at the University of Haifa – Butrus Abu-Manneh, David Kushner, Amalia Levanoni, Gadi Gilbar, Uri Kupferschmidt and Fruma Zachs with whom I consulted at various stages of the project. Their advice was always helpful and timely.

My friends Ran Aaronsohn, Eyal Ginio, Johann Büssow and Avi Rubin gave me excellent feedback and meaningful comments on various sections of the project. I am grateful to Ami Ayalon and Ehud Toledano from Tel-Aviv University for their insightful comments during the early stages of the project.

At the University of Haifa, graduate students Omri Eilat, Ziv and Idan Orenstein, Aamer Marisat, Nicole Khayat and Sucina Naarani assisted me in a variety of capacities and contributed to making this challenging project a reality.

The staff of the library at the University of Haifa – and, above all, Yardena Lewenberg, Amer Karkabi and Manhal Zreik – was extremely helpful and forthcoming in facilitating all my requests and needs for the project. I am thankful to them and wish to acknowledge their contribution to this project.

In Turkey, I would like to thank the staff of the Istanbul branch of the American Research Institute in Turkey (ARIT), where I stayed during my visits to the archive. The hospitality and assistance of Toni Greenwood, Gülden and the other members of the staff made the trips to Istanbul a wonderful experience. In this city, for their advice and guidance, I would also like to thank the staff of the Ottoman archive at the *Başbakanlık Devlet Arşivleri*, where most of this research was carried out. Finally, in Istanbul, I would like to thank my friend Muharrem Varol from Marmara University with whom often I consulted about my work.

Esther Singer deserves special thanks for her careful editing of the book. Tammi Soffer also deserves many thanks for preparing the maps for the book. I would also like to express my appreciation to Maria Marsh from I.B.Tauris Publishers who oversaw the project and who responded to my needs and concerns quickly and efficiently.

Finally, I would like to thank my wife Shira Offer and my lovely daughters Adva and Noga for all their support, patience and understanding throughout this long journey.

INTRODUCTION

"Because on top of the vergi tax we are asked to pay a fifth of our income, the rich people in our village have become totally destitute and they need alms, and for the same reason some of the people from our village have abandoned their place of birth and fled to other lands. Therefore, we beg you to save us from this miserable and gloomy situation."

The villagers of Sarafand al-ʿAmar in a petition
to the Grand Vizier, 1879

About this Book

This book aims to explore petitions, *arzuhal*s,[1] sent by Ottoman subjects in Palestine to the sultan and his representatives in Istanbul through officials and functionaries between 1865 and 1908. Using textual analysis, it examines the interactions between the two parties, their envisioned moral worlds, and the dialogue between them. The study of these petitions provides a window on the nature of the age-old Ottoman institution of petitioning the ruler at this time, and the transformations it underwent over the course of the nineteenth century.

Concomitantly, these petitions and their associated official correspondence provide a unique opportunity to explore developments in Palestine, a small Ottoman territory which, although it has attracted the attention of modern scholars, is only infrequently studied on the basis of Ottoman sources and the Ottoman perspective on events. This approach is particularly important as regards the end of the nineteenth century where the roots of the unresolved Jewish–Arab conflict are to be found. Notwithstanding the fact that the loyalty of the vast majority of Palestine's population at the time was undoubtedly to the sultanate and not to national ideologies, to date this conflict still shapes, if not to say distorts, the historiography of late Ottoman Palestine.

The institution of petitioning the Ottoman sultan by the Empire's subjects was not a unique Ottoman invention. In fact, mechanisms for petitioning the ruler have existed in many societies since writing was invented. Influenced by the empires around them with which they came into contact, the early Islamic empires incorporated the institution of petitioning the ruler into the Islamic world where it took on its own special characteristics.

Unlike the claim made by some researchers, and despite major differences with the "classical" Islamic institution of *mazalim*, the Ottomans inherited the institution of petitioning the ruler, attributed great importance to it and made broad use of it at both the provincial and imperial levels. As the head of the state, the source of its legitimacy and the embodiment of its just rule, the sultan was always willing to accept petitions by commoners who thus circumvented the regular procedure in the *kadı* court, where they would normally apply for justice. Petitioning Istanbul was in some cases a form of appeal system against decisions taken by *kadı*s in the provinces.

Given the massive legal, bureaucratic and administrative reforms in the Empire, the modernization and standardization of the state apparatus and the availability of modern technology, was there still a place for the 'archaic' centuries-old institution of petitioning? After all, the Empire's subjects had many other avenues readily available and closer to home to resolve many of the matters raised in the petitions, such as the branches of the various state bureaus, the reformed *shari'a* courts, the newly-established *nizamiye* courts which operated in several instances or (with regard to certain issues) even the administrative councils in the provinces that operated on several tiers.[2] What was the point of appealing directly to the sultan in faraway Istanbul, at times without even trying to pursue other alternatives first? Was the goal of petitioning at all the same as in previous centuries? Or, should it be considered a new institution given its goals and the way it operated?

Various elements related to these questions will be discussed throughout this book, based on a selection of petitions from Palestine at the end of the nineteenth century that I was able to locate in different sections of the Ottoman archives. In all, I examined some 500 petitions, and although it is impossible to provide firm and meaningful statistics for the entire collection of petitions from this period, as discussed below, roughly 65 percent of these petitions were submitted by the urban population, about 15 percent by the rural population, and some 5 percent by Bedouin groups. The remainder was submitted by Ottoman officials, foreigners residing in Palestine, Jewish colonists, and the like.

Petitions are a historical text that must be read critically and interpreted with great caution, perhaps even more so than other texts.[3] Nonetheless, the study of petitions allows us to explore state–subject relationships, their moral worlds, and the social order they support. One of the main claims made in this volume is that in the period discussed the institution of petitioning the Ottoman ruler, while definitely a continuation of a time-honored imperial and Islamic tradition, concomitantly witnessed considerable transformations that reflected the changing circumstances in the Empire, the nature of the reforms and modernization in the nineteenth century, and the availability of new means of communication and transportation which considerably reduced the previous limitations and barriers of geography. Thus, although it did not constitute a new phenomenon, the traditional institution of petitioning the Ottoman imperial center was nevertheless adapted to fit the *zeitgeist*. Furthermore, in some cases it even became more relevant than before for subjects who could not find redress in the reformed judicial-bureaucratic system, as well as for political purposes.

By using the mail and the newly introduced telegraph, Ottoman subjects in the nineteenth century had unprecedented access to Istanbul and were able to contact the imperial center easily and quickly over the head of the local authorities in the provinces. They could raise their concerns and grievances, demand justice and follow up the decision making process and implementation of decisions taken on the ground including sending variations of the same petition a number of times. In the words of Roderic Davison "the essence of the telegraph was the annihilation of distance, the divorce of communication from transportation, the emphasis on speed."[4]

With the progress of the reforms, the Ottoman sultans of the period, for their part, ruled over a centralized bureaucratic state, unlike the prevailing situation in most preceding centuries.[5] Compared with past practices, the nineteenth-century sultans from the time of Mahmud II (r. 1808–39) onwards were absolute rulers, despite the gradual loss of Ottoman territories in regions such as the Balkans and the semi-independent status of regions such as Egypt.[6] This new reality affected the institution of petitioning the ruler in the sense of preserving its value despite the reforms which, at face value, were expected to undermine and diminish its importance, if not make it completely obsolete. In such a situation, the sultans continued to be perceived as the ultimate address for justice and the entity that could receive petitions and provide redress in the most effective way.

For the sultans at the time, the institution of petitioning served as yet another means of centralization and control that allowed them to balance local nuclei of power, monitor the activity of the bureaucracy and the local authorities in the provinces and gather valuable information about their conduct. In other words, despite the reformed nature of the state and the improved division of labor between its institutions, the long-lasting Ottoman mechanism of petitioning the sultan still served to strengthen the ruler's position vis-à-vis the lower echelons of the administration and the bureaucracy and make clear who possessed ultimate authority, especially in the case of a suspicious and paranoid sultan such as Abdülhamid II (r. 1876–1908/9). This sultan even established a special office called the *Maruzat-ı Rikâbiyye Dairesi* in the Yıldız Palace to handle petitions, and his representatives continued the age-old practice of collecting petitions from subjects during Friday prayers and on religious holidays,[7] despite Abdülhamid's fears of assassination.[8]

Even more importantly, as in previous periods and in the spirit of Islamic tradition of the 'just ruler,' the institution of petitioning also continued to be a means to reinforce legitimacy and portray the sultans as just and benevolent rulers who cared about the well-being of their subjects, while diverting possible criticism of their conduct towards various intermediaries in the chain of command between the ruler and the ruled. This is nicely phrased by John Chalcraft in his analysis of petitions sent to the Khedive in Egypt by peasants in the 1860s and 1870s. Despite considerable differences with the Ottoman Empire – under whose jurisdiction it remained *de jure* – Egypt also went through a process of centralization under an absolute ruler from a dynasty that enacted an ambitious modernization plan of reforms:

> Petitions were addressed to the khedive or his ministers, who were depicted as the embodiment of justice and order and acclaimed as merciful, compassionate, benevolent, glorious, mighty, and worthy of a long life. Such high-flown praise was not just the flattery of simple-minded and fawning peasants. These salutations in part

simply reflected the demands of protocol and applied not just to peasants but also to merchants and even – one might say, especially – to high-status officials addressing the khedive. At another level, however, they performatively affirmed peasant loyalty to the khedive and ensured that all social transgressions were seen as stemming from corrupt intermediaries of one kind or another. This trope was so powerful that peasants were able to use it to criticize all but the highest reaches of government [...]. In other words, the discourse of the "Glorious Ruler" sought to project the notion of an alliance between the khedive or minister and his flock. The discourse reiterated also the public myths enunciating and reaffirming the bargain between ruler and ruled, in which subordinate and powerful alike held stakes.[9]

The Ottoman political system was by no means as rigid as the that developed under the khedives in Egypt, and its subjects had more leeway and mechanisms to find redress and achieve justice. As in Egypt, however, the petitioners endeavored to incorporate references to a benevolent, just and glorious Ottoman ruler, thus underscoring an alleged contract between the ruler and the ruled. Nevertheless, the sultan and the petitioners did not necessarily share the same aims. Whereas the subjects sought justice according to their own terms and understanding which would grant them rights and protect them against various kinds of injustice, real or perceived (often there was no genuine legal basis for their complaints), the ruler mainly sought legitimacy and stability.[10] The need to bolster legitimacy in the Empire at the time, both internally and internationally, heightened the importance of the institution as a way to garner public support.[11]

At the same time, the greater accessibility of Ottoman subjects to the imperial center and their growing interaction with state agencies, which gradually penetrated many aspects of their lives and in the eyes of many had ceased to be an amorphous, ill-defined entity, heightened the people's expectations for redress from the state.[12] This is apparent in the numerous petitions on a very wide array of topics that flooded the system. These developments also raised the petitioners' hopes that the sultan would hear their pleas. Not surprisingly, their frustration and disappointment intensified when their pleas were not answered, orders were ignored, or verdicts were not implemented. Thus, often, subjects sent angry telegraph after telegraph to Istanbul claiming that they had yet to receive an answer despite repeated approaches. They often insisted that the sultan could not let certain acts continue unabated because they contradicted Islamic and imperial laws. Other missives argued that the sultan and the Empire's interests were at stake and were jeopardized through judicial inaction. Consider the plea of villagers from the *kaza* of Gaza who, in 1891, asked the Grand Vizier to lower the rate of the *vergi* (land) tax (see Appendix 4):

> It is known to your highness that the mercy and compassion of the ruler, may God save him, is given to all the dominions of the Empire and does not discriminate one over the other, but encompasses all. Is it possible that the just rules and orders will let us continue to suffer from this injustice and unfairness? [. . .] We have nothing else to do in this situation but to contact your gates of justice with a request to receive your mercy and the benevolence of our exalted state.[13]

Versions of this petition were sent to Istanbul by mail and telegraph at least four times in the course of 1891, since the villagers were not satisfied with the answers they received (or worse, did not receive at all).

Particularistic Versus Imperial Histories: The History of Palestine as Part of Ottoman History

At the end of the nineteenth century, Palestine did not constitute a separate geo-political entity or a recognized well-defined national state, as is often erroneously implied or assumed in research. Above all, it was an integral part of the Ottoman territories, a region with shifting administrative borders (see Map 1).[14] Nevertheless, Palestine's history during this period is rarely examined from an Ottoman perspective even though Ottoman sources will have been used. Similar to other cases of national historiographies in some of the dozens of states inheriting the areas previously ruled by the Ottoman Empire, especially in their formative classical periods, the history of Palestine is still mostly examined through the paradigms, frameworks, and periodizations set by the national discourses and analysis is greatly influenced by later national and political agendas.[15]

Hence, the year 1882 is usually defined as the point of departure for analysis, and later events are interpreted as stemming from and relating to this point.[16] "Classical" Zionist historiography, for example, largely views the course of events from 1882 onwards in a teleological sense as inevitably leading to the creation of a separate Jewish national entity in Palestine in 1948, and tends to examine events retrospectively and interpret them as stages along an allegedly linear path of development (the various *'aliyot* – waves of 'ascendancy'; i.e., immigration to *Eretz Yisra'el*).[17] Conventional Arab and Palestinian historiography also tacitly accepts the importance of 1882, and often treats the unfolding of political events in Palestine in the twentieth century, particularly the *nakba* (literally catastrophe, the Palestinian term used to designate their defeat in the first Arab-Jewish war) in 1948, as the inevitable outcome of developments that began during the late Ottoman era. Thus, the sources are read retrospectively in light of nationalist narrations.

As a consequence, the Ottoman era is often described in both historiographies as a period of oppression led by a corrupt regime that consistently violated national rights. Zionist historiography, for instance, focuses on Ottoman restrictions on Jewish immigration and colonization activity in Palestine, which are considered sheer repudiation of the Jews on the part of the Ottoman authorities. By contrast, Arab historiography often argues that the Ottomans, by allowing Jewish immigration and settlement activity to materialize in the first place, were responsible for the initiation of the conflict in Palestine.[18]

Moreover, studies on Palestine during the late nineteenth century for the most part tend to focus on political, ideological and diplomatic dimensions,[19] and research predominantly concentrates on urban elite groups, especially when examining Arab responses to Zionist activity. With notable exceptions, analyses of the social, cultural and economic dimensions and their intricate ties to contemporary developments in the Empire at the time are few and far between.[20]

Moreover, due to the overemphasis in research on the subsequent development of the Jewish–Arab political conflict in Palestine, especially during the Mandate period and onwards, analysis of processes and developments taking place during the late Ottoman era have been marginalized and in many cases only serve as a prelude to considerations on other matters. Hence, the Ottoman era is often summarized in a brief introduction or a historical overview chapter based on Western secondary sources and simply serves as background information for the discussion of other topics and later periods.[21]

This approach does not fully account for the historical context in which the proto-Zionist[22]-Arab encounters unfolded and treats events as isolated from earlier complex social and economic processes that had lasting influence at both the local and imperial levels. Ongoing processes whose roots predate the beginning of proto-Zionist colonization in 1882, and that were related to broader developments taking place in the Ottoman Empire at the time (such as the efforts to achieve better centralization and governmental control over the state's resources, reorganize the bureaucratic and legal systems, register ownership of land and reorganize the tax collection system) had a crucial influence and ramifications on the development of relationships between the two communities. The same is true for the Ottoman administration of the regions comprising Palestine and the government's position on the question of the Holy Land, particularly with regard to foreign involvement there.

Moreover, examining the Ottoman perspective of the events makes it possible to expand the debate beyond its customary confines, while negating some of the most common arguments (and stereotypes) in the national historiographies and bypassing the dominant paradigms and periodizations they perpetuate. Such an approach can be used to delve into frequently neglected bureaucratic, social and economic issues, as well as the question of center–periphery relationships, which all have considerable bearing on later events in Palestine. It also serves to better contextualize and situate the discussion by embedding it into its larger (Ottoman) imperial setting.

In this regard, this volume, by examining petitions, official correspondence and other archival Ottoman sources, pursues a dual agenda. First, it presents a bottom-up examination of developments in Palestine at the end of the nineteenth century, from the period preceding proto-Zionist activity in the early 1880s to the turn of the century. Second, it strives to situate events in their larger Ottoman imperial setting and the existing literature on the changing Empire and its institutions. By doing so, it adopts a perspective which is often lacking in the particularistic research on Palestine at the end of the nineteenth century.

New Sources for the Study of Palestine at the End of the Nineteenth Century

Even today, most research on Palestine during the late Ottoman period remains largely based on various European or Jewish/Zionist sources[23] whereas the Ottoman and Arabic material available to researchers is much more rarely used.[24] Aside from the dominance of historiographies connected to and based on these sources, as discussed above, in part this state of affairs also had to do with the real shortage of primary sources in Arabic about the history of many regions in Palestine during the late Ottoman period. This can be attributed to the fact that the rural Arab population of Palestine was mostly illiterate and left little written evidence behind for future generations,[25] the destruction of hundreds of Arab villages in the war of 1948 and the dispersal of their populations, and the lack of organized Palestinian national archives to date.[26]

One field of research on Palestine that has developed considerably in the last few decades, and one that provides a unique perspective on Ottoman society at the end of the nineteenth century by using sources in Arabic and in Ottoman Turkish, is the study of the *sicill* records of the *shari'a* courts. Nevertheless, it should be recalled that the *sicill*s mainly reflect the atmosphere, whereabouts, and norms of urban society, whereas the representation of the rural population in the *shari'a* courts was relatively limited.[27] Moreover, by the end of the nineteenth century, after the implementation of a series of extensive legal and administrative reforms in the Empire, these courts increasingly dealt with family and personal matters,[28] whereas criminal cases and civil and commercial matters were for the most part referred to the *nizamiye* courts[29] and, in specific instances, to the administrative councils in the provinces.[30]

Research based on primary materials located in the Ottoman archives can thus serve in many ways as a complement to the study of the *sicill* records.[31] Linguistic difficulties and the question of access to these sources impeded such work on a large scale in the past, but the difficulty posed by these two problems has diminished in recent years with greater accessibility to archives in Turkey and the training of a new generation of scholars who have the skills to utilize the historical treasures found there.[32]

Using sources from the Ottoman archives helps better integrate events and processes in their broader Ottoman context while detaching the researcher from national paradigms and their implicit research frameworks.[33] It facilitates comparative research regarding other parts of the Empire on issues such as policies concerning questions of immigration and settlement in the Empire, the effects of land reforms and penetration of foreign capital, the notion of justice and the prevalence of petitioning, and similar key questions. These sources also provide a refreshingly new outlook on events and can complete the picture gleaned from other materials, as well as close existing information gaps, particularly regarding Palestine's understudied rural population.[34]

Finally, these sources help clarify a whole range of administrative, social and economic issues that traditional sources only deal with tangentially. For instance, much can be learned about these matters from using understudied documents in Arabic and, more often, in Ottoman located at the Ottoman section of the prime ministerial archives in Istanbul, the *Başbakanlık Osmanlı Arşivi*, the world's largest Ottoman archive. Of great interest are the collections of the Ministry of the Interior (*Dahiliye Nezareti*), the Ministry of Foreign Affairs (*Hariciye Nezareti*), Yıldız Palace (*Yıldız Sarayı*), the Council of State (*Şûra-yı Devlet*) and the various registrars of imperial decisions (*irade*).[35]

As previously mentioned, this book is largely based on petitions written in Arabic and Ottoman submitted to the central Ottoman government by all segments of the population in Palestine, as well as official correspondence between Ottoman officials and functionaries regarding the concerns raised in the petitions, the appropriate response, and the decisions rendered. The petitioners, urbanites (both Muslim and non-Muslim), villagers and Bedouins alike, as well as Ottoman officials serving in Palestine, and even foreign nationals and Jewish settlers, complained about such varied topics as unjust treatment and abuse of power by government officials and notables, the tax burden, dispossession, allegedly illegal changes in the status of land, misconduct by officials, new measures taken by the government, unjustified punishment of office holders, various moral issues, the conduct of rivaling individuals or coalitions, and even personal quarrels and business disputes. Tracing the petitions and the way they were handled in Istanbul and locally in Palestine is thus a valuable tool for exploring some of the issues discussed above.

The Ottoman central archives also house other sources such as official correspondence between Ottoman officials and functionaries dealing with Palestine, either directly or indirectly, which sheds light on Ottoman attitudes regarding developments there, as well as various bureaucratic and administrative dealings. This correspondence provides a basis for comparison of the case of Palestine to the general policies of the central government on issues such as immigration and settlement activity in the Empire, European activity in Ottoman territory, center–periphery relations, the implementation of Ottoman reforms, policies towards non-Muslim minorities and the holy places and the like.

Periodization

This volume deals with the period between 1865 and 1908, 43 years covering the rule of the Ottoman Sultans Abdülaziz (r. 1861–76) and Abdülhamid II (r. 1876–1908/9). It is based on petitions and associated official correspondence sent from the sub-districts of Gaza and Jaffa in the *mutasarrıflık* of Jerusalem. The year 1865 was chosen as the starting point of this periodization since it marks a change in the type of documents from Palestine preserved in the Ottoman archives. First, petitions began to be sent by telegraph and mail to Istanbul in massive quantities (the telegraph first began to operate in Palestine in the mid-1860s).[36] In addition, in 1864 the new Provincial Law (*Teşkil-i Vilayet Nizamnamesi*) was approved, which introduced a new phase of reforms with far-reaching implications in the Ottoman provinces.

The archives preserve considerably fewer petitions from Gaza and Jaffa before the mid-1860s, and these tend to be different from later petitions. Since the Ottoman institution of petitioning Istanbul operated continuously, the archives may very well still house undiscovered petitions from the period preceding the mid-1860s. However, the combination of new means of communication and transportation and the administrative and bureaucratic changes at both the local and imperial levels, which gradually reached the Empire's provinces, make it plausible to assume that a real quantitative, as well as qualitative, change took place in the 1860s.

The year 1908, on the other hand, marks the end of Abdülhamid's actual rule and, in fact, the end of effective rule by the Ottoman sultans. Interestingly, however, this did not mean the end of the institution of petitioning the imperial center, although naturally it took on new characteristics, a topic that goes beyond the scope of this study.

One of the advantages of this periodization is that it starts well before 1882 and the initial proto-Zionist–Arab encounters that have skewed research and periodization of late Ottoman Palestine so greatly. Another advantage is that by the early 1860s the Ottoman government had almost totally regained control over Palestine's hinterland, about two decades after the end of the occupation of this territory by the forces of the Egyptian Khedive Muhammad 'Ali. Various hotbeds of autonomy and resistance under local leaders, such as in Galilee and in the mountains of central Palestine, had been subdued.[37] Thus, the Ottomans could start thoroughly implementing their reforms in earnest in this part of the Empire. Finally, the *mutasarrıflık* of Jerusalem was established in 1872, a development that many researchers justifiably perceive as crucial in the process of shaping a unique local Palestinian identity.[38] Much can be learned by examining the nature of petitions from regions within that district's jurisdiction before and after this administrative change. Moreover, the fact that there are so many petitions from the *kaza*s of Jaffa and Gaza – perhaps even more than from the city of Jerusalem itself, where the district headquarters were located, as well as from this city's surroundings – makes this comparison even more informative and promising.

The Geographic Region Examined

The petitions analyzed here were sent from the sub-districts (*kaza*s) of Jaffa and Gaza in the *mutasarrıflık* of Jerusalem, on the central and southern Palestine coast, respectively (see Maps 2 and 3). In the 1880s, the two coastal towns of Jaffa and Gaza had some 18,000 and 10,000 residents, respectively.[39] Jaffa was Palestine's major port and its main gate to Europe from the mid-nineteenth century. Thus it went through a rapid process of expansion, modernization and development, including settlement of foreigners (Templers, European Jews, Egyptians and others) in and around the city and the inauguration of numerous new infrastructure projects.[40] The planting of numerous citrus groves in the vicinity of Jaffa spurred the town's quick development and led to an exponential rise in exports from the port. The growing economic activity in and around the town is reflected in many petitions, and apparently the economic boom led to growing friction concerning various matters such as tax collection, registration of land, concessions and the like.

Gaza, on the other hand, lost its prominent position as the leading economic center on Palestine's southern coast in the second half of the nineteenth century and largely remained outside the massive development and expansion processes experienced in Jaffa. It still remained a very important regional center for its agricultural hinterland and for the Bedouin population, as well as the hub of a number of main roads, including the pilgrimage route from Egypt to the holy places in the Hejaz, but had a relatively marginal importance in terms of connections with Europe and the other provinces of the Ottoman Empire, other than the

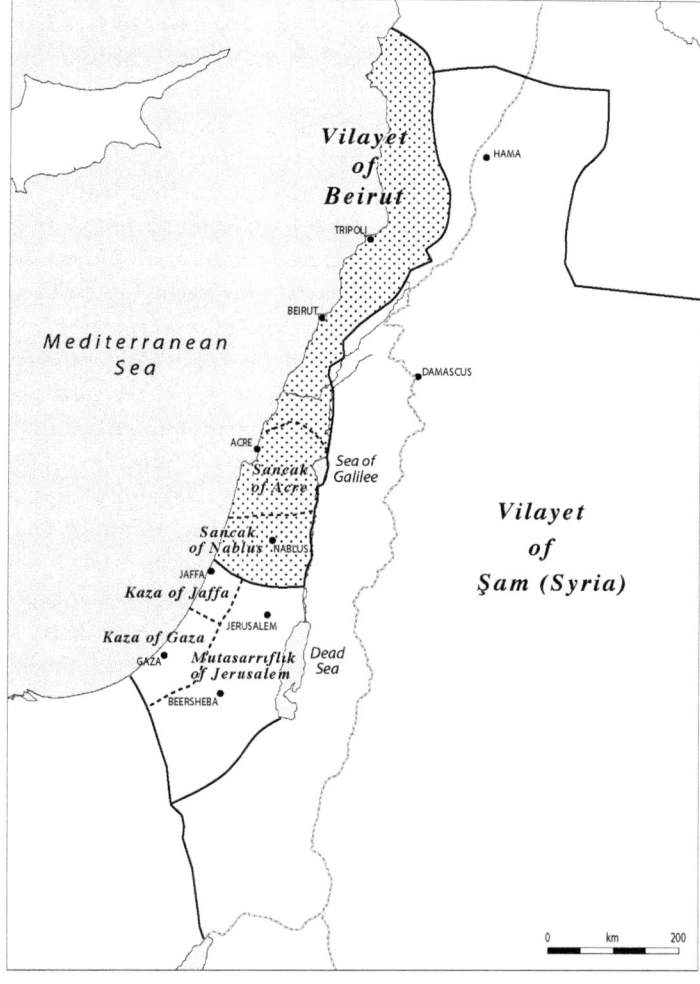

Map 1 The *Mutasarrıflık* of Jerusalem at the End of the Nineteenth Century

profitable grain trade with England.[41] Gaza, as portrayed in the petitions, was the seat of very strong intra-communal struggles over positions and local influence.[42]

Excluding its southern part, most of the region examined was not heavily populated in comparison with other regions in Palestine, such as the central mountain range.[43] Its western part, along the Mediterranean shore from Jaffa to Gaza, consisted of dunes and did not include permanent settlements (see Maps 2 and 3). A few larger villages and towns such as Ramle, Yibna, Isdod and al-Majdal were located on the fringes. The heart of the region was home to dozens of small to moderate-sized villages, consisting mostly of mud brick buildings, whose sources of livelihood were a combination of grain farming and subsistence agriculture.[44] Plantations were located mainly on the outskirts of the towns (oranges, olives, dates).

Some villages in the area were ancient and some even appeared in Ottoman tax lists dating back to the sixteenth century.[45] Others, however, were settled by Egyptian immigrants, who reached Palestine over the course of the nineteenth century.[46] These newcomers were poorer than the other villagers, usually did not own land but rather worked as tenants, and were viewed with contempt by the rest of the rural population who refused intermarriage.[47] Some Egyptians also settled in poor neighborhoods (*saknat*) established in the outskirts of Jaffa.[48]

Besides villages, several small semi-sedentary Bedouin groups who did not possess title deeds to the land where they grazed or resided were present in the area. Eventually, some of them went through a process of sedentarization.[49] The southern part of the region was exposed to occasional migration by Bedouin groups from the Negev desert that caused great damage to agricultural crops on their way north. Bedouins appeared in petitions either as the subject of complaints by the sedentary population or, more rarely, as petitioners.

A dozen or so absentee landlords owned estates in the region, mostly in the vicinity of Jaffa and south-east of the town, but less so further south, where a handful of local families from Gaza held large estates.[50] At times these absentee landlords, often Christians from nearby Jaffa, established mansions in the center of their agricultural fields, although in most cases their permanent residence was in nearby towns.[51] As many issues concerning landownership still remained contested at the time, and given their prominent status and capabilities, these absentee landowners often appear

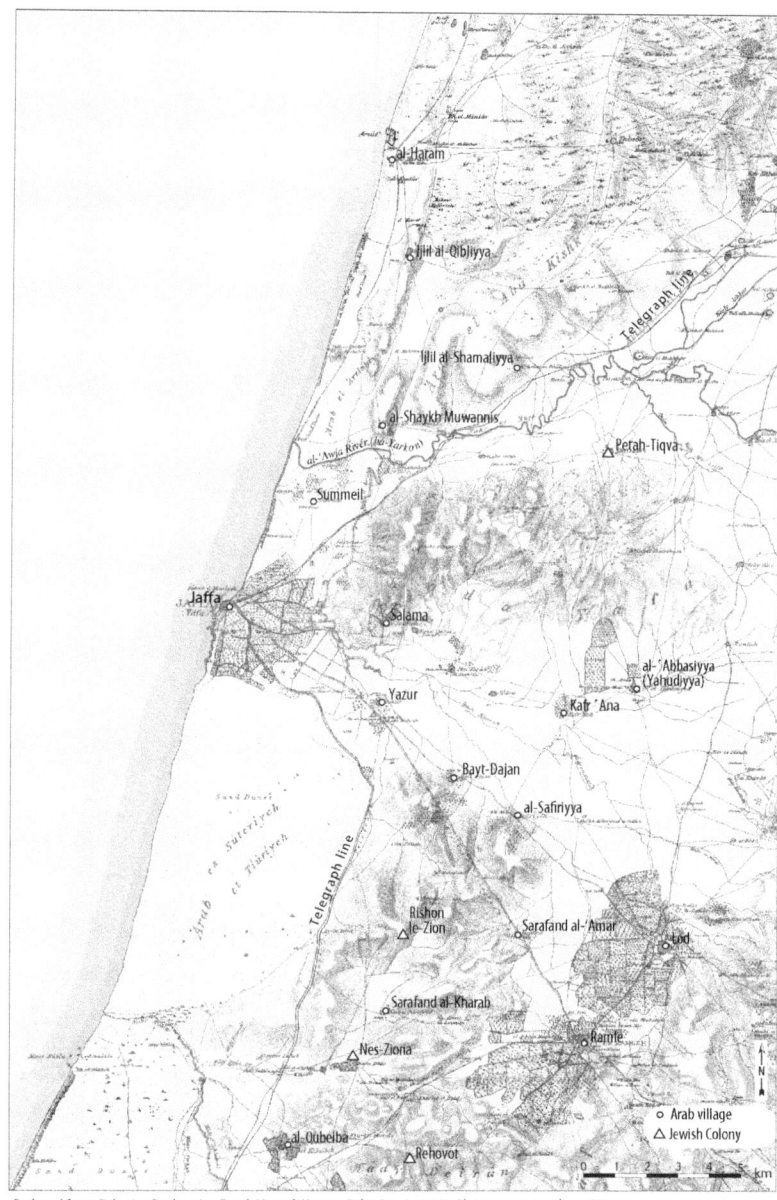

Reduced from: Palestine Exploration Fund. Map of Western Palestine, 1:63,360, Sheets 10,13, London, 1880

Map 2 Arab Villages and Jewish Colonies in the *Kaza* of Jaffa, 1882–1908

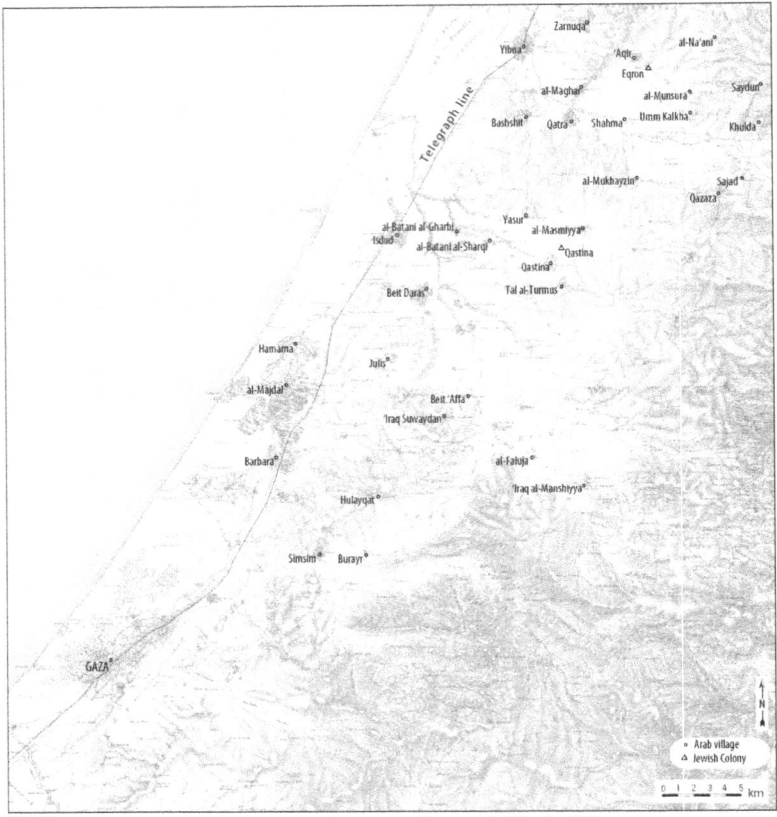

Reduced from: Palestine Exploration Fund. Map of Western Palestine, 1:63,360, Sheets 13,16, 19, 20, London, 1880

Map 3   Arab Villages and Jewish Colonies in the *Kaza* of Gaza, 1882–1908

in petitions, for the most part as petitioners, but sometimes also as those accused of various manipulations and misdeeds.

Many sources indicate that a considerable part of the land in the Arab villages in the region studied was held commonly (*musha'*), although it is not clear whether an annual redistribution of the plots, as in the classical system of *musha'*, indeed took place. The *musha'* system continued to exist even at the end of the Ottoman era despite attempts to abolish it.[52] In the petitions discussed here, however, *musha'* lands are not mentioned very often.

With regard to proto-Zionist activity in the region, Jaffa emerged at the end of the nineteenth century as a leading center of the "new *yishuv*" and its Jewish population increased increased rapidly. In addition, several Jewish colonies, known as the Judean colonies (*moshvot Yehuda*), were established south-east of Jaffa between 1882 and 1890, and a few others after the turn of the century, turning it into the area with the most intensive Jewish colonization activity in Palestine at the time. The importance of the Judean colonies stems not only from their number, but also from the relatively large size of the colonies, their close proximity to each other, and the leading role they assumed in the development of the "new *yishuv*" and its institutions. To a large extent, the Jewish colonies established in that period laid the foundations for future expansion of Jewish agricultural settlement in Palestine. Hence, their significance for understanding Jewish–Arab relationships is tremendous. The Jewish colonization activity appeared in petitions from time to time, both those submitted by the local population, as well as by the colonists themselves, but not on a massive scale.

A Brief Overview of this Volume

Chapter 1 discusses the institution of petitioning the ruler as a global phenomenon, in the Islamic world and specifically in the Ottoman Empire. This institution, which had pre-Islamic roots, was incorporated into the early Islamic Empires and its existence was anchored in Islamic political thought and the notion of the 'just ruler.' The Ottomans made vast use of this institution from the onset of their rule and, under their aegis, it went through various transformations over the years, reflecting not only Islamic tradition, but also the nature of the Ottoman state, its definitions and self-perception. This chapter also discusses the nature of the institution of petitioning the sultan in light of the massive reforms throughout the nineteenth century.

Chapter 2 discusses technical issues concerning the petitions such as their archival location today, the addressees, the identity of the petitioners and the concerns raised in the petitions, language and the usage of stylistic formulas and leitmotifs, methods of sending the petitions, and the intermediary of professional petition-writers. The chapter lays the groundwork for the content analysis presented in subsequent chapters.

The subsequent chapters provide a historically-based content ana-lysis of the petitions and a discussion of key issues they raise. Chapter 3 discusses petitions by the urban population, mainly from the towns of Jaffa and Gaza. It illustrates the huge variety of topics raised in the peti-tions submitted by the urban population to Istanbul, the personal and group interests represented in these petitions and the different concerns of the people in Jaffa compared with those of Gaza.

Chapter 4 focuses on petitions concerning the rural population, as well as the Bedouins who operated in the region. These two overwhelmingly illiterate groups, which composed the majority of Palestine's population at the time, made vast use of the institution of petitioning the ruler. The chapter provides a first-hand glimpse at the actions, concerns and dynamics of these two subaltern populations which are underrepresented in the literature, especially in the case of Palestine. The petitions by the rural population shed light on its relationships with the Ottoman authorities and with the urban population, whose influence on Palestine's hinterland increased during this period. Finally, the rural petitions indicate the exist-ence of regional networks and various modes of cooperation among the villagers, which have received scant attention in the literature thus far.

Chapter 5 examines petitions sent by Ottoman officials and function-aries serving in Palestine, mainly those who were not local residents of this land. These officials petitioned Istanbul not only regarding personal matters, but also about matters concerning the Empire's interests and the situation in Palestine.

Chapter 6 discusses various social and economic issues raised in the petitions such as inter- and intra-communal conflicts, moral issues, business disputes, the effects of tax and agrarian changes and the like. At a time of tremendous social and economic change in the Empire, and in Palestine particularly, the institution of petitioning the ruler was well adapted to a great variety of topics and reflected the growing visibility of the state in the daily lives of its subjects, increased state regulation of many facets of the subjects' lives and the latter's expectations for redress. Moreover, to an unprecedented extent the institution of petitioning Istanbul became a political tool at the hands of its subjects to engage in negotiations with the imperial center.

Chapter 7 examines the conduct of the Ottoman bureaucracy as reflected in the petitions, and the attitudes and moves of the authorities in the imperial center, including the transfer of the petitions to professional bureaus, the decisions taken, the role of intermediaries, the definition of corruption, referral to *nizamiye* and *shari'a* courts and the like. The petitions demonstrate the Ottoman bureaucracy's dual role at the time and the incomplete nature of its transformation. On the one hand, it went through major transformations and modernization in the course of the nineteenth century and acted as a modern, effective bureaucracy. However, on the other hand, it maintained many of its previous paternalistic features, as exemplified in the functioning of the petitioning system itself as an extra-judicial mechanism with political overtones.

Chapter 8 focuses on petitions concerning the Templers and proto-Zionists, two groups of Europeans who settled in Palestine during the period discussed. In many respects the Templers' activity was a forerunner (on a small scale) to the Zionist colonization project which followed roughly a decade later, a fact which is reflected in the similar nature of the petitions sent to Istanbul by the colonists themselves, as well as by the local population who complained about the colonists' activity. In contrast to the small-scale German activity, proto-Zionist activity has received considerable emphasis in the historiography of late Ottoman Palestine. This chapter, however, reveals that the nascent proto-Zionist activity was far from being the local population's main concern, as opposed to the growing Ottoman interest and opposition to Zionist activity which was expressed in official correspondence.

The concluding chapter brings together the insights gleaned throughout this book. Its main goal is to assess whether the institution of petitioning the Ottoman sultan at the end of the nineteenth century was simply a continuation of former practices adjusted to the *zeitgeist*, or whether it differed completely from former practices. It evaluates the uniqueness of the petitions from Palestine in comparison with other regions in the Empire and shows what can be learned from them about state–subject relationships at the time, namely whether these petitions were the forerunners of modern public opinion.

CHAPTER 1

THE OTTOMAN
INSTITUTION OF PETITIONS
TO THE RULER IN GLOBAL
AND ISLAMIC PERSPECTIVES

This chapter is designed to place the institution of petitioning the sultan in the Ottoman Empire in its global, Islamic and Ottoman contexts. First, it briefly discusses the global phenomenon of petitioning the ruler, the purpose of these petitions and their rationales. Then, it presents several Islamic versions of this institution, as a prelude to examining the petitioning system in the Ottoman Empire. Finally, it presents the operation of the Ottoman petitioning system, its historical development up to the reform era in the nineteenth century, the role of the sultan, the mechanisms for submitting petitions to the imperial center and the main changes it underwent during the time of the reforms.

Petitions as a Global Phenomenon

The institution of petitioning the ruler is not a unique Islamic or Ottoman invention. It has existed in many societies throughout history, even thousands of years ago, in fact since writing was invented.[1] In the words of Lex Heerma van Voss, "writing petitions was a common human experience".[2] Moreover, there are cross-cultural influences among different civilizations with regard to the operation of this institution and surprisingly similar patterns of submitting petitions exist in places far removed from each other on the globe.[3]

Complaints against abuse of power and special requests, two fundamental reasons behind petitioning, can also be found in the Bible after the Israelite tribes had adopted a form of central government, a monarchy. For example, in Kings II 8: 1–6 there is a story of a woman whose land was taken from her after she had abandoned it for seven years while she was elsewhere. She approached the king with a request to get her land back and be granted ad hoc justice despite her absence, which legally deprived her of her rights over the land.

There are also examples of petitions in archaeological findings. In the well-known *Mesad Hashavyahu*[4] ostracon that dates to the seventh century BC a peasant appeals to an unknown ruler for redress, claiming that a local tax collector impounded his garment unlawfully:

Let my lord, the governor, hear the word of his servant!
Your servant is a reaper.
Your servant was in Hazar Asam
and your servant reaped
and finished
and he has stored (the grain) during these days
before stopping.
When your [ser]vant had finished the harvest,
and had stored (the grain) during these days,
Hoshaiah came, the son of Shobai,
and he took the garment of your servant,
when I had finished my harvest.
It (is already now some) days (since) he took the garment of your servant.
And all my companions can bear witness for me
– they who reaped with me in the heat of the [harvest] –
yes, my companions can bear witness for me.
Amen! I am innocent from gu[ilt].
[Do give back] my garment,
so that I may be vindicated!
It is incumbent upon the governor to give ba[ck the garment] of [his] serva[nt!].
[And sh]ow pi[ty] on him!

[And you should he]ar the [word] of your [servant]
and you should *be silent* [. . .]!."[5]

In this particular case, the element of abuse of power as well as the
peasant's awareness of his rights are noteworthy. Throughout history,
petitioning the ruler was one of the main forms of recourse subjects had
at their disposal to appeal for justice. Although the generic title "petition"
covers various types of approaches to a higher authority, several typical
patterns can be found across civilizations and eras.[6] A petition can be
broadly defined as a plea that subjects submit to a ruler to authorize
steps in an extra-judicial manner that bypasses or supersedes the regular
justice system when all other avenues have been exhausted or are believed
to be devoid of utility. For the most part, but not always, appeals concern cases of abuse of power by lower ranked officials and institutions.
Petitions could also include requests for pardon, conversion, special monetary allowances and the like. Petitions, however, are not merely a judicial
tool, as political aspirations are intrinsic to them. Thus, common people
often used the right of petitioning as a political tool to secure their rights
by manipulating the system in their favor.

There is an ongoing debate among scholars regarding how to read
petitions as historical texts. Repetitive patterns and motifs that appear in
the petitions are not necessarily an indication that they should be looked
upon merely as literary compositions with fictional and rhetorical variants rather than as valid historical texts. Historians who are skeptical
about the documentary nature of petitions often refer to them merely as
rhetorical constructions or literary *topoi* written within specific complex
social systems. The historian Natalie Zemon Davis, for example, in her
book *Fiction in the Archives* which deals with remission letters submitted
in sixteenth-century France in cases of the death penalty, argues that the
decision whether to pardon people was actually made in a process that
had little to do with what was written in the petitions.[7] Although judges
went over these petitions, petition-writers wrote them in a way which
would serve those who a priori had very good chances of being pardoned.
Davis focuses on the fictional aspects of these pardon requests, which
might mislead modern historians who are unaware of the greater latitude
afforded to the petitioners to explain their circumstances and determine
the course of justice.[8]

J.E. Shaw takes a somewhat different approach to petitions. In his view, petitions:

> [A]ppear to offer a genuine insight into the mentality of suppli-cants. Yet this was not so much a 'voice' as a discourse, shaped by prevailing norms, institutions, and power structures. The voice of supplicants was typically mediated by anonymous clerks, lawyers, and notaries, whose role was to present the story so as to achieve the desired result.[9]

In fact, in most cases petitions were not written by the petitioners themselves, who usually were illiterate, but by professional petition-writers in return for a fee. These writers had the technical and legal skills to for-mulate these often flowery and highly codified texts. There were even manuals for petition-writers that explained how to write various kinds of petitions, depending on the nature of the appeal and the addressees.[10]

The aims of different petitioning systems across time and civilizations are also surprisingly similar. Petitioning the ruler enabled subjects to "let off steam," to feel that someone was attuned to their distress and suffer-ing and to initiate a hopefully meaningful dialogue with the ruler which otherwise would have been impossible given the imbalanced power rela-tionship between them. For the ruler, it was an efficient way to take the pulse of developments on the ground, to maintain a semblance of open channels of direct communication with the subjects and to monitor the scope of activity of the bureaucracy. After all, bureaucrats were always suspected of misconduct, misrepresentation and pandering to the ruler. Hence, the petitioning system was crucial for the ruler to glean infor-mation on their stratagems and regulate institutions that, although subordinate to him, gave the elites considerable leeway, which under cer-tain conditions could be used to challenge his authority.

Moreover, the institution of petitioning the ruler allowed the latter to divert criticism from himself in cases of corruption, misbehavior, misdeeds and immoral behavior, and place the blame squarely on the shoul-ders of intermediaries. It also shifted possible anger and frustration away from the ruler and contributed to his image as a just and benevolent sovereign who cared about the well-being of his subjects and rewarded them in kind. The flip side of this institution, however, was the ruler's moral obligation to fulfill the expectations of his subjects. Failing to find a solution to his subjects' complaints could fuel resentment and even lead to rebellion and tarnish the image he had so carefully cultivated.

Petitions in the Islamic World

Mechanisms to handle grievances of commoners against institutions and officials existed in the ancient East before the rise of Islam, such as in the Sasanid Empire.[11] The Byzantine Empire also had an equivalent institution.[12] To a large extent, the *mazalim* court – the classical Islamic institution which addressed grievances submitted by subjects to the ruler and his representatives concerning injustices done to them by officials – can be seen as a continuation of this procedure,[13] which is not a surprising development given that the early Islamic Empires incorporated a non-Muslim majority and were greatly influenced by the civilizations of the region. Many earlier judicial institutions carried over and were furthered by the Muslims' familiarity with Mesopotamian, Byzantine and Persian norms, even if they did not rule over a centralized state at the beginning.[14]

The Islamic thinker whose writing had the greatest influence on the Sunnite perception of the just ruler and the functions of the *mazalim* courts was al-Mawardi (d. 1058). His book *al-Ahkam al-Sultaniyya* (Ordinances of Government) is considered one of the best expressions of the classical Sunni theory of governance.[15] Al-Mawardi cites ten main types of cases heard in the *mazlim* courts which can be broadly split into two categories: abuse of power by officials and the enforcement of decisions made by a *kadı* court:

[1] oppression and maltreatment of the public by the government officials [. . .]
[2] the remuneration due to public officers for the taxes collected [. . .]
[3] the secretariat of government departments, who have the responsibility for keeping exact records of what Muslims must pay and what they must be reimbursed for [. . .]
[4] complaints concerning the inadequacy of pensions, delay in issuing them, or bad treatment of the recipients [. . .]
[5] restoration of usurped property [. . .]
[6] the monitoring of endowments [. . .]
[7] the implementation of sentences when judges are too weak to enforce them due to the sentenced person's power or social stand-ing [. . .]

[8] investigation of such matters of public welfare as the flaunting of reprehensible behaviour, assaulting passers-by, or other infringements that public morals officers are unable to deal with [. . .]

[9] ascertaining that such public acts of worship as the Friday prayers, the Feasts, the pilgrimage, and military duty are performed [. . .]

[10] settlement of quarrels and disputes in accordance with what is right and lawful, never contravening legal practice.[16]

Moreover, al-Mawardi specifies in great detail how the *mazalim* court should operate:

> A person delegated as a magistrate to look into torts should proclaim that he has set a certain day for petitioners and adversaries to make their appeals, reserving the rest of the week for other matters of policy and administration assigned him, unless he is appointed exclusively to perform this function [. . .]. There are five classes of persons who are indispensable and must all be present for the session to be valid and for action to proceed. These comprise: first, guards and lieutenants to subdue the strong and chasten the bold; second, judges and administrators to provide information on established rights and how they deal with litigants; third, jurists to be consulted on problematic issues and asked to clear ambiguities and other sources of obscurity; fourth, clerks to record what goes on between opponents and decisions made for or against them; and fifth, notaries to witness the decisions taken. Once the magisterial council is complete with these five categories of officials attending, business could be started.[17]

Al-Mawardi, however, did not introduce the institution of *mazalim* to the Islamic world, but rather conceptualized its operation in a period when the caliphate faced the invasion of the Seljuks and its existence was threatened.[18] In the words of Ann Lambton, he wanted "to give a legal exposition of the theory of government speculatively derived from the basis of theology and to set out the formal basis of government so that the ruler, knowing his rights and duties, might fulfill the charge laid upon him."[19] Jørgen Nielsen argues that al-Mawardi's theory was "formed at a particular stage in the history of the Islamic state [. . .] as part of a development which turned out to be an aberration in the course of Islamic history." He adds that this theory has been overestimated by his successors, as well as by modern scholars.[20]

Be this as it may, clearly, judiciary authority was initially an integral part of political Islamic authority. The Prophet Muhammad was invited to Yathrib as a judge and was asked to rule according to Arab tribal norms. The judicial aspects of the newly established Islamic community were agreed upon by Muhammad's successors, *al-khulafa' al-rashidun*,[21] and the early Islamic Empire was based on this tradition. Hence, for example, one of the obligations of provincial governors at that time was to serve as judges. Later on the growth and development of the Islamic bureaucracy led to a separation between the actual judicial authority, the *kaza* (in Arabic: *qada*), the main part of the judicial system, and the symbolic representation of the caliph as the guardian of the *shari'a* and the source of justice. From then on, there was no longer a complete overlap of the political and judicial systems, a situation which created an inherent tension between the state and the regular judicial system. The focal point of this tension was often the *mazalim* courts.

Al-Mawardi claims that the *mazalim* institution was introduced into the Islamic world by the Umayyad Caliph 'Abd al-Malik bin Marwan (r. 685–705).[22] Nielsen, however, insists that the *mazalim* was founded as an Islamic institution only under the Abbasids. At any rate, the operation of the *mazalim* courts remained a constant source of tension between the caliphs and their bureaucracy, on the one hand, and the judiciary apparatus, on the other.[23] To a certain extent the *mazalim* courts became a governing tool at the disposal of the rulers in everyday practices of ruling and assisted the subjects in dealing with cases of bureaucratic abuse of power. *Mazalim* courts were also used by the caliphs to increase their power at the expense of the judicial system and the *kadi*s.[24]

During the Abbasid period, the "classical" period of the Islamic *mazalim* system, the *mazalim* courts dealt with petitions concerning injustice and the abuse of power and office by officials, in addition to appeals of decisions made by *kadi*s,[25] which led some scholars to argue that *mazalim* courts actually served as a court of appeal.[26] The petitions were not exclusively submitted to the ruler; they could be submitted to his senior representatives, provincial governors, senior army officers and others.[27] Often, however, the authority signing decisions regarding a petition was the ruler or a senior representative acting on his behalf, and there was no direct connection to the bureaucratic chain of command where the decision was made. The functionaries and officials who received the petitions discussed them in an organized way which was supervised by the bureaucracy.[28]

An important question in this regard is whether the *mazalim* courts can be perceived as a secular institution. In spite of the political overtones of the *mazalim*, the fact that caliphs were monarchic rulers with a claim to possess divine legitimacy should not be ignored. Moreover, *kadi*s were often asked to participate or even to head *mazalim* sessions to provide legitimacy to the judgment.[29]

In fact, the development of the *mazalim* courts was inherent to centralized governments led by absolute monarchs. It embodied the ruler's political need to regulate the power of institutions over commoners and to prevent abuse of power. It also enabled rulers to execute policies in a way that evaded *shari'a* restrictions as, for instance, in the case of double sales to overcome the prohibition to charge interest.[30] The advantage of the *mazalim* over other types of courts was its ability to accept evidence and documents, as well as provide a means of investigation which the *shari'a* courts and the *kadi*s rejected.[31] It acted as a meeting ground between politics and religion and made it possible to ease the latter's restrictions.[32] In the words of Schacht, "the very existence of these administrative tribunals, which were established ostensibly to supplement the deficiencies of the qādīs, shows that at an early period, much of the administration of justice through the qādī had broken down."[33]

The end of the "classical" Islamic institution of *mazalim* came about under the Seljuks. Nonetheless, the famous Seljukid vizier Nizam al-Mulk still perceived it as the duty of the sultan to head the *mazalim* court,[34] although in practice under the Seljuks it was usually the vizier who headed *mazalim* sessions.[35] In later periods other variations of the institution were created and continued to operate.[36] Moreover, the different variations of the *mazalim* institution in the mediaeval Islamic period went through a process of "increased bureaucratization," as will be discussed below.[37]

Under the Mamluks in Egypt, for example, there was an overlap between the system of *mazalim* and the regular Islamic judicial system, which led to a power struggle between the sultanate and the courts. Although *kadi*s were legally involved in decisions in the *mazalim* courts, the sultans strove to reduce their authority.[38] Moreover, some researchers go as far as to argue that, under the Mamluks, the Mongol *yasa* started to play a role in some cases involving Mamluks, whereas the ordinary people were still judged according to the *shari'a*, but this claim is largely rejected today by most scholars.[39] This controversy notwithstanding, there was a clear tendency by the sultans to acquire judicial power and autonomy at the expense of the *shari'a* courts.

In the second half of the thirteenth and the fourteenth centuries, under the *Bahri* Mamluks, the earlier tie between the *dar al-'adl* (Hall of Justice), the court where *mazalims* were heard, and the system of *mazalim* was weakened substantially, and it mostly became a secondary activity of the *dar al-'adl* which dealt with a whole array of regular governmental and bureaucratic matters.[40] Moreover, abuse of power was not the only or even the main reason for the submission of petitions at the time. Rather, the *mazalim* courts handled all sorts of petitions, including requests for fiefs, protection and allocation of state resources, *waqf*s, trade, rituals and theology and the like.[41]

The Notion of Ottoman Justice and the Role of the Sultan

The Ottoman Empire, from its establishment as a border principality in north-west Anatolia at the end of the thirteenth century and throughout its history, was headed by a male descendant of the House of Osman, bearing the title of Sultan, who constituted the state's legitimating symbol and source of identity. As a just Islamic ruler, the sultan's duty was to "command good and forbid evil" and to ensure that justice, *adalet*, was rendered to the Empire's subjects, particularly as regards the tax-paying subjects, the *reaya*, on whom the whole structure of the state depended.

The ruling Ottoman elite, the *askeri*, which included not only military men in the limited sense of the word, but also senior bureaucrats and *ulema*, was considered part of the sultan's extended private household and was thus subject to special sultanic regulations and to a legal system.[42] Christians and Jews, the 'people of the book' who remained within the Empire's borders, were not forced to convert. Instead, they enjoyed a great measure of autonomy in running their own communal affairs, as long as they acknowledged their secondary status and paid the special poll tax, *cizye*, which concretized this reality, and also adhered to a few other, mostly symbolic, restrictions placed upon them.

As heads of state, the source of its legitimacy and the embodiment of its just rule, the sultans set up a mechanism that allowed their subjects to complain directly to the imperial center about injustices done to them. By so doing they were upholding the Islamic institution of petitioning the ruler and were always willing to accept petitions by commoners who wished to circumvent the regular procedure in the *kadı*'s court, to which they would normally turn for justice.[43] The function of the institution of petitioning the ruler was consistent with the structure of the Ottoman Empire as a patrimonial society, in which the sultan was considered the "father" of his subjects and was personally responsible for their welfare.[44] It was also consistent with the notion of the "Circle of Justice" which the Ottomans adhered to and adopted as part of their ideological system.[45]

Subjects' Means to Protest and Demand Justice

What avenues were available to Ottoman subjects to plead for justice to alleviate their plight? As recent research has shown, the workings of the Ottoman Empire were far removed from the typical literary depictions of "oriental despots" who ruled with an iron hand over their heavily taxed subjects who had no legitimate way to voice their protests over certain policies that violated their best interests, depictions which were very common in descriptions of the Empire in the West, even in modern scholarship until a few decades ago.[46] In fact, throughout Ottoman history, Ottoman subjects, particularly the tax-paying *reaya*, had various direct and indirect means at their disposal to protest, express their dissatisfaction, and demand justice and redress for their concerns.[47] As Suraiya Faroqhi argues, some of these activities were political in nature, although these were not officially acknowledged as such by state ideology.[48]

One of the most common reactions to the heavy tax burden, the encroachments of tax collectors and other officials, or impending conscription, particularly among the rural population, was simply to run away.[49] Massive abandonment of their land by peasants threatened the stability of the Ottoman state since it weakened not only the tax base on which the edifice of the Empire depended, particularly its vast army, the most important pillar of rule, but also the elaborate bureaucracy and the imperial court.[50] In addition, it undermined the legitimacy of the Empire headed by the sultan because it portrayed it as unjust, disdainful of the plight of its subjects, and as violating the notion of Islamic justice which it had embraced as its guiding ideology. As a last resort, as a drastic means to convey its dissatisfaction, the peasants could also revolt, a step that was breached in various provinces throughout Ottoman history, for the most part due to a combination of factors and developments and not merely one simple cause.[51]

The most readily available way for Ottoman subjects to attempt redress throughout Ottoman history (until the establishment of *nizamiye* courts in the last quarter of the nineteenth century) was to approach the local *kadı* in a nearby town, the authority delegated by the state to maintain justice and enforce *kanuni* and *shariʿa* laws. However, subjects could also send a petition to the imperial center through the *kadı* of the *shariʿa* court in the nearby town or send a representative or delegation to Istanbul to submit the petition in person.[52] As recent research has shown, petitions could also be submitted to the governor of the province, who held special *mazalim* sessions similar to those held at the imperial level but on a local basis, with the participation of the local *kadı*.[53]

Towards the end of the Ottoman era, with developments such as the expansion of journalism and printing, the renewal of parliamentary and political activity (albeit limited and partial), the introduction of new means of communication and transportation, and the spread of modern secular education and various liberal ideas, more modern methods of protest and demanding justice emerged, particularly in the Empire's urban centers. These included demonstrations, strikes and public gatherings, boycotts, seizure of government buildings, letters to newspapers, pamphlets, and various other political or semi-political activities.[54] These signified the rising importance of public opinion at the time. Thus, given the variety of methods available at the disposal of the Ottoman subjects to demand justice and redress, it is worth examining why petitioning the sultan remained so pervasive throughout Ottoman history.

The Characteristics of the Ottoman Institution of Petitions

As has been mentioned, the institution of petitioning the Ottoman sultan by the Empire's subjects has very deep historical roots which go back as far as the Empire's early days.[55] The Ottomans attributed it great importance and made broad use of it both at the provincial and imperial levels, although it changed considerably in comparison with past practices and the way it operated in its Islamic classical and later forms, as noted above. In a sense, the *mazalim* system continued to operate under the Ottomans and the claim that they did not continue this practice needs to be reconsidered.

Theoretically, every Ottoman subject, even the simplest peasant in the most remote province, had the right to submit a petition to the sultan and beg for justice, in person, through a representative, or by sending a petition. The *Divan-ı Hümayun* (Imperial Council – later during the reform period in the nineteenth century the Council of State, *Şûra-yı Devlet*) discussed the complaints.[56] Matters of lesser importance were addressed to the Divan of the Grand Vizier.[57] Petitions were also discussed at the provincial level in special sessions called *meclis-i şer* which were headed by the local governor, with the participation of senior officials and the local *kadı*.[58]

Even though the main purpose of the Ottoman institution of petitioning the sultan was to serve the mass of taxpaying subjects, in practice, those who submitted petitions were often subjects with considerable means at their disposal who possessed the knowledge and ability to deliver the petition to Istanbul, and knew how to use their influence and connections in the Ottoman capital to make sure their concerns were attended to, and later could also control whether steps had been taken pursuant to their claims. Moreover, given the limitations of geography and the limited means of travelling, appearance in person at the sultan's court was easier for people who lived relatively close to Istanbul or close to the main routes taken by sultans and viziers during campaigns.

As a way to give more weight to the petition and since sending a representative or a delegation to Istanbul was often a process that was expensive and complicated, in many cases petitions were written in the name of a collective group of people (*arz-ı mahzar*) and not by individuals.[59] This had another advantage, given that petitioners were often afraid of recriminations from those cited as wrongdoers in their claims,[60] especially in areas and during periods when central control was weak and to a large extent every region was autonomous.

Frequently, the petitions were appeals against a decision handed down by a *shari'a* court in one of the towns in the provinces. In these cases the petitioners usually did not ask for a retrial and reconsideration of their case based on the same facts, but rather claimed that they did not receive a fair trial, that earlier imperial orders and decisions had not been implemented, that there was some flaw in the judicial process and the like.[61]

Petitions were also used in the Ottoman Empire in an institutionalized way to ask for special favors from the sultan, for example by newly converted Muslims who applied to receive monetary allowances and jobs (*kisve bahası*, literally "clothing allowance").[62] In other cases petitions were regularly used to protest over-taxation and corruption by tax collectors,[63] or in order to receive restoration permits for minority places of worship.[64]

In response to petitions referred to it, the Imperial Council or a handful of other senior office holders in the central government issued a sultanic degree (*ferman*), in the name of the sultan.[65] The *ferman* was sent to the province, to the office holders or parties concerned and registered in the *sicill*s of the local *kadı* in the *shari'a* court.[66] Often, the *ferman* was given to the petitioner on the spot upon submitting the petition,[67] and he was in fact the one who delivered it to the *kadı* in his district for registration purposes and for future reference. When executive power was needed to carry out the stipulations of the *ferman*, the governor or other senior military officers in the region were addressed alongside the *kadı*, who had no enforcement capabilities at his disposal.[68] Aside from registering the *ferman* in the *sicill*s, the *kadı* also had to make sure that the decisions in the *ferman* were sent to the local bureaus and functionaries responsible for its implementation, verify that they were indeed carried out and notify the petitioners about the decision taken by the sultan, so that they could have the decision in their personal records in case the same problem or a similar one arose in the future.[69]

In the imperial center itself, from the mid-seventeenth century onwards, responses to petitions were inscribed in separate volumes called *Şikâyet Defterleri*, "Registers of Complaints," whereas beforehand they were simply written in the "Registers of Important Affairs," *Mühimme Defterleri*.[70] This practice continued until the early nineteenth century and stopped in 1813.[71] The fact that, as of the nineteenth century, petitions submitted were no longer registered in one place in the Ottoman bureaucracy makes it almost impossible to obtain reliable statistics on petitions from this period such as their actual numbers, their senders, requests made, treatment of the petitions or addressees. The petitions and the associated correspondence on the way they were handled are housed in several places in the Ottoman archive. Thus, further research may uncover other petitions among the collections.

The Ottoman Institution of Petitions under the Ottoman Reforms

At the end of the nineteenth century, after several decades of reforms and efforts at modernization in the Ottoman Empire which was gradually taking on the characteristics of a modern bureaucratic state, it made sense to assume that the importance of the traditional institution of petitioning the ruler would decrease considerably if not vanish completely and give way to other means of pursuing justice and redress from the state, its representatives and institutions. In the words of Avi Rubin:

> [T]he passage of Ottoman law to modernity in the nineteenth century did not result in a complete disappearance of this centuries-old pact between the ruler and his subjects. However, justice increasingly came to be defined in terms of procedural standards and universality of judicial practice.[72]

Among the legal-administrative reforms that should have affected this trend were the establishment of *nizamiye* courts in several instances in the Empire's provinces and their differentiation from the *shari'a* courts which were also reformed, the codification of the Ottoman civil law starting in 1869 and throughout the 1870s based on the *shari'a* (the *Mecelle*), the establishment of modern style state bureaus with branches in the Empire's provinces, and the operation of administrative councils in the provinces in several instances. Despite the existence of the reformed Ottoman institutions and the real change in the nature of the Ottoman state, the numerous petitions sent to Istanbul from the provinces at this time (in fact, in growing numbers) suggests that the institution's role and importance did not diminish. Apparently, it took on new importance and went through a process of revival and transformation due to both technological progress, as well as more fundamental institutional, bureaucratic and legal changes.

Technological Changes

The introduction of the telegraph to the Empire in the mid-1850s played a major role in the transformation of the petitioning system. The telegraph had a tremendous influence on Ottoman society, economy and politics. As noted by Davison, the advent of the telegraph greatly affected factors as varied as the control of the center over the provinces, the Empire's technological progress, law, trade, infrastructure, language, the press and information distribution.[73] Other researchers such as Yakup Bektas emphasize the role of the telegraph in achieving centralization:

> The real value of the telegraph to the Ottoman Empire [...] was demonstrated when it developed into an effective device for the centralization of power. Before railways or telegraphy it was impossible for the sultan and his officials to exercise effective control over the most distant provinces. [...] It became an even more powerful political tool during the long reign of Sultan Abdul Hamid II (1876–1909), who ruled autocratically for thirty two years. Under his rule more than 30,000 kilometers of lines were built, extending the system to remote corners of the Empire. [...] The telegraph played a vital role in extending Abdul Hamid's authority. His internal network of spies and secret agents depended mostly on telegraphic correspondence. Their reports were sent directly to the telegraph office established in the Yildiz Palace, the sultan's favorite residence.[74]

Davison mentions almost in passing that the telegraph allowed the Empire's subjects to send petitions to the central government, thus circumventing limitations of geography and long distances. His main argument in this regard, however, is that the telegraph allowed Ottoman subjects to contact foreign bodies with requests to put pressure on the Ottoman government:

> The telegraph operated further as a check on local authorities because citizens could wire their grievances to the central government. Individual and group petitions seeking remedies are not unusual among Ottoman documents. This facility had, however, one side effect deleterious to the central government, as individuals or groups could also appeal by wire to representatives of foreign powers to

support them against some act of Ottoman authorities. Minority peoples were most likely to use this channel.[75]

The first part of Davison's claim, however, is much more crucial here. Although the introduction of the telegraph was carried out with other goals in mind in the mid-1850s, within a short span of time the accessibility of the Empire's subjects to Istanbul, at a time of comprehensive reforms in the Empire, completely transformed the relationships of the Ottoman subjects in the provinces to the state. Hence, petitions to Istanbul became much more important than the subjects' ability to exert pressure by approaching foreign consuls. For the first time they enjoyed real direct contact with the center without geographical and physical barriers and the need to use intermediaries. Even when residing in the Empire's most remote provinces, they could now quickly and easily have direct contact with the central government above the heads of the bureaucracy and the local authorities. It eliminated the need to travel personally to Istanbul, send a representative there, or complain through the local *kadı*. All one had to do was to get to the nearest post and telegraph office (which were located in all the major towns of the provinces, and gradually also in small towns), write the petition with the help of professional petition-writers (*arzuhalcis*) in return for a fee, pay the required transmission fee, which was not tremendously expensive (see Tables 1 and 2), and send the petition to its destination in Istanbul.[76] Bektas described the effects of this process in detail:

> Pashas were dismissed or transferred in response to public telegraphic petitions. Further, citizens in remote parts of the empire saw the telegraph as a way of connecting to the sultan's palace directly. Believing their complaints would not be properly conveyed because of the bureaucracy and inefficiency of local administration, groups of people in many towns [. . .] marched to the telegraph stations in unruly crowds and demanded to be put into direct communication with the sultan.[77]

Bureaucratic and Legal Changes

Aside from new technology and means of transportation, broader processes and transformations expanded the nature of the petitions sent by the Empire's subjects as a whole. The reforms of the nineteenth century led

Table 1   Prices of sending Telegraphs from Palestine, 1895/6

Europe	
Country/City/Colony	Price (in francs) 1895/1896
Austro-Hungarian Empire	0.46
Italy	0.48
Algeria	0.67
Germany	0.55
Bulgaria	0.38
Belgium	0.60
Bosnia and Herzegovina	0.38
Great Britain	0.76
Gibraltar	0.69
Denmark	0.60
Netherlands	0.60
Western Tripoli	0.96
Greece	0.38
The Cyclades	0.42
Luxemburg	0.60
Malta	0.69
Morocco	0.83
Montenegro	0.38
Norway	0.72
Serbia	0.38
Portugal	0.69
France	0.56
Romania	0.43
European Russia	0.72
Asian Russia	—
Sweden	0.69
Swiss	0.51
Spain	0.65
Tunisia	0.67

The Rest of the World	
Country/Colony	Price (in francs) 1895/1896
Australia	11.44
USA	2.45
Bukhara	—
Bushehr	1.20
Brazil	8.325
India	3.23
Zanzibar	—
New Zealand	12.89

Table 1 Continued

The Rest of the World	
Country/Colony	Price (in francs) 1895/1896
Hejaz	—
Hina	8.89
Transvaal South Africa	—
Java	6.89
Japan	[?].89
Malaka	[?].14
Minnesota	3.00
Manitoba	3.10
Mississippi	2.75
Macao	9.39
Egypt (department a)	1.00
Egypt (department b)	1.25
Egypt (department c)	1.50
Siam	—
Sumatra	6.89
Singapore	6.33
Aden	—
Philippines	—
Persia	—
Sri Lanka	—
Cyprus	—
Penang	5.39
Persia	1.35
Chile	3.48
British Columbia	3.40
Columbia	2.65
Cap of Good Hope	—
Korea	15.69
Kushanshin (Indo-China)	5.39
Yemen-Hejaz	3.50
Yemen	—

Source: Luncz, Abraham Moshe, *Lu'ah Eretz-Yisra'el li-Shnat Hatarnav, Shana Rishona* (Eretz-Israel Almanac for 5656, the First Year) (Jerusalem, 1895/6) [in Hebrew].

Note: The price of a telegram was calculated according to the rate per word as well as a constant price, which was equivalent to the price of five words. The price per word inside Greater Syria was 20 standard *para*, in other parts of the Empire 40 *para*, which was one piaster or *kuruş*. Prices to other parts of the world were generally fixed according to distance. Petitions to external destinations were paid in francs.

Table 2   Comparative Cost of sending a Telegraph in the mid-1890s

Item	Price
Telegram from the District of Jerusalem to Istanbul	5 *kuruş* +1 *kuruş* per word
Price of a letter (writing and sending), up to 15 grams, within the Empire	2.5 *kuruş*
Regular train ticket from Jaffa to Jerusalem	25 *kuruş*
Man's robe in the Jaffa market	21 *kuruş*
Crate of oranges in the Jaffa market	22.08 *kuruş*
Donkey in the Jaffa market	130 *kuruş*
Monthly salary of a primary school teacher (1890s)	150 *kuruş*
Monthly salary of a government official (1890s)	450–500 *kuruş*
A Rotel* of Honey in Sefad (1890s)	36 kuruş
A Rotel of Sugar in Sefad (1890s)	16 kuruş
A night in a luxury hotel in Jaffa (1887)	6 francs (=35–40 kuruş)
Transport (by camels) fee for 1 ton/km in Jaffa (1890s)	1.25 kuruş

Sources: Büssow: *Hamidian Palestine*, p. 564; Luncz: *Lu'ah Eretz Yisra'el li-Shnat Hatarnav*, p. 19; Avitsur, Shmu'el, *Daily Life in Iretz Israel in the XIX Century* (Tel-Aviv, 1972), pp. 287–8 [in Hebrew].
Note: *2.564–2.885 kg, depends on the region within Palestine

Note: It can be seen that petitioning the sultan through the telegraph was an affordable procedure, all the more so in comparison with the official and unofficial prices of approaching the judicial system such as the *nizamiye* courts. Rubin, for example, in his book *Ottoman Nizamiye Courts* (p. 106) writes that "According to the official tariff in 1879 that regulated attorney's fees, clients had to pay their lawyers 50 *kuruş* for the first 150 words in an appellate petition, and an extra 10 *kuruş* for any additional 100 words. Each plea in court cost the client another 60 *kuruş*. In addition, court users had to be able to pay for a wide range of judicial fees in accordance with the official tariff. Further expenses caused by travel and loss of workdays should be considered as well." Nevertheless, petitioning via telegraph was still not very cheap. Based on the price of a telegram to Istanbul (which was the price for every telegram within the Empire and outside Greater Syria), petitioning could cost no less than 30–40 *kuruş*, similar to the cost of a major purchase. The cost of a single petition might also explain the frequent use of collective petitions by marginal populations, such as peasants and Bedouins. Their standard of living, it must be emphasized, was much lower than that of the urban subjects and the financial burden is more difficult to estimate since their economy was in part based on non-cash transactions. Interestingly, the period from the mid-1860s to World War I was an era of relatively very stable prices within the Empire.[78]

to greater centralization and gave unprecedented strength to the sultans as never before in Ottoman history.[79] The Tanzimat reformers tried – and succeeded only partially – to restrict the sultans' power by introducing new measures that guaranteed the right to life and property. There were also attempts to introduce a European style constitution and a parliamentary regime in 1876, but these were short-lived and were not reinstated before the Young Turk Revolution of 1908.

The reforms and the state's efforts to achieve greater centralization in the Empire led to much greater interference on the part of the state in its subjects' lives. The state started penetrating areas which it had previously neglected, partially or completely (e.g., the census, conscription, registration of lands, tax surveys and tax collection, education, health, the election of *muhtar*s who were part of the bureaucracy and so on).

Concomitantly, its acts and the changes it brought about encouraged its subjects to act more like citizens of a modern state (*tebaa*) and not merely as an undifferentiated mass of unrecognized subjects (*reaya*), despite the long reign of Abdülhamid II in the last quarter of the nineteenth century. The subjects increasingly expected the state to provide redress for their concerns and regulate a growing number of aspects in their daily lives, as reflected in their petitions.[80] Not surprisingly, the right of petitioning was even anchored in the first short-lived Ottoman Constitution of 1876, where it is stated that petitions would be referred to the appropriate Ottoman bureaus or to the parliament for consideration. In the section on the "Right of Petition," it was stated that "one or more persons of Ottoman nationality have the right to present petitions in the proper quarter relating to the breaking of law and regulation, done either to their own or public detriment, and may likewise present in protest signed petitions to the General Ottoman Assembly, complaining of the conduct of state servants and functionaries."[81]

However, had the short-lived parliament addressed petitions, this naturally would have contradicted the essence of the institution of petitioning the ruler as the head of an absolutist regime. Since the first Ottoman Parliament was dissolved by Sultan Abdülhamid II soon after it was convened and did not reconvene before the Young Turk Revolution its task of responding to petitions became a moot issue. And yet, as Hakan Karateke writes, "The idea that the sultan should not rule his lands with absolute and unquestionable power, but must be a servant of his people, was consonant with the norms of constitutional monarchy that became prevalent during the nineteenth century."[82]

The massive number of petitions from the provinces to the center in Istanbul must be considered in light of the transformations discussed above. Petitions were sent to the imperial center concerning almost every issue affecting the local population, large or small, by individuals or groups who either preferred not to go through the regular reformed legal and administrative channels or the province's chain of command, or used this mechanism alongside parallel venues of legal action as a means to manipulate the system in their favor.

A similar process apparently took place in Egypt at the time, *de jure* an Ottoman province, *de facto* an autonomous province under the ruling house of Muhammad 'Ali. Chalcraft writes the following about petitions by the rural population of Egypt to the khedive in the 1860s and 1870s:

> Mehmet Ali's dynasty building in Egypt centralized state power and built up a bureaucracy but continued to admit petitions on similar grounds as his predecessors. [. . .] [T]he central state increasingly served as a regulator of intermediaries in the countryside, and its growing presence arguably presented a political opportunity to peasants with local grievances. Numerous petitions were submitted throughout the 1860s and 1870s to the government.[83]

Thus, the Egyptian dynasty imitated the traditional age-old Ottoman institution of petitioning the sultan. In both the Ottoman and Egyptian cases, the newly established centralized state of the mid- to late nineteenth century reverted to this institution despite the existence of new reformed and modernized institutions.[84] As Chalcraft notes, the growing interaction of the state with its subjects and its penetration into every aspect of their lives facilitated the longevity of petitions and encouraged the submission of petitions with the hope of drawing state intervention.[85] On the other hand, in lieu of a movement for Western-style reforms (especially in the Ottoman Empire) which would have undermined the ruler's special status, and given the autocratic nature of the regime, reverting to this ancient institution helped the sultan/khedive to preserve his status, legitimacy, relevancy and power at the expense of potential rivals and new methods of governance.

In relation to Western-style reforms and the methods undertaken by the rulers to subvert them, it is interesting to note what Irene Schneider writes about the institution of petition to the Shah in Iran at about the same period:

> As to what Nāṣir al-Dīn Shāh's political aims for the institution of *maẓālim* may have been, a combination of political factors spring to mind: a control and maintenance of absolute authority that was in line with and referred to the ideological aspects laid down in the mirrors doctrine, upon which the Shāh based his rule. It thus seems acceptable to define the *maẓālim* in late 13th/19th-century Iran as a system for controlling legal, political, and administrative affairs that operated under the Shāh's supervision. However, far from being an outright advocate for reforms in the Western style, Nāṣir al-Dīn Shāh might have chosen the classic, traditionally acknowledged system of the *maẓālim* as an instrument for controlling the provincial administrative system and as a counterweight to the demands voiced by some of his reform-oriented ministers.[86]

Similar to the situation in Iran, the continuing operation of the institution of petitioning the sultan despite all the reforms can be perceived as a traditional tool of governance which allowed the sultans, particularly Abdülhamid II, to preserve their status, gain an edge over the bureaucracy, and block unwanted measures and reforms.[87] However, whereas in Iran the Shah at the time demonstrated great weakness which encouraged subjects to defy his authority, argue with him, and even threaten him,[88] the situation in the Empire was different. Not surprisingly, after the 1906 Revolution in Iran petitions were discussed in parliament, a culmination of a chain of events caused by the Shah's inability to handle the petitions effectively. In a way, Iran witnessed a bottom-up process which put the Shah in opposition to the subjects and the state's institutions. In the Ottoman Empire, by contrast, the reforms were top-down, initiated by reform-minded bureaucrats within the state's institutions, but parliamentary life under Abdülhamid was short-lived. The fact that so many subjects chose to refer their grievances directly to Istanbul even at the end of the nineteenth century illustrates their perception of the sultanate's essential role. What made petitions so dominant in the political and judicial spheres was the nature of sovereignty more than its definition. In this sense, government centralization increased the significance of petitioning.[89]

Finally, it is interesting to note that unlike the situation in previous eras, most of the correspondence between the central government and the provinces concerning petitions was not carried out with the *kadi*'s *shari'a* court, but rather with the province, in the case discussed here the *mutasarrıflık* of Jerusalem which was directly responsible to Istanbul. It reflects, among other things, the transformation of the role of the *shari'a* court, which now mainly focused on family and personal matters.

Petitions in the District of Jerusalem at the End of the Nineteenth Century

The advent of the telegraph lines and the regularization of the postal services by the end of the 1860s resulted in a flood of petitions from the *mutasarrıflık* of Jerusalem to the central authorities in Istanbul.[90] In Jerusalem, as in other provinces, the telegraph, which was mainly introduced as means of control and centralization, concomitantly allowed subjects "to reach all levels of government, to express opinions, make complaints, and petition for change."[91]

This development raises the issue of the conduct of the local Ottoman authorities and their handling of complaints. Haim Gerber demonstrated in his pioneering study on this province during the late Ottoman period that the District's administrative council, *meclis-i idare*, regularly received petitions from residents of the district and meticulously investigated their complaints. Among the most common topics raised in the petitions were the status and registration of land, the collection of taxes such as the tithe (*öşr*) and *vergi*, and various matters concerning *waqf* endowments.[92] Some of the petitions were submitted to the council as appeals against decisions made by the administrative councils at the level of the sub-districts, such as Gaza and Jaffa, as the higher authority for the whole district. Other petitions, in particular those submitted by residents of the region close to Jerusalem, were referred to the council acting as a first instance administrative council for the sub-district of Jerusalem itself (similar to the situation in the *nizamiye* court system, the administrative council of Jerusalem wore several hats: council of the whole District of Jerusalem, council of the sub-district of Jerusalem, and appeal court for the other sub-districts in the province).

Gerber's research on the conduct of the council, which is based on rare minutes from its deliberations over a period of several years, demonstrates the efficiency and professional nature of the council. It was established as part of the reorganization of Ottoman rule in the provinces during the Tanzimat reforms, and carried out a vast array of tasks assigned to it by law. In principle, many of the concerns raised in the petitions sent to Istanbul were the prerogative of the *meclis-i idare* at the provincial level and should have been handled there, without the intervention of the imperial center. What then accounts for the abundance of complaints sent from the District of Jerusalem to Istanbul?

A partial explanation might have to do with Gerber's observation that the influence of the council and the degree to which it was able to carry out its tasks was higher in the region close to Jerusalem as compared with more remote regions in the province, such as the sub-districts of Jaffa and Gaza (particularly the latter). In other words, the fact that there were more petitions addressed to the imperial center from the regions of Jaffa and Gaza than from the vicinity of Jerusalem might be related to the dominancy of the council of the district in regions closer to Jerusalem as opposed to its weaker position in the more remote regions. There, the operation of the sub-district councils, local politics, and the influence and jockeying by local notables somewhat limited the influence of the district's administrative council and its involvement in and control of various matters.

A good example was the method of tax collection. In the more remote areas, particularly in the sub-district of Gaza, collection continued to be based mainly on the old style *iltizam*, with all its disadvantages and flaws, rather than more direct methods of tax collection, or governmental bids which were closely monitored and supervised by the council. Thus, it was more exposed to manipulations and attempts at extortion by several dominant local urban families.[93]

Yet another possible explanation is reflected in the oft-made claim by petitioners that their approaches to the local authorities at the provincial level went unanswered or were rejected without due consideration, and therefore they had no other choice than to contact Istanbul directly to obtain redress. Other reasons such as the cost of approaching the *nizamiye* courts, the intricacies of the Ottoman bureaucracy, opposition to new measures and reforms introduced by state and the like will be discussed below.

In this regard, one of the most intriguing questions regarding the submission of petitions from Palestine to Istanbul in the last decades of the nineteenth century is the extent to which the case of Palestine was unique in comparison with other areas in the Empire. Were there more petitions sent from the Holy Land to Istanbul than from other regions, or the opposite? Within Palestine itself, what were the factors that influenced the geographical distribution of the petitions and the petitioners? For example, were there more petitions from the coastal areas than from the mountainous ranges? From the towns and their vicinity than from more remote places? And finally, were there differences in the proportion of petitions from different towns? While some of these questions await further comparative research, partial answers regarding the nature of the petitioners can be found regarding Palestine's central-southern coast and are presented throughout this book.

CHAPTER 2

GENERAL FEATURES
OF THE PETITIONS

This chapter provides basic information on the petitions discussed in this book. It covers their current location, the identity of the petitioners, the role of the petition-writers, the topics presented, formulas and language, the petitioners' expectations and the requests they made, the petitions' addressees, geographical distribution of the petitions and other data. This background material sets the stage for the thematic analysis of the petitions and their content in the next chapters.

Current Archiving of the Petitions

All the petitions examined in this book are located today in the Ottoman section of Turkey's Prime Ministerial State Archives in Istanbul, known among researchers as the *Başbakanlık Osmanlı Arşivi*. Even though the petitions were for the most part sent to the office of the Grand-Vizier (*Sadaret*) in his capacity to handle complaints in the name of the sultan, many of them are now grouped in the collections of the Ottoman Ministry of the Interior (*Dahiliye Nezareti*) or the collection of the Ottoman Ministry of Foreign Affairs (*Hariciye Nezareti*), for reasons which will be explained below. A substantial number of petitions or correspondences regarding them can also be found in the collections of Yıldız Palace, *Şûra-yı Devlet* (the Council of State), the *Bab-ı Âli Evrak Odası* (the Sublime Porte Secretariat) and, to a lesser extent, in other Ottoman ministries.

Most of the petitions, it is important to note, are traceable today through the archive's advanced computerized catalogue system, which is improving and expanding constantly.[1] As mentioned previously, as opposed to past practices, after 1813 answers to petitions were not registered in the *Şikâyet Defterleri*, and thus there is no one location in the archive in which the handling of petitions was concentrated, a fact which makes it almost impossible to gather reliable, accurate statistics on them.[2]

Much of the handling of the petitions sent to Istanbul in the period discussed here was carried out at the Ministry of the Interior, where the correspondence between the Ottoman bureaus was coordinated. The ministry typically sent copies of petitions to the appropriate bureaus and officials with a demand to investigate the complaint quickly, provide necessary data and explanations, question people or take any other measures before reporting back to Istanbul. The bulk of the correspondence examined in this volume took place between the Ministry of the Interior and the *mutasarrıflık* of Jerusalem, which had jurisdiction over the region under discussion. Many times the latter only learned about the petitions and the complaints when it received a copy from Istanbul and was asked to deal with the matter or investigate it.

Since the Ministry of the Interior had no translation services, it sent petitions that were not written in Ottoman to the Translation Bureau (*Tercüme Odası*) at the Ministry of Foreign Affairs. There, the petitions were translated from Arabic (or at times from other languages, such as French) into Ottoman. For this reason, drafts of translations from Arabic into Ottoman are found in the collections of the Ministry of Foreign Affairs, even though the administrative regions which constituted Palestine were within the Empire's borders.[3]

For the most part, however, the original petitions have not been preserved with the drafts. These drafts are often very hard to read as they are working sheets full of erasures. The petition translator (*mütercim*) wrote his name and the date of the translation at the top of the draft. In addition, he added a header to the translation with complete information about the petition, such as the date of submission, the language in which the petition was written and the identity of the submitters. The following is a typical header of a petition translated from Arabic to Ottoman at the Translation Bureau (see Appendix 1):

This is the translation of a petition in Arabic sent to the exalted Grand Vizier on the 29 of [the month of] Rabiyülevvel 1296 with the signature and seal of the *muhtar*s, imam, and people of the

village of Sarafand-ı Kubra [Sarafand al-'Amar], which is located in
the sub-district [*kaza*] of Jaffa in the District of Jerusalem.[4]

In the next step, a proofreader (*musahhih*) went over the translation and made
whatever corrections he saw fit (hence all the erasures, see Appendix 1). The
musahhih's name appears at the top of the form under a separate heading. His task was to go over the translation, correct it and erase wrong or
inaccurate sections that did not correspond to the original petition.

Occasionally, the archives have preserved the full correspondence
concerning a specific petition between the Ottoman bureaus and officials
such as the Grand Vizier, the Ministry of the Interior, *Defter-i Hakani* (the
Imperial Register of Land Revenues), the local authorities in Palestine,
and others. It is much harder, however, to find a complete set comprised
of the petition, the correspondence and the final imperial decision issued
(*irade*), although such examples surface from time to time. More often,
decisions were taken at the bureaucratic level and the problem was solved
or was terminated without the need to issue an official order. We can
assume that some cases did not reach a conclusive stage and were 'lost'
within the bureaucratic process.

The Petition Addressees

The fact that the vast majority of the petitions were addressed to the
Sadaret suggests that it was widely known to the public and the professional petition-writers, the *arzuhalci*s who wrote the petitions for the
petitioners, that the Grand Vizier was the authority delegated by
the sultan to handle the people's complaints on his behalf and supervise
the institution of petitions. Thus, all kinds of petitions were sent to the
office of the Grand Vizier, even those concerning matters for which there
was a clearly designated Ottoman authority, such as in the cases of evaluation and collection of land taxes and the registration of land. It is likely
that the petitioners were fully aware of who was responsible for handling
their specific complaint but still assumed that the petitions would have
more clout if they first reached the highest Ottoman authority and only
then were sent down the chain of command with operative orders directly to the appropriate bureaus and office holders, a process which indeed
took place.[5] Other reasons for their insistence on contacting Istanbul are
discussed below.

Some petitions were still sent directly to various Ottoman offices and functionaries in the capital, such as the Ministry of the Interior, the Ministry of Foreign Affairs, the Ministry of Finance (*Maliye Nezareti*), *Defter-i Hakani*, the Ministry of Justice (*Adliye ve Mezahip Nezareti*), the Council of State and the Palace of the sultan himself through his secretariat (*Mabeyn*).[6] At times, petitions had several addresses, perhaps under the assumption that this would improve their chances of obtaining redress.[7]

Identity of the Petitioners

During the period examined in this book, the ease of sending a petition to Istanbul in the form of a letter or a telegram reduced many of the geographical and physical barriers which had previously discouraged people or groups from submitting petitions to the imperial center. Nevertheless, ordinary peasants or Bedouins rarely petitioned individually. Rather, it was the heads of the village (*muhtar*s) or the tribal groups (sheikh) who signed the petition on behalf of collective groups (*ahali*, literally "the people of").[8] In part, as discussed above, this probably had to do with the price of the telegraph where payment was made per word, but social and cultural considerations were also involved. The picture only differed for the urban based population, where there tended to be a considerable number of individual petitioners including urbanites who possessed lands and property in the rural regions outside the main towns.

Hence, rural petitions were signed by the *muhtar* (in Arabic: *mukhtar*) or *muhtar*s of the villages involved. In the header of the translation of many petitions from Arabic into Ottoman at the Translation Bureau, it is often mentioned that the petition was submitted jointly by the *muhtar* and people of a certain village, or in collaboration with other office holders in the village such as the *imam*, *hatib*, members of the council of elders and the like.[9] Ordinary villagers, however, did not sign the petition with their own name and their mention as a group was only formulaic to emphasize that the *muhtar* represented the interests of the entire village.[10] Occasionally, several *muhtar*s from the same village signed a single petition or else petitioned together with *muhtar*s of other villages in the vicinity, with sometimes as many as several dozen *muhtar*s together.[11] In original petitions that have been preserved

in the archive in the form of letters, the seals of the *muhtar*s who signed
the petitions appear at the bottom of the document alongside the speci-
fications of their positions or responsibilities, but no personal signatures
are added (see Appendix 3).[12]

When Bedouins were concerned, the petitions were usually signed
by the sheikhs of their group, including a mention of their status.[13] At
times, however, members of the group associated themselves with the
petition and are mentioned by name alongside the sheikh's name, in addition to their seals, a fact that shows they were most probably members
of the leadership of the tribal group or relatives of the sheikh but not
ordinary members (see Appendix 3).[14] There are instances in which a
well-known figure in the region submitted a petition as the head of a
group of petitioners, such as in the case of Jaffa's *Nakibüleşraf* (in Arabic:
naqib al-ashraf), who headed a group of dozens of landowners from this
town.[15] This was apparently believed to give the petition extra weight and
increase its chances of fulfilling its objective.

It is noteworthy that petitions sent collectively usually concerned
people from the same social group. That is, almost no petitions have been
found in which urbanites, villagers and Bedouins (or any combination of
two of these three groups) collectively petitioned in the name of one cause,
a fact which might indicate that their interests and concerns were largely
at odds.[16] However, there are petitions sent by people who belonged to
different religious faiths, particularly Muslims and Christians, usually
from the same socio-economic group in matters concerning them all
such as taxes and the status of lands (see Appendix 2).[17] I did not come
across petitions representing a "confessional mix," for example either by
Catholics and Orthodox Christians in matters unique to their own communities or joint petitions by Sephardic and Ashkenazi Jews.

Individual petitions were sent to Istanbul mainly by men, although
in rare cases women also petitioned as individuals.[18] Individuals who
submitted petitions complained about injustices inflicted on them,[19] government officials and tax collectors who allegedly misused their power,
matters concerning ownership of land and evaluation of various taxes such
as the *vergi* (in Arabic: *wirko*, in Hebrew: *verko*) and *öşr* taxes, familial
disputes in which the authorities were involved, the security situation in
their towns, and business matters.[20] Most individual petitions were submitted by urbanites, mainly from the region's major urban centers, and

more so from Jaffa than from Gaza. As mentioned, practically no individual petitions came from the rural regions.

A large group of petitions was sent by landowners from various backgrounds, both individually as well as collectively, to complain about changes in the assessment of the taxes on their land, make requests for tax deductions and exemptions, protest the takeover of lands they claimed were theirs by other people or changes in the status of their land, and to present demands to revert to previous arrangements which had been abolished.

Interestingly, people who did not possess Ottoman citizenship, such as European settlers, foreigners who lived in the cities, and the proto-Zionist colonists, also occasionally sent petitions to Istanbul, a fact which challenges the prevailing claim in the literature that they preferred to exert influence on the Ottoman authorities only through their consuls rather than through the Ottoman system (see Chapter 8).

Ottoman officials, whether they resided in Palestine or only served there as part of their duty, also occasionally petitioned Istanbul. They complained about the treatment they received, delays in their promotions, accusations leveled against them and punishments inflicted upon them for alleged misdeeds they denied doing, or about abuse of power of their peers in the Ottoman bureaucracy. At times, they asked for raises in their salaries, claiming they could not provide for themselves or for their families with their current income (see Chapter 5).

Petitions about business disputes and commercial interests were also fairly common at this time (see Chapter 6). There were also personal requests which cannot be categorized easily.[21] Finally, collective petitions signed by several people or more in favor of a certain official or against him were very common, at times bringing together people of different faiths.[22] Such petitions were connected for the most part to domestic urban politics in the region's main towns, as will be discussed in Chapter 3.

The Intermediary of the *Arzuhalcis*

The vast majority of the petitions examined here were written by *arzuhalcis* (the plural in Turkish: *arzuhalciler*), professional petition-writers who offered their services to the general public.[23] Only a small percentage of the petitions were written by the petitioners themselves without the help of *arzuhalcis*. These were usually short telegrams which were not written in the form or style of the professionally written petitions. As can be seen in the pictures below (Pictures 1 and 2), the *arzuhalci*s sat at the entrance to the Ottoman post and telegraph offices, in the markets or in cafés,[24] and offered their services to the public in return for payment, similar to the document-writers one can see even today at the entrance to courts and public offices in the Middle East, including in Turkey.

There are several indications that *arzuhalci*s rather than ordinary people wrote most of the petitions. First, many of the petitioners were no doubt illiterate and could not write the petitions themselves.[25] Second, the fact that almost all the petitions were sent to the bureau of the Grand Vizier indicates that there was some guidance behind the organization and sending of the petitions, and no mere coincidence led the petitioners to send their petitions there. Third, many of the petitions are composed of similar and repetitive phrases and a specific jargon is used throughout. The structure of the petitions is often similar and includes repetitive parts and similar reasoning.[26] Finally, there are descriptions by contemporary people of the *arzuhalci*s and their activity, which was needed by large segments of the population.[27]

Little is known about the social background of the *arzuhalci*s or their training.[28] They were literate people, although not necessarily with formal training, who did not emerge from the higher echelons of society. For the most part they were private local people, perhaps retired scribes who had formerly worked in the Ottoman bureaucracy and possessed general knowledge of languages (particularly Ottoman), the art of correspondence and law.[29] There is evidence that a guild of *arzuhalci*s existed in Istanbul at the end of the eighteenth century and that they needed a special permit to work in this profession.[30]

The services offered by the *arzuhalci*s were well-known to the general public, as can be seen from the wide variety of people who approached them and paid for having their petitions written professionally. In fact, they served as intermediaries between the petitioners and the Ottoman central authorities, replacing the court scribes who, for the most part, wrote petitions in the past. They allowed the petitioners to express their claims within a framework and mechanism authorized by the authorities while using the jargon, language and codes of literary expression sanctioned by the Ottoman system. Hence, familiarity with the language, structure and line of argument of the petitions, which often were based on

formulas provided by special manuals with sample letters written especially for such a purpose (see Document 1),[31] makes it possible to hear the
voices of the petitioners, and extract the details of the specific events from
the heavily structured and formulaic writing.[32]

In this regard, Christa Hämmerle writes that "petitioning letters are
characterized by an especially strong tension between 'life' and 'forum'

Picture 1   Petition-Writer (*arzuhalci*)
Source: Wright, George Newenham and Charles Henry Timperley, *The Gallery of Engravings*, Vol. III
(London, 1844), between pages 56 and 57.
Notes: Notice the usage of the petition-writer's services by women, the location of the petition-writer in a
public place accessible to all potential clients and the stand used by the petition-writer when writing.

which, depending on the particular letter, tends more in one direction or the other."[33] This observation notwithstanding, as van Voss notes "it is generally possible to determine what was the influence of the professional scribe (preacher, schoolmaster), and what is the voice of the real petitioner."[34] It should recalled, however, that some of the petitions were

LETTER WRITER.

Picture 2   Letter-Writer
Source: Thornbury, George Walter, *Turkish Life and Character,* Vol. I (London, 1860), between pages 102 and 103.

"Not far off, under a stuccoed wall, pierced by ponderously barred gratings, sits the sagacious letter-writer, with a gossip on one side of him, and a customer on the other; three pair of huge red slippers, like crab-shells, are lying before them. The writer sits cross-legged on a thin plank platform, held up from the ground by three transverse beams, and spread with a dry hide of red and brown striped carpet, which gives it a domestic look though it is in the full open streets. The correspondent is very anxious, the writer very grave and consequential, the gossip very deferential and attentive. Before the writer is a small box of paper, reed-pens, pen-cases, inks, and seals; his chibouk has gone out, neglected in the hurry of business. The three men represent three types of Turks: the one, a bigoted, dull day-dreamer; the letter-sender, a man, puzzled, opium-eating knave; the centre man, a full brained but sorrowful, simple-hearted, and honest Mussulman. He looks quite the pasha with his yellow turban, red fez, light-coloured robe, and blue-stripped inner dress; the gossip, with broad red sash and purple robe, is the thorough old Turk; while the correspondent is a feeble, miserable admixture of European and Asiatic dress, flapping, buttonless waistcoat, and trousers of dirty gray plaid silk."

"organized" by people of interest or powerful people, who exerted their influence to convince individuals or groups of people to send petitions that would serve their interests or help them take revenge on their rivals. Apparently, there were also cases of fraudulent petitions that the modern historian should take into account.[35]

An interesting point regarding the work of the professional petition-writers is how soon after the 1908 Revolution and the reinstitution of parliamentary life and a constitutional regime this change was reflected in petitions sent to Istanbul. The petition-writers adopted the discourse about constitutional rights, the new era which was opened in the Empire, the end of the period of oppression and tyranny during Abdülhamid II's reign and the beginning of a new period of just rule, all of which were ideas floating in the urban milieu of Palestine, as elsewhere.[36] Moreover, some of the petitions were published in the press, which blossomed after the abolishment of Abdülhamid's censorship and the reinstitution of a parliamentary regime.

Means of Sending the Petitions: The Post and Telegraph

Until the second half of the nineteenth century, Ottoman subjects who wanted to submit a petition to Istanbul had to travel there themselves, a journey which was arduous given the means of transportation at the time, the dangers awaiting them on the road and the limited financial means at the disposal of most Ottoman subjects. Other options to send petitions to Istanbul were to ask the local *kadı* to do so, to organize a delegation which would represent a large number of people with a shared interest and would reduce the costs involved, or even to ask merchants and traders to take the petition with them to the Ottoman capital. Obviously each of these options had considerable limitations and disadvantages. This situation changed in the nineteenth century with the advent of new technologies and means of transportation which allowed quick and relatively easy communication with the center, without the intermediaries that had previously been necessary. In this regard, David Watenpaugh argues that the "adoption of new technologies that increasingly collapsed space and time" was an important component in the process of modernizing society in the Middle East.[37]

Alongside the Ottoman post, most of the major European powers operated postal services in Palestine in the second half of the nineteenth century, particularly in Jerusalem and the booming coastal town of

٦

الباب الاول

في الاعراضات

(١)   صورة عرض محضر

المعروض الى اعتاب الدولة العلية الابدية القرار ∗وذوالشوكة
الشاهانية العظيمة الاقتدار ∗ خلد الله سرير ملكها السلطاني ∗
وادام علينا ظل لوائها الشاهاني ∗ وابد لنا عمر وشوكة ولي نعمتنا
ومولانا بدون امتنان السلطان الاعظم ∗ والخاقـان الافخم ∗
السلطان ابن السلطان ∗ السلطان عبد الحميد خان لا زالت
ايام دولته السعيدة مرفوعة الاعلام ∗ بالعز والنصر والاكرام
يعرض هولاء العبيد ان فلان من حين حضوره لهذا الطرف
قد بذل الجهد بتسوية امور مامورينه توفيقاً للعمليات الموسسة
وتفرغ بالاتقان لاجراء الوسائل الموجبة لتحسين حالها وقد احسن
المجرى مع الجميع فاصبحوا منه ممنونين ومن حسن مسراه
واقدامه ∗شكرين وبما ان الذين يبذاون الجهد لاتقان مامور يتهم
تطبيقاً للرضا العالي مقرر بحقهم الوعد الملوكاني بالمكافأة السنيـة
وقد وجد فلان المومى اليه متصفاً بهذه الاوصاف الحميدة فالان

Document 1 Excerpt from a Manual explaining to Ordinary People how to write Petitions and Letters of various Kinds (both Official and Personal) themselves without outside Assistance

Source: Yusuf Efendi al-Shalfun, *Turjuman al-Mukataba* (Index of Writing/Compendium of Correspondence), 7th edition (Beirut, 1887) {in Arabic}

Jaffa.[38] In fact, the activity of the postal service became one of the key indications of the Powers' growing involvement in the Holy Land. Thus, in addition to the services of the Ottoman post, postal services were also provided in Palestine's major cities by the Austrian, German, Russian, Italian and French postal services. The opening of the Suez Canal in 1869

Source: BOA. HR. TO., 390/56, 22 Zilkade 1302 {2 September 1885}

Document 2   Envelopes of Petitions Sent by Mail
Source: BOA. HR. TO., 391/95, 23 September 1886

increased steamboat traffic connecting Europe with the Holy Land which had begun a few decades earlier when the first steamboats reached the region.[39] Consequently, as of the late 1860s, the postal services offered in Palestine were more regularized and improved.[40]

Some of the petitions examined here, particularly the longer ones, were sent to Istanbul via sea mail in the form of letters (see Appendices III, IV). This can be seen from the original envelopes and letters which have been preserved in the archive (see Document 2); the translation of the petitions from Arabic into Ottoman Turkish, where often the mode of delivery is mentioned; and the fact that petitions sent through the telegraph system were, for the most part, shorter and more concise than ordinary letters (for instance, they lacked the long greetings and flowery phrases at the beginning and at the end that were so typical of letters).[41]

With regard to telegraph services that first became available in Palestine in the mid-1860s and soon spread to major towns and even smaller localities,[42] there are cases in which the original telegraph forms have been preserved including details on the way they were sent to Istanbul, such as the date, place and time of sending, the transmitting officer, the route through which the telegram was sent, the price paid and so on.[43] Given that the telegrams had to be deciphered in Istanbul once they arrived there, often there are spelling mistakes which probably stem from this translation, particularly when it comes to names of places and people. To conclude, the relatively cheap price and simple procedure of sending a petition through the mail or the telegraph, in comparison with the complex and expensive "regular" venues of pursuing justice, made the petitions a sort of a "court for lower classes."

Formulas and Structure

Most of the petitions discussed here were originally written in Arabic, fewer in Ottoman Turkish and only a minority in French.[44] In the petitions written in Arabic, there are phrases in Ottoman embedded throughout the text, particularly at the beginning and at the end where there are honorific blessings and pleas for mercy and justice.[45] In the translation of the petitions from Arabic into Ottoman made at the Translation Bureau, however, most of the honorifics and flattery were replaced by standard blessings for the Grand Vizier, such as *mesned-i celil-i sadaret-i 'uzmaya* (to the glorious great Grand Vizier).[46]

The petitions to the Grand Vizier were written in a highly polite style, but often, especially when they were sent by telegraph where every word counted, the long exalting lines of praise which are so typical of official letters and direct approaches to the sultan himself are missing. The telegraph thus had a considerable influence on the language of the petitions, and forced the petitioners to get to the point right away when petitioning. One can even argue that it forced the petitioners to convey the bare bones of their narrative and shed much of the formulaic writing. In some petitions in Arabic there are words and phrases from the vernacular. In this regard, there is considerable variation in the eloquence of different petitions written in Ottoman Turkish, probably as a result of the petition-writers' level of mastery of this language, as well as the seniority of the addressee.

The petitions often repeat the same leitmotifs, such as diminishing of one's status ("Jaffa's poor people"),[47] glorification ("we have complete trust in the Sultan's justness"), exaggeration ("we are on the verge of catastrophe due to high taxes," "we will need to flee or immigrate to other lands because of our dire situation") and the like.[48] The most typical symbolic expressions used in the petitions are various Islamic religious phrases.[49] For instance, the sultan is termed the *Amir al-Mu'minin*; the name of the Prophet is praised as a symbol for the just; the *shari'a* laws are seen as the law of the state alongside *nizami / kanuni* laws, as are claims regarding the petitioners' rights according to these laws;[50] praying that God will protect and glorify the sultan or punish evil-doers who do not follow his path; the desire expressed by the petitioners to be able to continue blessing the sultan if – God willing – he ensures that justice is rendered; and even swearing in the name of the Prophet's pure virgin daughter.[51]

Short personal petitions sent by telegraph which were written by the petitioners themselves and not by professional petition-writers were, for the most part, not written according to the "rules" of the professional petitions, but were rather freely formulated.[52] This may have better reflected the voice of the petitioner and the narrative they wanted to convey.

The Petitioners' Expectations

In general, the petitioners' expectations fall into two categories. First, in most cases there is a general wish by the petitioners, expressed in polite flattering words, that justice will be rendered and that they, as loyal subjects of the sultan, will not be the only ones for whom justice will not be wrought; that the *shari'a* and *kanuni* laws will be upheld and adhered to; that *Amir al-Mu'minin*, the sultan, whom they trust, will protect them and ensure that justice is done; and that the evil-doers, according to the petitioners' claims, will be punished and the just rewarded. While invoking religious symbols and figures, the petitioners express their belief that the sultan cannot allow their unjust situation to continue and hence he will issue orders to make changes immediately. At times there is also an implied "threat" by the petitioners that if the sultan will not grant their demands they may abandon their land and run away, not be able to pay their taxes, or alas will not be able to pray for the sultan's well-being and strength as wholeheartedly as before. Consider the words of dozens of landowners in Jaffa who submitted a petition in 1891:

> Hence we ask for the issuance of an imperial order which will forbid unfair treatment of our property, something which does not correspond to the religious and *nizami* laws, both of which are the sources of the rulership's continuation [*madar qawm al-mulk*] and the preservation of public order and the people's well being. And in this way, our blessings for the continuation of the existence of the exalted state, may God save its generous existence, will multiply. And the decision is in the hands of the one who commands authority.[53]

The framing of requests for justice in these general terms appears to be an effort to create a shared moral world with the imperial center based on Islamic and Ottoman law, faith and history.[54] These are meant to convince the sultan to act in favor of the petitioners even if, legally speaking, they had no case. If he fails to do so, it is tacitly implied that he risks losing his image as a just and benevolent Islamic ruler, and the ability of the state, headed by him, to rule will be jeopardized.[55] Placing the petitioners and the sultan on the same side of the equation as adherents to Islamic law and justice, and depicting the sultan as a just, ideal Islamic ruler who cares about the well-being and conditions of his subjects and strives to implement *shari'a* rule, reflect more than simple rhetorical devices. They are, in fact, effective tools to compel the sultan to grant the petitioners their request. This was not a new device, but rather an old practice rooted in the Islamic and Ottoman institution of petitioning the ruler (which existed in other societies as well). In this regard, Chalcraft notes as follows regarding petitions submitted by peasants to the Egyptian khedive in the 1860s and 1870s:

> Peasants were not "instinctively deferential to a glorious ruler; lovers of despots by habit and tradition; mired in an immature, primitive, or prepolitical consciousness; and unable to "represent themselves." Instead, peasants made tactical use of the figure of the just ruler in a dangerous and power-laden context. They adopted a language that gave them permission to speak, drew in state intervention, and allowed them to (re)define in some measure the meaning of justice, even while ostensibly sticking to the terms of officially acceptable discourse.[56]

Alongside the general request for justice appearing in the petitions, there is usually also a specific request and an expectation that an order will be issued by the sultan to grant the plea. In this category, there are varied requests such as to stop collecting tithe from certain lands, order a reduction in the amount of *vergi* tax due from other lands, reinstate officials who were unfairly dismissed, investigate allegations against certain officials who were claimed to have misused their power or misbehaved, order the local authorities to stop implementing certain policies, send an investigative committee or an official to probe the petitioners' allegations, summon the petitioners and the person/s against whom a petition was submitted to court such that justice can prevail, order a new trial in cases where allegedly justice was not done by a lower court, find substitute arrangements for people who were evicted from certain lands, revert the status of certain lands, officially acknowledge local arrangements and norms which were rejected by officials as being unlawful, change administrative borders of certain regions such that specific places will be included/excluded from them, halt measures on the ground regarding specific matters until the court decides about pending issues and so on.

Consider the following quote taken from a petition by several villages in the sub-district of Gaza to reduce the *vergi* tax that they were forced to pay, which demonstrates the usage of both a general aspiration for justice alongside a specific practical request:

> We have nothing else to do in this situation but to contact your gates of justice with a request to receive your mercy and the

benevolence of our exalted state. Hence we ask for the issuance of an imperial order to accept the change in the value of our land, which took place according to the exalted regulations and directions, and abrogate what was imposed upon us out of injustice, and protect us from this damage. We appeal to the honor of the most respectful of human beings [the Prophet] may he rest in peace, for ensuring the justice, and strength and greatness of our Sultan, *Amir al-Mu'minin*, and the mercy of your state, and those who give mercy enjoy mercy from God and from the people.[57]

Mentioning the name of the Prophet as well as God's mercy is evidently an attempt by the petitioners to create a shared moral world with the sultan so that their specific request will be granted.

In another example, sent by residents of Gaza in support of their *mufti* and against his rivals who tried to bring about his replacement, there are several general requests alongside one implied specific request to send an investigative committee to look into the allegations raised in the petition. The objective is to make sure that the "evildoers" will be punished and that the *mufti* and his supporters will be protected (see Appendix 5):

If an edict had been issued to inquire about them or investigate their complaints in the sub-district and in the district, or by [sending] a special officer, or [by inquiring] in the vicinity, their acts, which are opposed to the exalted will [of the sultan], and the truth behind their baseless claims, signed by them and by their supporters, which [includes] names without real people behind them, would have been clear.

Since we know the justice of our master, may God support him, we dare to submit a petition to beg for justice, to punish the intriguers, in the sake of God and his Prophet, and to protect the honest people and the people of [religious] knowledge, so that the good prayers of the public for the supporter of truth, our master *Amir al-Mu'minin*, will multiply.[58]

Obviously, if the general moral claim of the petitioners is accepted, there is no other option but to accede to their specific request and order an investigation of the misdeeds committed by the accused, which after all was the petitioners' original goal.

CHAPTER 3

PETITIONS BY THE URBAN POPULATION OF GAZA AND JAFFA

Previous chapters have described the reasons for submitting petitions, and the mechanisms and technicalities of submission. This chapter and those that follow analyze the key thematic features of these petitions. It begins by examining petitions sent by the urban population of the two major urban centers of the region, Gaza and Jaffa. These petitions should not be confused with petitions sent by the rural population from post and telegraph offices in these two towns (see Chapter 4).

The age of the Tanzimat led to a growth in petitioning activity, which was not only the result of the introduction of more efficient and rapid forms of communication. The reforms gave many sectors more reasons to petition the sultan. Changes in customs and long-established bureaucratic procedures led to a significant rise in grievances. The range of topics broached by the urban population was enormous. Petitions by urbanites appear to have been used as an efficient mechanism to conduct its affairs with the central government, convey messages and leverage its interests. The pattern of petitioning the sultan in bureaucratic cases was thus by no means merely motivated by legal issues. Much more than before, it had clear political overtones.

Most of the petitions discussed in this study were submitted by the urban population of Gaza and Jaffa. Urbanites submitted numerous personal petitions about specific matters that concerned them as individuals, as well as collective petitions about issues affecting groups of people. Generally speaking, the petitions sent by the urban population of Jaffa were much more diversified than those sent from Gaza; the latter were primarily made up of group petitions and overwhelmingly dealt with the internal politics of this city, reflecting the strife within its elite. There were not many individual petitions from Gaza.

While some of the issues raised in the urban petitions will be discussed in the following chapters, the essence of this chapter is to convey the characteristics of urban individual and collective petitions, and the politics behind their submission.

Politics of Notables

Before discussing the urban petitions themselves, it is worth briefly characterizing the politics of the urban population of Palestine in the second half of the nineteenth century as regards both the local and central authorities.[1] To a large extent Palestine's politics was dominated by several Muslim Arab families, for the most part from Jerusalem, who enjoyed countrywide prestige and influence. These families included the Husaynis, whose power in terms of resources and influence was unmatched, the Khalidis, al-ʿAlami, and al-Dajani.[2] These were respected families with social standing that had a long tradition of religious learning and had held religious and administrative posts in the Ottoman system for generations. In the nineteenth century, they adjusted to the new conditions brought about by the Tanzimat reforms and preserved their privileged status in the Ottoman system despite attempts at centralization and the strengthening of the government's power over local elites.[3] Rashid Khalidi commented as follows on the response of Palestine's elite to these reforms and the shift in the nature of Ottoman rule:

> Given the material and other resources of these notable families, and their experience in adjusting to the realities of power over the centuries, it should not be surprising that they accommodated rapidly to this shift from a system which had long been in place and from which they had benefited substantially, to a new one, and in doing so largely managed to preserve their standing and influence. Within a generation, most of the same families who had for

centuries produced the judges, teachers, officials, and preachers who dominated the old system had secured privileged access to the modern educational institutions which were the path to positions in the new legal, administrative, educational, and political order. Although there they had to compete with others from more humble backgrounds trained like them in the new secular schools, or in the growing number of new schools run by western missionaries, they still retained many of their advantages.[4]

Thus, for example, when administrative councils were established in the provinces as part of the Tanzimat reforms, the local seats allocated to Muslims were usually filled by members of these families, and they dominated the activity of these councils within the limits set by the government. This gave them tremendous power and influence, but at the same time led to infighting and contestation, as reflected in the petitions. The councils approved the provincial budgets, initiated infrastructure projects and held tenders for implementing them, supervised the activity of the various governmental offices in the provinces, made decisions regarding the ownership of land, conducted land surveys to evaluate property tax (*vergi*), supervised the collection of land taxes in the provinces including bids for the tithe tax, dealt with various issues concerning endowments, addressed appeals from lower-instance councils, and supervised the movement of people in and out of the district in addition to conducting censuses.[5]

Lower instances of the administrative councils were dominated by powerful families in Palestine's secondary towns such as Jaffa, Gaza, Nablus and Nazareth, at times in concert with the elite of Jerusalem. These families, which had various sources of wealth and clout, dominated town life and exerted their influence over their towns' hinterland and sub-districts.[6] Jaffa was dominated by families such as al-Dajani, Tayyan, Baydas, Abu-Khadra' and al-Sa'id.[7] Gaza was in the hands of the al-Shawwa, Saqallah, Abu-Khadra', Abu-Sha'ban and, above all, the Husayni family.[8]

A new source of wealth for Palestine's elite families came from landholding. A good number of individuals from these families acquired large tracts of land in various regions of the country in the second half of the nineteenth century, following the introduction of the 1858 Ottoman Land

Law and the process of the commercialization of the land, particularly in the coastal plain and the low regions.[9] They leased out the land to tenants in return for a share of the profits, developed it for commercial purposes, or sold it later on the land market at a profit.[10]

The mayors elected in the main cities usually came from among the ranks of the leading families, as did many officials in the local bureaucracy and the *muftis* of the major towns in Palestine.[11] Members elected to the first Ottoman parliament in 1876 and to the second in 1908 were also members of Palestine's limited circle of notables, mainly from Jerusalem.[12] The governors and *kadis*, however, were appointed by Istanbul, and the appointees were usually of Turkish origin and not Arab.[13]

During the second half of the nineteenth century, a new elite gradually emerged in Palestine whose wealth and influence differed from that of the traditional group. For the most part, it was composed of entrepreneurs, bankers, tradesmen and merchants who were often Christians and members of minority groups. Some of them lived in the booming coastal towns of the Levant (Beirut, Haifa, Jaffa) and took advantage of growing economic ties with Europe and the better security conditions in the country to accumulate large plots of land as a commodity that could be marketed for profit.[14]

The various members of Palestine's elite, as noted above, appear disproportionally often in petitions, either as petitioners or as targets of petitions. Because they had considerable means at their disposal, as well as proven capabilities and knowhow, members of this elite group frequently sent petitions to Istanbul to complain about the conduct of Ottoman officials serving in Palestine, particularly with regard to the collection of taxes, registration of land and fulfillment of governmental orders. On the other hand, numerous petitions also level accusations against members of these elite families, arguing that they use their influence and connections in the administrative councils for personal gain, take advantage of their status and influence and oppress ordinary Ottoman subjects, disregard existing norms, practices and habits, break the law and so on.

Coalitions of leading urban families tended to submit mutual complaints against each other, in particular in Gaza. For instance, the *muftis* of Gaza and contenders for this job were the subject of numerous petitions, both in favor and against their candidacy, and each side tried to obtain as many signatures as possible on the mass petitions it submitted, as will be seen below. At times, such coalitions were connected socially and politically with members of the Jerusalem elite.

Administrative Matters

The changing borders of the region's administrative units, which were redrawn as part of the ongoing reforms in the Ottoman administration in the provinces, are clearly reflected in petitions.[15] For instance, "the inhabitants of Ramle," some 15 kilometers east of Jaffa, frequently complained that their town's importance as a center for its rural hinterland had been diminished by the new administrative division. This had given Jaffa more importance, had turned it into a *kaza* and had attached Ramle to it as a dependent *nahiye*. They wanted to return to the old status quo, turn Ramle into a *kaymakamlık* and cede from Jaffa.[16] In terms of the extent to which the petitioners represented *all* the people of Ramle, the wording of the petition should not be understood at face value. Rather, it was a common mode of expression which probably reflected a popular sentiment prevailing in this town at the time.

The inhabitants of Ramle also complained that the *kışla* (barracks) in their town had been moved to Jaffa and that, as a result, they had to go there when called to enlist and "sleep in mosques and stables." They enumerated their town's advantages such as its location, air, beauty and abundance of water, as well being a center of religious learning. They even promised to help finance and construct the *kışla* in Ramle if the decision were revoked.[17] The subjects of Ramle did not ask for personal or communal ad hoc justice but actually attempted to change a decision made by the government, by acting as a pressure group.

In another case, this time in the *kaza* of Gaza, the people of the small town of al-Majdal, some 15 kilometers to the north of Gaza, petitioned collectively against a decision to abolish the telegraph in Gaza, rumors of which they had read in the newspaper (they were probably referring originally to a decision about the telegraph in their own village). Their petition was sent to the *Serasker* in Istanbul, and from there to the *Sadaret* with the former's note of support for the request given the presence of a military unit nearby. The Ministry of Post and Telegraph was asked to handle the matter.[18]

Internal Dissent and Support/Objection to Local Office Holders

Dozens of petitions involved complaints against members of rival factions within the urban elite. These were usually collective petitions signed by any number of petitioners, ranging from several people up to hundreds, although there are individual petitions in this category as well. Apparently, the institution of petitioning served in this case as a way to settle old local accounts and to weaken rival groups while trying to get Istanbul involved. As noted, there are many more petitions reflecting the power struggle within the urban elite of Gaza than from Jaffa, suggesting that the internal struggles within this city's elite were much more severe and intensive.

The main bone of contention in Gaza was competition over offices in the local bureaucracy such the *mufti*, membership in the local administrative councils, and the like. Some of the local office holders targeted by petitions from rival groups were connected to members of the Jerusalem elite through countrywide alliances. Others were apparently associated with Ottoman officials in the local administration who were not natives of Palestine, such as the local *kaymakam*s of Gaza and Jaffa or even the *mutasarrif* of Jerusalem above them.

For instance, "Islamic jurists, *muhtar*s, respected elders and notables from Gaza" sent a joint petition to protest the practices of the *mufti* of Gaza at the time, Ahmad Muhyi al-Din Efendi, of the Husayni family (1808/9–1878). They argued that he had oppressed the people and exhibited poor conduct, and demanded that he should be replaced by Muhammad Saqallah (1812–96) who was "a respectful and honest man."[19] The opposing group wasted no time in counteracting with a petition sent several months later signed by 19 Islamic jurists and notables asking the government to dismiss *mufti* Muhammad Saqallah for lack of religious knowledge and general incompetence. They claimed that they had already presented the issue before and demanded the reinstatement of Ahmad Muhyi al-Din Efendi to the post of *mufti*.[20] The new *mufti* himself applied to the *Sadaret* to examine allegations against him which appeared in the newspaper *al-Jawa'ib*, and demanded a government inquiry into the running of this newspaper, hinting that the preceding *mufti* and his supporters were behind this publication.[21] It is worth noting in this regard that newspapers apparently emerged as a parallel arena for conflict and account-settling among Gaza's elite, in addition to the submission of petitions.

Petitions continued to pile up against Ahmad Muhyi al-Din al-Husayni and his family even after he finished his term in office. In one case, several people complained that Husayn, the son of Muhyi al-Din, collaborated with the Bedouin tribes in the region of Gaza with whom the Husaynis maintained close ties, and with the *kaymakam* 'Umar, who was allegedly their friend.[22] They claimed that the Bedouins were encouraged to attack the farmers in the region and to harass them as well as the people of Gaza, who thus lived in fear. Moreover, they stated that, in the year 1287 (1870/71), the former *mufti* and his sons had already been expelled from Gaza.[23]

As far as I can tell from the petitions, about a decade later the issue surfaced again. Members of the Husayni family submitted a series of petitions concerning several of their rivals in Gaza whom they accused of collaborating with senior Ottoman officials in Palestine to undermine their family's influence and sources of power. They point out that they had already submitted petitions and state that Yusuf Diya' Efendi al-Khalidi[24] from Jerusalem (1829–1907), who was an opponent of their father Ahmad Muhyi al-Din al-Husayni, the former *mufti* of Gaza, incited the *mutasarrif* of Jerusalem Muhammad Ra'uf Paşa (r. 1877–89)[25] against them. Moreover, together with the Husayni's rival in Gaza, Khalil Abu-Khadra' (d. 1887/8), they brought about the resignation of Muhammad al-Hanafi al-Husayni (d. 1902/3)[26] from his post as director of education in Gaza and excluded 'Abd al-Hayy Fa'iq al-Husayni (1849/50–1912)[27] from membership in the administrative council of Gaza.[28] In another similar petition signed by the four and sent a few days later, they raise similar accusations and blame al-Khalidi for undermining their friendly relationships with Khalil Abu-Khadra', and for inciting their rival 'Abdalla al-Ghusayn[29] to submit slanderous petitions against them and convincing the *mutasarrif* of Jerusalem to take steps against the Husaynis (see Appendix 6).[30]

In the early 1890s, the Husaynis in Gaza were yet again involved in a struggle with their rivals over the post of *mufti*. At the time, the town's *mufti* was Muhammad al-Hanafi Efendi al-Husayni. The Husaynis claimed that the former *mufti* of Gaza, Muhammad Saqallah, who was "dismissed a month after taking office for incompetence and malpractice," took steps with the *komandan* (military commander) of Jerusalem, Rüstum Paşa, against the current *mufti*. Thus, they filed various complaints and encouraged other individuals to follow suit. The Husaynis stressed the family's loyalty to the Empire, its tradition of religious learning, and the harm done to it by the lies and trumped up complaints of its rivals. Moreover, they claimed that Saqallah was appointed *mufti* in the past only due to the intercession of the former *mutasarrif* of Jerusalem, Fa'iq Bey,[31] whom they claim was also dismissed because of his implication in this affair.[32]

The struggle over the position of the *mufti* of Gaza during this time also involved Saqallah. The latter and his followers, on the one hand, and Muhammad al-Hanafi Efendi al-Husayni and his followers, on the other, continued squabbling over this position for several years. Each side tried to garner supporters and tarnish the name of its rivals. The Husaynis claimed that Saqallah and his followers ('Abdallah al-Ghusayn, Salih al-Shawwa and Ramadan Abu-Khadra') submitted fake petitions to bring about the dismissal of Muhammad al-Hanafi Efendi and his replacement by Saqallah.[33]

Supporters of Muhammad Saqallah in Gaza also submitted petitions in his favor and against *mufti* al-Hanafi that criticized his family's history and attitude towards the local population. They even put forward a claim that, in the year 1294 (1877/8), members of his family were forbidden to hold the office of *mufti* in Gaza.[34] At one point, Saqallah was offered the office of *kadı* in Jaffa, and petitions in his favor and against *mufti* al-Hanafi were also sent from there, probably after hearing about the offer he received. Jerusalem, however, reported that the behavior of *mufti* al-Hanafi was perfectly acceptable, a situation which made it impossible to dismiss him. Nonetheless, complaints against him continued to pile up.[35]

Given that *mufti* al-Hanafi's term in office continued to elicit controversy, and petitions for and against him were sent to Istanbul, the matter was eventually referred to *Şeyhülislam* with a *mazbata* (decision) from the District of Jerusalem praising his good services.[36] *Mufti* al-Hanafi himself complained in the mid-1890s in a petition to the Ministry of the Interior that his relationships with the *kaymakam* of the *kaza* of Gaza, Hasan Bey, were strained after he had protested five months earlier about the misconduct of the *kaymakam*. The latter, it was claimed, collaborated with the *mufti*'s rivals in Gaza. They filed complaints against the *mufti* and convinced many others to do likewise, a situation which led to several investigations.[37] A few years later, *Mufti* al-Hanafi, his son and his brother were exiled by the central government to Ankara. From there, they sent petitions and begged to be pardoned and be allowed to go back to Palestine (see Document 4).[38]

As opposed to the situation in Gaza, there are very few petitions in the archives reflecting a power struggle within Jaffa's elite. There are, however, a considerable number of petitions from Jaffa against incumbent *kaymakam*s, their activities, mistreatment of the local population and collaboration with unknown negative elements, all of which led to unrest among the local population. Possibly these petitions were connected to economic or political rivalries among the city's elite but they are too vague to yield definitive conclusions.[39]

Abuse of Power, Malpractice and Misconduct by Officials

As discussed earlier, one of the main aims of the institution of petitioning the ruler was to allow the common people to complain directly to the central government about misdeeds by the local bureaucracy and various office holders, especially those in the lower and middle ranks. In this sense, the institution of petitioning continued to serve its original purpose, as numerous petitions were indeed submitted by the urban population in the *kaza*s of Gaza and Jaffa against office holders in the local Ottoman bureaucracy, both locals as well as outsiders who only served in Palestine for a limited time. The power struggle within the elite for jobs, influence and distribution of resources and revenues must be kept in mind given that, at times, the real reason for submitting a petition is very difficult to ascertain.

Complaints by the urban population about Ottoman officials were submitted either by a group of petitioners or individually; the former were more common in Gaza, the latter in Jaffa. Some of the petitions are very specific with regard to the accusations they level (e.g., taking bribes, mishandling bids, using violence routinely, changing the status of certain lands illegally and the like). Other accusations, however, are very general and appear to be generic (e.g., corrupt and immoral behavior, mistreatment of the people, collaboration with criminals and evildoers, incompetence, disturbing the peace and so on).

Petitions by the urban population against abuse of power and mismanagement by office holders were submitted against officials holding a very wide range of posts, such as the *mutasarrıf, kaymakam, müdür, mufti, muhasebeci, tapu* and *yoklama* officials, and *waqf* officials. Beyond doubt, the function generating the greatest number of complaints in Gaza and Jaffa was their respective *kaymakam*, the governor of the sub-district, *kaza*, under the reformed administrative system. This should come as no surprise since this was the most senior official most subjects had dealings with in towns such as Gaza and Jaffa, and he was thus perceived as the embodiment of Ottoman reformed rule in the provinces. Given the scope of the material involving complaints against officials, only a few representative examples are presented here.

For example, a group of people from Jaffa complained that on various occasions the *kaymakam* Mustafa Hikmet Efendi al-Qanawati mistreated them, took bribes, imposed arbitrary fines and the like. The petitioners enumerate several instances in which the *kaymakam* violated their rights, interfered with the commercial activity in the town and misused his power.[40] No concrete evidence is cited by the petitioners, which might suggest that the *kaymakam* was connected or on good terms with a rival group within the town.

Petitions against *kaymakams* were also submitted in general cases of slander. For instance, a certain "Nathan the German" applied to the *Sadaret* with a request to take the *kaymakam* of Gaza to court for insulting him for no good reason.[41] A similar claim against the *kaymakam* of Gaza was made by Husayn Abu-Khadra', a merchant from Gaza. This complaint was most probably connected to the power struggle among Gaza's elite since he also mentions "the people of the *kaymakam*" as among those who wish him harm.[42] Abu-Khadra' complains that the *kaymakam* acted against him illegally and that he is even contemplating leaving his home town because of his situation and his tarnished reputation. This is, of course, a frequently used threat appearing throughout the Ottoman history of petitioning the ruler.

As indicated, officials such as the accountant of the *mutasarrıflık* of Jerusalem (*muhasebeci*) were also the subject of petitions. Such petitions were more concrete in nature and often involved arguments concerning the government's tax and fiscal policies. For instance, dozens of orchard owners in Jaffa claimed that the decision to take tithe from their land, unlike in the past when they paid only the *vergi* tax, had to do with the corruption and incompetence of this official. Possibly, this policy had to do with the decision not to treat Jaffa's land as *mülk* land (freehold property whose owners possessed the rights of possession and usufruct), but rather as *miri* land (whose occupiers had only the right of usufruct) as part of a larger move to reorganize the registration of land and the tax collection system, while abolishing previously granted illegal exemptions (see Chapter 6 for more details).[43]

As noted, petitions against incumbent local *mufti*s were usually connected to a power struggle within the urban elite, at times also involving the leading Jerusalemite families. This was most probably the case (although we cannot tell for sure from the evidence) for the *hanafi mufti* of Jerusalem, Tahir Efendi al-Husayni (1842–1908), who was accused of helping his friends and relatives be awarded the *iltizam* of the village of Resim [?][44] in the *kaza* of Gaza where he owned lands by striking a deal with the local *muhtar*.[45] Istanbul wrote to Jerusalem that people such as the *mufti* should not be involved in *iltizam*s due to their official position.[46] This case, at any rate, shows the extent to which the elite of Jerusalem extended its influence all over the entire *mutasarrıflık* of Jerusalem and even beyond.

At times, several officials were accused of jointly breaking the law. For example, a petition by an unknown person(s) sent from Jaffa accused the *kaymakam*, *mufti* and registration clerk of manipulating conscription lists by taking names of individuals off the register of recruits in return for bribes from village *muhtar*s.[47] As is well-known, the issue of conscription was one of the most pressing political and social concerns in Palestine at the time and it led to a great deal of squabbling, an issue in part revealed by this petition.

In another interesting such case in Gaza, 'Abd al-Hayy al-Husayni accused the *kaymakam* and the *kaza* accountant of sending poor quality grain to the Hejaz "for personal interest" even though they knew that it would be rejected there. The grains were allegedly sold cheaply and the damage to state coffers was huge.[48] Possibly, this petition was related to the *kaymakam*'s quarrel with the *mufti* of Gaza, the brother of 'Abd al-Hayy, at the time. The grain was probably needed for the pilgrimage, which gives the petition extra weight and importance.

Some petitions of a general nature submitted by the urban population were actually a manifestation of discontent with officials serving in the Ottoman administration and a demand to replace them. Usually, petitions

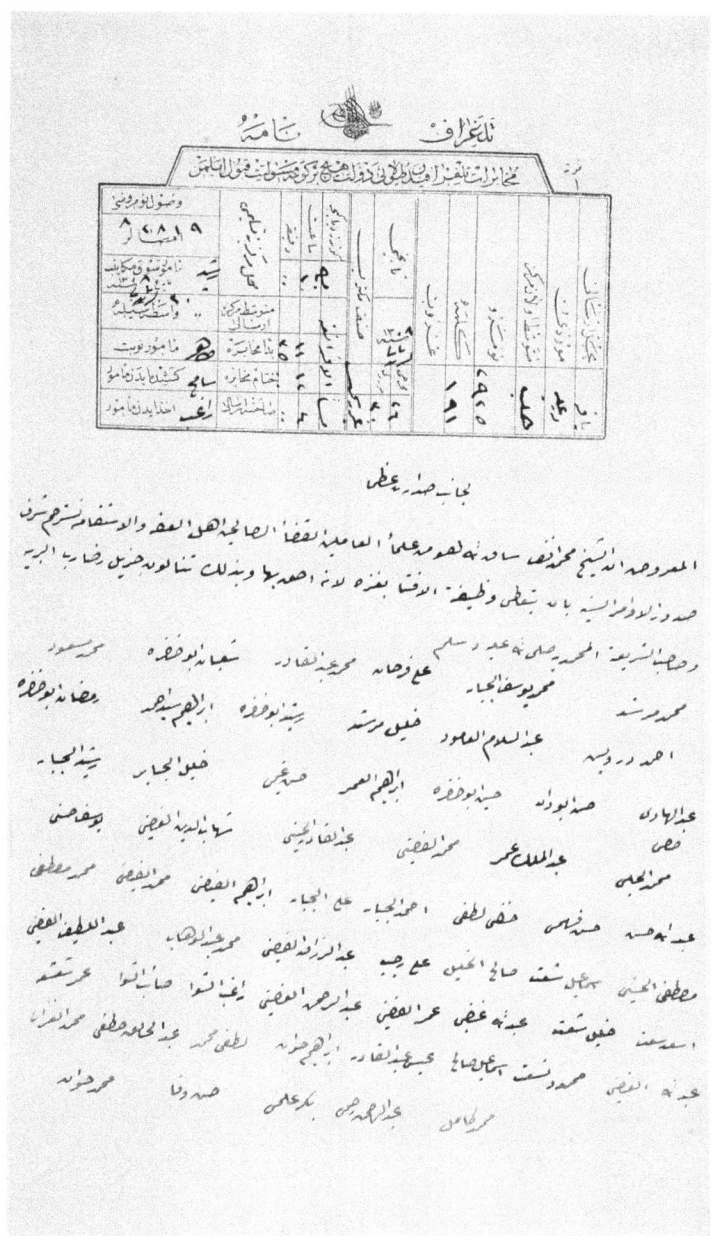

Document 3 A Collective "Invited" Petition from Gaza in support of nominating Muhammad Saqallah to the Post of *Mufti*
Source: BOA. HR. TO., 398/53, 26 Teşrinisani 1308 [8 December 1892], p. 1

Document 4   A Pardon Request by the Former *Mufti* of Gaza, his Brother, and Son

Source: BOA. Y PRK. AZJ., 40/89, 22 Haziran 1316 [5 July 1900], p. 1

Source: BOA. Y PRK. AZJ., 40/89, 22 Haziran 1316 [5 July 1900], p. 2

of this kind were signed by a group of unidentified people. For instance, "the poor people" of Jaffa asked the *Sadaret* to investigate the behavior of the *kaymakam* of Jaffa and the head of the *nizamiye* court, who were accused of attacking the people of the town and seizing their property. The details of one of these attacks allegedly even appeared in the press.[49] A similar petition was sent from Jaffa to protest the decision to appoint Ihsan Bey, the *kaymakam* of Gaza, to Jaffa's sub-district for a second term. The reasons mentioned were his past record, the controversies he stirred up in Gaza, and his lack of capability and training. Opposition was also expressed to sending an official called 'Ali Bey to Gaza to replace Ihsan Bey for similar reasons and his alleged illiteracy.[50]

Petitions dealing with Internal Family Matters

Familial quarrels where the parties involved, or at least one of them, considered it beneficial to appeal to Istanbul are especially telling. The issues prompting these quarrels were related to many of the topics discussed in this chapter, but the act of asking Istanbul to intervene in private disagreements in which local authorities had been unsuccessfully involved nevertheless deserves attention.[51]

For example, in one intriguing case from Gaza, Mustafa, Husayn and Sh'aban Abu-Khadra' petitioned the *Sadaret* against their brother Muhammad with whom they had an argument over the inheritance of their late father, al-Hajj Hasan Abu-Khadra'.[52] They claimed that the brother tried to disinherit them from property belonging to their father, whom it was understood had several wives. The brother, with the encouragement of the sons of the former *mufti*, allegedly filed fake complaints against the petitioners and their uncle Khalil Efendi Abu-Khadra'.[53] An appeal to the local court to divide the inheritance according to Muslim law was apparently unsuccessful. The brothers thus asked for an order which would protect their rights according to Islamic law and prevent their relative from depriving them of their inheritance.[54]

In another case involving a member of the Abu-Khadra' family from Gaza, Rashid Abu-Khadra' submitted dozens of petitions to various Ottoman offices with complaints against his relatives in Gaza, Hasan Abu-Khadra', his father, and his uncle who all are accused of an unspecified forgery in collaboration with "corrupt court officials."[55] In one of his telegraphs, Abu-Khadra' even claims that he was jailed.[56] It is worth noting that, a few years earlier, the *mutasarrif* of Jerusalem wrote to *Şûra-yı Devlet*, following a request to look into petitions it received, that Rashid Abu-Khadra' "was one of a group of people who submitted calumnious petitions constantly against officials," in this specific case against the *kaymakam* of Gaza at the time, a certain Lutfi Paşa.[57] Aside from this particular instance, Ibrahim Lutfi Paşa was indeed arrested in 1902 for taking bribes.[58]

Serial Petitioners

There were cases in which individual urbanites bombarded the system with numerous petitions, at times regarding one specific case, but in other instances regarding various different issues, large and small, taking advantage of the ease of sending a petition at the time.[59] Serial petitioning was a new phenomenon that may have been facilitated by the advent of mail and telegraph services. The flooding of the system with petitions by specific individuals who did not get along with officials and office holders led to significant manifestations of impatience towards the petitioners on the part of officials who handled these complaints.

One such serial petitioner was Rashid Abu-Khadra', discussed above, who submitted numerous petitions, in what seems an obsessive manner, against his arrest.[60] No wonder the *mutasarrif* of Jerusalem, when asked to deal with Abu-Khadra's petition, complained that "there was no law against serial petitioners who make false accusations, sign their name on every petition they come across, and overload the system while increasing corruption."[61]

Another person who submitted numerous petitions and was apparently involved in numerous fights and struggles, to the dismay of the local Ottoman authorities, was the Jewish Maghrebi entrepreneur from Jaffa, Yosef Moyal.[62] His petitions counter the overly rosy depiction often found in the literature of the ways in which Palestine's urban elite of different faiths at the time got along or shared a common mission. Moyal was involved in various commercial activities, served as an agent of Iran in Jaffa (*kargozar*), and helped various Jewish enterprises and initiatives. At the beginning of 1891, Moyal submitted a petition in French to the Grand Vizier against the *kaymakam* of Jaffa whom he claimed wanted illegally to take over his lands. Moyal asked Istanbul to order Jerusalem to investigate the matter and to compel the *kaymakam* to pay for the legal expenses.[63]

A few years later, Moyal applied to Istanbul against the *kaymakam* of Gaza and the head of the finance office in the sub-district of Gaza who taxed him in grains valued at over 400 liras, claiming that he owed *vergi* tax for a plot of land he rented, even though Moyal denied the allegation and said he had no debt whatsoever.[64]

In 1899, Moyal was apparently involved in a business argument with several persons that deteriorated into a fight. He was arrested by the order of the *naib* of Jaffa, Derviş Efendi, who at the time was substituting for the indisposed *kaymakam*. Moyal submitted a petition to Istanbul that he

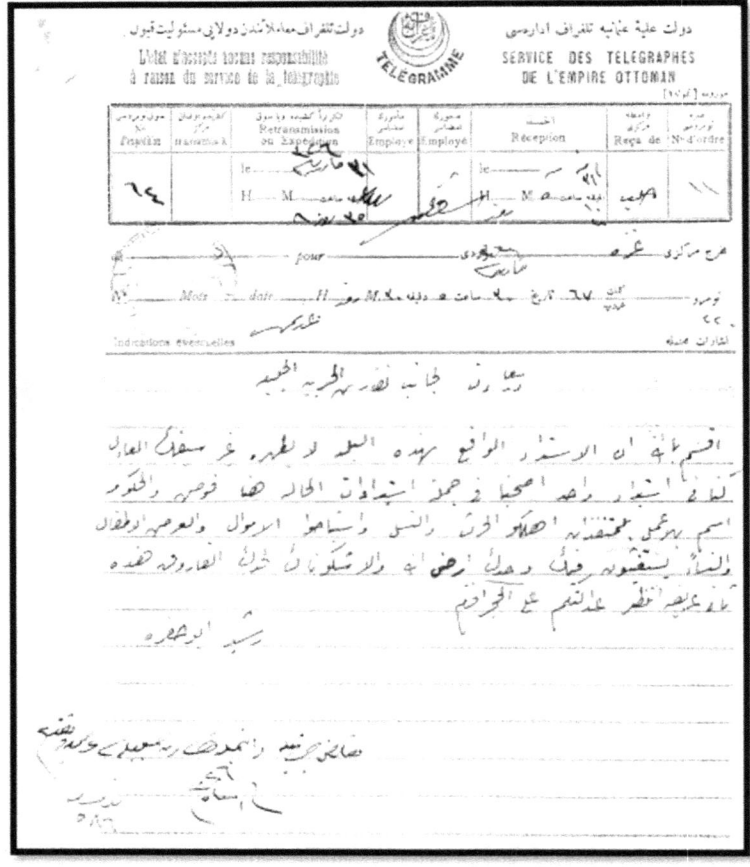

Document 5   A Petition by the "Serial Petitioner" Rashid Abu-Khadraʾ from Gaza
Source: BOA. DH. MUİ., 87–1/37, 20 Mart 1326 [2 April 1910]

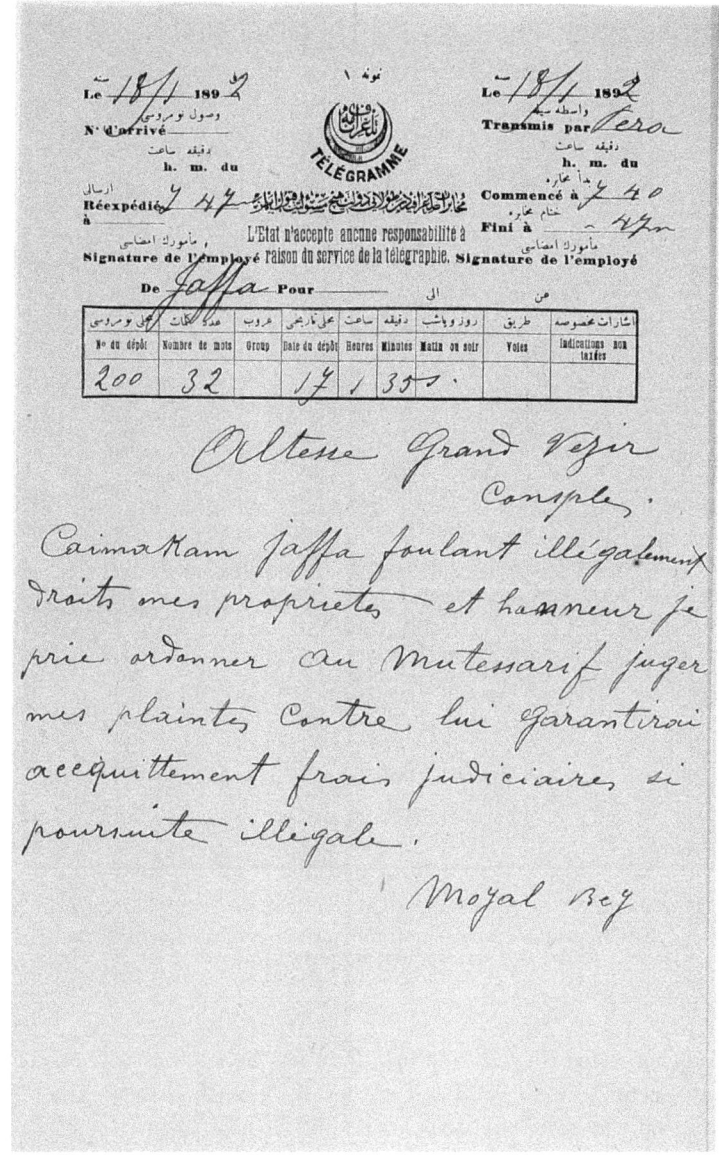

Document 6 A Petition in French by the Jewish Entrepreneur Yosef Moyal from Jaffa against the *Kaymakam* of the *Kaza* of Jaffa
Source: BOA. HR. TO., 536/77, 18 January 1892

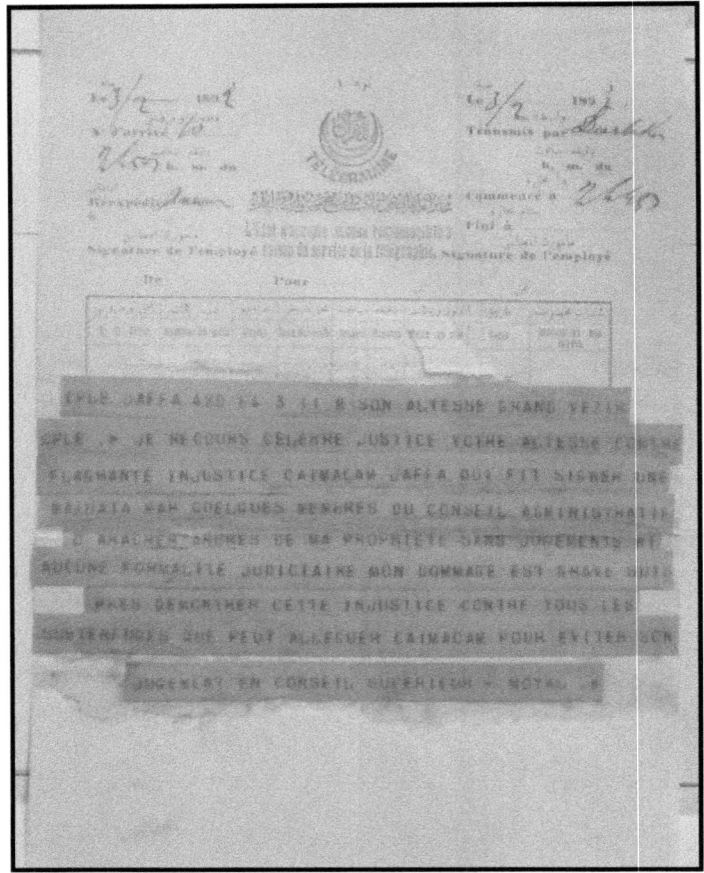

Document 7   A Printed Petition in French by the Jewish Entrepreneur
Yosef Moyal from Jaffa against the *Kaymakam* of the *Kaza* of Jaffa
Source: BOA. HR. TO., 536/79, 3 February 1892

had been arrested illegally and held for a few days in custody. His complaint was found to be valid and as a result Derviş Efendi was tried by a special court for state officials.[65]

Yet, Moyal's constant petitions led the Ottoman authorities to realize that his complaints could not be handled effectively in the sub-district of Jaffa and needed to be transferred elsewhere. In a case involving ownership of an orchard in Jaffa, Moyal had a violent dispute with a person named

Beshara Tasu [?], and submitted several petitions to Istanbul. A trial failed to resolve the issues between the parties, which led Moyal to petition for the replacement of the judge. It was apparently explained to him that there was no basis for his demand and that, in order to appoint a new judge, certain procedures had to be followed. Since it was felt that Moyal would continue sending petitions until there was a new trial and since his complaints against the judicial authorities were biasing the case, the Ministry of the Interior, based on the recommendations of an investigative committee, asked the Ministry of Justice to relocate the trial from Jaffa.[66]

In another case showing the wide spectrum of topics involving Moyal, he appealed to Istanbul to allow him to complete a land transaction in the *kaza* of Gaza where he had been awarded a tender from the Agricultural Bank. According to the correspondence, Moyal claimed that he was an Ottoman citizen and that there was no basis for preventing him from buying the land. The decision of the Council of Ministries in Istanbul was to allow him to complete the transaction, if he promised not to settle foreign Jews on this land.[67]

Moyal himself, not surprisingly, was the subject of numerous petitions by his rivals who also took advantage of the institution of petitioning for redress. In one particularly interesting case, a person named al-Hajj 'Ali Haykal Efendi,[68] a member of Jaffa's administrative council, applied to the *Sadaret* against Moyal, arguing that Moyal insulted him as well as other officials and subjects. He further accused Moyal of collaborating with a person named Istiryadi Efendi (Asteriadis), "a member of the administrative council of Jerusalem," to turn *miri* lands which Moyal bought near Jaffa into lands with *mülk* status (see further details in Chapter 7).[69]

Finally, the same Beshara with whom Moyal had a fight appealed several times to Istanbul against Moyal, arguing that even though he had a court order against Moyal, the latter took over an orchard which belonged to him whereas another part of the orchard was occupied by the local police force (*Zabtiye*).[70]

Demands to Investigate Crimes

Occasionally, urban petitioners contacted Istanbul in criminal cases when they thought there had been a miscarriage of justice. They complained about the local authorities' treatment of the case, their lack of competence, indifference, or inability to solve the crime and bring the offenders to trial. The normal channel for such complaints was naturally the *nizamiye* courts which dealt with crimes and their appeal system.

For instance, 'Abd al-Qadir al-Dabbagh from Jaffa petitioned the *Sadaret* in 1876 to order the authorities in Jerusalem to make an effort to find the murderers of his son, who was killed in the street by a group of people. The local authorities, he claimed, fell short of completing the investigation, a situation which he argued damaged the government's stature in the eyes of the public and weakened public security.[71]

In another case, Ahmad Mustafa Khatab, a merchant from Gaza residing in Egypt complained to the *Sadaret* that his son Muhammad was murdered in Gaza by a person with whom he worked named Muhammad Ibn al-Hajj Husayn al-Ghad. The father demanded that the governors of the Provinces of Syria and Jerusalem make sure the offender who was arrested received the punishment he deserved (See appendix 8).[72]

The third case is a petition to the *Sadaret* by Muhammad Saqallah[73] an *'alim* from Gaza (not to be confused with his relative the *mufti* who bore the same name) whose son Sa'id was murdered on the way to the town. The father claimed that ten people attacked his son, robbed him, and then murdered him. Among the offenders were four guards from the region and six more people. All of them, aside from one named Muhammad Shahin, were arrested. The father requested Istanbul to order the District of Jerusalem and the public prosecutor to find this person, arrest him and bring him to trial, and to prevent the release of the other nine offenders.[74] Jerusalem answered the *Sadaret* that 12 people were involved and convicted, three in absentia, but there was still an ongoing appeal process in court.[75]

Miscellaneous Personal Requests

There are, at times, personal petitions dealing with odd requests which cannot be categorized under any specific heading. For example, a Jewish person from Jaffa asked to be allowed to take exams to become a physician, arguing that he did not have time to go to medical school and that he was not able to take the required exams on time. The Ministry of the Interior referred the matter to the Ministry of Health. We can assume by the sound of the person's name, Mughanzivich [?] that he was an immigrant from Eastern Europe and, based on the nature of his request, that most likely he had medical experience from abroad and only needed the Ottoman certificate to practice medicine in Jaffa.[76]

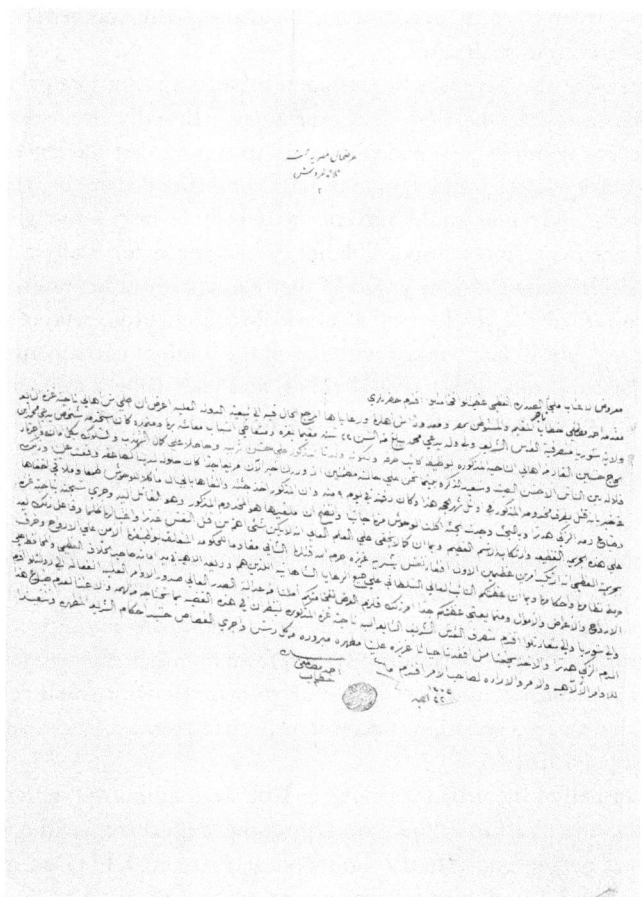

Document 8   A Petition by a Father whose Son was murdered to bring the
Perpetrators to Justice
Source: BOA. HR. TO., 391/95, 22 Zilhicce 1304 [21 September 1886]

Petitions by the Urban Population against Foreign Activity

The urban population in Palestine at times petitioned against foreign
activity. In one interesting case, the people of one neighborhood in
Jerusalem complained about several Jewish women in their neighborhood
whose conduct was out of place. It is extremely likely that these were
newly arrived immigrants who were not familiar with the local customs
and norms. Istanbul ordered the District of Jerusalem to make an effort

to remove them from the neighborhood and find them another place, "as was the custom in such cases."[77]

There were also petitions by Ottoman subjects against foreigners who won bids in tenders held by the government, allegedly in an unlawful manner. For example, a person who failed to be awarded the tender for a certain water project in the region of Jaffa complained that changes were made in the bid so he would lose the contract in favor of a foreigner. He blamed the department responsible for public works for undermining a former decision by the *Şûra-yı Devlet* that had approved his project. The person awarded the tender was a certain Mr. Lombardo, who offered a better price, but in fact worked with one of the original participants. This sleight of hand took place several times, and each time a foreigner was awarded the contract when a new tender was held.[78]

Conclusion

As seen throughout this chapter, the urban population sent petitions to Istanbul about numerous subjects and concerns. The multiplicity of subjects and the rise in the number of petitions are indicative of the transformation of the petitioning system from an institution whose main goal was to address injustices and deal with personal or small community issues, to an institution concomitantly characterized by considerable political participation.

About half of the urban petitions in Jaffa were submitted individually while the other half took the form of group petitions concerning a large number of people who shared a common interest or goal. In Gaza, most of the petitions I found were collective petitions and there are considerably fewer individual petitions. Gaza was immersed in internal power struggles between rival groups. As a result, Jaffa petitions dealt with a much broader range of subjects. The economic boom in Jaffa during this period, the economic activities and infrastructure projects initiated there, and the diversity of the population who resided in and around the city all contributed to the wide array of petitions sent from Jaffa and to the personal nature of so many of them. This might indicate a greater process of individualization in Jaffa than in Gaza (see also the following chapters).

The urban petitions are striking in that the institution of petitioning was, at times, used for purposes which were beyond the customary confines of this institution as we know it, such as promoting the interests of a certain town or group of people, not necessarily against the backdrop of misdeeds or oppression. As will be seen, it was also used for asking for concessions and permission and for putting pressure on official institutions to receive them.

CHAPTER 4

PETITIONS BY THE RURAL POPULATION AND THE BEDOUINS

"When peasants act alone, it is generally through foot-dragging, dissimulation, or surreptitious harassment of the powerful. When they act collectively, an outside agent of some kind is almost always present."[1]

Introduction

This chapter focuses on petitions concerning the two main groups living in the peripheral hinterland of Palestine: peasants and Bedouins. It discusses petitions submitted by these two groups, their uniqueness, advantages and limitations, as well as petitions submitted by others concerning the rural population, such as petitions against Bedouin activity. Because these two marginal groups, which demographically constituted the majority of Palestine's population at the end of the nineteenth century, had a very limited tradition of writing and documenting their activities, it is much more difficult to research and learn about their aspirations, whereabouts, concerns and deeds from first-hand accounts than those of the more educated urban population, which had closer contacts with centers of government and rule and left a variety of written evidence behind.[2] Not surprisingly, peasants and Bedouins are often considered to be on the sidelines of events, and secondary players in a game whose rules were dictated from the outside or above, particularly in an area such as Palestine with its turbulent history in the modern era.[3] However, as Joel Beinin writes with regard to the Tanzimat reforms, "subalterns resisted or evaded aspects of the reforms that extended the reach of the Ottoman state, its European allies, and their administrative, economic, and cultural practices."[4]

Moreover, these two populations themselves are often cast in the literature as two mutually exclusive groups who were involved in constant squabbles and whose interests were at odds. Research in the last decades, however, has shown that the situation in this regard is much more complex than has been portrayed, and that these two groups were intertwined in dynamic relationships of both cooperation and conflict.[5] In addition, splinter groups within the Bedouin population gradually went through a process of sedentarization and, in fact, did not differ substantially from the sedentary population in their region. Thus, the demarcation between the sedentary population and semi-Bedouin groups is not straightforward.

Demographic Background

The demographics of the rural population of Palestine in the late Ottoman era still elicit academic debate. Overall, Palestine was not very heavily populated, but the distribution of the population and its density varied greatly. The most populated areas were the hilly and mountainous regions in the center and north of the country, where hundreds of small agricultural villages were located. The inhabitants of these villages cultivated most of the arable land in their vicinity, which was suitable for traditional modes of agriculture. By contrast, most of the lower valleys and coastal plains were not densely populated, with the exception of the southern coastal plain to the north-east of Gaza, which was populated by dozens of villages and was heavily used for grain farming (see Map 3).[6] Historically, these lands often comprised sand dunes, fallow land and swamps, and were less suitable for traditional agriculture – a situation that did not change until the second half of the nineteenth century (for instance, see the large area of dunes near the Mediterranean Sea, between Jaffa and Gaza, in Maps 2 and 3).[7] These regions were also more vulnerable to Bedouin incursions and were considered unsafe, a fact that contributed to their depopulation.

Starting in the early 1840s, when the Empire regained control over Palestine after almost a decade of Egyptian occupation, it gradually subdued all the local warlords operating in various parts of the country, especially in the mountainous regions of Galilee and central Palestine, a process that took about two decades to complete fully. This effort was motivated by the Empire's objective to strengthen central control over the hinterland and introduce measures of centralization in running the province's affairs. It was part and parcel of the larger goals of the reforms in the Empire at that time.

The improved security conditions, together with the pressure created by the population increase, led to a slow process of repopulation in some of the coastal and lowland regions, often by establishing "daughter villages" at the foot of the hills where the "mother" villages were located.[8] Concomitantly, the Ottoman Land Law of 1858 made land a transferable commodity and enabled private individuals to register the right of usufruct (*tasarruf*) over land. This led to an accelerated commercialization of land and the development of a land market in Palestine. It also contributed to the process of integrating the Empire, including its Arab provinces, into the global capitalist system of the time. Consequently, many plots of land in the relatively less populated coastal plains and lowlands were acquired by a group of absentee landowners,[9] both locals who lived in the urban centers of Palestine and the Levant, and occasionally also European citizens and institutes.[10] At times, this process was carried out in underhanded ways at the expense of the indebted villagers, who became sharecroppers on land they had formerly held, a process which is well-documented in the literature but very rarely based on first-hand accounts by the subaltern population.[11]

The historical-geographer Yehoshua Ben-Arieh estimates that, in the late 1870s, the total population of Palestine stood at 350,000 sedentary inhabitants in addition to some 20,000 to 30,000 semi-sedentary Bedouins. The bulk of the rural population, the majority of Palestine's population at the time, lived in roughly 700 villages of various sizes spread throughout the country.[12] The population of the *kaza*s of Jaffa and Gaza in the early 1870s is estimated by Ben-Arieh at 40,742 in the former (of which 13,500 resided in towns and the remainder inhabited the rural region) and 55,454 in the latter (of which 16,500 resided in the town of Gaza and the remainder inhabited the rural area), thus totaling 96,196 persons (see Maps 2 and 3).[13]

The villages were headed by elected *muhtar*s who served as the official representatives of the Ottoman bureaucracy in the provinces, despite being at the lowest junior rank. For the most part, the *muhtar*s came from families that controlled village life and had greater financial-administrative clout. Some villages had more than one *muhtar*, a fact which reflected the size of the village and its social divisions. Semi-sedentary Bedouin groups were also asked to elect *muhtar*s.

Voices of the Rural Population

It is often claimed that the rural population did its best to avoid contact with governmental representatives because it feared taxation, conscription, retribution and similar acts by government representatives, and thus made efforts to run its own affairs as much as possible and settle its internal disputes and strife alone.[14] To a certain extent, the petitions contradict this assertion and reveal a wealth of information about Palestine's illiterate rural population, which has received insufficient scholarly attention. However, despite the potential of this untapped source, it is first worth inquiring into its value, given that these individuals could not write petitions alone.

As seen, some researchers view the whole genre of petitions to the ruler as no more than literary works which are informative as to the rules of petition writing and the discourse authorized by the state and the rulers, rather than as reliable historical texts with authentic information. When it comes to the illiterate subaltern populations, the situation is obviously even more complicated.[15] Others, however, such as Chalcraft, who wrote about petitions submitted by Egyptian peasants to the Khedive in Cairo in the 1860s and 1870s, adopt a more positive approach:

> Social interests expressed were not preconstituted in some authentic peasant space. However [...] although elite languages helped constitute even the nature of the demands lodged by peasants, these languages were simultaneously filled out, colored, and defined by the concrete projects of peasants themselves. The encounter between the petitioner and ruler, although heavily asymmetrical, was also dialogic in that peasants manipulated, contested, and partially redefined official terms. Collaboration with petition writers was a part of this inevitably "fallen" construction, not simply an inauthentic and repressive new layer of representation.[16]

Chalcraft adds that the Egyptian peasants:

> [E]voke not passivity, silent subversion, or outright revolution but, surprisingly, sophisticated engagement and negotiations with state

practice and discourse. Peasant discourse, constructed in collaboration with professional petition writers, was not tradition-bound, groveling, or immature; nor was it authentic, nationalist, and revolutionary. [. . .] Instead of the complete erasure implied in the claim that the "subaltern cannot speak," peasants arguably did convey elements of their moral economy through their petitions, especially by manipulating the meaning of and adding context to officially sanctioned discourse.[17]

The petitions by the rural population discussed here were also clearly written by professional petition-writers who adhered to semantic conventions, including the specific jargon which was authorized and accepted by the Ottoman bureaucracy in the framework of the petitioning system. In most cases, the petitioners did not even have the basic skills to review the contents of the petition independently, a fact which curtailed their ability to present their case in a full and free manner. Moreover, as suggested by the quote at the beginning of this chapter, some petitions were backed by interested parties and were initiated by people who sought to promote their own agendas or those of the group they represented. Hence, there is always a likelihood that the rural population was corralled by powerful urbanites (whose influence on the rural areas of Palestine grew tremendously during this period) or dominant rural notables to send petitions and did not necessarily send them on its own initiative in a way that represented its independent self-interests and concerns.[18]

These reservations notwithstanding, the rural petitions discussed here still contain the kernel of an "authentic" narrative that can yield important information. First, in the period discussed here, unlike most previous periods, there are abundant sources available to historians such as newspapers, official documents, memoirs, diaries, maps, pictures and the like. Thus, our ability as historians to confirm/deny some of the facts in the petitions through external sources can go a long way towards historicizing their content. Second, as opposed to khedivial Egypt in the 1860s which was the focus of Chalcraft's work, the Ottoman system was less strict and oppressive. It is widely acknowledged that the rural population could submit petitions directly to Istanbul without being punished for their wording or content, and without forms of censorship other than those required by the rules of petitioning. Third, many of the petitions discussed here were, in fact, prompted by centralization measures and reforms implemented by the state that undermined long-standing practices and customs (see Chapter 6). Fourth, the fact that many petitions were sent by telegraph forced the petitioners to get to the point immediately. Such petitions were thus probably less formulaic and closer to "reality," as experienced by the petitioners. Other than the services of the professional petition-writers who helped put the petition on paper, no other intermediary was needed. All this suggests that the rural petitions in this period were much more than simple formulaic literary compositions.

The Concerns of the Sedentary Rural Population

One of the most striking features concerning the scope and nature of the petitions submitted by the rural population, as compared with petitions submitted by urbanites, is the limited nature of the topics they discuss. The rural population submitted very few personal petitions or requests, as can be seen from the number of signatures on the petitions. For the most part, it was the *muhtar* or *muhtar*s of the villages who signed petitions in the name of their communities, at times with other leading public personalities such as the *imam* or *khatib* of the village. Thus, the bulk of the rural petitions were collective, in that they were submitted by representatives of any number of villagers and villages.

The vast majority of the petitions by the rural population deal with disproportionate or exorbitant taxes, both the *öşr* (tithe) and the *vergi*, the former appearing more as a problem in the region of Jaffa, the latter preoccupying the villagers in the sub-district of Gaza, as can be seen in the following example which was sent by villagers in the region of Gaza to the Grand Vizier (see Appendix 4):[19]

> Presented to you are the dutiful prayers of your servants, the people of the villages of the sub-district of Gaza which belongs to the District of Jerusalem, who are weak and poor and suffer a great injustice due to the *vergi* tax imposed annually on our land. Because of the exaggerated value of the *vergi* tax, and according to the just orders issued to abolish injustices imposed on every exploited person, and with the hope of obtaining the mercy of the exalted state, we ask you to abolish the injustice which we suffered and treat us comparably to others in our situation and to our neighbors.[20]

A related claim which often appears in petitions dealing with the land taxes levied on the rural population concerns the methods used to assess and collect the taxes. Complaints were filed for graft and extortion against the tax collectors, as well as Ottoman officials who supervised the collection process. The villagers complained that members of the urban elite in Jaffa, Gaza and Jerusalem were able to control and manipulate tax collection in the district in their favor because they dominated the district's administrative councils at both the level of the *mutasarrıflık* and the *kaza*. Hence, they were easily appointed *mültazim*s in the district, by taking advantage of the longstanding *iltizam* practice (which officially the Empire had promised to abolish since the Tanzimat). They attempted to extort as much money as possible from the peasants to recover their investments and, at the same time, make a huge profit. In addition, they used their connections with Ottoman officials to put pressure on the farmers to acquiesce to their demands or be subject to fiscal and property sanctions or even physical injury.

For instance, in 1879 the villagers of Sarafand al-ʿAmar, some 15 kilometers south-east of Jaffa, petitioned the Grand Vizier to reduce the rate of the *öşr* tax they were told to pay by the tax collector for *waqf* land they farmed (see Appendix 1):

In 1292 [1875/6], after an imperial order concerning the collection of tithe from our village had fixed the sum at 20,000 *kuruş*, and even though [the land of] the village is part of the endowments which are administered by the state [*evkaf-ı mazbuta*],[21] a member of the *meclis-i temyiz* in Jerusalem, Nakibzade Rabah Efendi [al-Husayni],[22] claimed that he had purchased [the collection of the tithe of] our village from the hands of the administrator [*mütevelli*] of the endowment of Sinan Paşa,[23] peace be upon him. Based on his claim, the District of Jerusalem granted him the collection of tithe [from our lands]. Despite this decision, the above-mentioned person was not satisfied and collected another tithe from your servants such that the total sum that is taken from us has now reached a fifth [of our income]. Because this individual is from amongst the influential people, and his relatives and friends serve in governmental offices, each time that we submitted a petition about him to the district [of Jerusalem, they] hid [the petition]. In addition they sent the gendarmerie after us to chase us away from the city.[24]

Regional Cooperation among the Rural Population

As Gabriel Baer has pointed out, there were considerable differences in urban-rural relationships across regions in Ottoman Syria and Palestine, a fact which makes it difficult for historians to make broad generalizations about them.[25] In general, however, the bureaucratic, social and economic processes taking place in Palestine in the second half of the nineteenth century were accompanied by a strengthening of the connections between the cities and their hinterlands. In the words of Michelle Campos:

> Palestine was very much a part of Ottoman administrative reforms as well as of the economic trends of the nineteenth century—the commercialization of agriculture, the incorporation of province and empire into the world economy, the rise of coastal trade, and the commoditization of land. These economic changes precipitated several important social developments, namely, the emergence of a large landowning class with strong patronage and other ties to rural hinterlands and the rise of minority merchant communities in the cities.[26]

As far as the regional aspects of the relationships among the rural populations of Palestine in the nineteenth century are concerned, these are usually discussed within the framework of the Qays/Yaman division which cut across Palestinian society, especially in the mountain region of central Palestine, and brought together urbanites, villagers, Bedouins and even people of different religious beliefs.[27] Notwithstanding this division, which had lost much of its importance in the final decades of the nineteenth century and a priori had less influence on Palestine's coastal region,[28] there is evidence that regional connections and cooperation existed among the Arab rural population, a topic that has received only scant attention in research. These regional ties were not very intense and did not create a close-knit socio-economic network, but nevertheless deserve attention.

The rural population was not monolithic. Rather, it was divided along several lines, notably semi-sedentary Bedouins and the sedentary population, landowners and tenants, relative newcomers and villagers whose forefathers had settled the land many generations earlier, and villagers originally from Egypt as opposed to villagers who migrated within Palestine itself. Moreover, internal conflicts were common among the rural population, primarily over resources such as land, grazing and water.[29]

Despite the existence of these internal divisions and sources of tension, several factors contributed to bringing together the rural population in the region, and possibly even led to the development of a shared sense of regional identity. Some of these factors were new, whereas others had existed before, but were ascribed new meanings. For example, revering notables, pilgrimages to holy places and marriages between villagers from different localities were not necessarily new phenomena. However, there are indications that these were more common in the second half of the nineteenth century given the better security conditions, the improved means of transportation, the development of regional markets as a result of enhanced economic activity and similar developments. All these extended the villagers' scope of interactions with their peers beyond the immediate locality where they lived, as well as with the population of the towns in the region. Such preexisting factors were incorporated into other new manifestations of regionalism.

In this regard, it is important to remember that regional identity was often one of several identities concomitantly held by Palestine's Arabic-speaking population at the end of the Ottoman period (Ottoman, Muslim or Christian, regional, local, familial and, at times, places of origin outside of Palestine).[30] To a large extent, these identities overlapped and complemented rather than contradicted each other.[31]

Regional connections between villages were manifested in joint petitions to Istanbul about common issues and problems, a feature which was found more frequently in the *kaza* of Gaza than in Jaffa. At times, representatives of several villages or more were associated in a joint petition. The specifics of these collective petitions may have been worked out in the major towns in the region where the *muhtar*s of the villages often met, perhaps in coffee houses in these towns where they spent considerable time[32] discussing administrative, bureaucratic and fiscal matters involving the local authorities. Hence, the *muhtar*s of a varying number of villages came together and submitted petitions through mail or by telegraph about issues affecting them all, such as the evaluation of the *vergi* tax.[33]

Pilgrimages to local shrines and holy graves revered by the local population were other important preexisting nuclei of identification.[34] In the city of Gaza, for instance, there were several important holy places, primarily the site believed by locals to be the grave of Sayyid Hashim, the great-grandfather of the Prophet Muhammad. Both a mosque and an Islamic *madrasa* were constructed nearby.[35] The annual celebrations held at Nabi-Rubin, some 15 kilometers south of Jaffa near the Mediterranean shore, and at Nabi-Salih in Ramle attracted large crowds from all over Palestine, but particularly from nearby localities, and were second only to the annual celebrations held in Nabi-Musa near Jericho every spring.[36] The celebrations in Nabi-Rubin lasted several weeks, and included a fair, cultural events and a market.[37] Obviously, this gathering was a major opportunity for socializing and exchanges and for important economic activity. Several other local shrines and holy graves existed in the region and were revered by the local population.[38]

Another major factor which brought the Arab rural population together was the important role played by the towns of Gaza and Jaffa as the economic, administrative, cultural-social and political hubs for their hinterland. The social and economic processes taking place in Palestine in the second half of the nineteenth century, and the emergence of a group of absentee landlords was accompanied by a strengthening and intensifying of the connections between the rural population and the urbanites (i.e., loans to the rural population, penetration of the cash-crop economy to the villages, social and cultural ties). For example, the elite of Jaffa acquired large tracts of land in the town's immediate and more remote vicinity and exerted its influence over the rural population and some of the smaller towns in the region.[39]

In Gaza, as well, several prominent families owned large tracts of land in the sub-district and exerted their influence there, although in comparison with Jaffa their number was much lower. Nevertheless, petitions from Gaza dealing with issues related to the rural population demonstrate the extent to which the rural population was entangled in the competition among the urban elite, as seen in Chapter 3. This elite maintained networks of alliance with leading Bedouin sheikhs and village leaders, including social and cultural ties.[40] Its members used their dominance in the administrative council of the sub-district and the fact that Gaza was far from the Ottoman regional ruling center in Jerusalem to carve out *iltizam*s in the sub-district and benefit economically from their influence.[41] The tithe collection in the Gaza sub-district was also in the hands of several urban *efendi*s who controlled their towns' hinterland and manipulated auctions held in Gaza, the administrative center of the sub-district.[42]

The urban elite's influence over the hinterland of their towns served as a key factor in the process of creating a sense of regional identity among the rural population, although in the coastal region it was not as strong as the one described by Beshara Doumani in his study of Nablus and its hinterland in Jabal Nablus.[43] However, it must be stressed that the same processes which gave rise to the emergence of large absentee landowners who resided in the cities also created new tensions and conflicts between the latter and the rural population over issues such as borders of plots, the registration and status of certain lands, the collection of various land taxes, accumulating debts and the like.

Also to be considered as contributing to regionalism is inclusion in the same administrative entity. The strengthening of the Ottoman hold over Palestine and the gradual influence of the reforms in the second half of the nineteenth century increased the importance of the regional administrative centers such as Gaza and Jaffa, located at the hub of the *kazas* bearing the same names, and promoted common activity among the rural population. Beyond the conscious influence of being part of the same administrative entity, a feature whose importance should not be underestimated, this inclusiveness at a time when the Ottoman administration was being reformed and transformed often necessitated cooperation between the villages vis-à-vis the Ottoman authorities on issues such as taxes, conscription and development plans. This, among other things, found its expression in the submission of joint petitions to Istanbul by the villages.

Another factor was the prestige and the influence of prominent individuals who resided in the region and were revered by the local population. For example, one such person was a sheikh from the village of Qatra, who was known as an important religious authority in the region. His funeral in 1886 was attended by many villagers from the vicinity and apparently also included a Sufi ceremony. Consider the following quote by Haim Hissin, a young colonist from the nearby colony of Gedera:

A while ago I had the opportunity to witness how the Arabs bury an important person. Such a large ceremony is rarely attended by a European. In Qatra lived an old respected man, a member of a family considered holy by the Arabs. He had much authority among the villagers, who considered him a holy man. In all the towns and villages in the area, the most common oath was "I swear in the name of al-Qatrawi."[44] Arabs came to him from faraway places to settle disputes, get advice and blessings. [...] It was not long before processions started to come to Qatra from different places. From every village a solemn delegation arrived. The flag of every village was carried at the head of the procession, followed by players who drummed and played musical instruments, and at the back marched the elder sheikhs and the most observant men in the village singing dirges.[45]

Other prominent figures included various notables who often mediated in confrontations among the Arabs and between the latter and the proto-Zionist colonists by drawing on their good relationships with both sides.[46]

Marriages between villagers from different localities were yet another manifestation of regional relationships between the villagers in the area.[47] There are indications, however, that some villages refrained from marrying members of other villages who were of Egyptian origin.[48] The phenomenon of inter-village marriages clearly had a history, but one can assume that it was reinforced in the second half the nineteenth century due to the developments discussed earlier and the rapid social and economic changes. Based on an analysis of the Ottoman census of 1905, Johann Büssow, for example, writes about women who married villagers from the village of Qastina in the *kaza* of Gaza that "more than half of them came from other villages in the Gaza region [...] marriages were arranged in connection with social and market relations, which all centered around Gaza. The important markets that were held in the city might have been used to arrange marriages as well as to strike business deals."[49]

Finally, the activities of the Jewish colonies in the region as of the early 1880s, in particular the joint aspects of their policies, often brought the Arab rural population together.[50] Word of mouth about the various clashes which took place from time to time between individual colonies and the Arab population spread rapidly and played a role in crystallizing these inter-village networks. The Jewish influence over the rural population was naturally stronger in regions where Jewish settlement activity was more intensive and where the colonies developed a close-knit network of relationships that influenced their attitudes and policies towards the Arab rural population in their vicinity.[51] In the *kaza* of Gaza, even though Jewish settlement activity at the end of the nineteenth century was rather limited, it is nevertheless mentioned in the villagers' petitions. The villagers demonstrate an awareness of developments taking place in their vicinity, including specific details regarding Jewish activity, which prompted them to make collective demands for equal treatment and rights.[52] Moreover, information concerning clashes between the Arab rural population and the Jewish colonies in their vicinity rapidly spread in the villages and, at times, led to their mobilization to act together against the Jewish colonies in the region.

An example that vividly demonstrates this feature is a joint petition submitted by representatives of dozens of villagers in the *kaza* of Gaza to complain about the activities of the two large Jewish colonies of Rishon le-Zion and Rehovot to their north in the adjacent *kaza* of Jaffa, following a severe clash between the village of Zarnuqa and the guards of Rehovot, known in Zionist historiography as "the Zarnuqa incident" (see Chapter 8, for more details).[53] The petition is written in the name of the villagers of Zarnuqa, but dozens of *muhtar*s from the *kaza* of Gaza and one tribal group from the *kaza* of Jaffa added their seals in an act of solidarity (see Appendix 10). This negative encounter with people considered by the local rural population to be foreigners obviously reinforced the crystallization of a shared identity among the villagers in the region, who defined themselves in opposition to the colonists, the "others." Thus, similar to the petitions concerning the *vergi*, there was a mobilization of village representatives in the name of a common cause within the framework of the *kaza*.[54]

Bedouins and their Activity

Bedouins were parties to three main types of petitions. The first covers petitions that sedentary Bedouin groups, mainly in the sub-district of Jaffa, submitted to Istanbul. These were signed by representatives of the groups such as the sheikhs and leading figures in the name of the whole group. The second type of petition was submitted by the sedentary population to complain about Bedouin activity that damaged crops and property. These were much more common in the sub-district of Gaza, an area which bordered the Negev and the Sinai deserts and was vulnerable to constant encroachment by the Bedouins in the region. The third type was sporadic petitions with no real common denominator between them concerning matters in which Bedouins were involved, either as petitioners or as the subject of the petition. It is worthwhile, however, to examine first the government's official policies towards the Bedouins, which often found its expression in the petitions, directly or indirectly.

Generally speaking, the Ottoman government viewed Bedouin activity in southern Palestine, as elsewhere in the Empire's Arab provinces, in a highly negative light. As part of its centralization measures and efforts to regain control over the provinces and strengthen its rule in the periphery, the government attempted to settle the Bedouins in permanent localities, stop their seasonal roaming and link them to specific lands through registration of landownership.[55] As far as the authorities were concerned, the Bedouins disrupted agricultural activities in settled areas caused damage to crops and property and undermined the collection of taxes for state coffers by reducing crops, disturbing the peace and draining away considerable armed forces.[56] The Ottoman policy concerning the Bedouins was partially dictated by a desire "to bring civilization" to people who were considered savage and disobedient.[57] The establishment of Beersheba at the turn of the century can be perceived as part of this "civilizing mission" vis-à-vis marginal groups in society such as Bedouins.

However, as recent research suggests, the Bedouin population cannot be viewed merely as a constant source of harassment to the sedentary population through its illegal activities, such as highway robbery, occupation of fields, damage to property, acts of violence, collection of protection money and the like. Hence, the frequent claim that they were the major reason for the depopulation of large areas in the plains of Palestine prior to the nineteenth century[58] is considered today by most historians and historical geographers as merely a partial explanation. Rather, the suitability of certain lands for traditional pre-modern agriculture was a significant factor that must also be taken into account.[59] The fact that one of the most densely populated regions in Palestine was the coastal region in the vicinity of Gaza, a region which was close to the desert and did not have natural physical defenses, calls into question the notion that the Bedouins were the major force behind the depopulation of most of Palestine's lowlands prior to the nineteenth century (see Map 3).

The Bedouins, moreover, played an important role in shaping the economic and social fabric of society and maintained complex relationships with its diverse sectors.[60] For instance, Bedouins supplied city dwellers with certain products and economic services which only they could provide (e.g., transportation of goods, provision of meat and wool, protection on the roads) and, in return, enjoyed services which were available only in the towns. At times, the Bedouins were part of local power alignments and participated in struggles between the villagers or joined coalitions headed by leading urban notables. Moreover, some of the Bedouins became sedentary or semi-sedentary and earned their livelihood in basic agricultural farming in addition to grazing.[61] Bedouins also took part alongside the sedentary population in social gatherings and events such as pilgrimages to local shrines, festivities and veneration of sages in their region of residence. Some Bedouins were entangled in urban politics while siding with different rival groups, as can be seen in the petitions.[62]

Petitions against Bedouin Activity

Infrequently, groups of Bedouins from the Sinai and the Negev deserts migrated northwards with their herds in search of new grazing grounds, causing tremendous damage to the fields of the Arab villages and Jewish colonies they encountered on their way, a problem which the Ottoman authorities were well aware of and did their best to eliminate.[63] The villages in the region of Gaza submitted a considerable number of petitions complaining about Bedouin attacks, damage to fields and crops, and takeover of lands.[64] The government's immediate response was usually to send armed reinforcements to deal with the unrest. The picture that arises from the correspondence between Ottoman officials regarding this matter is of a negative occurrence which must be prevented by any means in order to let the rural population continue with its normal life and avoid losses to state coffers. Consider the following quote from a decision by the *Şûra-yı Devlet* concerning the payment of salaries of reinforcements sent to help pacify the tribal groups in the region of Gaza:

> Bedouin tribes such as Tarabin, Tiyaha and others who live in tents in the sub-district of Gaza are busy fighting each other and for a while now they stopped cultivating and plowing their land. These [Bedouins] naturally [*bil-tab'*][65] destroy the district's and the villages' agricultural lands and attack passengers and locals [on the roads].[66]

More generally, however, it took vigorous measures to strengthen the government's hold over southern Palestine, while trying to tie the Bedouins to specific lands. This involved the founding of Beersheba in the early twentieth century as an administrative-bureaucratic center around which the Bedouin tribes were to be settled; the establishment of the border town and new administrative sub-district of 'Awja al-Hafir and al-Hafir, respectively, near the border between the Negev and Sinai; an investment in infrastructure (telegraph lines, bridges, roads, railroads) in this region, whose strategic importance vis-à-vis the frontier with British-ruled Egypt grew with time; a reorganization of the region's administrative units; registration of the tribal land with the *tapu* registrars and collection of taxes from it; and an effort to co-opt the leadership of the Bedouins and strengthen their affiliation with the Ottoman state.[67] Interestingly, similar efforts were carried out in the second half of the nineteenth century in Transjordan and in its southern part only shortly before the turn of the century.[68]

In the region of Jaffa, there were not many petitions complaining about Bedouin activity. One such example, from an earlier period, was submitted by villagers of al-Yahudiyya (al-'Abbasiyya), located some 15 kilometers east of Jaffa. Its people, together with a few "respected individuals," complained that a tribal leader named Mustafa Darwish from the Banu-Hamad seized land the village and the notables had owned legally for 15 years. They wanted the District of Jerusalem to be ordered to intervene to stop the aggression and injustice. Istanbul ordered the governor of Jerusalem to investigate the matter in the administrative council as well as in the *shari'a* court.[69]

Petitions by the Semi-Sedentary Bedouin Population

The petitions from the region of Jaffa which deal with Bedouins are different in nature from those originating from the region of Gaza. Unlike the situation in the south, only several small sedentary Bedouin groups resided in the Jaffa region (see Maps 2 and 3).[70] At times, such as in the case of Arab Abu al-Fadl Bedouin group (al-Sutriyya),[71] located in Khirbat Duran east of the colony of Rehovot, the Bedouins leased agricultural land on a yearly basis.[72] Such splinter Bedouin groups went through a process of sedentarization and cultivated agricultural land. The problem which clearly emerges from their petitions, however, is that they did not possess title deeds for the land where they resided, even though they perceived it as theirs and claimed to have occupied it for many years (*aba 'an cedd*),[73] or that there was some sort of contention and ambiguity over the land's ownership and status. The Bedouins of Khirbat Duran, who according to their claims had been there for many generations, allegedly first became tenants on their own previously held land when it was bought by an Arab landowner from the region. Later, they were asked to leave when the colonists of Rehovot bought it from him and became its legal owners. In their own words, as written by the *arzuhalci*, they state that (see Appendix 3):

Our tribe numbers 32 families comprising approximately 200 people, from amongst the loyal subjects of the exalted state, residing in tents in Khirbat Duran [...]. This tribe, from olden times and from [the time of our] fathers and forefathers, does not know any other land than the above mentioned Khirbat Duran, makes its living from it, and does not have any other place of residence other than this Khirba. Recently, the exalted government sold this farm to certain people from amongst the residents of the state [*watan*] [...]. These servants [the Bedouins] did not express any opposition since the new landowners clearly knew that the farm [*mazra'a*] was cultivated and held by us from olden [times]. They did not express any opposition to us and did not expel us from our [place of] residence or from our farm [...].

[But] as we were in this situation, the farm was suddenly sold to a group of foreign Jews [*Isra'iliyyin*], who came to this land, and possessed capital and had economic means at their disposal. They succeeded in buying this land with the help and support of 'Ali Efendi Haykal, a member of the administrative council of the sub-district [*kaza*] of Jaffa and the chamber of commerce [sic: *muba'i'yat*, should be *mubaya'at*], who is notorious for interventions of this kind.

Later, these rich Jewish buyers, who already had built a few buildings on the land of this Khirba without official permission, with the help of the above mentioned Efendi, were not satisfied with what they had done. They started to chase us away from our place of residence, and to prevent us from cultivating [our crops on] the above mentioned farm, so that only their people would benefit from it. The more we made concessions to them, with the aim that both sides would derive advantages, [the more] they continued to upset and annoy us, and opposed us with stern resistance, in order

to prevent [us from fulfilling] our wishes [. . .] [a]nd the blame for
this damage and the mistreatment we received, can only be attributed to the unacceptable [acts of] the above mentioned Efendi.[74]

Interestingly, the Bedouins of Arab Abu al-Fadl, together with another
group called Tyur were involved a few years later in a dispute with the
nearby Municipality of Ramle over a tract of land they claimed they were
cultivating and the Municipality sold.[75] Apparently, they demanded substitute land and approached religious leaders in Istanbul to help them.
For unknown reasons, Nazim Paşa, the former governor of Syria who was
allegedly in Jerusalem, was asked by the Ministry of the Interior to look
into the matter and reported back about the case.[76]

Similar to the case of the Bedouins of Khirbat Duran, the Bedouins
near Nahr al-'Awja apparently also occupied and farmed the land where
they had resided for many years. They argued that it was *miri* land and
that they paid an annual tax for its use, and furnished receipts as proof
(*senedat*). They resented the confirmation of the land as *waqf* land whose
management was in the hands of two brothers named Salim and 'Abd
al-Hadi and claimed that the latter treated them like tenants and that, as
a result, they were unjustifiably and unlawfully asked to pay much higher
taxes than before (see Appendix 9):

> Due to their voracious greed, they claim that all the land which
> we possess belongs to the *waqf* of the Sufi lodge [*dergâh*] and that
> we are tenants. However, an exalted *ferman* which was issued on
> 17 Rebiyülevvel 1271 [8 December 1854] proves and supports the
> claim that our land is not *waqf* land but rather [regular] *miri* land
> [held by the state].
>
> The 1,500 tribal people who occupy the above mentioned two
> plots of land earn their subsistence solely from this land. We have
> occupied it for many years and we have [always] paid *miri* payments.
> Based on this, if we remain under these oppressive *waqf* adminis-
> trators [*mütevellis*] it will bring us to the verge of extinction, as a
> result of such corruption.[77]

The Bedouins' complaint in this case may have arisen against the
backdrop of a revival of an old *waqf* which was abandoned for many

years, a phenomenon which was common during the reign of Sultan Abdülhamid II. Possibly, the Bedouins, who were used to seeing this land as *miri* land and paid taxes accordingly, were upset that now they had to deal with the *waqf*'s administrators and pay higher taxes, a development which may have been accompanied by misconduct by the latter.

General Petitions concerning Bedouins

The third category involving Bedouins consists of various petitions that Bedouins submitted, or in which they are the subject of the petition. Although there is no direct connection between these petitions their content reveals important information about the Bedouins' modes of behavior and their role in society. They demonstrate the extent to which the Bedouins were integrated in society, as well as their recourse to the institution of petitioning to Istanbul despite their inability to read and write, the limited resources at their disposal and their lack of social and political capital.

For instance, the tribe of Tarabin, which "resided in tents in the district of Gaza," petitioned against the attitude of Gaza's *kaymakam* and the local government's treatment of the tribe. It pleaded with Istanbul to send an officer to investigate their claims. This trust in the government on the part of the Bedouins seems, in a way, to contradict the well-established stereotype of Ottoman enmity towards the Bedouins.[78]

In a second interesting case involving Bedouins, a person named Ibrahim Abu-Rabah, a famous resident of Jaffa, allegedly assembled followers in a location outside Jaffa and committed various illegal activities.[79] Among his followers were villagers and "Bedouins who resided in tents."[80] The issue at stake was most probably Abu-Rabah's activity in the *Khalawatiyya* Sufi order. Abu-Rabah, a graduate of al-Azhar, who served in the 1890s as the Director of Education in the *kaza* of Jaffa, belonged to a branch of the well-known Dajani family. He is often cited in the sources for his use of his considerable influence and connections to instigate anti-Christian feelings in Jaffa.[81]

Conclusion

The rural populations discussed in this chapter, both the peasants and the Bedouins, are two under-represented subaltern groups that did not leave abundant evidence behind. Moreover, they needed intermediaries to convey their requests to the central authorities, such as professional petition-writers who wrote the petitions for them in return for a fee. Thus, even more than in the case of urban petitions, it is still questionable whether these documents reflect truly authentic voices that mirror the desires, aspirations, concerns and activities of the rural population. Added to this problem is the ever-present possibility that the rural population was enlisted by various influential people, such as notable urbanites, to submit petitions on their behalf in support of their interests.

These reservations notwithstanding, the petitions of Palestine's rural population were clearly based on their interpretation of certain events and developments around which the petition-writers constructed their story in order to adhere to the stylistic, logical and persuasive rules of the game, while emphasizing certain parts that favored the case and downplaying others that weakened it. In fact, the mere act of going to a nearby urban center and hiring the services of petition-writers in an effort to influence the policy of the central authorities shows that the way historians look at the rural population of Palestine at the end of the nineteenth century should be reconsidered and reevaluated. Evidently, they were not as passive and subordinate as suggested in the quote at the beginning of this chapter.[82]

The rural petitions reflect the growing resentment of the rural population with urban notables who controlled the collection of taxes and manipulated land transactions in their favor, while collaborating in one way or another with the local Ottoman authorities. Thus, the increased influence of the urban notables over the hinterland of their towns as witnessed in the second half of the nineteenth century also led to new sources of friction and contestation.

Finally, the petitions submitted by the rural population are indicative of growing regional cooperation among the villages in matters in which they had a common interest vis-à-vis the reformed state apparatus and bureaucracy. This cooperation was one example of other manifestations of regionalism, some of which were enhanced and ascribed with new meaning, to create a nucleus of regional identity alongside the other identities concomitantly held by Palestine's population at the time.[83]

CHAPTER 5

REQUESTS BY OTTOMAN OFFICIALS SERVING IN PALESTINE

The institution of petitioning Istanbul at the end of the nineteenth century was not solely restricted to the local population. Ottoman officials who served in the region also submitted petitions on a variety of topics through the postal and telegraph services which allowed direct and instant communication with the imperial center. Among the issues raised were benefits and salaries, complaints about their peers, claims of abuse of power by supervisors, accusations against subordinates who failed to implement imperial decisions and/or accepted bribes, requests to be transferred/returned to specific locations, repudiation of accusations of various kinds against them, and general complaints about the situation in Palestine and the threats to the continuation of Ottoman rule. In this regard, Teyfur Erdoğdu's claim that most officials did not believe "that they could obtain redress for grievances of any kind through the law" perhaps needs to be modified.[1]

The official petitioners were either local inhabitants of Palestine who served in the Ottoman bureaucracy or outsiders who were positioned there temporarily. This chapter, however, mainly deals with petitions by the latter group, whereas the issue of petitioning by local officials is largely covered in Chapter 3 when discussing the power struggle within the local Arab elite. Some of the petitions discussed here were sent directly from towns in the region but others were sent from elsewhere in the

Empire after the officials had already completed their tour of duty in the region and had been assigned elsewhere.

Ottoman Officials in Palestine at the End of the Nineteenth Century

It is worth briefly examining the structure of Ottoman bureaucracy at the provincial level at the time, which sets the stage for a better grasp of the dynamics of petitioning by officials. In the aftermath of the Tanzimat reforms, the power of the Ottoman governors in the provinces was strengthened. As the imperial center became stronger, they were given many more powers that had been denied them in the past under the pretext that officials could foment a drive for autonomy. The governors were, for the most part, graduates of the new schools established during the Tanzimat era and had a broad modern secular education based on European models. They were appointed by Istanbul and were dependent on the center, but within the province itself could wield wide authority in matters of administration, police, monetary regime and law enforcement. In the case discussed here, the governor was the *mutasarrif* of Jerusalem who reported directly to Istanbul. Below him were the *kaymakam*s of Jaffa, Gaza and a few other sub-districts (Jerusalem, Hebron and also, after 1900, Beersheba) and, below them, the *müdür*s who headed the *nahiye*s.[2]

The administration at the provincial level was more diversified than in the past and mirrored both the growing scope of daily life administered by the modernizing state and the situation in the imperial center, albeit writ small. Thus, the Ottoman ministries had representation at the provincial level whose officials were responsible for reporting both to the ministries in Istanbul as well as to the governor (i.e., the *mutasarrif* of Jerusalem). Some officials, particularly in senior posts such as most of the *kaymakam*s, came from outside of the region, but others were locals, primarily from elite families who were intent on preserving their influence, powers and sources of wealth by their incorporation into the reformed Ottoman system. This dual system of reporting gave Istanbul a greater degree of oversight concerning provincial officials and their whereabouts but, on the other hand, made it very difficult for governors to fire ineffective or corrupt officials.[3]

At all levels of the Ottoman bureaucracy in the provinces there were administrative councils set up to assist the governors. These councils, whose composition and structure fit the needs of the various administrative units in the provinces, gave the local population a say in the decision making process and served as a way to curb any overreaching of authority on the part of the governor. The local representatives in the councils were mostly from the elite urban families, whereas the other members of the councils were from members of minority groups and senior Ottoman officials.[4] Thus, officials found themselves embedded in a complex situation of checks and balances, rivalries and coalitions. In this situation, petitions were an effective means of bypassing the strictures of the system, as was the case for other sectors of society as well.

Salaries and Conditions of Service

Officials petitioned Istanbul with very specific requests concerning their salaries, benefits and ranks. They used various justifications to convince the central government to yield to their pleas which were not necessarily always based on recorded rights, but rather on their needs, proven loyalty, their situation in comparison with their peers, their hard work and extra responsibilities, and even the state's responsibility for their wellbeing. These justifications and the fact that the imperial center often yielded to such requests is another indication that the Ottoman bureaucratic system was still largely based on personal connections, irregular decision making, and networks of patronage and did not work solely "by the book."[5] The petitioning system, in that sense, continued to serve its age-old purpose as an extra-judicial mechanism and as a tool to demonstrate the benevolence of the sultan. This is perhaps not surprising given Erdoğdu's comment that officials "remained subject in matters of appointment, dismissal and promotion to the rules of traditional servitude in their relations with powerful authorities."[6] In other words, a distinction should be made between corruption and malfunctions in the system, on the one hand, and established customs which were in fact remnants of the older system, on the other.

For example, in one case Vehebi Efendi, the former head of the Ottoman post and telegraph office in Jaffa, applied to the *Sadaret* for a promotion, arguing that he was paid as if he had served for merely 25 years even though he had served longer. He added that two peers in a similar situation had been promoted, a situation which made him very sad, and that he had been out of a job for three years. He petitioned to become a member of the ministry's council, a promotion which meant a higher salary and return to work, and argued that the government should provide for his happiness (*mesrûriyyet*). The latter claim resonates with the famous Ottoman notion of *saadet*, happiness, although the direct connection between this official's salary and his happiness is intriguing since this notion was usually used in connection with severe injustices, wrongdoings, mistreatment and loss or damage to life and property, which all impeded calm and happiness. Be that as it may, the Ministry of Post and Telegraph was ordered to find ways to give him a promotion and ensure his happiness.[7]

The same person, referred to as Husayn Vehebi, petitioned Istanbul again about a month later, this time to the Ministry of the Interior, with a request to be given a raise in his salary and to be transferred to Istanbul. It is likely that he sent a new petition because the first one had failed to elicit a response. While providing a somewhat different explanation for his request, he wrote that during the 38 years he had served his salary had been eroded. He had been sent to Jaffa a few years earlier for only a short period of time but since then could not return and currently had been arrested. His income, he added, which totaled 150 *kuruş* a month, did not provide for his family's basic needs since the expenses in Jaffa were much higher than the salary he earned and could be as much as 600 *kuruş* a month.[8]

In another interesting case involving the salary of a local person, the *imam* (by the name of Muhammad) of the main mosque in Jaffa applied to the *Sadaret* twice with a request for a raise in his salary, arguing that his current salary did not provide for his basic needs and stressing his loyalty to the sultan and the fact that he also served as the *khatib* (preacher, in Turkish: *hatip*) of the mosque.[9]

Petitions by Relatives of Officials

Petitions were also submitted by relatives of officials who served in the region; for instance, regarding the rights of deceased relatives whose families wanted to preserve. For example, the wife of the deceased first *yüzbaşi* (captain) of the reserve unit (*redif*) in Jaffa applied to the *Sadaret* to receive his salary for the year 1315 [1900/1901] which she argued was desperately needed for herself and for her family.[10]

Requests to Return to Office and for Pardon

Former officials who served in the region often submitted petitions with requests to clear their names or to be pardoned for accusations or sanctions related to their service. At times, officials asked to be appointed to their former position or a similar one if their claims were proven to be correct. For instance, the former *kaymakam* of Jaffa, Muhammad Asif Bey, applied to the *Mabeyn*, the Palace Secretariat, with a request to return to his former job or a similar one. He argued that he had been dismissed and was in a difficult situation, adding that the government would gain from returning him to his post. Such a decision, he argued, would help the government regain its lost prestige and honor as regards Jews in Palestine, given that he was known for his stern stand against illegal Jewish activity and his endeavors to limit their operation there (see below).[11]

A similar case involved the mayor of Jaffa, a certain Ahmad al-'Ibadi, who claimed he was illegally fired by the *kaymakam*. Despite the fact that the *mutasarrıf* of Jerusalem issued an order to reinstate him, another person was appointed and the order was allegedly ignored.[12]

At times, officials insisted that they could not be fired or accused of various wrongdoings without a trial or the issuance of a court order to authorize such acts.[13] For instance, the former head of the *Tahrirat* (bureau of official correspondence) in the District of Jerusalem claimed he was illegally fired without a court order, citing bad behavior, even though he purportedly performed his duties beyond reproach.[14]

It is interesting to explore the ways former officials phrased their requests for reinstatement or appointment to a new position. The former *kaymakam* of Jaffa, for example, a certain Muhammad Rida Efendi, applied to the *Şûra-yı Devlet* with a request to be given a new position, saying that he had to leave his former post "due to fate" (*hasb-ul-kadar*). An investigation with Jerusalem revealed that he was fired due to his inability to govern such a complex and important *kaza* as Jaffa, and specifically his inability to resolve the clashes between the Afghani and Maghrebi guards in the town's orchards.[15]

Officials sometimes got into trouble after filing a complaint and their efforts were counterproductive. For instance, the former *serkomiser* of Jerusalem Tevfik Bey was fired after he was tried in court. When he was found not guilty, he petitioned for reinstatement or appointment to a similar position. The subsequent investigation discovered that he "professed opinions which were considered deleterious to the state and its law" and his name was stricken from the list of state officials. As a result, a much more thorough investigation was conducted and the authorities in his previous places of service were asked to provide details about his character.[16]

In this regard, there was often a huge gap between the way former officials presented their situation when petitioning Istanbul to be pardoned and the evidence on the ground, as revealed in investigations prompted by these appeals. For instance, the former head of census registrar (*nüfus memuru*) in the *kaza* of Jaffa, Muhammad 'Abd al-Salam al-Ja'uni applied to Istanbul claiming that he was fired for no good reason. An investigation revealed that he had been fired several years earlier for incompetence, and recently had failed a qualifying exam for a position in the *kaza* of Gaza.[17]

At times, complaints by Ottoman officials led to complications and exchanges of words between Ottoman bureaus about their responsibility and the way they handled certain issues. For example, the director of the education department in the District of Jerusalem was fired following complaints about him when he served on a committee of inquiry which was sent to the *kaza* of Gaza to settle disputes between rival Bedouin tribes. The investigation found him to be innocent, a situation which led to an angry exchange of letters between Jerusalem, the Ministry of the Interior and the Ministry of Education about who was responsible for firing him and how to reinstate him.[18]

Finally, there were also cases of pardon requests involving former local officials who were natives of Palestine. The most famous case was that of the former *mufti* of Gaza, al-Hanafi Efendi, his son and his brother, who petitioned the *Mabeyn* to be allowed to return to their hometown after their three-year exile in faraway Ankara. They took advantage of the Prophet's birthday to submit their request to İzzat Bey, the second scribe in the Palace Secretariat (for more details about this affair, see Chapter 3).[19]

Suggestions for Reforms and Reorganization

Officials would send Istanbul letters with suggestions for reforms and changes. These personal letters, which are not ordinary petitions, were possibly an attempt to attract the attention of higher authorities and demonstrate the petitioners' capabilities, with the hope of future rewards. On occasion, they were written after the officials hadconcluded their term in office in the region and had moved elsewhere. Some of these letters were sent anonymously. The sending of letters by officials to Istanbul – which were distinct from regular petitions – was not a new phenomenon. Uriel Heyd described how Ottoman officials sent letters (*mektubs*) to Istanbul over the course of the sixteenth and seventeenth centuries, as indicated in the *Mühimme Defterleri*.[20]

For instance, an official in the tax authority in Jaffa petitioned Istanbul arguing that the taxes on lemons and oranges exported from Jaffa were too low and should be raised to protect state coffers. The normal channel for such a suggestion would have naturally been for this person to approach his direct supervisors and not Istanbul.[21]

In one letter sent to the Ministry of the Interior from the *vilayet* of Şam, an unknown official who said he used to serve in the region warns about the dramatic increase in the number of Jews there and states that the measures taken by the Empire were in no way effective. He urges the state to take immediate steps before the region is filled with Jewish immigrants (see also below).[22]

Foreign Activity and Settlement Initiatives in Palestine

Officials who served in Palestine frequently sent petitions to the central authorities to warn of the consequences to the Empire of foreign involvement there. These approaches to Istanbul were often not petitions per se but, rather, general complaints and suggestions on how to bring about a policy change, often even without specific names of wrong-doers mentioned. The petitioners stressed their inability to enforce imperial decisions because of interference from foreign consuls who refused to accept restrictions on their subjects, the fact that some officials turned a blind eye to foreign activity in return for bribes and the ineffective nature of the Ottoman rules and regulations on the ground. Obviously, letters or petitions of this kind may have taken a line the petitioners knew the sultan favored in order to find grace in the eyes of Abdülhamid.

One key issue was Jewish immigration and settlement activity and the authorities' inability to curb it despite official policy and numerous decisions on this matter. A striking example was a letter sent to the Palace in 1894 by an Ottoman official, who signed his letter with the generic title "the slave of your slaves." The letter warns the sultan about the dire consequences of the Jewish settlement and colonization activity in the area for the local population. He states that he served in the region for seven years and witnessed the creation of a new political problem for the Empire which he compares to the Armenian problem. He blames the people of Cevat Paşa,[23] the Grand Vizier, for collaborating with Baron de Rothschild to bypass restrictions on Jewish immigration and settlement in Palestine. The official says that he was told that this activity contradicts the policy of the former Grand Vizier, whose name is not mentioned,[24] who opposed Jewish activity and refused to collaborate with Rothschild. While expressing typical stereotypes about Jewish money controlling the world and global power politics, the official describes how Rothschild is able to bypass Ottoman restrictions and promote Jewish activity in Palestine by spending money and pulling strings.[25]

A considerable number of petitions were sent by officials who claimed they were fired because of Jewish activity in Palestine and the government's inability to prevent it. For instance, the former *tapu* official in Jerusalem 'Abd al-Razaq Efendi complained that he was fired by the administrative council of Jerusalem because he was unable to halt Jewish settlement activity near Jaffa which took place on *miri* lands. The petitioner, however, claims that he constantly warned that measures should be taken and that he told the local government about the start of construction work in the Jewish villages in an attempt to stop it.[26]

In another such case, the former mayor of Jaffa, sheikh 'Ali, applied to the *Sadaret* with a request to return to office after being falsely accused and fired by the *mutasarrıf* of Jerusalem. According to the petition he submitted, he was appointed to investigate illegal acts committed by the *kaymakam* of Jaffa in cahoots with Jewish immigrants. When the *kaymakam* and the Jews heard about the investigation, they filed false complaints against him and brought about his dismissal despite his long and loyal service to the state. Other than getting back his job, the petitioner wanted the *kaymakam*, who was well-connected through family ties to Ahmet İzzet Paşa,[27] to be fired.[28]

At times, officials who were fired due to reasons which probably had nothing to do with Jewish activity applied to reverse the decision by playing the Jewish card in their favor. This was most likely the case for two petitions mentioned briefly above by Asif Bey, the former *kaymakam* of Jaffa, who applied to the *Mabeyn* with a request to be reinstated or be granted a similar position. He enumerates all the measures he took against Jewish immigration and settlement activity, while describing in great detail Jewish activity, its aims, the threats it posed to the state and the loopholes in the Ottoman system with regard to this activity. Asif Bey makes no attempt to conceal the connection between his request and the policy he implemented against Jewish activity and says his return to the job would increase the state's image and credibility.[29]

Anonymous Petitions against Misdeeds and Corruption by Officials

It is rare to come across signed petitions by incumbent officials against their peers and supervisors (see Document 12 in Chapter 7).[30] Such petitions were usually sent only after completion of their term of office and were frequently related to dismissals and deprival of rights, as seen above. However, some petitions were submitted anonymously and signed with symbolic names such as "honest informer" (*muhbir-i sadık*). It is impossible to determine who these individuals were, but from the nature of their complaints it is likely that they were highly familiar with the Ottoman bureaucracy from within and had inside information only accessible to officials.

In the case of the "honest informer," for example, the petition which was written in Arabic was sent from Jaffa. The informer complained about collusion between the *mutasarrıf* of Jerusalem (Ibrahim Paşa), the former *kaymakam* of Jaffa (Musa Kazim Efendi), police officers, and the *serkomiser* (police superintendent), who all ran a scheme to allow Jewish immigration activity and settlement to take place in return for bribes. The petitioner describes in detail how the process was carried out, how the registers in the port in Jaffa were altered, and how the officers were instructed to allow Jews in.[31] The same petitioner complains in another letter full of inside information that the *tapu* official in Jaffa, the *yoklama* officer in Ramle and the *Defter-i Hakani* officer colluded to steal sums collected as *vergi* tax.[32]

General Requests

Some petitions contained general requests submitted to Istanbul by officials. Among them were requests for clarifications, copies of certain decisions, guidance and the like. For instance, the head of the post and telegraph office in Jaffa applied to receive a certified copy (*ilam*) of the decision involving his trial in the court of appeal for state officials in Istanbul. He said he was tried by a local court for state officials in the administrative council of Jerusalem for losing ten French gold bars which were sent by secured mail and was found to be innocent, a decision which led the ministry where he worked to appeal to Istanbul against the decision. His request was immediately granted.[33]

Conclusion

Historically, the main goal of the Ottoman institution of petitioning the ruler was to allow the common people to complain about misdeeds by officials of low and middle ranks. Junior officials at various posts, despite theoretically being members of the ruling class, also reverted to this institution when need arose. In this sense, the situation at the end of the nineteenth century, despite the changes in the structure of Ottoman society and bureaucracy, was rather similar. Most of the petitions were submitted by the local population, often against incumbent officials, but the latter also occasionally submitted petitions. Many complaints by officials were submitted by former officials after leaving the region. They made requests such as to vindicate their names, be reinstated, investigate wrongdoings by their peers and punish them and so on.

The role of the Jewish activity in Palestine at the end of the nineteenth century was often cited in complaints by former officials who were fired over accusations about the way they handled this activity, failed to prevent it or even assisted it. Jewish activity also played a prominent role in general letters of suggestion sent by officials to Istanbul containing proposed reforms and measures to be implemented. This was possibly connected to the well-known policy of Abdulhamid, who opposed Jewish immigration and settlement activity in Palestine.

Finally, it is difficult to disentangle some of the petitions from rivalries within the urban elite of Palestine, as surveyed in Chapter 3. Some of the petitions against incumbent officials discussed in this chapter were most probably connected in one way or another to these rivalries.

CHAPTER 6

SOCIAL AND ECONOMIC MATTERS

Introduction

This thematic chapter analyzes some key social and economic issues reflected in the petitions. To a great extent, the common thread linking the topics discussed in this chapter has to do with center–periphery relationships and the implementation of imperial policies and reforms on the ground. A large body of petitions, for instance, was directly or indirectly related to new policies and measures implemented by the central government as part of the Tanzimat reforms designed to achieve a greater degree of centralization in running governmental affairs and improving state control over resources.[1] These included efforts (none of which fully materialized) at the reorganization and standardization of the tax collection system that strove to eliminate previous exemptions granted unlawfully and also longstanding practices that undermined tax collection, registration of landownership and the right of usufruct over land, consolidation of the state's ownership rights over *miri* lands, efforts to transform and more closely supervise the way taxes were collected and similar measures. These measures all reflected the central government's attempt to carry out what it perceived as a rationalization, systematization and regularization of central state control in the provinces, particularly with regard to the provincial administrative and financial systems.

Often, these new government policies represented an upheaval for the local population, who resented the fact that the new reforms and regulations were forced upon it from above by orders of the imperial center.[2] Moreover, many of the new policies were accompanied by considerable misconduct on the part of local Ottoman officials and other influential individuals, who often flaunted the central government's official policy and took advantage of their power and influence to promote their self-interests. Worse, at times the population received conflicting orders from various Ottoman bureaus and functionaries, all of which caused bewilderment and frustration.[3]

The Ottoman reforms were enacted at a time when the central government was much more accessible to its subjects in the provinces and had ceased to be an amorphous entity in the eyes of many, who had previously rarely encountered its representatives in their everyday lives. This was done through measures such as conscription, land and tax surveys, registration of land, censuses, law enforcement, better communication, health services and epidemic control measures, education services, the nomination of *muhtar*s, the operation of the administrative councils and the like. To some extent, this greater accessibility affected the nature of the petitions directed towards the center, which frequently called for state intervention in inter- and intra-communal affairs, ongoing business disputes, moral issues and similar issues which all were not the typical subjects of petitioning in the past. In addition, the petitions became much more political in nature than previously.

Another issue which is discussed in this chapter is the moral world envisioned by the petitioners in their pleas to Istanbul to obtain justice. In their effort to convince Istanbul to side with them, the petitioners had to appeal to the religious, ethical and traditional values of the Empire which would enhance their demands and convince the center to respond favorably to their request.

Agrarian Changes and Land Issues

Land was one of the most essential resources in the Ottoman economy. Moreover, to a great extent landownership defined the relationship between the subjects and the sultanate. Not surprisingly, one key element of the Tanzimat policy involved land reforms which were designed to achieve greater uniformity and centralization in the land system and increase revenues from land taxes.[4] Its centerpiece was "the registration of all lands in the land registry office, in the name of the actual possessors of the right of usufruct (*tasarruf*)."[5] Another aim was to "consolidate the state's rights and privileges over the land, which legally, of course, belonged to it as *miri*-land."[6]

In this regard, a major bone of contention which appears in many petitions was the differences in the perceptions of landownership between the local population and the government. It is clear from many of the petitions that the government was seen as reneging on longstanding precedents which, although not legally sanctioned, had been honored for years and instead recognizing only lawful and registered ownership and rights. The government had much to lose from acknowledging *de jure* existing arrangements, practices and concessions that had acquired a *de facto* status over the years. One case study concerning a dispute between the government and landowners from Jaffa with regard to the status of land in this town paints a clear picture of these conflicting views.

Landowners in the region of Jaffa were preoccupied for several years with an issue that led to considerable tension with the central governments. At stake were *miri* lands in the town's immediate environment which, over the years, had gradually come to be seen as *mülk* (privately owned) land. This step had been unlawfully accepted by local Ottoman officials and was concretized not only when these lands were bought and sold, but also in the type of taxes levied on the owners of these lands. The conflict was triggered when the state took steps to revert the classification of these lands to their original status.

The first manifestation of the landowners' discontent I came across appears in a massive petition sent in July 1891 by 58 Muslim and Christian landowners from Jaffa to the Grand Vizier to contest the government's decision to treat the land of Jaffa as *mülk* rather than as *miri* (see Appendix 2). The petition argues that the inspector of *Defter-i Hakani* in Beirut, Zekati Efendi, ordered the *tapu* official in Jaffa to change existing policy with regards to Jaffa's lands, a step which they claimed was illegal, violated the Islamic laws of inheritance and negated the accepted practice approved by past rulers.[7]

A few months later, another mass petition, signed by Jaffa's *Nakibüleşraf* and 38 other people, was sent to the Grand Vizier, arguing that the same Zekati Efendi had initiated a new land survey in Jaffa as part of a plan to carry out a land reform. The petitioners stressed again that they had documentary proof that they legally owned the land in Jaffa and that the survey was illegal in their eyes.[8]

In a similar petition signed by the *Nakibüleşraf* and 25 others, it was stressed that Zekati Efendi's activities were bringing economic activity in Jaffa to a halt, including construction work and trade, as well as the renting, selling and buying of land. In a veiled threat, the petitioners made it clear that support for the government would decline among the people of Jaffa if the situation did not revert to the status quo ante. Zekati Efendi's reports are characterized as "lies which are based on false assumptions."[9]

Interestingly, two years after the land survey, the *Defter-i Hakani* sent Zekati Efendi to the region again, with sultanic approval, at the head of a committee whose task was to prepare a map of landownership in Jaffa. Zekati Efendi was familiar with the complications of the land issue in Jaffa and his mission was prompted by the discrepancies between sultanic orders and the situation in Jaffa itself.[10] The problems included orders that were not implemented or that were implemented in a way that contradicted sultanic orders and also illegal construction that needed to be resolved with the local population. The existing map was apparently old, incomplete and did not reflect changes on the ground. Ostensibly, part of the reason for making a new map stemmed from various petitions the local population sent to Istanbul about the status of land in Jaffa.

The arrival of Zekati Efendi in Jaffa, probably in connection with the preparation of the map, thus sparked new tensions with landowners in the town who filed petitions against Zekati Efendi. Zekati Efendi himself complained that members of the committee who owned land in the town interfered with the work of his committee by defending their own interests. The Council of Ministers in Istanbul decided that the committee should continue with its work since halting all kinds of land transfers in Jaffa, including transfers unaffected by the new regulations, would be deleterious to the economy and would contradict state and public interests. The ruling was that complications concerning the land problems in the town should be resolved in line with previous decisions and the books should be corrected to comply with sultanic orders.[11]

An examination of the decision handed down regarding the petitions of the landowners from Jaffa, who complained their *mülk* land was treated as *miri* land, shows that the situation was much more complex than that described by the petitioners (see Documents 13.1 and 13.2; see also Appendixes 7.1

and 7.2). In particular, the decision sheds light on why Zekati Efendi was sent to Jaffa in the first place and asked to conduct a land survey.[12] In the inquiry prompted by the petitions, it was found that until the *hicri* year 1294 (1877/8) the land was considered *miri*. At that time, local *tapu* (land registration office) officials started distributing title deeds illegally as though the land were private *mülk* land. Houses were built on some of these lands and, in fact, whole neighborhoods were constructed, while other large plots of vacant land (*arazi-yi haliye ve-mahlule*) were seized.

Based on these findings, the records were reexamined and it was found that these lands had been originally *haraç* (in Arabic: *kharaj*) lands,[13] for which one quarter of the summer crops which one third of the winter crops were paid as tax. With the passing of time, however, the land status became *miri*, and in 1278 (1861/2) the sultan ordered that these lands should be treated as such, rather than as *mülk*. People who had already received title deeds for *mülk* land before that year were asked to replace their title deeds and register the land under the tithe regime imposed on *miri* lands. From then on, it was decided to avoid this type of occurrence. Lands which were already denoted as *waqf* before 1278 remained endowed lands, but they were still treated as *miri* and not as private *mülk* land. Thus, there was no legal basis for declaring land as *mülk* in 1877/8, as some officials had done.

Moreover, it was stressed that steps should be taken to comply with past decisions; that is to say, no *mülk* title deeds would be handed down for the lands discussed and they would remain *miri* lands whose holders only had the right of usufruct on them and not full ownership. The sultan approved the draft of the decision prepared by the *Şûra-yı Devlet* which was passed to him by the Grand Vizier.[14]

The Collection of Taxes

Other state measures and reforms whose implementation led to the submission of numerous petitions had to do with the reorganization of the tax collection system. The petitions reflect disputes over the collection of land taxes from landowners and cultivators. The root cause was the arbitrary and irregular way in which taxes were collected before the reforms of the mid-nineteenth century. As with the issue of landownership, many of the petitions dealing with taxes opposed the new state measures which countermanded traditional practices and habits, and led to higher and more systematic demands for payment.

For example, five people from Jaffa claimed they owned a piece of sandy land (*remliyye mukataasi*) in which they had invested a great deal of money.[15] In the past, they paid only *vergi* tax for this land but now they were asked to pay tithe as well, which they claimed they could not afford due to their "destitution" (probably used here as a literary device).[16] Their land was allegedly registered in the *tapu* and they had title deeds (*kushan*s) for it.[17] Foreigners in a similar situation were allegedly exempt from this new measure.[18]

A similar petition was submitted by three owners of vineyards (*kürum*) who claimed that previously they paid only *vergi*, but now several "corrupt officials" were forcing them to pay tithe for the yields of their fields. Moreover, their land was not suitable for cultivation and required tremendous investment and effort; thus, the payment of the tithe would lead to the failure of their crops.[19] Although the petitioners blamed intermediate officials for levying extra charges, in fact they were protesting the new governmental policy itself, which is a frequent feature of petitions worldwide that puts the blame on a group of intermediaries and low- to middle-ranked bureaucrats rather than on the ruler.

The vast citrus groves in the vicinity of Jaffa, which constituted one of the city's main sources of wealth in the second half of the nineteenth century, often stirred up controversy and led to the submission of petitions. For instance, in 1898, 29 merchants from Jaffa applied to the *Sadaret* to abrogate a tax of 20 *para* pocketed by the municipality for each box of oranges exported from Jaffa. They argued that the municipality had other sources of income and did not need their money. The Ministry of the Interior wrote to Jerusalem that, according to a previous edict, the municipality could take ten *para* from each box for a period of five years, if the annual support of 1,500 liras from the District of Jerusalem to which it was entitled was not sufficient.[20]

As far as I can tell from the sources, about a decade later the issue of taxing the oranges exported from Jaffa surfaced again. Jerusalem asked Istanbul to raise the tax (*resm*) on every box exported to 20 *para* instead of 20 *para*: 20 *para* for the development of Jaffa as before, and 20 *para* for the replacement of foreign guards in the orchards (most probably Afghanis and Maghrebis) with local guards since the foreign guards had created problems. The move was apparently approved by the growers themselves.[21]

Petitions about taxes, their collection and assessment were for the most part submitted collectively, since issues concerning more than one person were at stake. In some cases, however, private individuals also submitted petitions about tax assessments. One such petition was submitted by Anton Ayyub, a Christian tax collector from Jaffa who won the tender to collect the tithe in certain villages in the region of Jaffa and Gaza.[22] Ayyub submitted a petition in Arabic to the *Bab-ı Âli*, the Sublime Porte, arguing that the amount he paid as a *mültezim* to get the *iltizam* was unrealistic that year and he could not recover his expenses. There had been severe damage to the crops from locusts, bad weather, plagues and loss of manpower from conscription, all of which reduced yields to a fraction of the norm.[23] Interestingly, this petition is different in its structure, addressee and form from most of the petitions sent after the mid-1860s, when telegraph services became operational and the implementation of the reforms on the local level had attained a certain "maturity." For instance, later petitions were referred to the *Sadaret* and not to the *Bab-ı Âli*.

Petitions about taxes were not necessarily directly connected to land issues. For example, grain merchants from Beirut petitioned Istanbul claiming that they had deposited 7 percent of the value of the merchandise when sending grain from Gaza to Alexandria and from there abroad. However, this money was not returned to them, as had been the practice upon showing receipts.[24]

Inheritances and *Waqf*s

Complaints concerning *waqf*s covered a number of issues which were often unrelated. Urban dwellers sent petitions complaining about the right to administer certain *waqf*s and the status of certain lands as *waqf*s. The rural population often petitioned about the status of certain *waqf* lands, the collection of taxes from these lands, and abuse of power by tax collectors and *mütevelli*s (see Chapter 4). Finally, there were petitions by officials against mishandling and mismanagement of *waqf*s by fellow officials and *mütevveli*s.

Most petitions dealing with *waqf*s concerned their management and the right to their income. As part of the reforms, the government assumed control over the administration of most of the large *waqf*s and supervised the smaller private ones through the Ministry of Endowments (*Evkaf Nezareti*) and the administrative councils in the provinces. This was done at the expense of the *kadı*s who had traditionally carried out these tasks,[25] but numerous issues still remained contested and controversial.[26] Apparently, part of the problem was that certain lands were only partially supervised by the Ministry of Endowments, whereas their day-to-day management remained in the hands of the *mütevelli*s (*evakaf-ı mülhaka*). Moreover, the collection and distribution of *waqf* revenues apparently still provided many loopholes for corruption and administrative error. Below are a few examples which provide a glimpse into petitions concerning the *waqf*.

For instance, as regards complaints about the management of *waqf*s, a resident of Jaffa named Muhammad complained to Istanbul about the state official supervising *waqf*s in Jaffa, arguing that for ten years he had not been given receipts for a shop he rented from the *waqf* in the town and implied that the official put the money in his own pocket.[27] No further information is available regarding the context of this petition.

In another case, a person named Mustafa wrote to Istanbul several times to complain about the grandson of the deceased *mütevveli* of *waqf*, Bayazid Bastami, a certain Hafiz Bey, who misappropriated the endowment's money. The *waqf*, named after the famous ninth-century Sufi, was supposed to support two mosques and *tekke*s (dervish lodges) in Ramle and Jerusalem, financed by the income from 12,000 *dönüm*s, of which 5,000 were registered in the *tapu* in Jaffa. The grandson allegedly took a huge amount of this money illegally for his personal use. The petitioner claimed that complaints to the local authorities were ignored and that he did not get money to which he was entitled.[28]

Complaints about mishandling of *waqf*s were also raised in the context of power struggles within the urban elite, as seen in the case of the sons of the *mufti* of Gaza who appealed to the Ministry of the Interior against the *mutasarrıf* of Jerusalem whom they accused of collaborating with their rivals in Gaza. They claimed that, as a result of the governor's decision, the *waqf* they administered was taken from them and handed over to their rivals, a situation which brought a mosque supported by the *waqf* "to the verge of collapse." The mosque, they add, had been repaired by Sultan Abdülmecid (r. 1839–61).[29]

Another problem with regard to *waqf*s was whether certain lands were endowed land, and who had the right to administer them and benefit from their revenues. For instance, the above-mentioned Anton Ayyub from Jaffa wrote to the *Sadaret* to accuse the accountant of *waqf*s in the *mutasarrıflık* of Jerusalem of falsely declaring land which Ayyub owned, cultivated and developed as *waqf* and selling it in a public auction. Ayyub said that 14 years earlier he had been granted the land of Khirbat Cendas [?], where he planted trees, constructed several buildings and restored the area.[30] Based on the correspondence between Ottoman offices dealing with a similar complaint a few years later, it emerges that the land was uncultivated (*mahlula*) *waqf* land which the *tapu* and *yoklama* officials seized while destroying olive trees that had been planted there.[31]

Another interesting petition involving *waqf* in Jaffa was submitted by women, which is rather rare in the corpus analyzed here. Several sisters who were *mütevvelis* of *waqf* land wrote to the Ministry of the Interior that the *waqf* authorities in their town had confiscated some of their land illegally by claiming that the *waqf*'s management was in its jurisdiction (see Document 9).[32] Jerusalem informed Istanbul that the issue was in the *shari'a* court and, until a decision was handed down, it had to act according to the original endowment of the land. It is clear from Jerusalem's response that the situation was much more complicated than that described by the sisters. The land belonged to the Shakir al-Nabulsi *waqf* and the sisters had actually taken it over illegally, a situation which led to a trial. Jerusalem, moreover, stressed that the legal situation of the land as *waqf* was clear and incontrovertible.[33]

Some cases deal with intra-familial quarrels about the administration of a certain *waqf* and the issue of the authorities' intervention. For instance, the *mütevveli* of *waqf* Wehbe Muharram in Jaffa,[34] Muhammad Salim, applied to the *Şûra-yı Devlet* to contest a decision allegedly made illegally by the *shari'a* court in Jerusalem, which should not have had any authority over Jaffa, to transfer the administration of the *waqf*, which he claimed was established by his grandfather, to a woman from Jerusalem whose name is not mentioned. This was done despite the approval received from the *shari'a* court in Jaffa confirming Salim's status as the administrator of the endowment. Moreover, the decision was carried out by the local authorities by using force against the petitioner. He asks for an investigation and argues that the behavior of Jerusalem is against the laws of the *Mecelle* and the enforced *kanun*s.[35]

Petitions that were submitted a few years later by a person named Salim al-Dabbagh from Jaffa are most probably related to the same issue. Al-Dabbagh applied to various bureaus claiming that a familial *waqf* was taken from him illegally, despite a court decision, by a representative

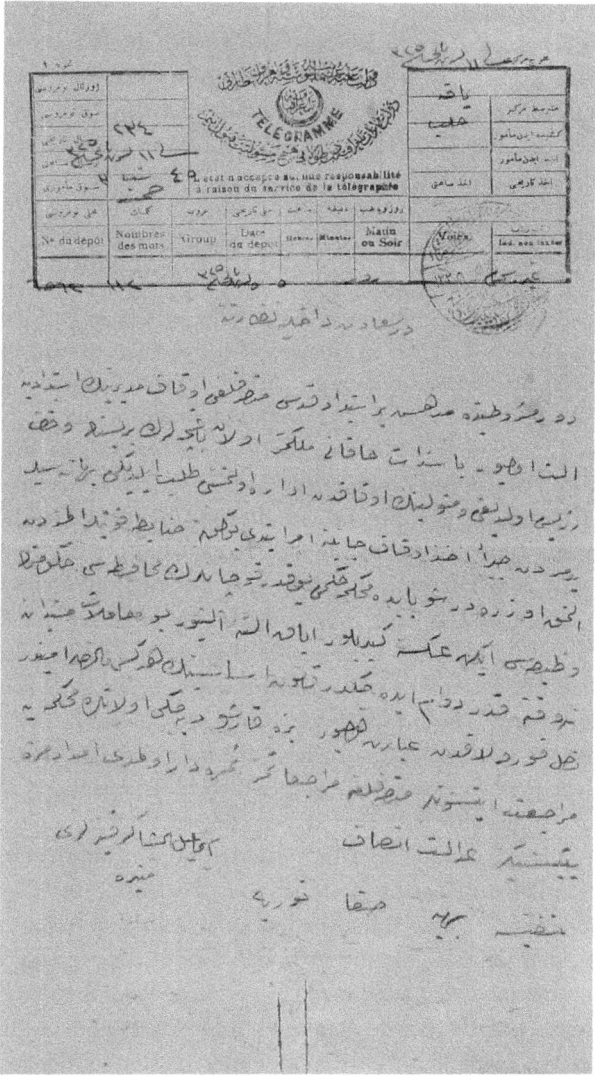

Document 9   A Petition by Several Sisters in Jaffa about the Status of *Waqf*
Lands they claimed they administrated

Source: BOA. DH. MUİ., 43–1/54, 11 Teşrinisani 1325 [24 November 1909]

Notes: Notice the change in the discourse after the Young Turk Revolution, and the emphasis
on constitutional rights and the rule of law.

of the *mutasarrıf* of Jerusalem who made use of a canceled court order (*mefsuh bir ilam*).[36] An investigation revealed that the issue at stake was *waqf* Wehbe Muharram in Jaffa whose administration was handed over to Labiba Bint Mustafa al-Dabbagh, a relative of Salim, by a *shari'a* court order which rejected Salim's claims, ordered him not to intervene in the *waqf* affairs and ruled in favor of his relative.[37]

Projects, Infrastructure and Commercial Matters

The rapid economic development of Palestine in the second half of the nineteenth century and the multitude of infrastructure projects which were planned or already under construction, especially in the booming region of Jaffa, were a source of petitions complaining about the tender process and the reliability of the participants, as well as suggestions for new projects and initiatives in various fields. These were not always typical petitions and, at times, no actual complaint was raised.

For instance, several people applied to the *Sadaret* in 1897 with a request to be awarded the contract for the construction of the port and wharf in Jaffa, claiming that they had the expertise and could get the required financial backing, whereas the company that had won the bid had neither. The latter was said to be unfit and incapable of completing the project or building in Jaffa a port similar to the one in Beirut which could serve its purpose and withstand the weather conditions and the waves. If the port were not built properly, the petitioners argued, delays in maritime trade with Jaffa were to be expected.[38]

The legality of development bids also stirred up controversy and led to the submission of petitions to Istanbul. For instance, Yosef Navon Bey (1858–1934),[39] the well-known Jewish Sephardic entrepreneur from Jerusalem, petitioned the *Sadaret* through two of his representatives to obtain information about a bid made by Adham Efendi for a water distribution project in Jaffa. Navon demanded information about a change his competitor had made in his bid and requested the authorities to examine whether it was indeed the best offer, something that implies that Navon was probably notified that he had lost the bid.[40]

Most probably in connection with this petition, Navon transmitted a letter to Sa'id Paşa, the head of the Council of State at the time, through an intermediary. Although not a regular petition, the letter still contains a veiled complaint, with a request to receive a concession for supplying water and for drainage in the city and the sub-province of Jaffa. He notes that he applied to the Grand Vizier several times but had received no answer, hinting that the matter was stuck in red tape. He describes the advantages that no other developer can deliver, promises to donate money to the poor people of Jaffa if he gets the concession, and takes it upon himself to pay a fixed annual amount of money to state coffers, in addition to 16 percent of the profits and a payment of five *para* for every cubic meter of water used in return for a 30-year concession (see Document 10).[41] Five years later, Navon applied to the *Sadaret* for the return of guarantees he deposited when applying to be awarded the water work concession mentioned above after his bid was not chosen.[42]

New development schemes in the region of Jaffa at times also elicited the residents' opposition and anger. For instance, the residents of the al-Ghazzawiyya neighborhood in this town applied the *Sadaret* to change the course of the planned railway line because it would cut through their fields. They wanted to move it to a nearby location which would not affect their fields and houses.[43]

In another case, 'Uthman al-Nashashibi from Jerusalem[44] applied to the Ministry of Commerce and Public Works claiming that the company building the railway in Jaffa confiscated a plot of land he owned while offering minimum compensation, which he rejected because it did not correspond to the value of the land. Hence, the company started working without settling the issue of the land properly. The petitioner wanted to get the land back or be given similar land, since his complaints to the commissioner of the railway had been ignored.[45] Interestingly, al-Nashashibi's petition is quoted as putting emphasis on the breach of commercial law by the company.

As discussed above, the boom in economic activity in Jaffa at the end of the nineteenth century was largely based on trade with Europe which made it Palestine's biggest port. This raised the issue of communication and contacts with foreign merchants. The Ottoman authorities wanted to appoint a French-speaking governor to Jaffa because of the region's growing strategic importance.[46] This issue was also raised in a petition by a person named Albert Just, who applied to the Ministry of Foreign Affairs to nominate an official who spoke French to the commercial court in the town. He argued that the Ottoman officials did not speak French, the *lingua franca* of international commerce at the time, and hence activities such as signing contracts, appointing legal representatives, obtaining

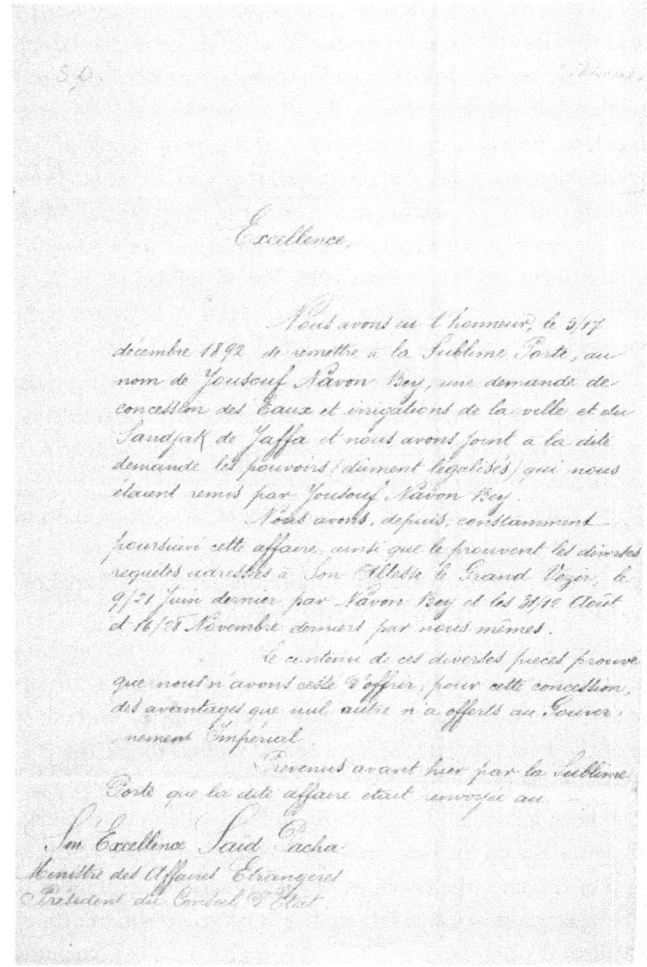

Document 10   A Letter submitted in the Name of Yosef Navon to Saʿid Paşa in
Istanbul concerning various Infrastructure Concessions in Jaffa

Source: BOA. ŞD., 2963/14, 11 December 1893, p. 1

loans, transferring bonds and so on. were all jeopardized. At the time,
there was no official who spoke French who could serve as a contracting
secretary.[47]

Finally, various entrepreneurs used the institution of petitioning Istanbul simply to suggest new plans and infrastructure projects.

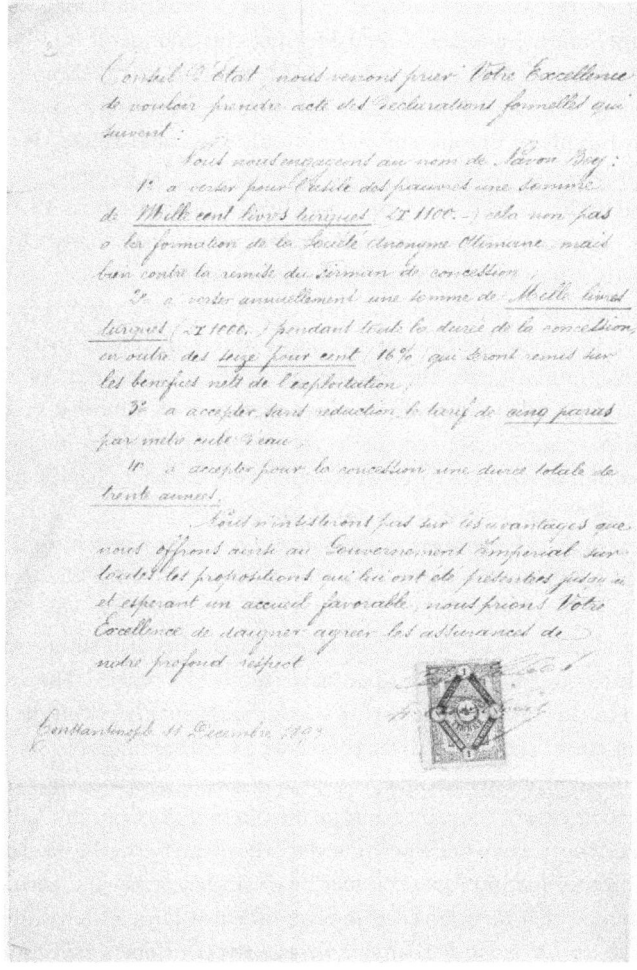

Source: BOA. ŞD., 2963/14, 11 December 1893, p. 2

For instance, two merchants from Syria applied to the *Sadaret* to get a concession to construct three fuel depots near Beirut, Jaffa and Tripoli.[48]

Non-Muslim Minorities

Minority groups enjoyed a great deal of autonomy in running their internal affairs in the nineteenth century under the Ottoman *millet* system.

At that time this system, which according to Ottoman (unfounded) tradition came into being when Sultan Mehmet the Conqueror (r. 1444–46, 1451–81) captured Constantinople in 1453, took on its full Empire-wide hierarchical structure. In addition, members of minority groups in the nineteenth-century Empire enjoyed not only the equal rights they were gradually granted by the Empire (for example, in the famous *ferman*s of 1839 and 1856, as well as in the short-lived Constitution in 1876), but also the protection of the European Powers which took many Ottoman individuals and minority groups under their auspices.

The minorities' ability to run their own affairs to a great degree can be seen in the operation of their own legal system in certain matters, the levy of communal taxes, the election of representatives and communal leaders and the like. However, at times members of minority groups or even entire communities sent petitions asking Istanbul to intervene in their communal affairs in cases where they were unable to handle internal conflicts alone and resolve these issues themselves.

For example, 11 members of the Greek Orthodox Church from Gaza, Ramle and Jaffa applied together to the *Sadaret* to dismiss the Patriarch Borkobious (Procopius II, 1872–75) and regain control over the Church's schools and places of worship. They claimed that they had submitted several petitions to that effect but had never received a reply.[49] The struggle reflected in this petition was part of a lengthy dispute between the Greek Orthodox clergy and the Arab lay people who were members of this church (the lay movement later became known as *al-nahda al-urthuduksiyya*).

In another case in the same Church, members of the Church's "administration and court" from Gaza petitioned for the dismissal of the head of their community for his improper conduct, maladministration and corruption. They claimed that he intervened in favor of Yusuf Diya' al-Khalidi in the election to the Ottoman Parliament, despite the petitioners' objections due to his alleged "lack of qualifications" (see Document 11).[50] In addition, he submitted defamatory petitions against the *kaymakam* and members of the local *meclis* and his presence stirred up tension between Muslims and Christians in the town. Possibly these allegations had to do with the rift between rival factions in Gaza, as described above, and al-Khailidi's alleged enmity towards the Husaynis in this town.

Members of the Jewish community in Jaffa also submitted complaints against their own *millet* authorities. For example, there is evidence for

Document 11   A Translation into Ottoman of a Petition by the Christian Greek
Orthodox (Rum) Community in Gaza against the Head of their Community
Source: BOA. HR. TO., 554/35, 20 Kânunusani 1293 [7 December 1876]

tensions within the established Ottoman Sephardic community in this town. These may have surfaced as a result of Jewish immigration from Eastern Europe to Palestine at the end of the nineteenth century, which altered the demography and makeup of the *yishuv*, as can be seen in a petition submitted by 15 members of the Jewish community in Jaffa concerning the representative (*vekil*) of the *hahambaşı* (Chief Rabbi) who allegedly misappropriated *waqf* endowments with the collaboration of foreign Jews, intervened in the process of electing *muhtar*s and engineered the election of two corrupt individuals, misused *bedel-i askeri* money (money paid by the Empire's minorities after 1856 as substitution for military service), created discord in the ranks of the community together with foreign Jews and so on.[51]

Moral Issues

In his discussion of petitions submitted by indigenous populations to the governing authorities in various regions of the British Empire in the late nineteenth and twentieth centuries, Ravi de Costa concisely conveys the essence of petitions:

> [P]etitions not only recognize and appeal to authority; they are implicit descriptions of the moral worlds in which particular claims are sensible and legitimate. Thus petitions act to articulate the identity and status of the petitioner and that of authority in a shared moral order. As we shall see, many petitioners rely on an enlarged vision of morality in order to justify their specific claims. Frequently, petitioners seek inclusion of themselves or marginal others in existing moral worlds, but petitions can also be the opportunity for the presentation of a transcendent moral order, in which identities and authorities shift into new relations and take on new forms.[52]

This depiction also applies to the moral dimensions raised in the petitions discussed here. The petitions clearly convey the moral world of the petitioners, and the social order they support. Idealistic portrayals of the ruler's piety, pursue of justice and care for his subjects, on the one hand, and, on the other, the society's norms, conduct, trust in their just ruler and the like serve as a yardstick against which the conduct of individuals cited in the petitions is evaluated.

The most common method used in the petitions to evaluate people's behavior was to assess it in terms of Islamic piety and morality while using Islamic justifications to appeal. Certain acts are described as *i'tisaf* (tyranny), *zulüm* (oppression), *istibdat* (despotism) and so on, which are obviously contradictory to the *shari'a* and the just rule of the sultan. Since the sultan and the Empire's raison d'être was to uphold the *shari'a* laws, this obviously accounts for the moral stances adopted by the petitioners.

A second set of accusations concerned deliberate rabble-rousing in the ranks of the population (*fesat*), violation of peaceful coexistence between groups (*ilka münaferet*) and attempts to undermine the social order – a concept which resonates with a very important Ottoman concept and with one of the main duties of Ottoman sultans; namely, preserve the social order and the subjects' well-being so they can work, produce, pay taxes and the like (as part of the notion of the "Circle of Justice").[53]

Corruption and felonious acts are very often described in the petitions as well, such as *su-i istimal* (abuse), *su-i idare* (maladministration), *su-i hâl* (misconduct) or *su-i hareket* (wrongdoing). Nonetheless, a conspicuous feature of many petitions is the extremely vague nature of the accusations; often, there is nothing substantial in them beyond typified complaints regarding corruption, immoral behavior and misdeeds.[54] In part, this has to do with the fact that in this period, as part of the petitions' politicization process, petitions were often used as a tool to settle old accounts between rival individuals and groups, especially among the urban population. In part, however, it also had to do with the policies of Abdülhamid II. This suspicious sultan was known for his distrust of officials and also the alacrity with which officials were dismissed from office, fired, transferred or punished. In such a situation, it was enough for certain allegations to be raised against specific officials to put them in a dire situation.[55]

Other themes often mentioned in petitions concern acts which violate the essence of humane conduct, practices prevailing among people in a certain place or region or among people exercising a certain profession. For instance, the Bedouins of Khirbat Duran presented a moral argument against the colonists of Rehovot in 1890, whom they termed *isra'iliyyin* (see Appendix 3): "The foreigners [*ajanib*] who do not want to treat us according to the accepted norms among farmers and according to human norms [al-sha'a'ir al-insaniyya] and compassion, took it [the farm] over. In short, [they reject us] even as their servants."[56]

Other claims include accusations such as drinking alcohol in public and performing unspecified immoral acts in public, whose nature is for the most part not disclosed. In one particularly interesting case, the head of the Greek Orthodox community in Gaza is accused of being "bored due to the closure by the local government of an illegal drinking establishment next to a church upon complaints by the people." The petition itself concerned internal strife within the Greek Orthodox community as well as within the Gazan elite, since his alleged ties with Yusuf Diya' al-Khalidi are mentioned, but the mention of the drinking habits of the head of the community were designed to garner support from those who received the petition (see Document 11).[57]

Conclusion

This chapter shows the extent to which petitions were submitted in response to centralization measures and reforms implemented by the central government, particularly as regards the status of land and the collection of taxes. As seen in the case of the controversy over the status of land in Jaffa or in the case of levying tithe from lands previously exempt from it, the state often chose to ignore preexisting arrangements including some that had received official or semi-offical approval. Another issue which led to the submission of petitions that diverged to some extent from the original aims of the institution of petitioning had to do with economic projects and concessions, particularly in the rapidly developing area of Jaffa. Minority groups often chose to let Istanbul handle their internal rivalries when they were unable to heal community disputes. Finally, the moral vision portrayed in the petitions strove to convince the sultan and his representative to recognize and address the petitioners' grievances and acknowledge various accusations against people who did not adhere to these moral standards, which is similar to former styles of petitioning in the Empire in the pre-Tanzimat period.

CHAPTER 7

THE OTTOMAN BUREAUCRACY AND ADMINISTRATION AS REFLECTED IN PETITIONS

Introduction

This chapter analyzes features of the Ottoman bureaucracy and administration as reflected in the petitions and the associated correspondence between the Ottoman bureaus and functionaries handling them. It examines whether the institution of petitioning at the end of the nineteenth century was indeed a continuation of a traditional institution and age-old practices or something new, given the new conditions prevailing in the Empire and the *zeitgeist*. Moreover, it tackles the question of whether certain aspects of modernity were reflected in the Ottoman petitioning system, not only with regard to the handling of the petitions by the bureaucracy and the legal system, but also with regard to the way the subjects perceived their place and role in the sultanate.

Why not rely on a Local Solution?

It is worth exploring, first, why petitioning Istanbul was still often preferred to local solutions by the population of the *kaza*s of Jaffa and Gaza. Michael Ursinus writes the following about the handling – at the provincial level – of complaints submitted by Ottoman subjects from the province of Manastır (Bitola) in Ottoman Rumelia at the end of the eighteenth century, which is worth quoting at length:

> On the provincial level, the administration of *mazalim* lay in the hands of the provincial executive and was dealt with in the provincial *divan*. On the other hand [. . .] the fact that the court ruling was eventually laid down in writing by the local kadi in the shape of *hüccet* and copied into his regular *sicil* suggests that the acting kadi played a regular and prominent role in the process of redressing injustice on the provincial level. [. . .] [B]y the late seventeenth and early eighteenth centuries (if not earlier), the governors of the province of Rumelia held formal court meetings within the *Divan-i Rumili* to answer petitions submitted by the local population. These meetings were convened in the governor's presence and attended by some of their own high-ranking officials, but acted under the immediate direction of the local kadi. Such hearings may have been considered distinct from (if not higher in rank than) the regular court meetings in the *mahkeme*. [. . .] On the other hand, the court hearings of the *Divan-i Rumili* around the turn of the eighteenth century are invariably described as sharia court hearings, just like those taking place in the *mahkeme* under the local kadi. But [. . .] such hearings belong into a category of their own. They were regarded as distinct from the regular meetings of the *meclis-i şer* whose primary function was the safeguarding and implementation of the Sacred Law. It would appear that the principal purpose of the court hearings convened in the Chancery of Rumelia was to redress wrongdoings which the regular judicial system itself had proved unable to resolve or was unwilling to address, or had not been charged with for a variety of reasons.[1]

Extant documents concerning the *mutasarrıflık* of Jerusalem at the end of the nineteenth century suggest that there was no separate *mazalim*-like institution parallel to that described by Ursinus in which the *kadı* and the governor sat together at the provincial level. Nevertheless, works by Haim Gerber and others indicate that concerning issues such as the registration of land, evaluation of land taxes, *waqf* lands, registration of population and so on, petitions were addressed to the administrative council of the province (*meclis-i idare*) which discussed them on a regular basis, conducted investigations and examinations, and made decisions.[2]

Councils also existed in lower echelons such as at the level of the *kaza* and addressed petitions of a similar nature, although their functioning in this regard was a world apart from the operation of the *mazalim* sessions at the provincial level as described by Ursinus. To cite one example, 'Ali Haykal Efendi, a prominent local politician and businessmen from Jaffa, sent a petition in December 1889 to the Grand Vizier against Yosef Moyal, a Jewish entrepreneur from this town, arguing that he insulted him as well as other officials and subjects, and that he collaborated with a person named Istiryadi Efendi (Asteriadis) to turn *miri* lands that Moyal had bought near Jaffa into privately owned *mülk* lands.[3] Moyal was said to have sold part of this land to Istiryadi as part of a deal between them and, in return, the latter, who was a member of the administrative council of Jerusalem, apparently voided complaints against Moyal sent to this council and helped Moyal avoid sanctions. As proof of his argument, Haykal attached a *mazbata* (decision) against Moyal issued by the administrative council of the *kaza* of Jaffa on 29 August 1889 and sent to Jerusalem after Haykal filed a complaint there and an investigation was conducted by the council. This description is informative as to the role of the local council in Jaffa as a body that discussed petitions on the local level.

Many petitions to Istanbul mention that the petitioners first unsuccessfully approached the local councils or the local authorities, thus justifying why an approach to Istanbul was needed. In other cases, petitioners thought that approaching Istanbul directly without referring first to local echelons (or alternatively approaching both simultaneously) would be more beneficial and fruitful.[4] A partial explanation can perhaps be found in Carter Findley's depiction (based on the "knowledgeable observer" A. Heidborn) of the ineffective way complaints were handled at the local provincial level in the Empire even as late as the early twentieth century, which is worth quoting at length:

A person with a petition (*arzıhal*) to submit in a provincial office would try to submit it directly to the chief administrative officer of the place, or at least to a member of his personal staff, and only failing that to the responsible department. From there, the petition would go to the records office (*evrak odası*) for registration, and the petitioner would be given a registry number in return for a payment of 20 paras. The records officer would forward the petition directly to the responsible official if the matter was important, otherwise to the head of the correspondence office (*mektubcu, tahrirat müdürü*) who would put on the document a note for its transmission (*havale*) to the head of the appropriate department and return the document to the records office, whence it would be forwarded to the indicated official after registration of a summary. The decision on the petition would normally take the traditional form of a marginal note (*derkenar*). [...] Since most requests passed through several bureaus – often for no clear reason – the ultimate result was usually a set of documents (*evrak takımı*), attached to one another, hard to handle, and dirtied and torn from being rolled up and unrolled. The petition would eventually be submitted, depending on its importance, to either the chief administrative officer or the head of the correspondence office, who would note on it an order for execution and return it to the records officer for him to communicate the decision to the petitioner at his next visit, no official initiative being taken to notify him.[5]

Clearly, some of the issues raised in the petitions discussed here were matters which normally fell within the jurisdiction of the regular *shari'a* and *nizamiye* court systems, particularly the latter which had gradually taken hold as of the 1870s, or the province's administrative councils. Yet, petitions continued to be sent to Istanbul regarding such matters as crimes of varying severity, business matters and commercial disputes, land and tax disputes and the like. In part, it had to do with the fact that approaching the *nizami* courts was not easy for subjects at the time and required considerable funds and resources, which gave an advantage to the well-off. In a recently published work on the unavailability of the *nizamiye* courts to commoners, Avi Rubin writes that:

[T]he *Nizamiye* justice was expensive, in part due to the growing dependency on attorneys. As a rule of thumb, the judicial opportunities created by the formalization of the Ottoman judicial sphere mainly served the interests of the wealthier classes and the various state authorities able to bear the costs involved in the appeal procedures, such as retainers and fees.[6]

Beyond this, however, it seems that people still sent petitions directly to Istanbul because they wanted access to power and a dialogue with the central government as a way of bypassing the administration and enhancing their position and maneuvering room in existing disputes and arguments, even though they probably knew they had no "legal" case.[7] The multitude of institutional bodies created by the modern state with all its new rules and regulations, the bankruptcy of the state and the chronicle shortage of financing faced by the newly-reformed institutions (which often led to corruption), together with the fees demanded from subjects approaching these institutions, all led to inefficiency and confusion. These circumstances doubtless prompted subjects to contact Istanbul directly as a tool which balanced the (often) inaccessible and more expensive reformed legal system. In other words, it was a cheaper and easier solution for the subjects' problems and provided a way out (however ephemeral) from the labyrinthine bureaucracy. The disenfranchised populations, hence, stuck to traditional *örfi* ways,[8] while transforming pre-modern procedures of petitioning into a tool to preserve their political, social and economic privileges in changing times. *Örfi* in this regard should be perceived as a pre-modern "constitutional" right which clashes with positive law.[9]

In addition, the petitioning system allowed subjects to raise claims and concerns which were not acceptable in the other more rigid court systems,[10] re-open matters on which a decision had already been handed down with the hope of overturning the verdict, put pressure on the local authorities in the provinces or on rivaling parties and beg for a sultanic ad hoc extra-judicial decision. The unprecedented accessibility of Istanbul by mail and telegraph, which lessened the barriers of geography, and the enhanced tangibility of the state in its subjects' lives far beyond its earlier incarnations also contributed to people's determination to beg the sultan directly for redress.

Finally, complaining to the local authorities about local officials and office holders was probably still considered more risky than referring the issue to Istanbul, whose intervention was considered to provide better protection against acts of revenge or retaliation, as seen in the case of the villagers of Sarafand al-ʿAmar who dared to complain in Jerusalem about their tax collector and were chased out of town by the police on a request from the Husayni family (see Appendix 1).

Hence, Istanbul was flooded with petitions from the provinces, and subjects considered the sultan and his representatives as the addressees for matters they could have resolved (and should have addressed) elsewhere.[11]

Handling Petitions: Offices and Procedures

Petitions were, for the most part, addressed to the Grand Vizier (*Sadaret*) in his capacity as the senior representative of the sultan or, to a lesser extent, to the ministries responsible for specific matters cited in the petitions. Petitions were also sent directly to the *Mabeyn*, the Palace Secretariat, or made their way there, but not in great numbers.[12] At a time when a clearer division of labor between Ottoman ministries responsible for different tasks was being implemented, continuing to address most issues to the *Sadaret* can be perceived as a continuation of a past practice well-rooted within Ottoman society.

When the petitions reached Istanbul, if they were written in other languages they were translated into Ottoman at the Translation Bureau, the *Tercüme Odası*, at the Ministry of Foreign Affairs. Despite the fact that most of the petitions were addressed to the *Sadaret*, much of the correspondence between the various Ottoman bureaus and functionaries whose reference was required for handling specific petitions – such as the *mutasarrıf* and *mutasarrıflık* of Jerusalem, *Defter-i Hakani*, and the Ministry of Justice (*Adliye*) – was coordinated by the Ministry of the Interior (*Dahiliye*), which eventually submitted all the information it gathered to the Council of State (*Şûra-yı Devlet*) in order for a decision to be made. Other matters that involved larger populations than the specific case involved or were of great importance were discussed in the Council of Ministers, the *Meclis-i Vükela*.[13]

Once all the information had been sent to the Council of State and had been read in one of its departments,[14] a draft of an imperial decision (*irade*) was prepared based on the information and then signed by members of the council (for instance, see Document 13a). Its summary was presented by the Grand Vizier to the Sultan whose decision was noted in handwriting by his Chief Scribe (*baş kâtibi*) in the margins of the summary (see Document 13b). A similar process took place in the Council of Ministers.[15]

The body that notified all the appropriate ministries, administrative units and the provinces about the decision and the steps to be taken was the Ministry of the Interior.[16] Unlike in the past, no glorious *ferman*s were issued; rather, the *irade* was written and distributed on a simple sheet of paper that resembled the workings of a regular routine bureaucracy. The above-mentioned steps constitute a theoretical description of the entire process of handling a petition from its submission to the imperial decision.[17] In most cases, however, petitions did not reach this stage; the issue was resolved along the way and an answer or decision was rendered by a specific bureau. In essence, the whole process was not so different from that described by Uriel Heyd in his study of *Mühimme Defterleri* in the mid-sixteenth–early seventeenth century Ottoman Empire:

> On important matters the Grand Vizier first submitted a brief account (*telḫīṣ*) or a memorandum (*taḳrīr*) to the Sultan, who returned it with his decision written on it with his own hand (*ḫaṭṭ-i hümāyūn* or *ḫaṭṭ-i şerīf*). Members of the Divan also presented certain matters orally to the Sultan during an audience and noted his approval, if given, on the document under consideration. It may, however, be assumed that a great many matters were neither submitted to the Sultan nor discussed in the Imperial Divan or the *paşa dīvānı*, but were decided upon by the Grand Vizier or another high official without any consultation. The Grand Vizier (or his subordinate) wrote his decision on the incoming communication or another paper in the form of a sentence ending in *buyuruldı*.[18]

The major difference was apparently that the process was more formalized and bureaucratic. Petitions were not submitted directly to the council by people or delegates who appeared in person and presented their cases. Rather, they were sent by mail or telegraph in large numbers. Orders were not issued on spot and given in situ to the petitioners themselves, as had often been the case in the past;[19] instead, a process of correspondence and investigation was carried out quickly and effectively using the telegraph and the mail (see Document 12). These allowed instant communication back and forth between Istanbul, the provinces, and the bureaus and functionaries concerned (often on the back of documents there are indications as to the petition handling process, such as where was it sent, when and so on).

The handling of a petition at each bureau was usually carried out within a matter of days to several weeks at most, except for cases where complicated processes were involved such as nominating an investigative committee, waiting for further clarifications from the province which itself needed to conduct an investigation, consulting the archives regarding previously discussed matters and decisions and the like. In general, every petition was processed, even those which seem marginal and unimportant.

The Role of Intermediaries

Suraiya Faroqhi highlights the importance of the presence of intermediaries in the Ottoman imperial center as regards the rendering of justice in the sixteenth and seventeenth centuries.[20] During the period discussed here, petitions were still entrusted to various intermediaries who were committed to intervene and exert pressure in the imperial center to promote the petitioners' interests. This type of approach apparently continued to play a significant role, particularly among the rural population, Bedouins and various minority groups. It can be perceived as an indication of the lingering effects of the old patrimonial system where connections and informal approaches to senior officials in the imperial center were crucial to obtaining justice and promoting one's interests, perhaps even more so than the written laws published during the reforms of the nineteenth century. It also underscores the fact that the quintessential signifiers of the age of modernity in the Empire, namely the efforts to introduce the rule of law based on a codified and coherent legal system and administration, were only partially successful.

For instance, as discussed in Chapter 4, the Arab Abu al-Fadl Bedouins who were involved in a dispute with the municipality of Ramle over a tract of land they claimed they had the right to farm and that the municipality had unlawfully sold, demanded substitute land and approached religious leaders in Istanbul to help them. Their approaches to these dignitaries are not preserved but information can be gleaned from the correspondence between the Ministry of the Interior and the former governor of Syria, Nazim Paşa, who was apparently in Jerusalem at the time and was asked to look into the matter.[21]

In another case, four members of the Husayni family in Gaza sent a petition in 1885 to Şakir Paşa, who in the translation of the petition into Ottoman is called "the brother of the Grand Vizier" (Kıbrıslı Mehmet Kamil Paşa, 1833–1913) against Yusuf Diya' al-Khalidi from Jerusalem for ruining their friendly relationships with people in Gaza, inciting their

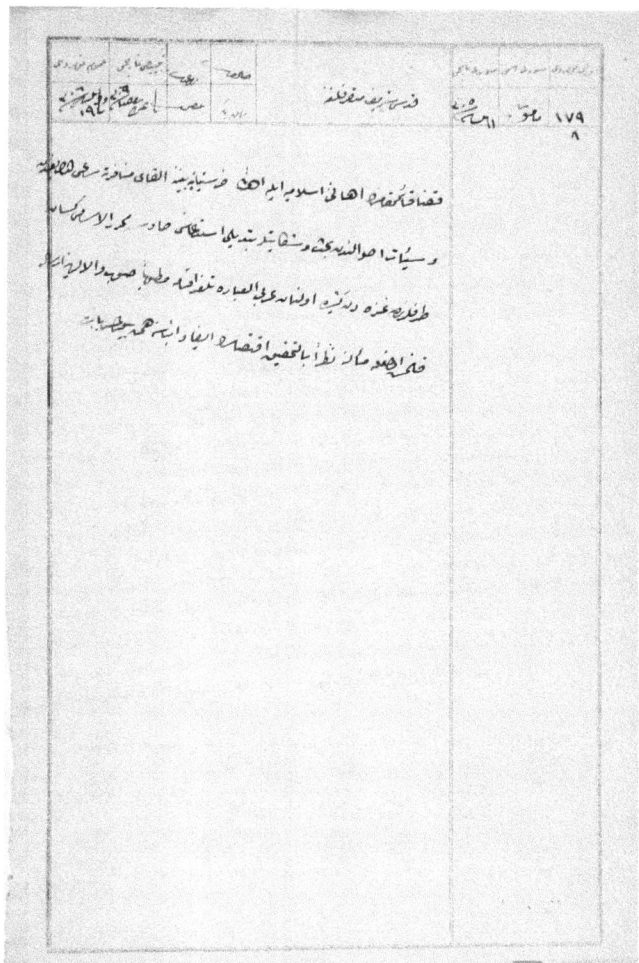

Document 12 An Order to Jerusalem to investigate a Complaint sent to Istanbul by an Official in Gaza against the Kaymakam who stirs up Muslim–Christian Tensions

Source: BOA. DH. MKT., 1620/123, 10 Ramazan 1306 [10 May 1889]

Notes: Often, the District of Jerusalem heard about the petition only when asked to refer to the matter by Istanbul. See the short laconic wording which cites the subject of the complaint and asks that the matter be checked and the situation reported back.

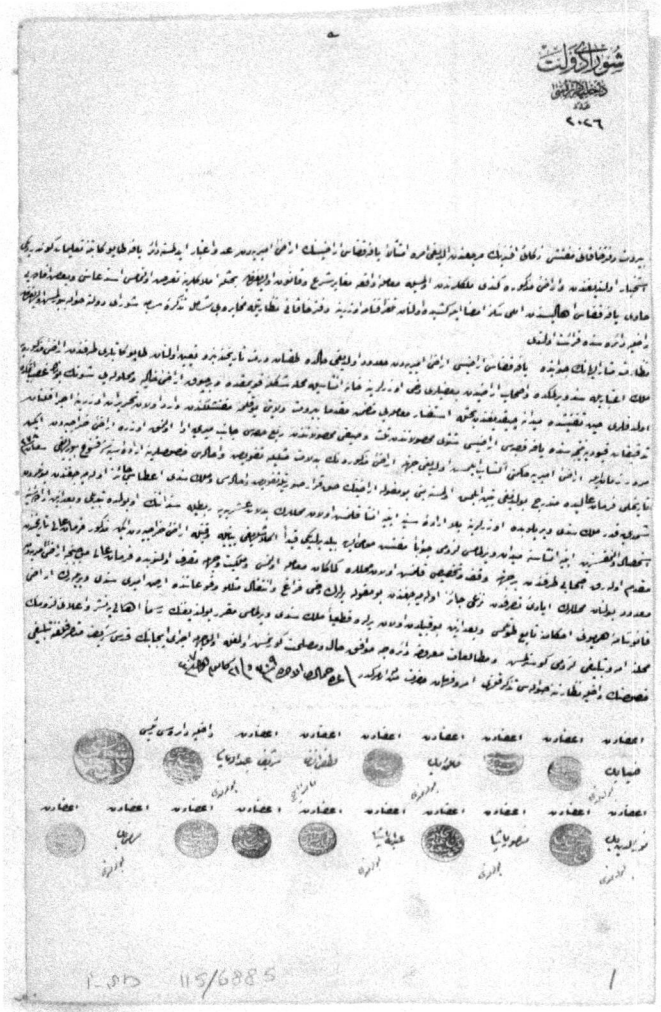

I.ŞD.00115

Document 13.1   A Proposed Resolution by the Council of State regarding the Status of *Mülk* and *Miri* Lands in Jaffa

Source: BOA. İ. ŞD., 115/6885, 21 Kânunuevvel 1307 [2 January 1892] (see Appendix 7.1, for a translation)

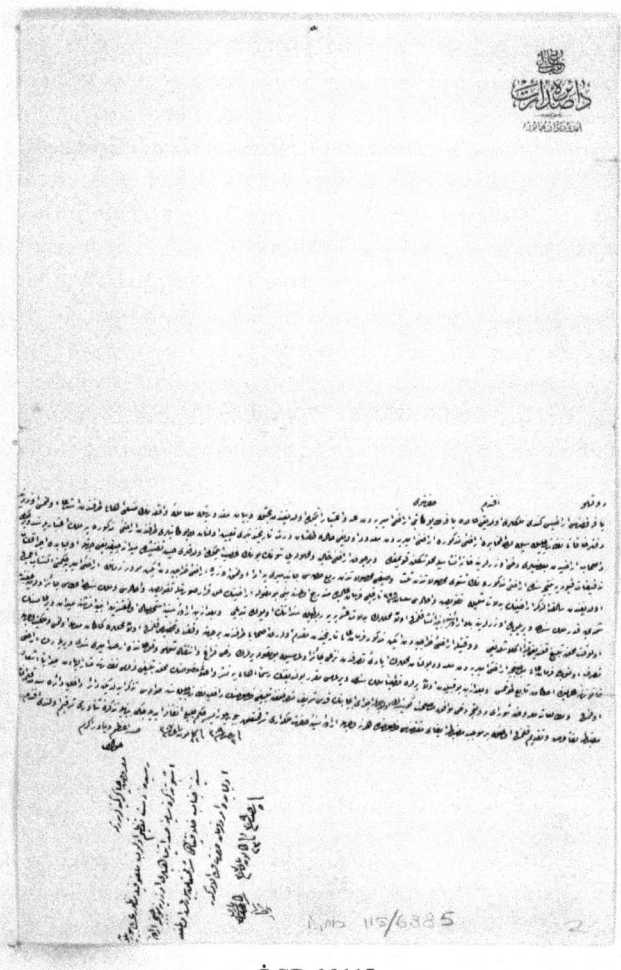

İ.ŞD.00115

Document 13.2 The Resolution by the Council of State transferred by the Grand Vizier to the Sultan for Approval

Source: BOA. İ. ŞD., 115/6885, 21 Kânunusani 1307 [2 February 1892] (see Appendix 7.2, for a translation)

Note: The Grand Vizier summarized the decision of the Council of State, at times copying sentences verbatim. The sultan's decision is written on the side, signed by the Chief Clerk of the *Mabeyn*. It was handed down two days after the Grand Vizier submitted the summary of the decision and about a month after the Council of State made its decision.

rivals to act against them and convincing the *mutasarrıf* of Jerusalem to act against their family (see Appendix 6).[22]

Jewish immigrants to Palestine also made use of intermediaries when petitioning. In the case of the Sephardic colony of 'Artuf (Har-Tuv), for instance, situated roughly halfway between Jaffa and Jerusalem, shortly after the colonists' arrival from Bulgaria at the end of 1895, the Ottoman authorities discussed whether to let them stay and whether they should be treated as Ottomans, given the somewhat ill-defined status of Bulgaria at the time. After receiving an order from the *mutasarrıflık* of Jerusalem, which rejected their request to stay and ordered them to evacuate the locality within eight days, the newcomers submitted a petition to the office of the deputy (*kaymakam*) Chief Rabbi in Istanbul through Rabbi Ya'akov Sha'ul Eliachar (1817–1906), the Rishon le-Zion Rabbi. Eventually, after a series of events which apparently included the intervention of the former, they were allowed to stay and convinced the government that they were Ottomans who moved within the boundaries of the Empire and were acting in accordance with imperial orders.[23]

In another interesting case involving Jewish immigrants, the acting Chief Rabbi in Istanbul approached the Ottoman high echelons in the name of the colonists of Rishon le-Zion with a request to settle the status of Sinan Paşa lands in the colony on which the colonists wanted to construct a school.[24]

How were the Petitioners Notified?

As shown in studies on petitioning practices in the past, petitioners were usually notified through the local *kadı* who received an order from Istanbul. His duty in such cases was to register the order in the *sicill* of the *shari'a* court, notify the petitioners concerning the decision handed down and give them the edicts sent from Istanbul to keep as future reference. In other cases, petitioners who went to Istanbul personally received the decision on the spot and took the order back with them to their place of residence, where they approached the local *kadı* in order to register the verdict in the records of the *shari'a* court.

In the nineteenth century, the *kadı*s who headed the *shari'a* courts had been divested of many of their former roles and mainly concentrated on personal and familial matters, such as divorce, marriage, endowments and the like.[25] Although there was some fluidity with regard to the duties and responsibilities of the *kadı* and the areas under his jurisdiction and although the *kadı*s also played a role in the *nizamiye* courts, the *kadı* was no longer responsible for notifying the petitioners about the decisions handed down in Istanbul with regard to their appeal or for the preservation of the records, as in previous centuries.

Possibly, the petitioners were notified by the staff of the *mutasarrıflık* of Jerusalem involved in the correspondence with Istanbul regarding petitions. More likely, however, as the quote by Findley above indicates with regard to the provincial administration, the petitioners needed to inquire in person about the outcome of their submission and ask for updates on the handling of their complaints (if the imperial orders had not been carried out in the meantime).

Settling Accounts

It is difficult to dispel the impression that the institution of petitioning during the nineteenth century was very often used as a mechanism to settle accounts or vilify rivals and opponents. The ease with which people could send a petition directly to the highest echelons in Istanbul can partially explain why this category of petitions was so common. In addition, the centralizing, autocratic nature of Abdülhamid II's regime, as discussed above, certainly favored denunciations and the exposure of real or imagined plots.

As seen in Chapter 3, account-settling petitions were for the most part sent by urban coalitions in Gaza and, to a lesser extent, in Jaffa. These petitions targeted rival individuals or coalitions, as well as their patrons and collaborators within the local Ottoman administration. The usage of petitions of this kind by the urban population is perhaps not surprising given the struggles for influence, power, jobs and resources in a changing administrative-bureaucratic and economic environment. The political game was largely played out in the major cities and towns of the region where the centers and representatives of state power were located and where economic activity was concentrated. There were also cases where officials settled their personal accounts with their peers, at times even anonymously, as seen in Chapter 5.

The Shari'a and Nizamiye Courts

As part of the Ottoman reforms, *nizamiye* ("civilian" or more precisely "regular")[26] courts on several hierarchical levels were established throughout the Empire and came to cover some of the cases previously tried in the *shari'a* courts headed by the *kadı*, whose jurisdiction was gradually restricted to familial matters. In principle, lower *nizamiye* courts were located in the centers of *nahiye*s. Above them were courts established at the center of *kaza*s, in the case discussed here in Jaffa and Gaza. Appeals in the *nizamiye* courts were made in larger urban centers such as Jerusalem, Beirut and Istanbul depending on the relevant instance of appeal. The *nizamiye* court on the *kaza* level was known as the *mahkeme-yi bidayet* and was headed by a *naib* from the *shari'a* court along with two judges, one Muslim and one non-Muslim. Moreover, the heads of the *shari'a* courts in the major towns often also ruled in the lower appeal *nizamiye* courts; thus, the separation between the two systems was not complete.[27]

At the level of the *mutasarrıflık* of Jerusalem, the *nizamiye* court served both for appeals from lower *nizamiye* courts in the *kaza*s under its jurisdiction such as Gaza and Jaffa (*mahkeme-yi istinaf*) and for the lower court for the region of Jerusalem itself. It was divided into two section, one that dealt with criminal matters and another which dealt with civilian matters. The court of appeal above Jerusalem was in Beirut. The highest instance of appeal in the *nizamiye* system was the *mahkeme-yi temyiz* (Court of Cassation) in Istanbul which was established in 1876.[28] This structure raises the question of why a "republican" institution such as the appeal system of the *nizamiye* courts was founded in the first place, considering the absence of a constitution in the Empire and the fact that the legitimate source of authority in the Empire remained the sultan, who held the ultimate power of decision.

Interestingly, in the petitions examined for this volume there are no examples of an appeal to Istanbul by an individual or a group of people that led to direct interference in the workings of the courts, such as orders to change or reconsider a verdict. In this sense, as far as we can tell from the documents, the separation of judicial authority was largely preserved. At times, the *mutasarrıflık* of Jerusalem, upon request from Istanbul to refer to a certain matter in a petition, simply answered that the matter was pending in court and that it could not intervene until a decision was made.

Such was the case, for instance, when several sisters from Jaffa applied to the Ministry of the Interior arguing that they were the *mütevelli*s of Shakir al-Nabulsi *waqf* and that their land had been confiscated illegally and forcibly by the *waqf* authorities in their town (see Document 9).[29] When requested to do so, Jerusalem informed Istanbul that the matter was pending in the *shari'a* court and meanwhile it could only act based on the original endowment of the land until a final decision was handed down.[30]

In other cases, Jerusalem sent Istanbul copies of decisions by the local courts when requested to do so, including appeals,[31] or informed Istanbul that the stipulations of a certain petition were unwarranted or incorrect and contradicted a court decision on this matter.[32] This was the case, for instance, with Salim al-Dabbagh from Jaffa who repeatedly applied to various bureaus claiming that a familial *waqf* had been taken from him illegally against court orders by the agents of the *mutasarrif* of Jerusalem who used an annulled court order against him.[33] Jerusalem replied that a *shari'a* court order had rejected Salim's claims and wrote that he must come to court with proof that he was the owner of the *waqf* if he wanted to challenge this decision.[34]

Other requests by petitioners concerning procedures in courts had to do with demands to dismiss officials who overstepped their powers and bring them to trial. This was the case, for example, for the Arab Abu al-Fadl Bedouins who wanted to bring to trial the former governor of Jerusalem, Rashid Bey, whom they accused of collaborating with the seizure and selling of their land.[35] At times, petitioners also asked Istanbul to delay certain steps until the court decided on the matter, arguing that it could only be implemented legally with a court order.[36] At other times, petitioners protested against the attitude and behavior of a certain court official or against plans to extend his term of office.[37]

Some petitions concerned an appeal against a decision by the *shari'a* court, while using the petitioning system as a high court of appeal. For instance, Mustafa, Husayn and Sha'ban Abu-Khadra' from Gaza applied to the *Sadaret* to intervene in a familial dispute with their brother Muhammad who disinherited them from the inheritance of their father al-Hajj Hasan Abu-Khadra'. The petition makes it clear that the brothers, who did not have the same mothers, had first applied unsuccessfully to the *shari'a* court to acknowledge their rights. They blamed the sons of the former *mufti* for collaborating with their own brother and for inciting him against them.[38]

Finally, there were petitions asking the government in Istanbul to force representatives of the local government (in Jerusalem, Gaza or elsewhere) to enforce or implement a decision by a local court that the local authorities had not complied with or ignored.[39]

Aspects of Modern Bureaucracy?

At the end of the nineteenth century, following several decades of reforms in the Ottoman Empire at both the imperial and provincial levels, many of the general features of a modern bureaucratic state were gradually introduced with varying levels of success in the Empire's provinces, including those which later constituted Mandatory Palestine. As a result, the Ottoman Empire, particularly its bureaucracy, was radically transformed and, from a patrimonial system, it slowly and gradually developed into a more professional, elaborate, differentiated and institutionalized system, with a clearer division of labor between its branches, standardized regulations and greater loyalty to the sultanate and to office rather than to an individual sultan or patron. At the ideological level, there was a gradual, slow shift from the previous system in which patrimonial relationships existed between the sultan and his subjects towards a system where equality before the law prevailed.

Nonetheless, despite all the reforms and efforts of modernization, the Ottoman bureaucracy still left considerable room for intermediaries and informal connections. Decisions were almost always open for renegotiation and subject to change, and various leverages were available to pressure the government to make decisions in favor of interested parties. Moreover, bribes were still a rather common practice, as seen in the numerous investigations against officials who were suspected of fraud. Decisions were not always supported by or anchored in legal practices and regulations and the sultan and his representatives at various ranks and echelons had considerable leeway to twist the law when there was a need. Finally, there was a wide gap in many cases between the normative level, as portrayed in correspondence and official documents, and reality on the ground. As Teyfur Erdoğdu, who summarized the dual nature of the Ottoman bureaucracy, pointed out "[i]n the bureaucratic structure of the Ottoman fin de siècle, modernizing accountability and arbitrary behavior existed side by side, as parallel mechanisms."[40]

This is the context that forms the basis for an examination of the nature of the Ottoman petitioning system at the end of the nineteenth century. At face value, the whole process of applying to the sultan over and above the head of the bureaucracy to demand justice ad hoc, rather than adhering to the regular procedures of the reformed bureaucracy and legal systems, appears to conflict with the notion of modernity and contrasted with modern impartial professional bureaucracy and the rule of law which the Empire tried to introduce and had declared to be its guiding light. Given that the status of Ottoman subjects gradually resembled that of citizens in a modern state more than the masses of unspecified *reaya*, their concerns and complaints should have been handled by one of the reformed institutions in the provinces.

Moreover, even in terms of serving as a kind of a court of appeal, there were now substitutes for the institution of petitioning Istanbul in the form of the hierarchic *nizamiye* court system in the provinces, the pinnacle of which was the *mahkeme-yi temyiz* in Istanbul, or the administrative councils in the provinces which operated in several instances and dealt with some of the issues raised in the petitions.

However, as seen above, there are several reasons for the continuing existence and even the flourishing of the petitioning system. From the sultan's point of view, relying on the traditional institution of petitioning for contact with the Ottoman subjects and allowing the latter to raise their complaints and grievances directly to Istanbul provided several clear advantages. It showed that the sultan was still an important figure despite all the reforms, it strengthened his status as the head of the state and the source of legitimacy and it boosted his image as a just and benevolent ruler who watched over his subjects personally and was responsible for their well-being. Moreover, the institution was used as a tool to gain recognition given the growing crisis of legitimacy the sultanate faced at the end of the nineteenth century.[41] For a suspicious sultan such as Abdülhamid II, petitions provided a wealth of information about the activity of his representatives in the provinces and the general mood of the population, especially given that many petitions at the time were sent collectively. The latter point is especially important if we take into account the turning of petitions in this period into a tool to conduct politics vis-à-vis the central government to an extent unknown thus far.

A hallmark of the reforms was the effort to introduce standardization and to regulate every aspect of the bureaucratic and legal systems, a step which of course necessitated the enlargement of the Ottoman bureaucracy and its red tape.[42] Unlike the very meticulous insistence at the time in anchoring the decisions in the *nizamiye* courts in specific laws and verifying that a trial as a whole was strictly carried out according to the judicial system,[43] the petition process was, for the most part, quite different. As in previous centuries, no specific laws or articles are mentioned, the considerations and justifications raised are, in the main, general and vague ("it is against the *shari'a* and the public interest," "it is against the law of the Sultan and his well known benevolence")[44] and there was much leeway for maneuvering.

Nevertheless, it must be stressed that there was by now a clear chain of command and division of labor for the petitions once they reached Istanbul, and there were hardly any cases of interference in decisions made by office holders responsible for certain duties and holding certain responsibilities. The process of handling the petitions was highly formalized and fixed, with very few exceptions. Most of the cases did not actually reach the sultan and were resolved beforehand in the warren of the bureaucracy. Many others ended in no more than bureaucratic correspondence which clarified that the petition was groundless or unjustified – doubtless to the dismay of the petitioners.[45] Some petitions that required a sultanic order, and were usually more principled in nature, were handed over to the sultan's staff for approval, which was granted almost automatically.

Conclusion

This chapter posed the question of whether petitions at the end of the nineteenth-century Ottoman Empire were a continuation of an old tradition modified or adapted to the *zeitgeist*, or whether under the prevailing conditions it was actually a new institution. Clearly, many characteristics of the Ottoman petitioning system in previous centuries remained in the petitioning system of the Ottoman Empire at the time. The source of legitimacy, law and power was still invested in the sultan and not in the people through their elected representatives and a constitution, despite the changing nature of sultan–subject relationships as part of the transition towards modernity. The system of petitioning continued to serve as an extra-judicial mechanism which bypassed regular procedures of the kind the Empire strove to instill in the period of reforms.

Even the procedures of handling the petitions by Istanbul were not completely unlike those implemented in previous centuries as described by Heyd, Faroqhi and others (see Chapter 1). Nevertheless, the process of petitioning was more regularized, open and accessible to all in a way that was both unprecedented and direct. There was also a clearer division of labor within the bureaucracy and the separation of offices and duties was preserved. Communication was faster due to the telegraph and mail, and there was no need for the petitioners to go to Istanbul in person or send a delegate to present their case. The procedure of petitioning was thus modernized by the essential removal of barriers or filters between state and subjects. Petitioning became a service which was accessible and affordable to the masses. The intermediaries in the procedure, the *arzuhalci*s, were professionals who sold their services independently rather than imperial official functionaries (such as the *kadı* or the staff of the *mahkeme*) who were the main pre-modern intermediaries.

In part, the decision to approach Istanbul had to do with the nature of the justifications and legal proofs raised in the petitions, which were insufficient to convince a regular court or council. The subjects wanted to conduct direct negotiations with the imperial center for their pleas to be heard and their request granted, even if there was no legal basis for them. Other considerations for contacting Istanbul were the cost of appealing to the *nizamiye* courts, the labyrinth of new institutions and procedures,[46] and the fact that the state now interfered with its subjects' lives to an unprecedented extent and was thus perceived as the final arbiter for their concerns.

To conclude, under the new conditions "justice increasingly came to be defined in terms of procedural standards and universality of judicial practice,"[47] whereas the petitions symbolized the extra-legal power of the sultanate. Nevertheless, in the context of Ottoman correspondence of the time, petitions were handled in a straightforward manner that favored legibility and simplicity over stylistic mannerisms as part of a broader attempt to achieve standardization that Ottoman officials at the time considered to be a symbol of rationality.[48]

CHAPTER 8

TEMPLER AND ZIONIST ACTIVITY AS REFLECTED IN PETITIONS TO ISTANBUL

Introduction

This chapter examines the Templer and Zionist activity in Palestine at the end of the nineteenth century as reflected in petitions sent to Istanbul, both by the settlers themselves as well as by the local population. At the time, various groups of Europeans settled in Palestine and contributed to its development and settlement, while at the same time eliciting direct European interest in the region.[1]

The German Templers, in particular, made an important contribution to Palestine's modernization in the realms of agriculture, industry, construction, transportation and technology.[2] They settled in Palestine about a decade before the proto-Zionist colonists and established several agricultural colonies and semi-agricultural neighborhoods in the outskirts of Haifa, Jaffa and Jerusalem. Their activity served as a model for the Jewish colonists in the 1880s, who learned a great deal from their experience and accumulated knowledge (although the Jewish colonization activity was on a much larger scale).[3] The Templers often maintained uneasy relationships with their Arab neighbors and the latter submitted petitions against their activities.

For the Ottoman administration, the clearest example of the threat of European intervention in the Holy Land was Jewish activity there at the end of the nineteenth century. Many of the Jewish immigrants enjoyed the protection of European Powers under the capitulations, either because they came from Europe or because European consuls in Palestine took them under their wing as part of their effort to increase their influence. Hence, the local Ottoman authorities were a priori restricted in their ability to confront the Jewish immigrants, restrict their activity or enforce Ottoman law. The Ottomans were afraid that a new national problem would arise in their troubled Empire and did not want to strengthen the European foothold in Palestine, although they were willing to accept Jewish immigration to other parts of the Empire, such as Anatolia.[4]

Despite what is commonly assumed, foreigners and settlers did not act only through their consuls. At times, they also approached the sultan through the institution of petitioning and asked for his intervention in various problems they encountered with Ottoman subjects, officials and institutions. Even though petitioning was not the approach of choice, foreigners nonetheless considered applying to Istanbul, perhaps alongside other steps such as asking for consular intervention, as a measure that would not harm their cause and could perhaps even promote it.

The Settlement of the German Templers

The Templers were a group of evangelist Christians from Württemberg in southern Germany. They aspired to gather their supporters in Jerusalem and save humanity by rebuilding the temple there (hence their name), and by preparing for the arrival of the Messiah.[5] In their view, the Holy Land was initially promised by the prophets to the Jews, but since they did not fulfill their historical task it was up to the 'People of God,' the association of the Templers, to inherit it. They wanted to create a pious Christian community in the Holy Land that would live according to the true spirit of Christianity, as they understood it, and not according to the rigid dogma of the Church. The religious community they envisioned was to serve as a model for both the Christians in the world and the people of the East.[6]

As an organized group, the Templers started immigrating to Palestine only in 1867.[7] They abandoned their initial plan to settle in the vicinity of Nazareth and preferred instead to establish colonies near existing urban and commercial centers, in particular the developing coastal towns of Haifa and Jaffa. They established three semi-urban colonies in the suburbs of Haifa (1869), Jaffa (1869) and Jerusalem (officially in 1878, but practically much earlier), as well as one agricultural colony a few kilometers north-east of Jaffa (Sarona, 1871) (see Map 4). The economic activity in the Templer colonies was very diverse and included agriculture, trade, commerce, transportation, industry and tourism.[8] In addition, a few Templer families resided alone in various towns in the country and ran various entrepreneurships (Ramle, Isdod, Nazareth).[9] A second group of Templer colonies was established in the first decade of the twentieth century in the vicinity of Haifa and Jaffa. Wilhelma was established in 1902 not far from Jaffa; Galilean Bethlehem (1906) and Waldheim (1907) were built close to Haifa (see Map 4). These three colonies were all based on agriculture.

The relationship between the Templers and the Arab population in Palestine was tense from the beginning.[10] Alex Carmel contends that the source of the unease was the Germans' negative attitude towards the Arabs, who, for their part, feared the newly-arrived foreigners. He notes that as early as 1858 – when the two leaders of the Templer society, Hardegg and Hoffmann, conducted a preliminary trip to Palestine – they reached the conclusion that the Arabs were "violent and dangerous, and that they hated foreigners." These observations apparently predetermined the German attitude towards the local population and encouraged the first settlers to distance themselves from Arab residents.[11]

Thus, an ambivalent pattern of relationships developed between the Templers and the Arab population. On the one hand, extensive economic cooperation developed. For example, there is evidence that Arab builders were employed in the construction of the German colonies.[12] Trade was also common between the Germans and the Arab population. The urban Arab population enjoyed the new services and high-quality products introduced by the Templers. For their part, the Germans purchased various raw materials from the Arab villages (manure, stones, whitewash).[13]

On the other hand, complaints, accusations and confrontations between the two populations were common and their daily relationships were often troubled. From the very early stages of settlement, the Templers had to deal with attacks on settlers and their transportation, theft, uprooting of trees and grazing on cultivated lands.[14] These occurrences forced them to

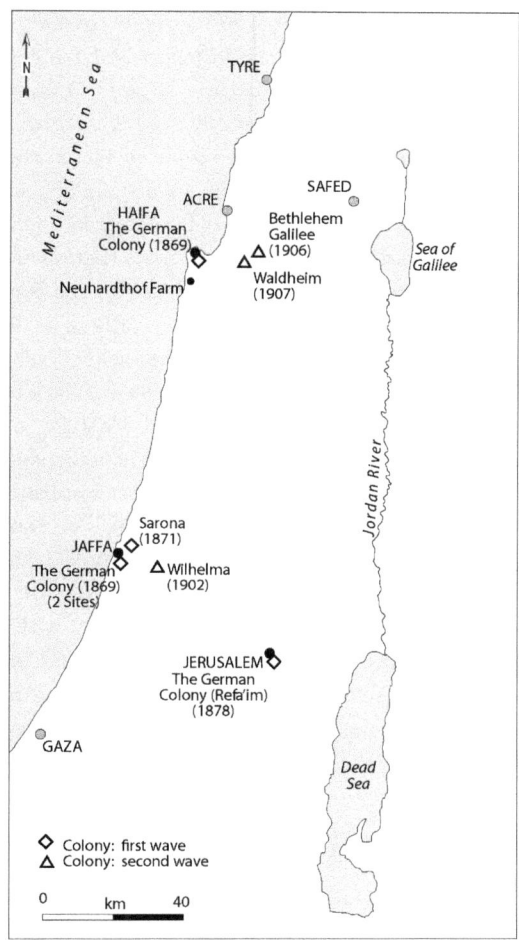

Map 4   Templer Colonies established in Palestine, 1860s–1908

take preventive measures, such as building a wall around their neighbor-hood in Jaffa, guarding the fields and putting pressure on the Ottoman government, often through the German representatives in the Empire and German public opinion, to protect them and their property.[15]

The first German colonies were established on land that was neither settled nor cultivated, and thus no Arab villagers were dispossessed. Yet,

there are reports that the success of the German colonies, which were
established on land considered by the villagers as having only limited
utility and hence sold cheaply, puzzled the latter.[16] Mahmoud Yazbak,
however, who examined documents from the *shari'a* court of Haifa argues
that, at least in the case of the German colony in Haifa, the colony was
established on land that had been previously farmed.[17] He cites evidence
that the Templers drove the prices down deliberately in order to convince
Arab owners to sell their land. Be that as it may, there is no doubt that
the second wave of German colonies, established in the early twentieth
century, involved dispossession of villagers, especially in Wilhelma where
the settlers were met with very stiff Arab opposition.[18] The confrontations between the two sides culminated in an armed attack on the colony
in 1909, an event that caused Germany to send warships to the coast of
Palestine.[19] Similar occurrences, although less severe, took place in Galilean
Bethlehem and Waldheim immediately after their establishment.[20]

These cases of confrontation notwithstanding, in some instances
friendly relationships developed between the Templers and the Arab
population to the benefit of both parties.[21] There is evidence that the two
groups exchanged expertise and know-how, especially with the villages
in the immediate surroundings of the German colonies. Contrary to the
common perception, the Templers also learned a great deal from the Arab
population, whose traditional agriculture was well-suited to the climate
and natural resources of the country.[22]

Petitions Involving Templer Activity

The tense relationship between the German settlers and the local population as described above found its expression in petitions sent to Istanbul
by the local population in Palestine. For example, the Maronite Church in
Jaffa, together with Muslim subjects with whom it had unspecified ties,
submitted a series of petitions to the Grand Vizier in Istanbul against the
Germans who allegedly trespassed on the Church's land and hit everyone
who approached the place. One of the persons they hit named 'Abdalla
al-'Aqiqi was "badly injured and could not get out of bed for two months,"
which caused him tremendous damage (see Document 14). The petitioners emphasized the fact that they were Ottoman subjects and that the
Germans refused to come to court to settle the matter, an accusation

similar to the one leveled occasionally against Jewish colonists.[23] About a year later the, Church sent a similar petition claiming that earlier approaches had not produced any outcome.[24]

Complaints by German Representatives Concerning the Templers

I was not able to locate significant evidence indicating that the Templers directly submitted petitions to the sultan.[25] Nevertheless, the German diplomatic representatives in Palestine and in Istanbul often approached senior Ottoman officials when problems were encountered by the Templers. This is an interesting point given that, at the beginning of the Templers' activity in Palestine, their relationships with the German authorities back home were strained and the government viewed them as a dissident group. Later on, however, relationships improved and the government realized the advantages it could derive from the Germans' presence in the Holy Land. A small, non-exhaustive sample of cases testifying to German contacts with the Ottoman authorities on behalf of the Templers is presented below.

In one case, in 1885, the German embassy in Istanbul complained about an attack on a group of Germans traveling between Haifa and Nazareth by a gang of 30 people. The embassy demanded that the offenders be found and punished.[26]

In another case, in 1891, a memorandum from the German Embassy was sent to the Ottoman Grand Vizier about a series of attacks in various places in the vicinity of Jaffa against German subjects, including Templers, and the failure of the local authorities to handle the situation. The attacks included robbery, theft, assault and obstructions to agricultural work. The letter states that German public opinion and the government were very concerned upon learning about these attacks.[27]

In yet another case, the Ottoman Embassy in Berlin reported a case of alleged attack on Germans near Jaffa which appeared in the newspaper *National Zeitung* in Germany and was ordered by Istanbul to deny the allegations that a German farmer and a mechanic were attacked near Jaffa since nothing had really happened on the ground.[28]

German complaints about attacks by the local population and the way the authorities in Palestine handled these cases continued well up to World

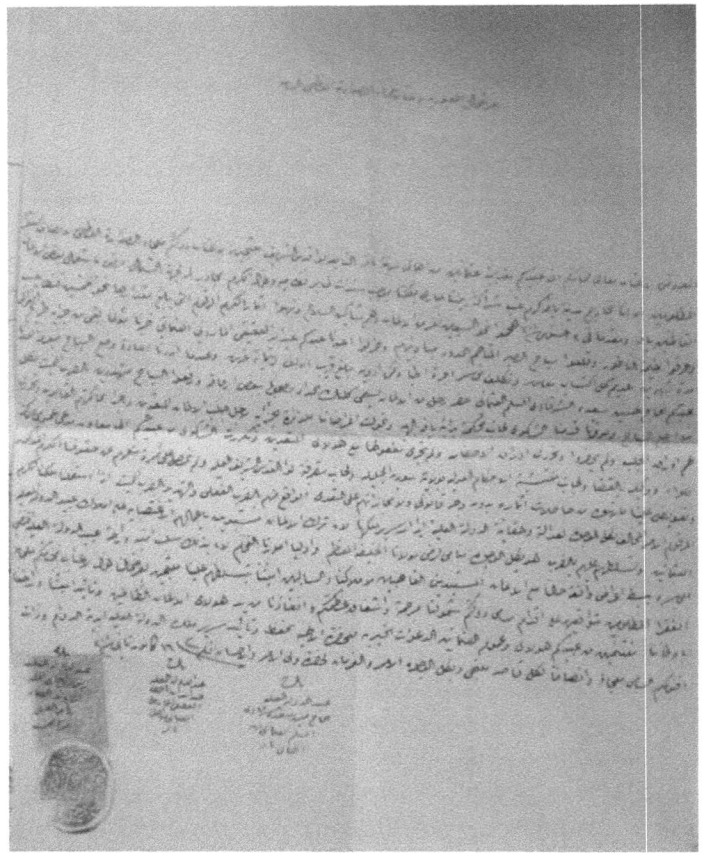

Document 14   A Petition by the Maronite Community in Jaffa against the German Colonists in this Town
Source: HR. TO., 391/13, 16 Kânunusani 1301 [28 January 1886]

War I. In 1913, the Grand Vizier Sa'id Halim Paşa (1865–1921) sent a letter to Baron Hans Freiherr von Wangenheim (1859–1915), the German ambassador in the Ottoman Empire at the time, most probably in response to the latter's complaint, concerning a series of attacks on Germans by local Arabs around Haifa and Jaffa. Particularly important was a case of a German girl from Haifa named Frieda who was kidnapped and sexually assaulted by a man called Beshara Samion, who later fled to Lebanon. The Grand Vizier updates the Baron about this case and claims that the Ottoman authorities investigated the event and found that the assailant hid in Beirut for a while and then fled to America with help from his mother who sent him money through the mail. Because he escaped, there was nothing the Ottoman authorities could do in terms of legal measures.[29]

Finally, there is evidence of the extent to which the protection granted to the German colonists by the German embassy helped them in cases in which the local population in a similar situation had no recourse. At stake was land that had progressively been considered *mülk* (privately owned) in Jaffa that the government wanted to revert back to its original status as *miri* land. As has been seen, petitions submitted by landowners in Jaffa concerning this type of issue were received negatively by Istanbul, which insisted on carrying out its plan. It turned out in this case that some of the landowners involved were Germans who had bought the land before Istanbul's decision to revert the land to its original status. With the help of the German Embassy in Istanbul, the Empire was forced to abandon its attempt as regards the Germans. Istanbul resented this situation, which it described as "very dangerous," but realized it could do nothing against it. Thus, the officials were ordered to change the records in accordance with the registrars held by the German Embassy, so they would reflect the situation on the ground and grant the colonists title deeds for their *mülk* lands.[30]

Jewish Immigration and Colonization Activity at the End of the Nineteenth Century

Zionist activity is customarily viewed as a key component in debates on late Ottoman Palestine as part of the controversy over the origins of the Jewish-Arab conflict which, as discussed above, to a great extent still shapes interpretations and defines attitudes towards this subject even today. In the petitions, however, Zionist activity occupies a rather minor place and is mentioned as only tangentially impacting other developments, processes and activities that preoccupied Palestine's population at the time. This perhaps reflects the relatively limited scope of Jewish activity during these specific years, other than in several specific regions where Jewish presence was concentrated. It contrasts sharply, however, with official Ottoman correspondence in which Zionist activity received considerable attention due to the government's overt opposition to it and its fear of the emergence of a new national problem in the Empire.

It is estimated that during the "first 'aliya" (1882–1903), the term used in Zionist historiography to designate proto-Zionist immigration to Palestine at the end of the nineteenth century, between 30,000 and 50,000 Jews immigrated in several waves. By 1904, however, fewer than 30,000 of those immigrants remained in the country. Of those who stayed, about 5,500 established some 30 agricultural colonies (*moshavot*) on an area of approximately a quarter of a million *dunam*s (see Map 5).[31] These colonies formed the backbone of the "new *yishuv*," the national sector of Palestine's Jewish community, and constituted the major contribution of the "first 'aliya" immigrants to the Jewish national project in Palestine.[32] The other Jewish immigrants during this period either followed in the footsteps of Jews who had previously immigrated to Palestine and joined the communities of the "old *yishuv*," the traditional non-national religious Jewish community in Palestine, or settled in the booming coastal towns of Haifa and Jaffa and in a few neighborhoods in Jerusalem outside the walls of the old city, which were all part of the "new *yishuv*."[33]

The initial wave of Jewish immigration to Palestine in 1882, following a series of pogroms in Russia starting in 1881, was fairly spontaneous. Most of the "first 'aliya" immigrants in the early 1880s were not necessarily motivated by ideological considerations but, rather, ended up in Palestine due to a lack of means or opportunities to move elsewhere. They were influenced by the unfounded belief that Palestine, the Biblical land of milk and honey, would lead to many economic opportunities.[34] At the same time, certain "first 'aliya" immigrants, particularly among those who established the first colonies, were determined to move to Palestine out of a combination of religious and proto-nationalist considerations. Unlike Jewish immigrants to the Holy Land in the past, they were not motivated solely by religious considerations but, rather, aspired to realize the dream of returning to Zion (*Eretz-Yisra'el*), which they perceived as the ancient Jewish homeland, and to establish a modern national society there.

The period between 1904 and 1914 is defined in Zionist historiography as the "second 'aliya." This period witnessed the arrival in Palestine of Jewish immigrants whose characteristics were noticeably different from those of the previous period. Members of the "second 'aliya," were often young, secular, single, socialist and without substantial private capital at their disposal. They came mainly from Russia and, beginning in 1908, established cooperative farms (this later became the *kibbutz* and the cooperative *moshav*) (see Map 5). They aspired to implement a revolutionary socialist ideology combined with Jewish nationalism, which led them to struggle to replace Arab workers and guards in the Jewish colonies with Jewish ones.[35]

Almost every newly-established colony clashed in the beginning with its Arab neighbors over issues such as borders of plots, grazing and water rights, theft and various kinds of assault. In some cases, minor quarrels, which can perhaps be interpreted as cultural misunderstandings, turned into violent confrontations culminating in injuries and even deaths.[36] Occasionally, tensions persisted for years and led to costly trials, boycotts and mutual complaints to the Ottoman authorities.

The petitions discussed above portray the rural society in Palestine in the period preceding the start of proto-Zionist colonization activity in Palestine in 1882, and well into the 1880s and 1890s, as one undergoing a process of transformation, whose features were largely dictated from above/outside. Many of these petitions were directly or indirectly related to new policies and measures implemented by the central government, which were apparently accompanied by considerable misconduct on the part of local Ottoman officials and other influential urban individuals.

This situation must be taken into account when dealing with the proto-Zionist colonization activity in Palestine from the early 1880s onwards because the colonists, who became part of this region's social and economic fabric, often confronted and became entangled in the lasting consequences of earlier tensions and unresolved problems. Moreover, the colonists settled at a time when changes in the agrarian system had already begun and they needed to cope with their effects, which in part remained contested and unresolved. Many of the daily clashes between the two populations during the early years of Jewish colonization must be interpreted against this backdrop rather than being merely viewed as "cultural misunderstandings,"[37] especially if we take into account the continuation of daily disputes between them even years after the beginning of Jewish colonization activity.[38] Hence, at least some of the anger voiced by the rural population towards the Jewish colonists stemmed from ongoing developments and processes that started well before their arrival in Palestine.[39]

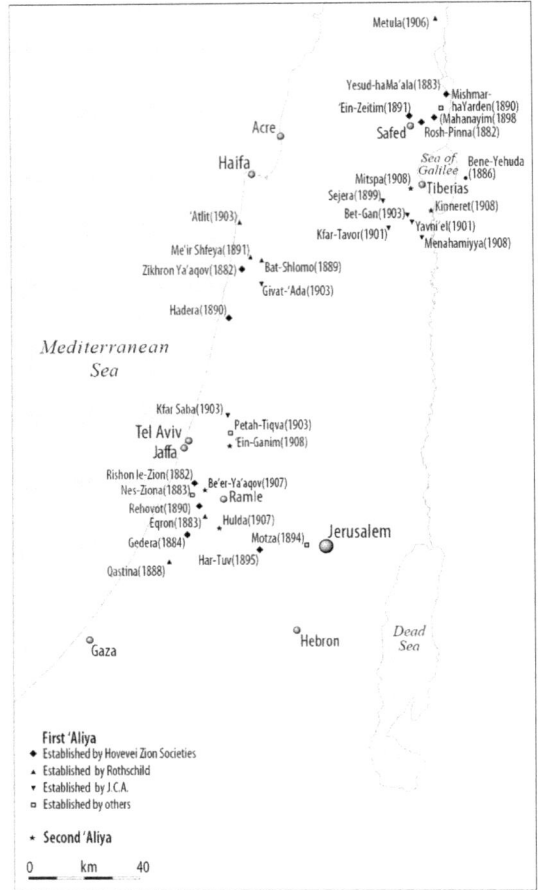

Metula(1906)

Yesud-haMaʻala(1883)
ʻEin-Zeitim(1891)   ◆Mishmar-
                    ▫ haYarden(1890)
Acre   Safed   ◆(Mahanayim)1898
                Rosh-Pinna(1882)

Haifa

Sea of
Galilee   Bene-Yehuda
Mitspa(1908)   (1886)
Sejera(1899)   ▫Tiberias
Bet-Gan(1903)   ▪Kinneret(1908)
ʻAtlit(1903)   Kfar-Tavor(1901)   ▾Yavniʼel(1901)
                        ▾Menahamiyya(1908)
Meʼir Shfeya(1891)
Zikhron Yaʼaqov(1882)◆ ▴Bat-Shlomo(1889)
            ▾Givat-ʻAda(1903)

Hadera(1890)

Mediterranean
Sea

Kfar Saba(1903)▾
Tel Aviv   ▫Petah-Tiqva(1903)
Jaffa   ▪ʻEin-Ganim(1908)

Rishon le-Zion(1882)◆
Nes-Ziona(1883)▫ ◆Beʼer-Yaʼaqov(1907)
Rehovot(1890) ◆   ▫Ramle
    Eqron(1883)▴   ▴Hulda(1907)
Gedera(1884)◆   Motza(1894)▫ Jerusalem
Qastina(1888)▴   Har-Tuv(1895)

Gaza   Hebron   Dead
                  Sea

First ʻAliya
◆ Established by Hovevei Zion Societies
▴ Established by Rothschild
▾ Established by J.C.A.
▫ Established by others

▪ Second ʻAliya

0   km   40

Map 5   Jewish Colonies established in Palestine, 1882–1908

Petitions against Proto-Zionist Activity

Despite many documented disputes and clashes between the Arab rural population and the proto-Zionist colonists,[40] relatively few petitions that deal with the effects of proto-Zionist colonization activity, directly or indirectly, have been located thus far in the archive in Istanbul. Several such cases are presented and analyzed below.

The first case deals with ownership claims made by the Bedouins of Khirbat Duran. As has been noted, representatives of the Bedouin group Arab Abu al-Fadl petitioned Istanbul several times around the time the colony of Rehovot was founded in 1890, arguing that the people of the new colony forced them to leave their land, prevented them from cultivating land they had been occupying for many generations and had chased them away (see Appendix 3):

> Based on this, and since we are Bedouins who live in tents in this Khirba from olden times and we have no other place aside from it, and also because we have no other land to cultivate, and since we are from amongst the Bedouins who are loyal subjects of the exalted and eternal State, which is our protector, without expecting anything in return, and based on the well known justice of the state and the justice and equity of your Excellency that are famous all over the world, with the hope that we will not alone be deprived of the justice and equity of the exalted state; we have no other choice but to submit this petition to beg for the issuance of an exalted order to let us stay in our place of birth where we reside, based on the current arrangement and not to let the Jews [*isra'iliyyin*] chase us away and prevent us from cultivating the land in a way which will guarantee their and our rest and benefit; or else issue an exalted order to allocate us land from the imperial property, which would be sufficient for our livelihood and the sustenance of our families and children.[41]

Zionist sources indicate that Rehovot clashed several times with the Bedouins living to the east of the colony during the first years after its establishment. This group leased some of the lands bought by the colony on a yearly basis and the first dispute between the two sides took place immediately after Rehovot was established.[42] Eliyahu Levin-Epstein (1864–1932), the head of the colony of Rehovot at the time, wrote the following about this dispute:

> As said, the land of Duran [Rehovot] is comprised of nearly 10,600 *dunam*s.[43] Of these, the previous landowner rented out around 600 *dunam*s to Bedouins, who were close neighbors to Rehovot, as well as rivals. Given that we were newcomers in the country, who did

not know the language, and the practices of the place were alien to us, the first quarrel between us and the Bedouins took place while they were sowing their land. We understood that after we had bought the land, paid its price, and received title-deeds from the government, we were the land's sole owners and no one else had a say [on this matter]. Thus, we did not want the Bedouins, they and their wives, children and herds, to come and occupy our land. We planted vineyards, and were afraid that their herds would destroy them. We asked them to leave the place, but they claimed that they had rented it for two years, had sowed it only once [thus far], with summer crops, and therefore had the right to sow it once more with winter grain crops, harvest it, thresh it, a task which would take the whole summer, and only then they would leave. We did not know if they were speaking the truth, therefore we asked Mr. Hankin[44] to come to us and explain the root of the issue. Mr. Hankin told us that the Bedouins were right. Thus, we compromised with the Bedouins: provided that they removed their tents from our land, they could come and cultivate the land they rented, until they collected the winter crops. In such a way, the first quarrel between us and our neighbors ended in a good way.[45]

The Bedouins, for their part, admitted in their petition that the land where they resided had previously been sold to a local landowner, but claimed that, before the arrival of the Jewish colonists in 1890 – whom they argued bought the land in an underhanded fashion with the help of a person named al-Hajj 'Ali Haykal Efendi, a member of Jaffa's Administrative Council and the Chamber of Commerce – they had reached an understanding with the landowner who let them stay and continue cultivating the land as tenants.[46] They claimed that they had not reached a similar arrangement with the Jews.

At face value, the events described above during the first year of Rehovot were resolved on good terms and did not lead to violence. However, a few years later the colony and the Bedouins clashed over a grazing dispute, which the author and popular historian Moshe Smilansky from Rehovot, who witnessed the events, argues were connected directly to the Bedouins' strong initial feeling that the land on which Rehovot was established was theirs.[47]

Petitions of this kind made by Bedouins demonstrate the disparity between the way they perceived the issue of ownership of land and

Ottoman law and the government's official policy. Following the introduction of the Ottoman Land Law of 1858, the government wanted to rigister all lands under the names of their actuall retainers (*tasarruf*).[48] As far as the Bedouins were concerned, however, the fact that they had occupied a certain land and farmed it for many years was sufficient to grant them rights over it.[49] In the pre-1858 system, the land was held by the cultivators, who had the right of usufruct, as long as the land was regularly cultivated and taxes paid. In the eyes of the rural population the land was thus theirs, even if there was an intermediary between them and the state, be it a tax collector or an owner. Hence their demand to force the colonists to compromise with them or grant them equivalent land to that from which they had been evicted.[50]

The second case involves villages in the region of Masmiyya-Qastina, in the northern part of the *kaza* of Gaza, which repeatedly petitioned together to demand a reduction in their *vergi* tax (see Appendices 4 and 8).[51] In one of these petitions, the villagers point to three recent examples of land transactions in their region, which allegedly demonstrated the land's real value.[52] The first case was uncultivated land (*mahlula*) in the Arab village of Zarnuqa to their north which was sold at an auction (*müzayededede*).[53] The second was land bought for the establishment of the Jewish colony of Gedera, also in their vicinity.[54] The third was land possessed by rich influential people whose identity is not disclosed.

In all three cases, the villagers claimed, the land sold was evaluated at much lower prices than theirs, although the price of these lands should have been similar and the property tax, accordingly, should have been calculated at lower rates.[55] While expressing their frustration at the tax rates they were required to pay, the petitioners refer directly to the Jewish colonization activity in their vicinity and provide specific details regarding it. In this context, it is interesting to see how they phrased their demand for justice from the sultan by referring to Jewish activity (see Appendix 4):

> It is known to your highness that the mercy and compassion of the ruler, may God save him, is given to all the dominions of the Empire and does not discriminate one over the other, but encompasses all. Is it possible that the just rules and orders will let us continue to suffer from this injustice and unfairness?[56]

The third case took place a little after the period discussed here but it still deserves attention as it is indicative of the deteriorating Jewish–Arab relationships after the Young Turk Revolution and constitutes an excellent comparison with the petitions concerning Zionist activity from the previous period. The well-known al-Fula incident took place in northern Palestine two years after the Revolution and symbolized the initial politicization of the emerging Jewish–Arab conflict and the involvement of the Arab urban circles in it.

Al-Fula was a village located in Marj Ibn ʿAmir (the Jezreel Valley) at the foot of the Nazareth Mountains. The Sursuk family from Beirut bought large segments of the valley from the Ottoman government in 1872, during the reign of Sultan Abdülaziz. In 1910, Ilyas Sursuk sold the land of al-Fula, some 3,500 *dunam*s, to a Zionist organization called the *Jewish National Fund* (JNF), which was established at the beginning of the century to purchase land and facilitate Jewish colonization activity.[57] The JNF's attempt to exercise its ownership rights and settle colonists there led to tensions and, eventually, to a clash between the villagers of al-Fula, who previously were tenants on Sursuk's land, and the Jews who settled there. The former were encouraged by the *kaymakam* of the sub-district of Nazareth, Shukri al-ʿAsali,[58] who refused to complete the transaction, and the generally negative attitude towards Zionist activity which had spread in the Empire and in Palestine after the Revolution, including in the press.[59] As far as they were concerned, they cultivated and possessed the land, had the right of usufruct over it and did not care whether the owners were from Beirut or elsewhere as long as the situation on the ground remained the same. The Jews, on the other hand, wanted to implement their full ownership rights as they saw fit and in accordance with Ottoman law.

The villagers of al-Fula submitted a petition to the Grand Vizier against Sursuk Efendi (Ilyas Sursuk) claiming that together with another person, an Ottoman middleman who helped facilitate the transaction, they had sold the lands of their village to Zionists who were not Ottoman subjects. Interestingly, the use of the terms "Zionist" and "sons of the religion of Moses" (in Turkish *siyonist musevi*) and "non-Ottoman" (in Turkish *yabancı ecnebi*) in the petition contrasts with the older petitions discussed above where Jews were called "Israelites" (in Arabic: *isra'iliyyin*) or *musevi* (sons of the religion of Moses). The villagers expressed concern for their livelihood and lands, and added that there were about 1,000 people living there who had no other land or sources of livelihood.[60] Moreover, they added that they rejected the oppression of foreigners and made an uneasy comparison with the Ottoman state which had ruled them for many years, while using the same vocabulary (*tahakkum*, i.e., oppression, arbitrary power). Thus, on the top of what we know and what was published about the incident of al-Fula, which deteriorated into a bloody fight and was widely reported in the Arabic press in Palestine and in the Levant, the villagers' petition provides information about their own perception of the event. The land transfer was perhaps legal by the book, but it affected their daily lives and deprived them of their sources of livelihood. This helps account for their resistance to the establishment of the cooperative settlement of *Merhavia* on land purchased from Sursuk by the JNF.[61]

The last case also occurred after the period discussed in this study, but nevertheless it deserves consideration due to its uniqueness and relevancy. It is a collective petition sent by villagers in the *kaza* of Gaza – interestingly, together with the Abu-Kishk tribal group located in the *kaza* of Jaffa near al-'Awja River – against the activities of the Jewish colonies of Rishon le-Zion and Rehovot in their vicinity (see Appendix 10). In July 1913, the villagers wrote to the Grand Vizier explaining that the Jewish colonies treated them in a very harsh manner, attacked passengers who passed by the colonies, hired Circassian (*cherkes*) and other foreign guards who behaved very aggressively towards the rural population and possessed illegal weapons. The villagers claimed, moreover, that the local court summoned several Jews but the colonies replied that these individuals were out of the country.[62]

Jewish sources record that the immediate cause for the petition was a severe clash between the colony of Rehovot and the adjacent Arab village of Zarnuqa on 23 July 1913. The event started as an argument over accusations of theft from fields owned by Jewish farmers between the colonies of Rishon le-Zion and Nes-Ziona. It quickly deteriorated into a series of clashes between Rehovot and the nearby village of Zarnuqa, where the accused fled and found refuge. The incident left an Arab and a Jew dead and resulted in tremendous bad blood between the two sides. The fact that a Jewish guard in Rehovot was found dead in mysterious circumstances a few days after the clash contributed to the tension. The clash in 1913 was apparently the culmination of a series of other daily confrontations and tense relationships between the Arab rural population and the Jewish guards of the *ha-Shomer* organization in the region.[63] This claim finds support in a recent study by Gur Alroey on *ha-Shomer* in Rehovot and its confrontational approach.[64] Tension was also high in the colony of Rehovot itself between the farmers of the "first *'aliya*" and the Jewish workers of the "second *'aliya*" who demanded a stiffer reaction to the village of Zarnuqa.[65]

Petitions by Zionist Colonists and Jewish Activists

Common wisdom has it that foreign nationals who confronted difficulties of various sorts in their dealings with the local population or local government representatives that required the intervention of the Ottoman authorities preferred to approach their consuls in Palestine or Istanbul with a request to intervene in their favor. This was apparently by far the tactic favored by most foreigners residing in Palestine, who could take advantage of the broad protection granted to them by their states in light of existing agreements with the Ottoman Empire, which reflected the latter's weak political position vis-à-vis that of former.[66] For instance, Levin-Epstein described how the colonists of Rehovot asked for the intervention of the Russian consul in Jaffa in their favor – despite all their reservations about asking for Russian help – when they had an argument with the *kaymakam* of Jaffa who refused to intervene in a fight with the adjacent Arab village of Zarnuqa:

> I went to the consul's residence [in Jaffa]. I woke him up and told him what had happened and was about to happen in Rehovot, and how the *kaymakam* had received me. The consul immediately sent to call the "chief translator" (dragoman) and ordered him to accompany me to the *kaymakm*, wake him up – if he was already asleep – and tell him in his own name that the *kaymakm* would be personally held responsible for everything that happens in Rehovot.[67]

In such a situation, even without referring to written laws or international agreements, it was enough for the consuls to intervene to swing events in favor of their nationals. The Empire was afraid that even minor incidents involving a foreigner, especially in a sensitive place such as the Holy Land which was attracting global attention, would quickly deteriorate into an international crisis.[68]

The above notwithstanding, both proto-Zionist immigrants and colonists who did not possess Ottoman citizenship, as well as representatives of the Jewish colonization organizations, sent petitions to Istanbul with various requests – at times, not in the normative petition format. These petitions by non-Ottoman Jews shed light on the sultan's status among Jewish immigrants who arrived in Palestine at the time and the extent to which they had grasped the mechanisms and modes of operation of the Ottoman system and made use of it. It shows that they did not merely go through the European consuls in the Holy Land – the more frequent method which is well-documented in the literature. Rather, they also attempted to achieve certain goals within the Ottoman system itself and, at any rate, they apparently did not consider sending a petition to Istanbul meaningless or hopeless and made the effort and expenditure to do so.

For instance, in one case four Judean colonies south-east of Jaffa – Rishon le-Zion, Eqron, Nes-Ziona and Rehovot – together with the colony of Petah-Tiqva (Malabes) which was located some 15 kilometers to the north-east of Jaffa, sent a telegram to the sultan via the Secretariat of Yıldız Palace (*Mabeyn*) with a request to permit the construction of agricultural buildings in the colonies, arguing that they paid taxes and fulfilled all the governments orders, and that there was not enough housing for their families (see Document 15). At the beginning and end of the telegraph, there are very long blessings to the sultan. The names of the signatories at the bottom of the telegraph are invented typical Jewish names written in their Arabic form in reverse order. For instance, the representative of the colony of Petah-Tiqva is Ibrahim bin Musa (Abraham the son of Moses) whereas that of Rishon le-Zion is Musa bin-Ibrahim and so on. The names of the colonies are written in their Arabic form rather than the Jewish versions (for instance, Rehovot is called Duran, Rishon le-Zion is called ʿUyun Qara, and so on).[69]

In another case, the colony of Petah-Tiqva petitioned to be allowed to drain the swamps in its vicinity which had caused considerable damage, and asked that the swamp land either be drained or sold at public auction.[70] Although we do not possess the original petition, the correspondence between the Ottoman offices suggests that the petitioners mention both the damage from the swamp, as well as the fact that the state could earn revenues from potential development of the swamp land.

These sporadic petitions by Jewish immigrants and colonists notwithstanding, petitions to Istanbul by activists and organizations involved in Jewish colonization activity with various requests in favor of the colonists were more common. These petitions were often in the form of a letter in French, written by individuals who were not professional petitioners and thus did not employ the standard flowery phraseology. For instance, Elie Scheid (1841–1922), the head of the Rothschild administration in Palestine, the largest sponsor of the "first 'aliya" colonization activity, often submitted such petitions and letters to various Ottoman officials explaining how the expansion of the Jewish colonies would benefit the Empire in general and the local population in Palestine in particular.[71] The former, argued Scheid, would benefit from the development and technology the Jews brought to Palestine which coincided with the Empire's development plans.[72] The latter, he added, received free medical treatment in the colonies and also were being taught Arabic by a local teacher.[73] Scheid repeatedly complained in his approaches to Istanbul that the local authorities in Palestine were creating obstacles to Jewish activity and did not let Ottoman Jews who were loyal subjects of the Empire buy land, construct houses or establish new villages (see Document 16).[74]

Scheid maintained regular ties with Ottoman officials in Istanbul and throughout the Levant. On each visit to Palestine, he met with senior Ottoman officials in Palestine and Beirut, lobbied in favor of the colonies and tried to eliminate obstacles to the colonization project. The vast official and unofficial connections between the Rothschild administration and the Ottoman authorities, at both the local and imperial levels, have not received much attention in the literature. These ties were often used to promote the colonization project, solve problems with which the colonies were confronted, protect them in times of need and attempt to annul orders issued against them.[75] Rothschild himself met senior Ottoman officials in the Levant and possibly was in contact with officials in Istanbul, a point which still awaits further research.[76]

Moreover, the Rothschild Bank in London made loans to the Empire which desperately needed cash, although it remains unclear whether Baron Edmond de Rothschild (1845–1934) himself was involved in these transactions or whether they decisively influenced Ottoman policy towards Jewish colonization.[77] As part of his efforts to curry favor with the Ottoman authorities, on several occasions Rothschild's aids made contributions on his behalf to charitable organizations, to the overt satisfaction of the sultan.[78]

In this regard, it is interesting to note the high degree of autonomy that the Ottoman authorities granted the Rothschild administration and the

Document 15 A Collective Petition by the Judean Colonies South-east of Jaffa
Source: BOA. Y. PRK. AZJ., 40/37, 21 Nisan 1316 [4 May 1900]

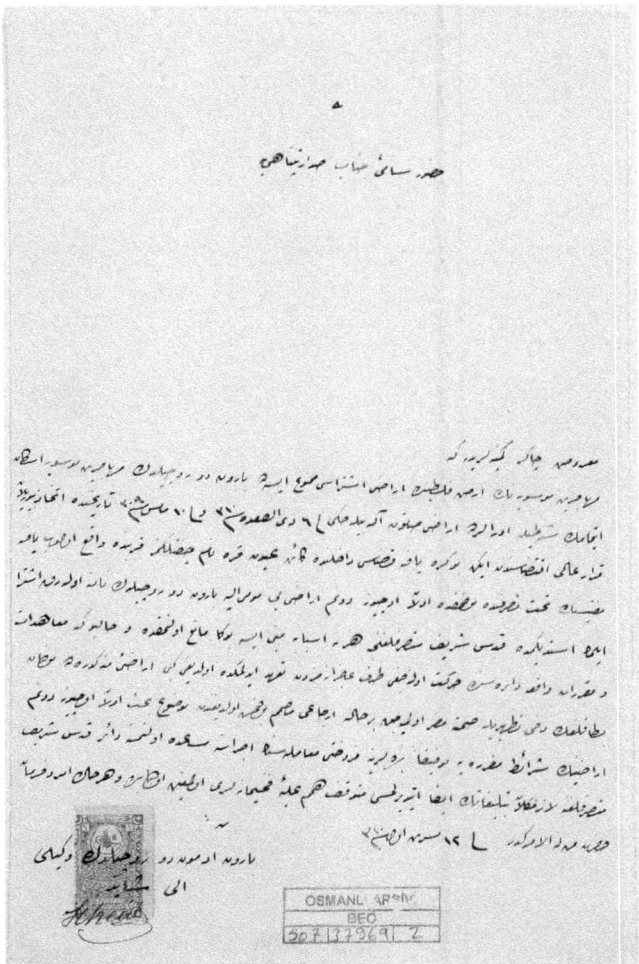

Document 16 A Petition by Elie Scheid, the Representative of Baron Rothschild
Source: BOA. HR. TO., 507/37969, 12 Teşrinievvel 1310 [24 October 1894]

Jewish colonies to run their own affairs. In most instances, the Ottoman
government did not intervene in the colonies' internal affairs and allowed
them to exercise self-governance in social, religious and cultural matters,
as well as regarding more practical issues such as the internal distribution of land.[79] It only took steps in rare cases when representatives of

the Rothschild administration (or later, after 1900, the Jewish Colonization Association [JCA] founded by Baron Maurice de Hirsch [1831–1896], which took over all of Rothschild's dealings in Palestine) asked the authorities to intervene in the colonies' internal affairs, as part of their struggle with colonists who did not accept their authority. In these cases, for instance in the colonies of Rishon le-Zion and Eqron, Ottoman police entered the colony, a step that elicited a sharp retort on the part of the colonists and among Jewish circles abroad, who perceived this behavior as a form of betrayal.[80]

Ottoman Jews who had a standing in the Ottoman system also petitioned Istanbul at times with the aim of helping the Jewish settlement activity. This use of intermediaries, which was very typical of the Ottoman system throughout the years, is striking in that large segments of established Ottoman Jewry vehemently opposed Zionist activity in Palestine during its early stages. For example, the bureau of the Empire's acting Chief Rabbi (*haham başı kaymakamlığı*) intervened in favor of a school which was planned in the colony of Rishon le-Zion. The plan ran into difficulty because the school was set to be built on the land of Sinan Paşa *waqf* and there was a need to resolve this problem before construction could start.[81] A similar intervention by an intermediary was recorded in the case discussed above of the colony of 'Artuf, established by Bulgarian Sephardic Jews.

Finally, there were sporadic petitions by Jews who immigrated to Palestine and petitioned Istanbul after running into difficulties of various types, either with a request for aid or with a complaint. For example, in one petition – which in fact does not involve a complaint but, rather, a request for mercy and a plea for the sultan's benevolence – representatives of 70 Jewish families who immigrated to Palestine from Russia, led by the Jewish activist Vladimir Temkin [Ze'ev Tiomkin],[82] sent a petition from Jaffa to the Grand Vizier with a request to receive agricultural land for settlement from the state (see Document 17).[83] We do not know how this naïve petition was handled but data from other sources indicate that this period, which in Zionist historiography is known as the "Tiomkin period" ended in bitter disappointment and frustration for the "new *yishuv*."

In another petition involving foreign Jews, representatives of 500 Jewish immigrant families requested to be granted Ottoman citizenship and claimed the local authorities in Syria were preventing them from doing so.[84] Finally, in a case involving a foreign Jew that took place after the 1908 Revolution, a certain Ilya Babayof applied through the Empire's acting Chief Rabbi to protest having been issued a "red note" in the port of Jaffa, which limited the stay of foreign Jews in Palestine to three months. Babayof refused to take the note at the port, arguing that in the period after the Revolution there was no place for such conduct. In response, Jerusalem notified Istanbul that it continued to uphold previous sultanic orders and that as far as it was concerned there were no changes in the official policy until new orders had been sent.[85]

Petitions by Ottoman Officials serving in Palestine Regarding Proto-Zionist Activity

The final type of petition concerning Jewish activity covers those submitted by Ottoman officials and office holders, some of whom were residents of Palestine, others simply serving there, complaining about corruption and misdeeds connected to Jewish immigration and settlement activity.

Many complaints dealt with alleged misdeeds by Ottoman officials who took advantage of their position and, in return for bribes, allowed Jewish activity to take place.[86] In other petitions, Ottoman officials claim that they were dismissed from office and were persecuted because they dared to complain about their peers who acted in violation of imperial orders regarding Jewish activity. They demanded government intervention to return them to office, the abrogation of legal sanctions against them and punishment of those who had unjustly persecuted them.[87]

The central Ottoman authorities frequently reiterated in their correspondence with local officials in Jerusalem and the Levant (Beirut, Damascus) that they opposed Jewish immigration and settlement activity in Palestine.[88] They pointed to numerous sultanic decisions to that effect and emphasized the need to take concrete measures on the ground to prevent these activities from taking place. Their reasoning was that Jewish activity would be harmful to the Empire's interests, as well as to the local population;[89] that a new political-national problem may be created in Palestine;[90] that, unlike America, there was not enough room for massive Jewish immigration;[91] that Jews created problems everywhere they go;[92] that the "enlightened" European states and Russia had also rejected the

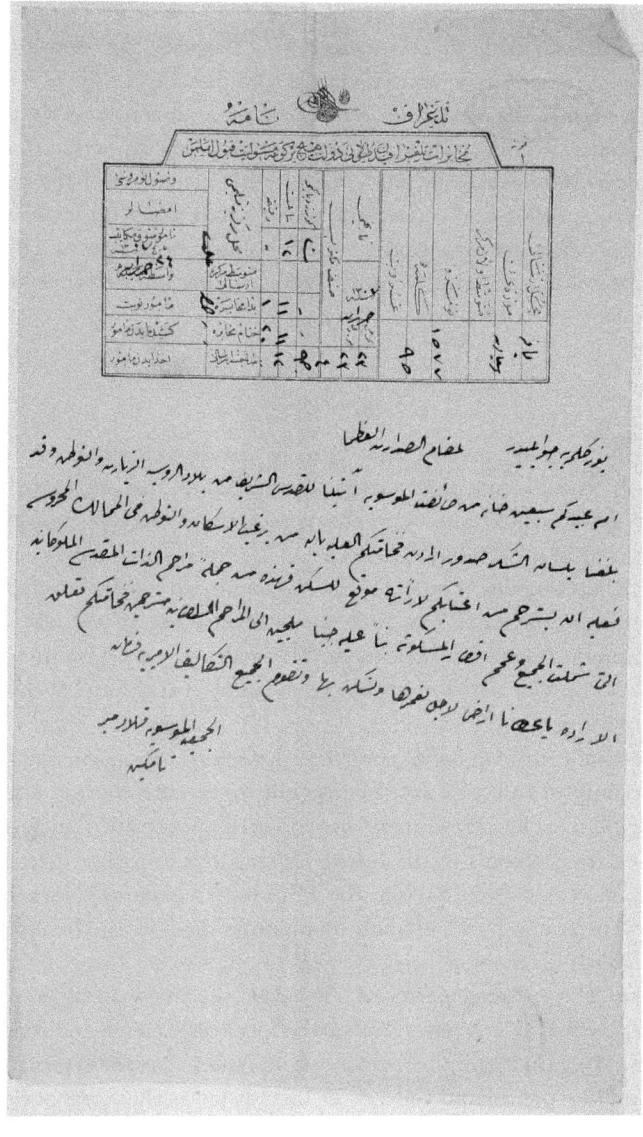

Document 17   A Petition to the Grand Vizier by Representatives of 70 Jewish Families who immigrated to Palestine from Russia, led by the Jewish Activist Vladimir Temkin [Ze'ev Tiomkin] asking to be granted Agricultural Land for Settlement

Source: BOA. HR. TO 396/5, 26 Haziran 1307 [8 July 1891]

Jews;[93] that a Jewish presence would serve as a pretext for foreign intervention; and even made statements reflecting European anti-Semitic ideas that Jews were not clean and that they spread disease.[94]

Ottoman officials serving in the region were obviously aware of this official imperial policy. However, the fact that Jewish activity continued almost uninterruptedly may suggest that they turned the issue of Jewish immigration and settlement activity into a tool to level accusations, thwart or exact revenge from rivals, colleagues and peers. There are numerous examples of this from the 1880s, 1890s and onwards (see also Chapter 5).[95]

Conclusion

The petitions discussed in this chapter demonstrate that, at times, foreigners who did not hold Ottoman citizenship also submitted petitions to Istanbul and also were themselves the subject of petitions by Palestine's local inhabitants. The former was often carried out in conjunction with other modes of operation such as approaching the local consuls. The petitions concerning foreigners are of diverse nature and often there is no common thread between them. Nevertheless, they give us another glimpse of the wide variety of petitions to Istanbul at the end of the nineteenth century.

In official Ottoman correspondence, Jewish immigration and settlement activity in Palestine at the end of the nineteenth century occupied a major place. The government vehemently opposed it and feared it would create problems in the future, especially given that most of the immigrants came from Russia, the Empire's archenemy. Nonetheless, very few petitions by Palestine's inhabitants dealt with the effects of proto-Zionist settlement activity, perhaps due to its limited scope at the time. The existing petitions, however, shed new light on Jewish activity, the way it was perceived by the local population and its consequences. We gain a unique perspective on issues that are typically only discussed in second-hand sources, at least as far as the Arab position is concerned. The archival material also demonstrates that proto-Zionist colonists and various Jewish activists also referred, at times, to the institution of petitioning in an effort to find redress and promote their interests.

CONCLUSION

OLD INSTITUTIONS, NEW CONDITIONS, A NEW MEANING OF JUSTICE?

The institution of petitioning the ruler is typical of monarchies, whereby the monarch balances tensions in his realm and serves as the supreme guardian of the common good. In the Ottoman Sultanate, this institution was a variant of a centuries-old Islamic institution and it endured throughout Ottoman history. Even at the end of the nineteenth century, it did not disappear or lose its importance against the backdrop of sweeping institutional and political change. Nevertheless, given the extensive reforms and efforts at modernization in the Empire, the conditions under which it operated were different. By that point in time, the Ottoman subjects had a whole range of new mechanisms at their disposal to raise their concerns and grievances and demand redress other than submitting a petition directly to their sovereign in Istanbul. And yet, they continued submitting petitions to the imperial center – in fact, in growing numbers – concerning almost every issue affecting them and preferred not to go through the regular reformed legal and administrative channels or the province's chain of judicial-bureaucratic procedures. Consequently, the imperial center was literally swamped with petitions by its subjects in the provinces complaining about matters large or small and demanding justice and rights as they perceived it.

There are several key factors that can account for the continued relevancy of the institution of petitioning. Above all was the unprecedented penetration of the state into every aspect of its subjects' lives and its centralized reach in the form of conscription, censuses, registration of land, education and unification of the tax collection system, to mention but few practices. This caused subjects to perceive the reformed state headed by the sultan as the direct addressee for their concerns. At the same time, the multitude of institutions to which the Ottoman subjects were subordinated under the reformed state, with all its regulations and its associated changes, also prompted a sense of confusion. Satisfactory resolution of issues related to these changes required leverage such as through petitioning the sultan. Moreover, the bankruptcy of the State and the chronic shortage of financing faced by the newly-reformed institutions often led to bitterness and complaints about corruption or bribery. Individuals may have preferred contacting Istanbul directly in search of a cheaper and accessible remedy or as a second track parallel to other avenues of pursuing justice, under the assumption that it might help and certainly would not detract from their cause.

Petitions can be perceived as a tool which completed top-down reforms from below, by guaranteeing, at least de jure, their enforcement and allowing claims to be scrutinized. Many of the petitions were written in response to centralization measures such as changes in the tax collecting system and the demand to register land, especially when these reforms undermined long-standing practices, norms and habits. As a direct result of the Ottoman reforms (such as in the field of education), larger groups enjoyed higher mobility and were more cognizant of their rights. At the same time, there were more individuals with a reason for petitioning the sultan after losing their "perceived rights" without their consent due to the implementation of governmental policies.

By the end of the nineteenth century, the new technologies and means of communication and transportation meant that ordinary, illiterate peasants could appeal directly, quickly and fairly cheaply to the central authorities, and demand justice and redress from the sultan's representatives. Moreover, the possibility of petitioning collectively made petitioning affordable for almost every group, as can be seen from the abundance of petitions by peasants and semi-nomads preserved in the archives. Not surprisingly, the imperial center was soon flooded with petitions from all segments of the population. Petitioning thus largely became a matter of service for money, and less about status and the ability to pull strings. One could petition for a reasonably cheap price through the postal and telegraph services. Moreover, unlike in earlier times, no judicial mediation (such as the *kadı*'s services) was needed to submit a petition, other than that of petition-writers. Handling of the petitions was also transformed as most correspondence was quickly done by means of the telegraph and post.

Most of the petitions discussed here were sent by city dwellers, including members of minority groups who enjoyed a higher degree of economic and social mobility due to the reforms, the newly-emerged bourgeoisie and the traditional urban Muslim elite. These relatively educated people, who had greater financial means, political awareness, and the wherewithal to protect their interests, made vast use of their ability to send petitions easily and cheaply. In a way, petitioning became a tool at the hands of local notables to conduct their affairs with the government and negotiate with it.[1] The ability to contact Istanbul quickly and easily also led to numerous cases of repeated petitioning ("serial petitioners") and what can anachronistically be termed "trash/spam petitioning."[2] The corollary was that, given the increased accessibility to Istanbul, the expectations of people for redress were also higher, as was their frustration when their pleas were ignored or rejected.

Another reason why Ottoman subjects continued to send petitions to Istanbul was that they sought dialogue and attention from the central government as a means to bypass local administration and improve their position and maneuvering space when dealing with mundane disputes and arguments. Often, they did so even though they knew they had no legal case to appeal. It was a way to beg for mercy and solicit the benevolence of the ruler. The latter, in turn, perceived the institution of petitioning as yet another means for preserving legitimacy and recognition and as a means for monitoring the activity of lower echelons. In this respect, petitioning in modern times was not very different from past practices; nevertheless, it became a mass phenomenon involving multiple institutions with parallel tasks.

Given the above observations, can one argue that, more so than in the past, petitions are a source that can be reconstructed in order to learn about the petitioners' deeds, moral world, concerns and expectations? Historians have at their disposal an abundance of sources on the late nineteenth century compared with previous eras in Ottoman history. This state of affairs makes it possible effectively to historicize key sources such as newspapers, memoirs, diaries, official and unofficial correspondence – and, of course, petitions. A proper contextualization and a nuanced reading of petitions reveal that they make a fascinating source for historical reconstruction.

In this regard, petitioning through the mail and telegraph required usage of a language that was rather different from the one employed in petitions submitted through earlier means such as the court, sending a delegation, a journey to Istanbul in person and the like. The process of petitioning the sultan took on a highly abbreviated form. The costly and timely delegation or journey to the capital was replaced by a quick process, which took a few hours or even less in the regional post and telegraph office. Payment per word had a bearing on the discursive aspects of this genre: telegraph petitions were shorter, leading to elimination of the normative blessings and embellishments.

What do changing patterns of petitioning tell us about changes in the notion of Ottoman justice at the end of the nineteenth century? Despite apparent continuities in the workings of the institution of petitioning the ruler, the prime rationale for this institution in the early centuries of the pre-modern Ottoman Empire was different. In theory, the basic objectives of petitioning did not change, but in practice there was a difference stemming from major transformations in the nature of the state and the changing times. Previously, the key goal of petitioning was to prevent abuse of power so as to allow tax collection from the masses of the *reaya* without delay and disturbance, and to strengthen the imagined paternal bond between the sultan and his subjects. All the other aims of the institution were considered secondary. Towards the end of the nineteenth century, the scope of the institution expanded, evolving – to a greater extent than before – into a political tool and serving as a means to garner public support and legitimacy in the face of threats to the Empire's integrity. At a time of mounting international and domestic pressures, the ruling elite needed to be attuned to its subjects' complaints to preserve its hegemony among the masses. While it could have simply referred grumbling subjects to the reformed or newly-created institutions, it chose not to do so. At the same time, as in other centralizing regimes – and not unlike traditional aims of the institution of petitioning – petitions were an important venue for monitoring the activity of bureaucrats suspected of disloyalty, especially during the time of Abdülhamid II.

For the Empire's subjects, on the other hand, recourse to the institution of petitioning was a plea to (and an expectation of) the state to regulate every aspect of life and thus ensure order (although many petitions still continued to serve their original purpose). Interestingly, unlike the institution's original function – to serve mainly the lower echelons of society; i.e., the masses of *reaya* – it was more often used by the urban population, frequently in the framework of internal strife and struggles, and less so by peasants and Bedouins.

Based on the content of the petitions, can we make a case for a new type of interaction between the sovereign and his subjects at the end of the nineteenth century? As noted, as a result of the reforms and efforts at centralization, Ottoman governance became much more tangible and concrete, making its presence felt in a whole range of unprecedented ways. Nevertheless, the subjects, who were no longer treated as the *reaya*, were still not yet looked upon as citizens of a modern state. Rather, they were often referred to as *tebaa*, a term used both for Ottoman subjects and for subjects of European states (obviously with the specification of the state involved).[3] An interesting point in this regard is the fact that many petitions were still not submitted individually by single subjects but, rather, collectively by a village or several villages together, a Bedouin group, or a group of urban dwellers such as landowners or simply "the people of" this or that place. Thus, in a way, beyond financial considerations, it was still largely assumed that a collective approach had more weight and better chances of being accepted and favorably received than an individual petition.

Another important question in this regard refers to the actual impact of public opinion in the Ottoman Empire at the end of the nineteenth century. The typified image of the Ottoman Empire as an "oriental despotism" has long been challenged and refuted. The enduring vitality of the institution of petitioning the ruler and the evident adherence to the notion of the "Circle of Justice" are but two examples that show the extent to which this image is fundamentally wrong.[4] After all, one of the main tasks of the sultan throughout Ottoman history was to ensure that the *reaya* would feel that justice had been rendered so that they would continue cultivating their land, paying taxes and not flee or revolt.

Nevertheless, one cannot really speak of public opinion in the Ottoman Empire in the modern sense of the word before the closing decades of the nineteenth century. At that time, despite the nature of Sultan Abdülhamid's regime, the situation with regard to the emergence of public opinion gradually changed, at least as far as the major urban centers were concerned. This was the result of several contemporaneous factors such as the expansion of secular education, more rapid circulation of ideas and information, the penetration of Western-liberal concepts of citizenship, liberty and equality, the founding of newspapers and printed media (despite the heavy Hamidian censorship) and the experience in constitutionalism and parliamentary regime (despite being only partial and limited).

Several comments are in order regarding the reflection of public opinion in the petitions. First, mass petitions by mail or telegraph representing dozens of villages – or, for the urban population, dozens (and, at times, even hundreds) of city-dwellers – was frequent and in numbers which are very significant given the size of the villages and towns at the time. Given the nature of the regime, the lack of free press and the restrictions on political activity, these mass petitions can be perceived as an indicator of the public's mood.[5] It can be assumed that in the past, given the obstacles of geography and communication, it was much harder to arrange such collective petitions. Second, the wording of many of the petitions – alongside flattery and adulation – included indirect references to reprimand and admonition in a way unthinkable in the past. Thus, it is not uncommon to find statements such as "how could your highness let such injustice go on?" and "how could a behavior which violates the *shari'a*, *kanuni* and *nizami* laws – and even the constitution [after 1908], and does not respect the name of the Prophet, continue?" Third, changes in the nature of the petitions and the flooding of the system with petitions represented a quantitative change related to the issue of public opinion. Finally, some of the petitions referred to or revolved around the growth of the new media that shaped public opinion, such as newspapers and journals (after the Revolution of 1908, collective petitions were even published in the press) or concerned the functioning of various newly-elected or semi-elected organizations or persons whose activity was criticized.

A question arising from the present study is the extent to which the petitions from Palestine were representative of other regions in the Empire. On the face of it, there is no reason to assume a priori that the submission of petitions from Palestine and their handling at the imperial center in Istanbul at the end of the nineteenth century was fundamentally different from the situation in other provinces. After all, many of the changes and transformations were experienced by Ottoman subjects across the Empire because they resulted from official policies, economic and social developments in the Empire, and global developments whose roots went beyond the borders of the Empire. Arguably, however, there was a heightened sensibility in the Empire to developments in the Holy Land, which was manifested in the general approach to and the treatment of petitions arriving from Palestine.

The growing symbolic and strategic importance of Palestine for the Ottomans at the end of the Egyptian occupation in 1840, which can be ascribed to rising European involvement and interference in the Levant, is well-known and documented. The creation of the *mutasarrıflık* of Jerusalem, which was directly governed from Istanbul in the early 1870s, reflects this development. In this regard, it can be argued that the Ottoman government wanted to avoid giving the European powers a pretext for further intervention in Palestine's affairs as a means to expand their influence. Thus, Istanbul arguably paid extra attention to grievances raised by the local population so that the European consuls would be less able either to extend their interests to embittered persons or even entire communities or to turn every local incident into an international crisis and an excuse for interference in the Empire's internal affairs. The overt Ottoman opposition to Jewish national activity partially stemmed from these considerations.

Finally, this study has highlighted the vast untapped potential embodied in the study of petitions sent from Palestine to Istanbul in the last decades of the nineteenth century. At the imperial level, these petitions reveal a great deal about changes in the traditional institution of petitioning the ruler and the sultan's image, the functioning of the Ottoman bureaucracy at both the local and imperial levels, and the interrelations between center and periphery against the background of Ottoman reforms. They also demonstrate the role played by the advent of new technologies and means of communication and their influence on the relationships between Istanbul and the Empire's subjects, as well as the radical changes in the land regime and the efforts to change the tax collection system and its evaluation.

Of equal importance, the study of petitions from Palestine at the end of the nineteenth century contributes to a bottom-up examination of the region's history, while concomitantly embedding the discussion in its broader Ottoman imperial discourse and setting. The petitions arriving from Palestine's rural population, which constituted the bulk of the total population, are particularly indicative in this regard. To date, most of the research on this topic is still based either on European or Zionist/ Jewish sources, whereas the extensive and diversified Ottoman and Arabic sources are more rarely used. Moreover, most of the research on Palestine's history during the period studied here is still influenced (at times, tacitly) by national perspectives, whether Arab/Palestinian or Jewish/Zionist. In this sense, the expression of early Zionist–Arab encounters and confrontations in petitions to Istanbul provides solid evidence of the importance of petitions as a historical source.

There is a need for further comparative research examining the petitions sent from the Jaffa and Gaza sub-districts with the situation elsewhere, both in Palestine and in other areas of the Ottoman Empire, to reveal shared patterns as well as differences in practice, motivations and objectives of petitioning. What was the impact of modern means of communication and transportation on the distribution of petitions? Comparative research of this kind can further integrate debates on Palestine's history during the late Ottoman period into the broader Ottoman discourse and avoid the worn clichés of national narratives.

For this reason, it is also crucial to expand the usage of Ottoman sources in the historical study of Palestine. Such sources will most likely allow a more effective treatment of historical gaps, provide new insights and a new outlook on events and processes, and reveal layers of information which cannot be found in other sources. The decision making process and its influence on events on the ground (and vice versa) is one example. Such an approach will help better clarify the extent to which Palestine was unique among the Ottoman territories (as a result of its history, symbolism, the nature of the population and geostrategic location) or whether it was similar to other provinces in the shrinking Empire.

A comparative effort will also serve to better understand petitions sent by the population of Palestine in the post-Ottoman period, based on the Ottoman tradition, to various organizations and officials. The American King–Crane commission, for example, received more than 1,850 collective and personal petitions from residents of Greater Syria when, in 1919, it explored options for the political future of the non-Turkish regions previously under Ottoman rule.[6] Many of these petitions were pre-organized and included the same language and content, but the committee still considered them a reliable tool with which to measure public opinion and even encouraged the submission of petitions.[7]

Later on, petitions were submitted to such different persons and organizations as the Mandate High Commissioner in Palestine,[8] the Permanent Mandates Commission in Geneva[9] and even the American president.[10] Jews and Arabs made use of the institution of petitioning to promote their goals and submitted petitions, often collective petitions that were initiated or even solicited by interested parties.[11]

The mechanism of petitioning was retained in other parts of the previously ruled Ottoman areas as well, in part along previous lines but also with variations.[12]

APPENDIX 1

A PETITION BY THE VILLAGERS OF SARAFAND AL-KUBRA TO THE GRAND VIZIER CONCERNING THE STATUS OF THE LANDS OF SINAN PAŞA *WAQF* IN THEIR VILLAGE

Source: BOA. HR. TO., 387/61, 29 Rebiyülevvel 1296 [23 March 1879]

Draft of a translation from Arabic to Ottoman produced by the Translation Bureau of the Ottoman Foreign Ministry. The petition itself was sent by the villagers of Sarafand al-Kubra (Sarafand al-ʿAmar) to the Grand Vizier. There are abundant erasures on the draft made by the translator at the Foreign Ministry. The first lines of the petition (italicized by the author), which include general details on the petitioners and the petition, were appended to the translation by the translator as follows:

This is a translation of a petition in Arabic that was submitted to the Grand Vizier with the signatures and seals of the people, the imam and the muhtars of the village of Sarafand al-Kubra, located in the sub-district of Jaffa in the District of Jerusalem, on the 29 [of the month] of Rebiyülevvel 1296.

[The income from] the tithe of the village of Sarafand al-Kubra which is part of the sub-district [*kaza*] of Jaffa was allocated in the past, for many years, to [support] a school in Damascus which belonged to [the *waqf* of] the late Sinan Paşa. In 1291, [1874/5] while [the land] was in the category of general endowments [*evkaf-ı cumla*], [its management] was taken over by the exalted Ministry of Finance. At the same time, according to an order that was issued, the amount [of the tithe] was sold [*bedel ile ihale ve-ilzam*] for 25,000 *kuruş*.

In 1292 [1875/6], after an imperial order concerning the collection of tithe from our village had fixed the sum at 20,000 *kuruş*, and even though [the land of] the village is part of the endowments which are administered by the state [*evkaf-ı mazbuta*], a member of the *meclis-i temyiz* in Jerusalem, Nakibzade Rabah Efendi [al-Husayni], claimed that he had purchased [the collection of the tithe of] our village from the hands of the administrator [*mütevelli*] of the endowment of Sinan Paşa, peace be upon him.[1] Based on his claim, the District of Jerusalem granted him the collection of tithe [from our lands].

Despite this decision, the above-mentioned person was not satisfied and collected another tithe from your servants such that the total sum that is taken from us has now reached one fifth [of our income]. Because this individual is from amongst the influential people, and his relatives and friends serve in governmental offices, each time that we submitted a petition about him to the district [of Jerusalem] they hid [the petition]. In addition they sent the gendarmerie after us to chase us away from the city.

Due to the fact that [the lands of] the village have been in our hands and possession for many years, only a tithe tax was collected on them, a condition whose stipulations are also clear from the particulars of the *koçan*s [in Arabic: *kushan*s] we possess. And according to the *vergi* receipts [we possess] an additional annual [land and property] tax amounting to 23,000 *kuruş* is paid for the land. There is no other *waqf* land for which one fifth of its income is paid in such a way. Since this [situation] is clear, clearly the Efendi turned the tithe into one fifth.

Based on what we have heard, according to which he [the tax collector] acquired the right to collect the tax in return for a very small sum, and based on the fact that the priority [for acquiring the tithe collection] should be ours, we hereby declare that we are willing to pay the amount

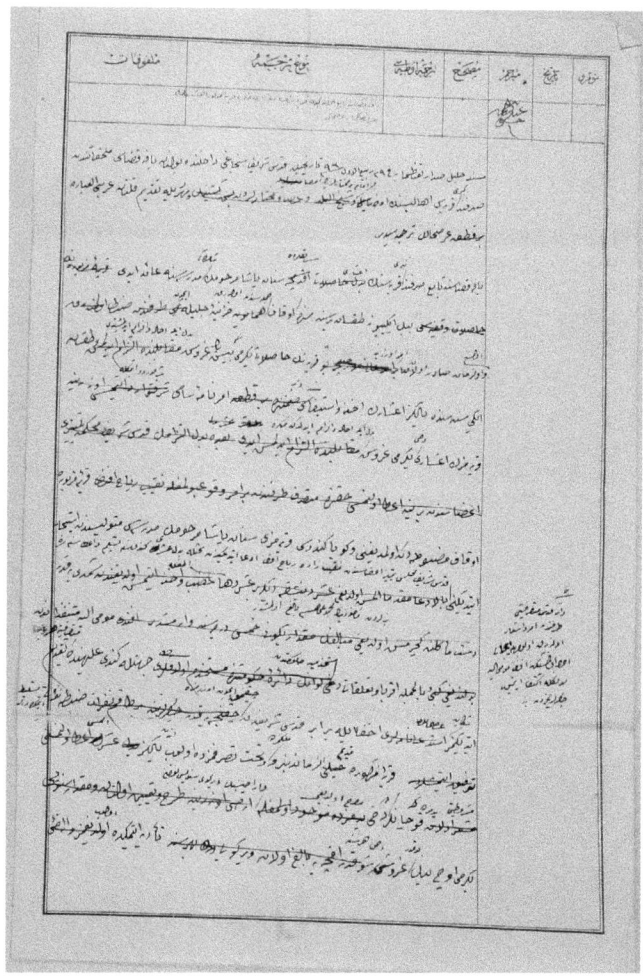

Source: BOA. HR. TO., 387/61, 29 Rebiyülevvel 1296 [23 March 1879], p. 1

that this person paid in addition to a supplementary [extra] amount, in return for [the collection of tithe from] our land.

Because on top of the *vergi* tax we are asked to pay one fifth of our income, the rich people in our village have become totally destitute and they need alms, and for the same reason some of the people of our village have abandoned their place of birth [*vatan-ı aslını terk*] and fled to other

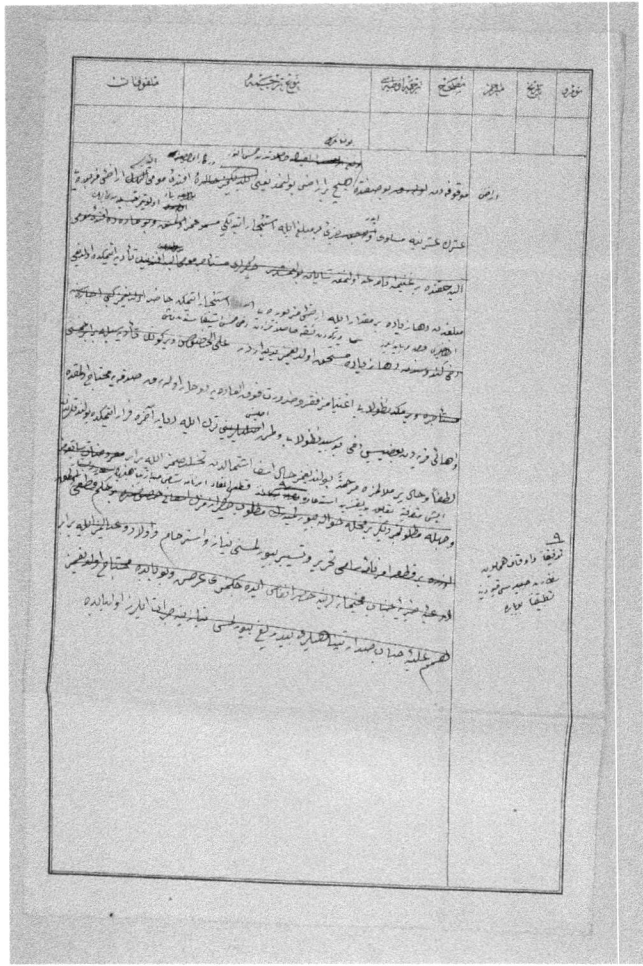

Source: BOA. HR. TO., 387/61, 29 Rebiyülevvel 1296 [23 March 1879], p. 2

lands [*diyar-ı âhara*].[2] Therefore, we beg you to save us from this miserable
and dire situation and ask the exalted Grand Vizier to issue an imperial
order that will clearly remove the handling of the [tithe collection] from
the hands of the District of Jerusalem, based on our request, and act in
accordance to the registrars of the imperial Ministry of Endowments on
this matter. And the decision is at the hands of the one who commands
authority.

APPENDIX 2

A PETITION BY DOZENS OF LANDOWNERS IN JAFFA TO THE GRAND VIZIER AGAINST THE CONDUCT OF A NEW LAND SURVEY IN THEIR TOWN WITH THE AIM OF CHANGING THE STATUS OF VARIOUS LANDS

Source: BOA. HR. TO., 396/16, 17 Temmuz 1307 [29 July 1891]

To the seat of the Grand Vizierate,

We bring to your attention that recently an order was received from the inspector of *Defter-i Hakani* [the office responsible for registration of land] in the *vilayet* of Beirut, Zekati Efendi, to the *tapu* official in Jaffa, which considers the land of the town of Jaffa as land with *miri* status. This caused great bewilderment and has led to a delay in daily activities and transactions because it neither corresponds to *shari'a* nor to *nizami* law.

As is well-known, the land in Jaffa is privately owned and is legally bequeathed. In the past as well as recently, a large part of it has been turned into endowed land, a development which even the great rulers

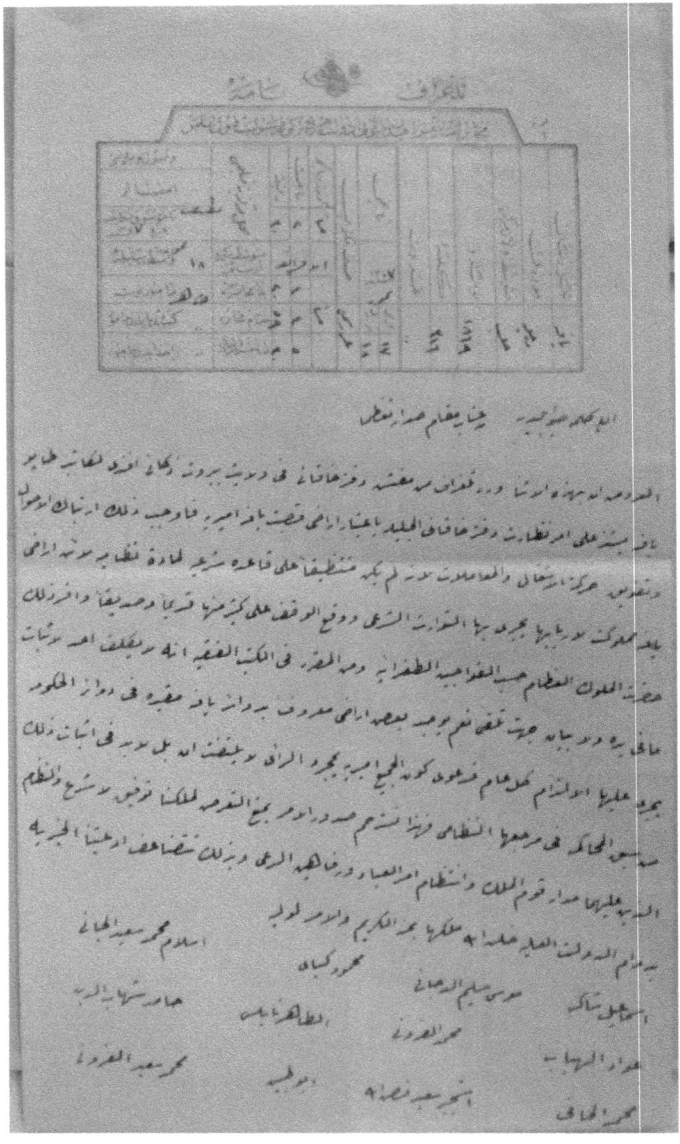

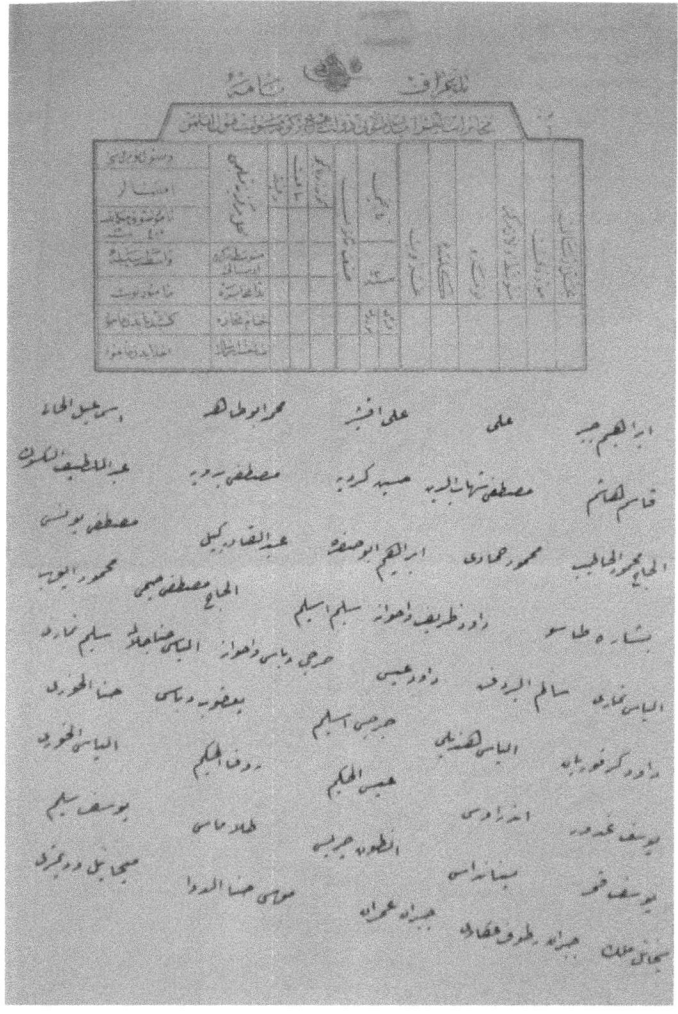

Source: BOA. HR. TO., 396/16, 17 Temmuz 1307 [29 July 1891], p.2

acknowledged based on certified deeds [kushans]. And it is known, based on jurisprudence, that a person does not have to prove ownership over something which he possesses or prove the way in which he received it.

Indeed, there are certain lands known among certain circles in Jaffa as registered in the government's offices as lands subjected to [a regime of] *iltizam* [lands for which the collection of tithe is rented out annually], which are sold out every year, but to argue that all the lands are *miri* is not a reasonable claim. Therefore, there is no other way but to prove this [claim] through a legal process in court. Hence we ask for the issuance of an imperial order which will forbid unfair treatment of our property, something which does not correspond to the religious and *nizami* laws, both of which are the sources of the rulership's continuation [*madar qawm al-mulk*] and the preservation of public order and the people's well-being. And in this way, our blessings for the continuation of the existence of the exalted state, may God save its generous existence, will multiply. And the decision is in the hands of the one who commands authority.

Signatures...

APPENDIX 3

A PETITION BY FOUR MEMBERS OF THE BEDOUIN GROUP ABU-HATABA FROM MAZRA'AT DURAN TO THE GRAND VIZIER AGAINST THE ESTABLISHMENT OF THE COLONY OF REHOVOT

Source: BOA. HR. TO., 395/32, 3 Kânunuevvel 1306
[15 December 1890]

A petition to his highness the threshold of grand-vizierate, let God keep his honored existence,

Our esteemed respectful master,

We Hamdan Abu-Hataba, 'Abd al-Hadi Abu Ehmeid, Mahmoud Abu-Rysheiha, and Muhammad Ibn Salem, Muslim Ottomans, the *muhtar* and elder males of the Abu-Hataba tribe, in our own names and in the name of all the members of the tribe, bring the following to the cognizance of your Highness:

Our tribe numbers 32 families comprising approximately 200 people, from amongst the loyal subjects of the exalted state, residing in tents in Khirbat Duran which belongs to the sub-district of Jaffa in the District of Jerusalem. This tribe, from olden times and from [the time of our] fathers and forefathers, does not know any other land than the above-mentioned Khirbat Duran, makes its living from it, and does not have any other place of residence other than this Khirba. Recently, the exalted government sold this farm to certain people from amongst the residents of the state [*watan*]. These [your] servants did not express any opposition since the new landowners clearly knew that the farm [*mazra'a*] was cultivated and held by us from olden [times]. They did not express any opposition to us and did not expel us from our [place of] residence or from our farm. On the contrary, they made it as easy for us as possible to cultivate this land, such that both parties were satisfied and benefited from it.

[But] as we were in this situation, the farm was suddenly sold to a group of foreign Jews [*isra'iliyyin*], who came to this land, and possessed capital and had economic means at their disposal. They succeeded in buying this land with the help and support of 'Ali Efendi Haykal, a member of the administrative council of the sub-district [*kaza*] of Jaffa and the committee of commerce [sic: *muba'i'yat*, should be *mubaya'at*], who is notorious for interventions of this kind.[3]

Later, these rich Jewish buyers, who already had built a few buildings on the land of this Khirba without official permission, with the help of the above-mentioned Efendi, were not satisfied with what they had done. They started to chase us away from our place of residence, and to prevent us from cultivating [our crops on] the above-mentioned farm, so that only their people would benefit from it. The more we made concessions to them, with the aim that both sides would derive advantages, [the more] they continued to upset and annoy us, and opposed us with stern resistance, in order to prevent [us from fulfilling] our wishes. In this way, all the members of the tribe experienced great distress, since we do not have another land [*watan*] or farm other than this. We are in a situation of confusion and do not know what to do. The farm, which was in our hands from [the time of our] fathers and forefathers was taken from us by force. And the foreigners [*ajanib*], who do not want to treat us according to the accepted norms among the farmers and according to human norms [*al-sha'a'ir al-insaniyya*] and compassion, took it over. In short, [they reject us] even as their servants, and the blame for this damage and the mistreatment we received, can only be attributed to the unacceptable [acts of] the above-mentioned Efendi.

Based on this, and since we are Bedouins who live in tents in this Khirba from olden times and we have no other place aside from it, and

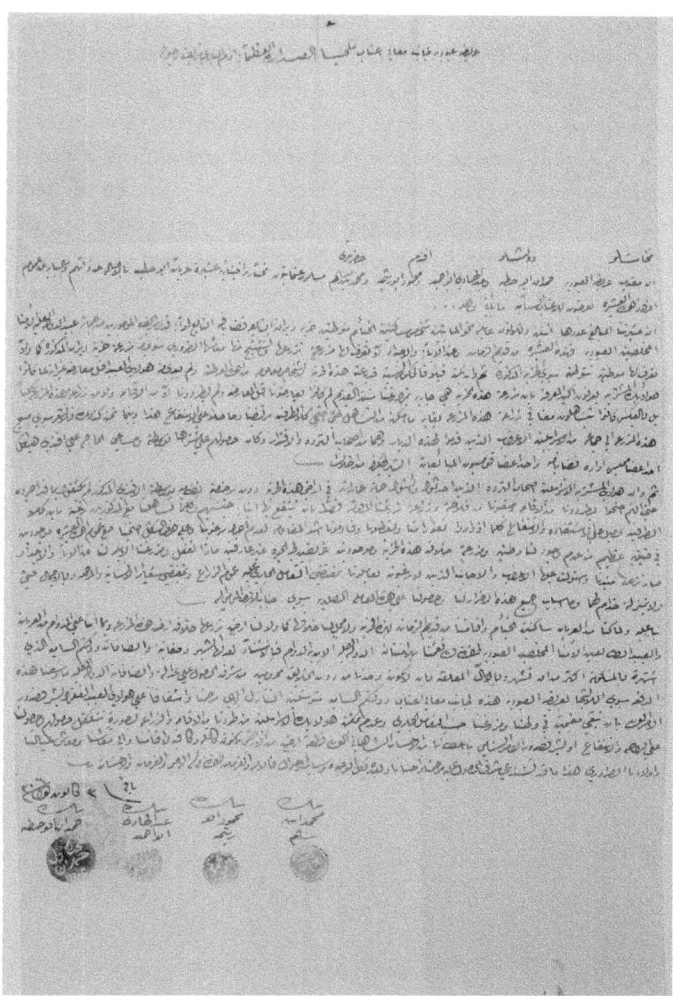

Source: BOA. HR. TO., 395/32, 3 Kânunuevvel 1306 [15 December 1890]

also because we have no other land to cultivate, and since we are from amongst the Bedouins who are loyal subjects of the exalted and eternal State, which is our protector, without expecting anything in return, and based on the well-known justice of the State and the justice and equity of your Excellency that are famous all over the world, with the hope that we will not alone be deprived of the justice and equity of the exalted State; we have no other choice but to submit this petition to beg for the issuance of an exalted order to let us stay in our place of birth where we reside, based on the current arrangement and not to let the Jews [isra'iliyyin] chase us away and prevent us from cultivating the land in a way which will guarantee their and our rest and benefit; or else issue an exalted order to allocate us land from the imperial property, which would be sufficient for our livelihood and the sustenance of our families and children. We are applying to obtain mercy, to the one who has the authority to issue imperial edicts and grant benevolence.

[Signatures]
Hamdan Abu-Hataba
'Abd al-Hadi Abu Ehmeid
Mahmoud Abu-Rysheiha
Muhammad Ibn Salem

APPENDIX 4

A JOINT PETITION BY SEVERAL VILLAGES IN THE *KAZA* OF GAZA IN PROTEST AGAINST THE RATE OF THE *VERGI* TAX

Source: BOA. HR. TO., 396/79, 18 Rebiyülâhır 1309
[21 November 1891]

A petition signed together by the *muhtar*s of several villages in the *kaza* of Gaza which was sent to the Grand Vizier by mail to protest the rate of the *vergi* tax they were asked to pay. Note the seals and names of the *muhtar*s who signed the petition at the bottom of the page.

A petition to the threshold of the exalted Grand Vizierate,
To our distinguished honorable master,

Presented to you are the dutiful prayers of your servants, the people of the villages of the sub-district of Gaza which belongs to the District of Jerusalem, who are weak and poor and suffer a great injustice due to the *vergi* tax imposed annually on our land. Because of the exaggerated value of the *vergi* tax, and according to the just orders issued to abolish injustices imposed on every exploited person, and with the hope of obtaining the mercy of the exalted state, we ask you to abolish the injustice which we suffered and treat us comparably to others in our situation and to our neighbors.

In 1306 [1888/9] the value of our land ['s *vergi* tax] was reevaluated and it was lowered, with the knowledge of the government's assessors, and it was approved by the councils according to the law. We were given a collective [*sharaki*] imposition [*murtabat*], according to the corrected value. After we paid our registered debt in accordance with the collective arrangement, we prayed to the creator and multiplied our prayers to keep and continue the strength and status of our master, the owner of our livelihood, *Amir al-Mu'minin*, the distinguished arbiter of exalted mercy and compassion.

After that, suddenly a telegraph order arrived from the Ministry of Finance not to accept the changes and to collect the taxes from us as before. This was done only based on fake unreliable information provided by several corrupt people who do not want our success and do not care about the damage caused to us which are known by God. However, the situation in this sub-district does not need further explanation. According to this order, all these discount sums were collected from us by force and imprisonment, and by the brutality of the mounted gendarmerie. When the situation of your subjects became too difficult, we decided to approach the Grand Vizierate to present our condition. We all came together and begged you to consider us with mercy and justice. A high order was issued to the district [of Jerusalem] to investigate the truth of the injustice done to us. And there was also an investigation by the government of the sub-district in response to our petition and an answer was sent that confirmed our claims and confirmed the exaggerated value of our land. Until now, however, it has not borne fruit. Thus we decided to ask for mercy through the telegraph as well as by submitting a petition. However, we did not receive any relief since our tax collectors demanded the former imposition which we cannot pay, other than by a great effort by borrowing money and selling our possessions and supplies, which are kept in order to buy food for our children and families and develop our agriculture, a step that is contrary to your justice.

At the same time an order was issued from the above-mentioned ministry to accept the reassessment of [tax on] profits and property [in Arabic: *tamattu' wal-amlak*][4] without correcting the [value of our] land despite its exaggerated evaluation which is so clear. The proof can be found in the previous decreases [in the value of the land] which were made in the past and still take place today. Moreover, the uncultivated lands [in Arabic:

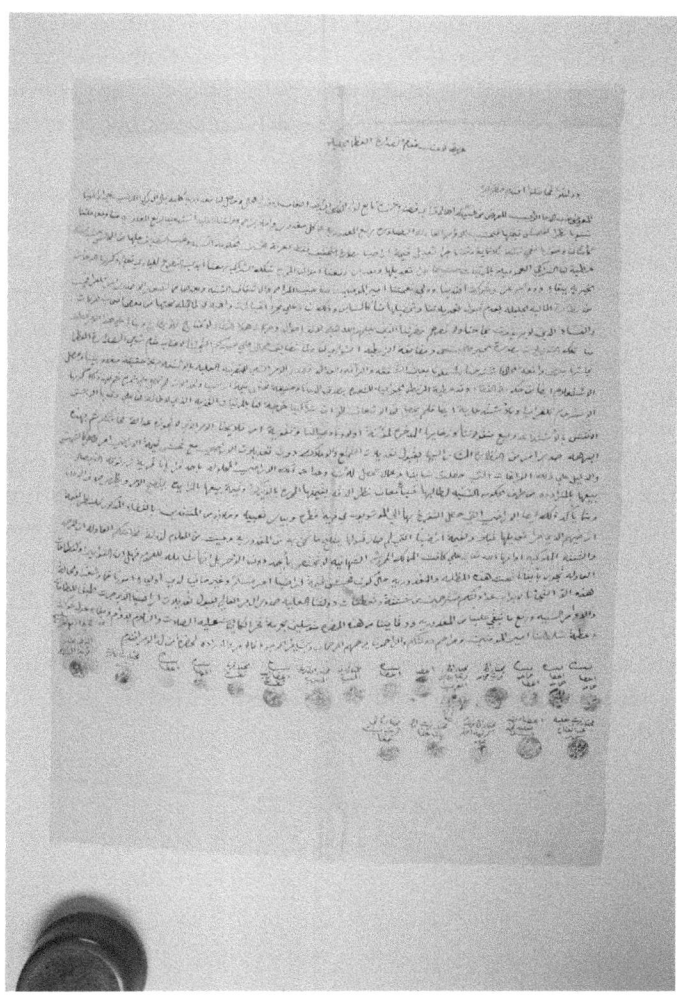

Source: BOA. HR. TO., 396/79, 18 Rebiyülâhır 1309 [21 November 1891]

al-aradi al-mahlula] in one of our sub-district's villages, Zarnuqa, was
sold at a public auction by the exalted state to its demanders. When one
looks carefully at its exact registered value in the *vergi* [files] and the value
of its sale at the public auction the issue becomes clear and the validity of
our claims emerges. What also proves this is the lands which were sold to

the Jews in the village of Qatra[5] and Biar Ta'abiyya [?] and to others from among the influential people in the above-mentioned sub-district. If one examines the value of their lands, whose value was changed previously, and the value of our land whose [change of] value was not accepted, he will see the injustice.

It is known to your highness that the mercy and compassion of the ruler, may God save him, is given to all the dominions of the Empire and does not discriminate one over the other, but encompasses all. Is it possible that the just rules and orders will let us continue to suffer from this injustice and unfairness? At the same time, the high value of our lands is a clear issue and not a secret known [only] by those responsible for our concerns. We have nothing else to do in this situation but to contact your gates of justice with a request to receive your mercy and the benevolence of our exalted state. Hence we ask for the issuance of an imperial order to accept the change in the value of our land, which took place according to the exalted regulations and directions, and abrogate what was imposed upon us out of injustice, and protect us from this damage. We appeal to the honor of the most respectful of human beings [the Prophet] may he rest in peace, for ensuring the justice, and strength and greatness of our Sultan, *Amir al-Mu'minin*, and the mercy of your state, and those who give mercy enjoy mercy from God and from the people, and the decision is at the hands of the one who has authority, our master.

APPENDIX 5

A MASS PETITION IN SUPPORT OF THE *MUFTI*, AL-SAYYID MUHAMMAD AL-HANAFI EFENDI AL-HUSAYNI

Source: BOA. Y. MTV., 77/140, 10 Nisan 1309 [22 April 1893]

This petition, in Arabic, was signed by about 150 people in Gaza, and was probably organized by the *mufti*'s close circle rather than being spontaneous. It has to do with the intense squabbles over the post of the *mufti* in this town between the Husaynis and their rivals from the Saqallah family.

To the distinguished great ghazi, Field Marshal Derviş Paşa,

After praying to God to save the power of our master, *Amir al-Mu'minin*, some of the *'ulama*, *ashraf* and merchants of Gaza beg, in the sacred name of the Prophet and in the name of our master *Amir al-Mu'minin*, may God give him victory, that you pass on our petition to the threshold of the Sultan. Like others, the people of our sub-district, with God's blessing, enjoy the Sultanic policy of justice, they are living in comfort like brothers without deceit or intrigue [which exists] in other places, and they pray continually to our merciful ruler.

[However] currently, Muhammad Saqallah, together with three people like him who are known for their bad reputation, have plotted since about a year ago, against our most learned and pious *mufti*, al-Sayyid

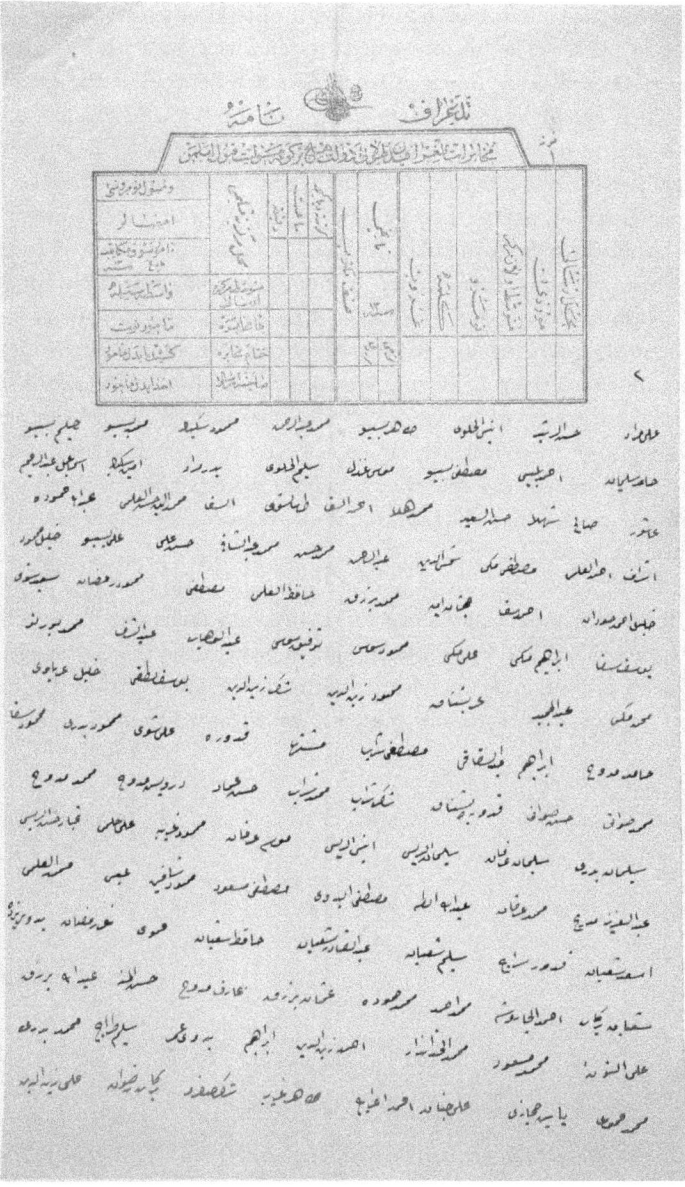

Muhammad al-Hanafi Efendi al-Husayni, who is known for his dedicated service to the state, as his forefathers, to nominate Saqallah in his place. Because the well-known attributes of Saqallah contradict the esteemed task, when his intrigues became known to the higher echelons, orders were issued to reject their baseless complaints, and as a result the public started blessing our just ruler [*malikuna*] who supports the truth.

Then Saqallah approached Istanbul to tarnish the good name of our *mufti*. Afterwards he came back to Gaza upon being appointed to serve as the head of Jaffa's *shari'a* court. A month after he came back, Saqallah returned to Istanbul together with his three supporters, 'Abdalla al-Fayid, Ramadan Abu-Khadra' and Salih al-Shawwa. If an edict had been issued to inquire about them or investigate their complaints in the sub-district and in the district, or by [sending] a special officer, or [by inquiring] in the vicinity, their acts, which are opposed to the exalted will [of the sultan], and the truth behind their baseless claims, signed by them and by their supporters, which [include] names without real people behind them, would have been clear.

Since we know the justice of our master, may God support him, we dare to submit a petition to beg for justice, to punish the intriguers, in the name of God and his Prophet, and to protect the honest people and the people of [religious] knowledge, so that the good prayers of the public for the supporter of truth, our master *Amir al-Mu'minin*, will multiply.

APPENDIX 6

A PETITION BY MEMBERS OF THE HUSAYNI FAMILY IN GAZA AGAINST THEIR RIVALS IN GAZA AND THEIR ALLIES IN JERUSALEM

Source: BOA. HR. TO., 390/74, 7 Hicce 1302 [17 September 1885]

To our master, the great Şakir Paşa,

God, we beg you in the name of the Prophet to preserve His Excellency endowed with generosity and excellent quality, our Lord.

The most important thing our father left us after his death and kept for us during his lifetime is our servitude to your Highness, and to the state of our master the respectful Nazir Paşa [a title ascribed to the Minister of Interior and not to a person's name], which we have legally inherited, and all the people of our land Syria can testify to this as well. It is known that servants have no role but the protection of their masters, and therefore we undertook to submit this petition to your highness, the depository of compassion and strength. We beg you to save us from the misfortunes that the passage of time has inflicted upon us and from the consequences thrust upon us by these unfortunate events, and with your help these terrible events will be cast aside and with your strength the one who is oppressed will be saved.

The old-time enmity of the al-Khalidi family in Jerusalem towards us is well-known and no further explanation is required. For this reason, they nurture the desire to do us harm and they hope to replace our tranquility with sadness. What has kindled these [evil] intentions is their status and their good relations with the exalted governors. We have already suffered various kinds of misery at their hands, and have tasted the bitter fruit of their perseverance. Among other things, one of the members of this family known as Yusuf Diya' Efendi [al-Khalidi] continues to cause evil things to befall us and damage us and he is even attempting to create enmity between us and our compatriots [ahl watanina].[6] People get close to him by manifesting enmity towards us.

Recently, he has made enormous efforts to create enmity between us and one of our friends, a person named Khalil Efendi Abu-Khadra'. The dispute took place between one of his sons and between one of our relatives. If Yusuf Efendi had not intervened in this dispute, when he visited Gaza ten months ago, [the problem] would have been simple. However, he put a person in charge affiliated with him and with his family named 'Abdallah al-Ghusayn from Gaza. The latter started to incite the sons and nephews of Khalil Efendi [Abu-Khadra'] to complain that we are causing them harm and to claim that we transgress against them, [but] only God knows who is oppressed. They raised several baseless complaints which are nothing but incitement. Even though people constantly intervened to resolve the conflict between us, they failed due to the influence of evil people upon the sons of al-Sayyid Khalil [Abu-Khadra'].

Later we heard that the above-mentioned Khalil Efendi sent a petition to our honorable master Nazir Paşa, complaining about your slaves. He entrusted it [the petition] to his nephew Hasan Efendi who was on his way to Istanbul to seek a position. When we learned about it, we became sad and our peace of mind was troubled, out of fear of a change in the attitude of our lord towards us. [Nevertheless] the more they complained about us, the more restraint we showed.

Apart from this matter, we do not have a shelter other than your Excellency and we cannot bear a change in his opinion. When we heard about sending an order by his highness to the governor of Jerusalem concerning this matter, we hastened to present the problem to you. When we heard that his order was also issued to Musa Efendi al-Husayni our fears were multiplied and the broad horizons of our world closed in on us. Afterwards, the governor of Jerusalem, who does not want to reconcile us, took advantage of the event and committed an act which increased the enmity between us and the people of our place of residence [*ahl watanina*], in accordance with the acts of Yusuf Efendi al-Khalidi mentioned above.

Supporting the position of our old enemies, when he [Yusuf Diya' al-Khalidi] visited Gaza a month ago, he fired one of your servants [named] Muhammad al-Hanafi from the chairmanship of the committee of education, as well as your servant 'Abd al-Hayy Fa'iq, from membership on the sub-district's administrative council without a justifiable reason.

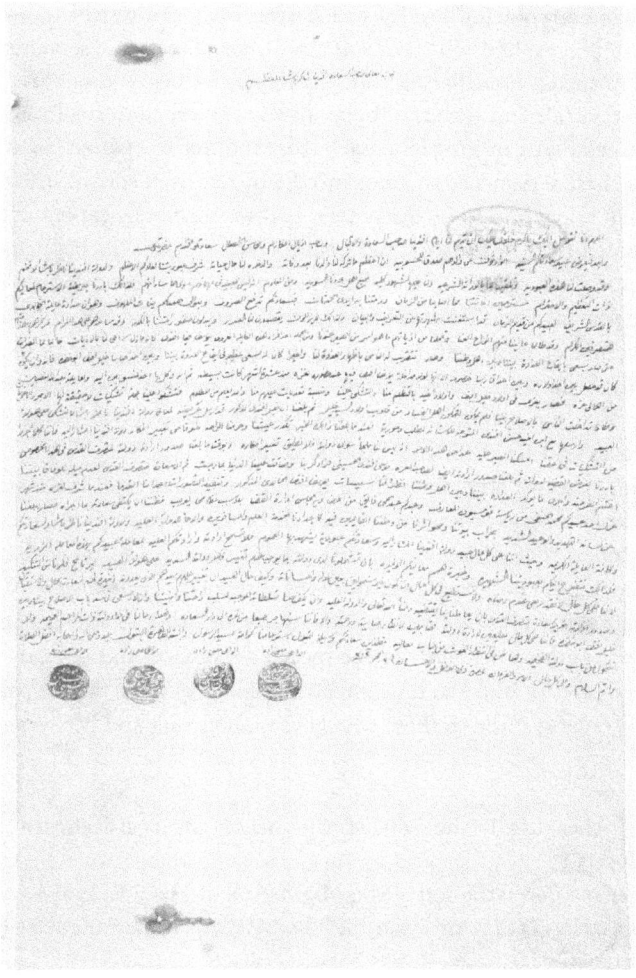

Source: BOA. HR. TO., 390/74, 7 Hicce 1302 [17 September 1885]

We thought that he [al-Khalidi] would be satisfied with what he had done, but then we received threats and strongly [worded] messages in his name [promising] to destroy our houses and to obliterate us from our homeland where we live, as our forefathers did, [and work in the] service of learning and travelers [the pilgrims to the holy cities in the Hejaz], and pray for the exalted state and for our master Nazir Paşa, and for your highness, and for all the members of the honorable family.

At any rate we are the servants of our master mentioned above and your highness, showing loyalty which everybody can testify to. [We are sure that] his exalted will and yours will not allow your servants to be treated in such a humiliating way. Therefore, we beg you because of our known servitude and with the abundant and earnest concern of your highness to include us in his highness' [favor] and not to change his attitude towards these servants so that our mind will rest from sorrow. At any rate we cannot allow him to be discontent, and we absolutely cannot accept to be excluded from his justice and benevolence. What will happen to the servants if the [attitude of their] master, whom they consider the source of their present and future happiness, will change? We ask him to order the governor of Jerusalem to treat us according to the favor of God and the exalted state and refrain from his exertions that will deprive us of our security and tranquility, and not to close the door to reconciliation between us and Khalil Efendi Abu-Khadra'.

In any case we obey the will of his highness and need his mercy and compassion because otherwise we will all be forced to migrate from Gaza to Istanbul to ask for his government's protection which encompasses everybody and we will not move away from the gates of his exalted state. We wait for salvation from his highness and we take your honor as the sign you will accept our petition, in honor of the messenger of God and his pure virgin daughter, pray for him and his companions and give them perfect peace. At any rate, order is given to those who have high virtues and benevolence.

[Signatures]

The preacher (*da'i*), the son of the *Mufti*: 'Abd al-Rahman Shafiq al-Husayni

The preacher (*da'i*), the son of the *Mufti*: 'Abd al-Hayy Fa'iq al-Husayni

The preacher (*da'i*), the son of the *Mufti*: Muhammad al-Hanafi al-Husayni

The preacher (*da'i*), the son of the *Mufti*: Husayn al-Husayni

APPENDIX 7.1

A DECISION BY THE *ŞURA-YI DEVLET* CONCERNING THE STATUS OF LANDS IN JAFFA

Source: BOA. İ. ŞD., 115/6885 (1), 21 Kânunuevvel 1307
[2 January 1892]
(for a reproduction of this document, see Document 13.1)

A decision (*mazbata*) prepared by the *Şûra-yı Devlet* concerning the status of lands in Jaffa that caused a controversy with the local population over whether their status should be *miri* or *mülk*.

Fifty-eight people from the *kaza* of Jaffa submitted a petition by telegraph asking for a halt to intervention on their privately owned properties [*mülk*] which is against *shari'a* and *kanuni* law. [They petitioned] after they learned that the *tapu* official in Jaffa was instructed to treat the lands in the *kaza* of Jaffa as *miri* lands by order of the inspector of *Defter-i Hakani* in Beirut, Zekati Efendi. The *Şûra-yı Devlet* has received correspondence with *Defter-i Hakani* including a note from *Sadaret* and it was read at the Department of Interior.

In the answer from the department mentioned above [*Defter-i Hakani*] the following is stated. During an inspection it was discovered that even though the lands in the *kaza* of Jaffa had been considered *miri* lands, since the year 1294 [1877] appointed *tapu* officials [in Jaffa] started considering these lands as *mülk* and issued certificates to this effect. Some of the landowners built houses on these lands and [eventually] formed localities resembling neighborhoods. [Moreover] vacant land and land which was not cultivated [*mahlula*] were seized by certain people. Earlier, upon receiving information from the *yoklama* [land survey] official in the District of Beirut as part of the investigation, the records in the archives were consulted. [It turned out that] for the lands of Jaffa one third of the winter crops and one quarter of the summer crops was paid as tax to state coffers. Although the lands were defined as *kharaji*, with the passing of time they took on the status of *miri* lands. It emerged that an imperial *ferman* dated Şaban 1278 [1861] sanctioned the exchange of these lands for similar lands [or financial compensation].

Given the above, the aforementioned inspector wrote in his answer that according to the above-mentioned *ferman* it was irregular to issue *mülk* certificates for such lands and to legally transfer them in such a way. As for the areas on which houses were built without imperial consent based on these [erroneous] *mülk* certificates, they should be linked to the tithe tax regime, and their certificates should be replaced. From now on it is forbidden to build houses on these lands without an imperial order.

[Based on this answer] the local authorities [in Palestine] must make the following decisions known to the people [of Jaffa] officially: Places which were considered *kharaji* lands and which were designated by the owners as *waqf*s and other declarations before the issuance of the above-mentioned *ferman* should be treated as before. In terms of ownership, according to the *ferman* mentioned above, since it is not proper to seize *miri* lands from the hands of their possessors, in cases of buying and selling such lands, *miri* certificates should be issued and they should be maintained under the provisions of the imperial land code. From now on, no *mülk* certificates should be issued for such places under any circumstances.

The department [of the interior in the *Şûra-yı Devlet*] found the considerations presented to it to be proper and suitable and therefore decided to refer the matter to the Ministry of the Interior to take the necessary steps and inform the District of Jerusalem of its decision on this matter. The order is in the hands of the Authorities.

APPENDIX 7.2

A LETTER FROM THE GRAND VIZIER TO THE SULTAN TO APPROVE THE DECISION

Source: BOA. İ. ŞD., 115/6885 (2), 23 Kânunusani 1307
[4 February 1892]
(for a reproduction of this document, see Document 13.2)

Our honorable master,

People in the *kaza* of Jaffa submitted a petition asking to halt an injustice inflicted on them by the *tapu* official in Jaffa, who considers lands in the *kaza* that they own [as *mülk* lands] as *miri* lands, and to prevent [the act of registration] from taking place. A consultation with the *Defter-i Hakani* has revealed that despite the fact that these lands have been *miri* lands, since 1294 [1877] local *tapu* officials in Jaffa have started treating these lands as *mülk* and distributed land certificates to this effect. [As a result] some landowners have started building houses on these lands [gradually] creating neighborhoods. [Moreover], it was discovered during an investigation that many vacant lots and lands which were not cultivated [*mahlula*] were seized by some people. A verification of the records revealed that these lands were [originally] *kharaji* lands for which one third of the winter crops and one quarter of the summer crops were paid to state coffers.

With time these lands acquired the status of *miri* lands. As a result, an imperial *ferman* issued in Şaban 1278 [1861] [authorized] substituting these lands with similar lands [or money]. [However] it was not proper to distribute *mülk* certificates for such lands or to authorize their replacement based on the content of this *ferman*. It was understood that at that time the [people of the] place were informed officially of the following restrictions: Places in which houses were previously built without imperial approval, based on these *mülk* certificates should be linked to the tithe [*miri*] tax system and the certificates should be replaced accordingly. [Moreover, it was decided that] from then on no houses would be built without imperial permission.

[Now, upon being asked to handle this matter] the ministry referred to above [the *Defeter-i Hakani*] responded that the local government [in the District of Jerusalem] should officially notify the local people [of Jaffa] of the following decisions. Parts of the *kharaji* lands which were designated by their landowners as *waqf* lands and other designations prior to the issuance of the above-mentioned *ferman* should be maintained as before. In terms of ownership, according to the *ferman*, it is not proper to take places which have the status of *miri* lands from the hands of their holders. In case of buying and selling such places, *miri* certificates should be issued and they should be administered as areas under the imperial land code. From now on areas such as these should under no circumstances be issued *mülk* certificates.

The proposed suggestions presented [by the *Defter-i Hakani*] were found by the Council of State to be proper. Hence, the District of Jerusalem should be notified as to what needs to be done by the Ministry of the Interior, as specified in the *mazbata* [proposed decision] prepared by the Department of Interior [in the *Şûra-yı Devlet*] which is attached and presented to you. To comply with the matters specified in the *mazbata*, a note is presented to you by the Grand Vizier. Whatever the imperial [center] commands us will be carried out. Our master.

Grand Vizier Cevat

APPENDIX 8

A TELEGRAPH SIGNED BY THE *MUHTARS* OF FOUR VILLAGES IN THE *KAZA* OF GAZA CONCERNING THE RATE OF THE *VERGI* TAX

Source: BOA. HR. TO., 395/61, 5 Şubat 1306 [17 February 1891]

To the exalted Grand Vizier,

Your slaves are from the sub-district [*kaza*] of Gaza. The people of our villages are poor. The [assessed] value of our property is very excessive. As your Excellency has long been aware, the *vergi* [tax] payments have caused our impoverishment [and therefore] our weakened situation makes it an absolute need to clarify the issue of transferring and renting property [in Arabic: *al-faraghat al-ijara*], and especially land [defined as] *mahlula* [uncultivated]. [For example, the value of the land of] the village of Zarnuqa which was sold by the government in a public auction supports our claim that justice has not been done. A Sultanic order was recently issued to the [appropriate] ministry to examine the claims [that the value of the land] was excessive and to adjust the value of the land to its real value. [Hence] we rushed to the gates of justice and submitted a petition. When our claim was proved to be right, the value of our land

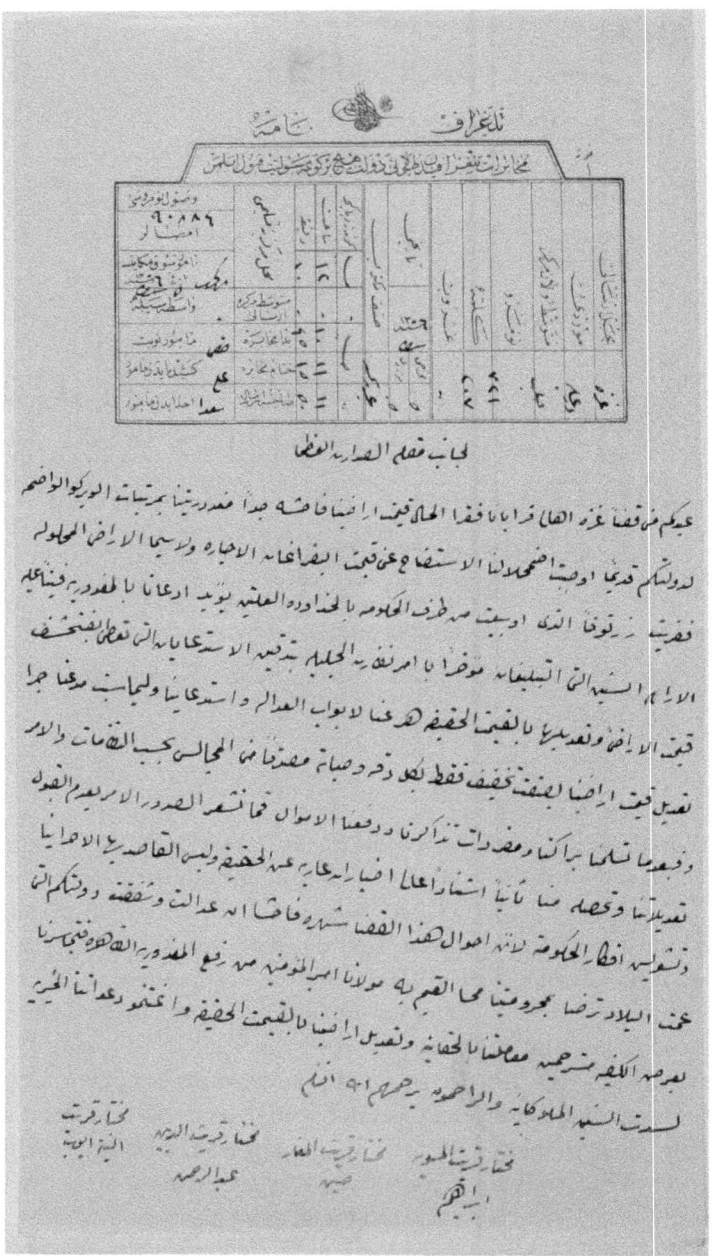

was adjusted by a reduction, in an accurate way which was approved by the councils according to the regulations and orders.

After we received the titles and the separate [payment] invoice, we paid the money. Suddenly [however] we were surprised to learn that an order was issued not to accept the change and to collect it [the original value] from us again based on false information [provided by those] whose only aim is to ruin us and confuse the views of the government, at a time the [destitute] situation of this district is obviously known. Indeed the justice and mercy of your Excellency that are known throughout the land will not tolerate denial of what our master, *Amir al-Mu'minin* ordered, [namely] to revoke this clear injustice. We have dared to present the case and beg you to treat us with justice by reassessing the value of our land at its true value. [By doing so] you will merit our benevolent prayers for the exalted Sultan. Those who show mercy, God will give them mercy. Our master.

[Signatures]
Mukhtar [in Turkish: *Muhtar*] of the village of al-Masmiyya, Ibrahim
Mukhtar of the village of al-Maghar, Husayn
Mukhtar of the village of Dibin [?], 'Abd al-Rahman
Mukhtar of the village of al-Tina, Ayyub

APPENDIX 9

A PETITION BY THE BEDOUINS OF ARAB AL-ʿAWJA CONCERNING THE STATUS OF LANDS THEY CULTIVATED AND THE TAXES DEMANDED FROM THEM

Source: BOA. HR. TO., 389/104, 12 Şaban 1301 [7 June 1884]

A draft of a translation from Arabic into Ottoman of a petition by the Bedouins of al-ʿAwja (located near Nahr al-ʿAwja, ha-Yarkon), who claimed the land they occupied was *miri* land and not *waqf* land. The first sentence containing the details of the petition (my italics) was added by the translator at the Translation Bureau in the Foreign Ministry.

A translation of a petition in Arabic which was sent from Jaffa to the Ministry of Finance on 12 Şaban 1301 [7 June 1884] signed by the sheikh of Arab al-ʿAwja, Muhammad Yusuf Abu-Kishk together with two of his companions:[7]

As we presented recently and previously [to this petition], receipts [*senedat*] which we hold in our hands prove that until the year 1271 [1854/5] we paid the tithe of the two tax farms [*mukataalar*] of Qula and Za'faraniyya [?], which have been in our possession for many generations and we legally own, directly to the imperial treasury. Even though there is no need to prove that this place is ours, two persons from [the province of] Syria [*Şam ahalinden*] named Sa'id and 'Abd al-Hadi showed up claiming that they were the descendants of *Sayyidna* 'Ali bin 'Alil and that the above-mentioned lands were allegedly part of the endowment for the upkeep of the grave of their grandfather which was left to them as such. However, the tithe from the above-mentioned two pieces of land was given in its entirety by the exalted government to cover the expenses of visitors to the Sufi lodge [at the place].

In the year [12]64 [1847/8] the government took over the management of these lands. In 1271 [1854/5] the above-mentioned two persons submitted a petition to the Ministry of Endowments and to your exalted ministry [regarding the status of these lands]. An answer was sent to them upon discovering [in the investigation] that all the land in the two plots was *miri* land. On 17 Rebiyülevvel 1271 [8 December 1854] the exalted Sultan, may his place be in heaven, Abdülmecid Khan, God bless his grave, ordered that the above-mentioned land is *miri* land whose tithe income of 55 *irdabb* will be dedicated to the [maintenance of the] grave mentioned above.

When the two claimants died, their children Salim and 'Abd al-Latif Efendis upon receiving the endowment for the grave's management [*makam-ı tevliye*] took the entire income of the grave as their forefathers had done and spent it as they wished. However, they were still not satisfied. [Thus] with the help of several corrupt officials, while acting against the law, they started to deploy force to collect one fifth [*hums*] of our land's yields. In addition, they claim that all the tithe of the village of Jalil [Ijlil] in the [sub-] district of Balqa, and one quarter of that of the village of Jarisha, and three quarters of the village of Jammasiyya [al-Jammasin] [both of] which belong to the [sub-] district of Jaffa is included in our *waqf*. They divide the payment received [profits] from these places between themselves. According to this calculation, the yearly income of the above-mentioned Salim and 'Abd al-Latif Efendis is more than 1,500 liras, but they are still not satisfied with that. Due to their voracious greed, they claim that all the land which we possess belongs to the *waqf* of the Sufi lodge [*dergâh*] and that we are renters. However, an

Source: BOA. HR. TO., 389/104, 12 Şaban 1301 [7 June 1884], p. 1

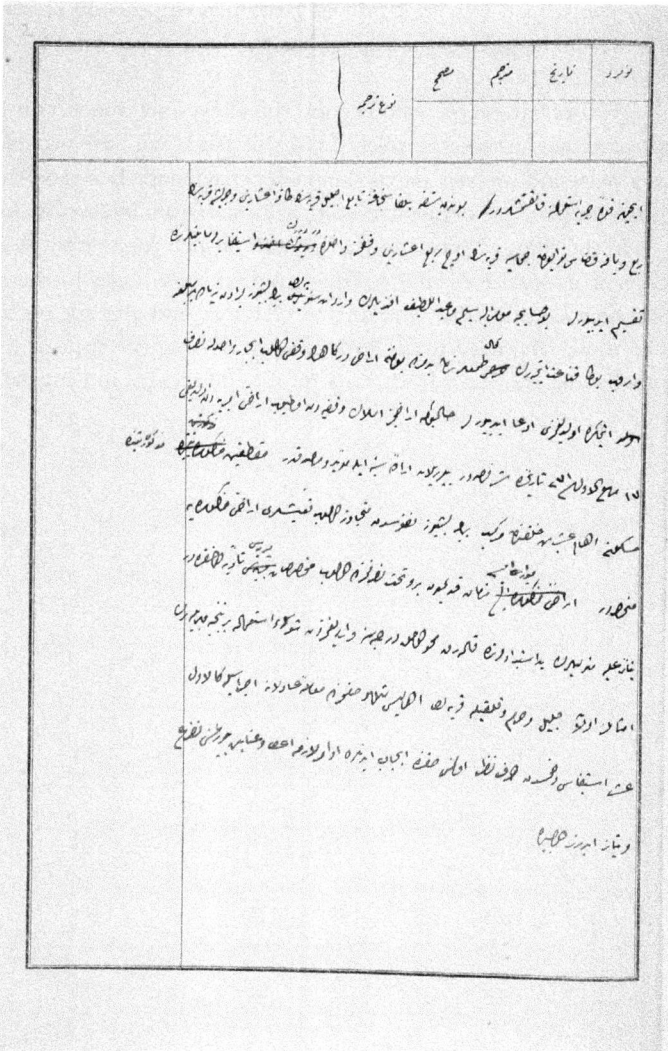

Source: BOA. HR. TO., 389/104, 12 Şaban 1301 [7 June 1884], p. 2

exalted *ferman* which was issued on 17 Rebiyülevvel 1271 [8 December 1854] proves and supports the claim that our land is not *waqf* land but rather *miri* land.

The 1,500 tribal people who occupy the above-mentioned two plots of land earn their subsistence solely from this land. We have occupied it for many years and we have [always] paid *miri* payments. Based on this, if we remain under these oppressive *waqf* administrators [*mütevelli*s] it will bring us to the verge of extinction, as a result of such corruption. We beg you to grant us justice similar to [that granted to] villages in the same situation such as Jalil [Ijlil], Haram and Qalqilya, and give the necessary orders to those who need to act to levy from us only the tithe as before while abolishing the *hums*. In this matter [the decision is in your hands].

APPENDIX 10

A PETITION BY THE VILLAGE OF ZARNUQA TOGETHER WITH DOZENS OF OTHER VILLAGES IN ITS VICINITY AGAINST THE JEWISH COLONIES

Source: BOA. EUM. EMN., 30/5, 16 Temmuz 1329 [29 July 1913]

A petition in Arabic by the village of Zarnuqa, in the northern part of the *kaza* of Gaza, submitted together with dozens of villages and one semi-Bedouin group in the vicinity to the Grand Vizier. The petitioners complain about the activities of the Jewish colonies in the region, following the "Zarnuqa Incident" in 1913 between the guards of the colony of Rehovot and the village of Zarnuqa.

To our master the honorable great Grand Vizier,

It is well-known that the exalted state works continuously for the welfare of the people and the numerous decrees it issues clearly testify to this. The state does not discriminate when applying justice and conferring mercy between poor and rich, peasant and townsman, Muslim, Christian and Jew. However, the above-mentioned Jews attacked the people of our village, robbed and looted our belongings, killed, and even violated our families' honor, all this in a way which we cannot find words to describe. One example of their attacks, is that they appointed Jewish and foreign

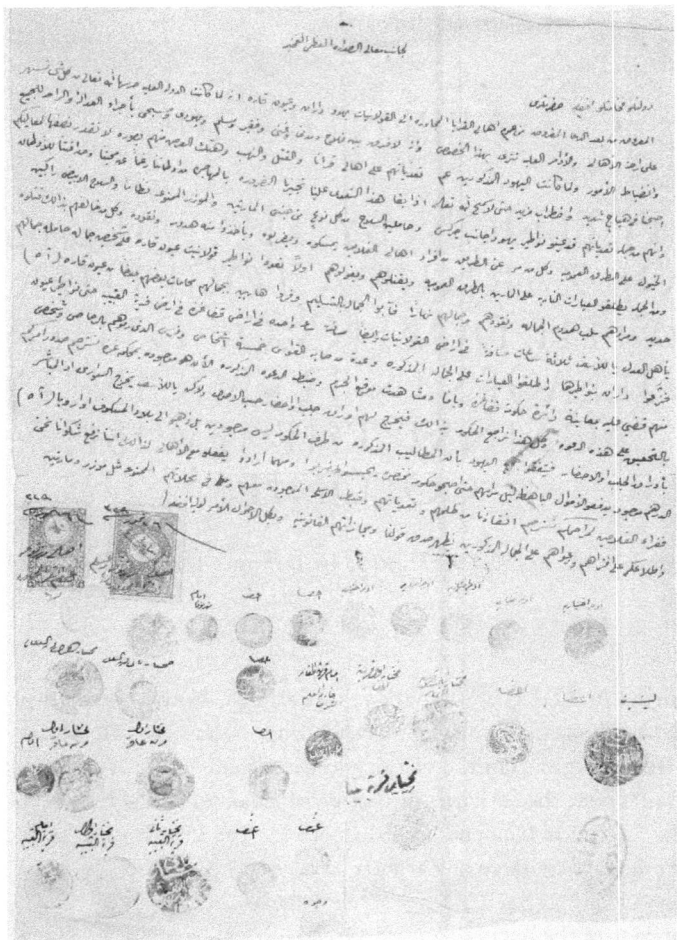

Source: BOA. EUM. EMN., 30/5, 16 Temmuz 1329 [29 July 1913]

cherkes [Circassian] guards and put them on duty armed with various weapons, including illegal ones such as Martins [guns], Mausers [pistols] and knives, to ride with their horses on the public roads. They catch every villager who travels along the public road, beat him, and take his clothes and money. They kill whoever opposes them. They also shoot passersby on the public road, and murder them.

At first, the guards of 'Uyun Qara [Rishon le-Zion] attacked two camel owners who were transporting iron. They wanted to take their clothes, money and camels, but they refused to hand over their camels and fled from 'Uyun Qara with their camels, while protecting each other [in order to find refuge] with the people of justice. But unfortunately, they had to walk for three hours in the lands of the Jewish colonies [of Rishon le-Zion, Nes-Ziona and Rehovot] and another hour in the land of the village of al-Qubeiba in the sub-district of Gaza [before they reached their village Zarnuqa]. Meanwhile the guards of 'Uyun Qara had time to call the guards of Duran [Rehovot] who opened fire on the above-mentioned camel convoy, injuring five servants [*qawas*] and a horse which they shot. One person from among them was sentenced by the local government in Gaza and Jaffa which examined the scene of the crime.

Given that the prosecutor's report on this matter is filed today at the local court in the *kaza* of Gaza we beg the issuance of your order to investigate this matter. Each time that we approach the local government with a request to summon them [the Jewish colonists] to court according to the rules, the Jews reply to the court official that the wanted persons are not present since they have travelled to Russia or to Europe. With the help of money, they do whatever they want as if they have a little government of their own inside the country.

Therefore, we the poor peasants submit this petition to confiscate the illegal weapons they carry [with them] and possess in their villages such as the Martins and the Mausers. If you investigate our complaints and the lies they tell about the camels' owners mentioned above you will find that we are right and will punish them according to the law. At the end the decision is yours.

NOTES

Introduction

1. '*Ardahal* (عرضحال) in Arabic means a "petition" (literally "presentation of the situation," '*ard al-hal*). This term, however, is much more commonly known in its Turkish form, where it is pronounced *arzuhal*. It should be distinguished from *şikâyet*, the term used in Ottoman Turkish to define "both the act and concept of petitioning." See Ursinus, Michael, *Grievance Administration (şikâyet) in an Ottoman Province: The Kaymakam of Rumelia's 'Record Book of Complaints' of 1781–1783* (London and New York, 2005), p. 3.

2. For more on the workings of the administrative council and the *nizamiye* court at the provincial level in the District of Jerusalem at the end of the nineteenth century, see Gerber, Haim, *Ottoman Rule in Jerusalem, 1890–1914* (Berlin, 1985), chapters 5 and 6, respectively.

3. In the words of the sociologist David Zaret, to verify what is claimed in petitions, they should be read "in conjunction with other printed and manuscript materials." See Zaret, David, "Petitions and the 'Invention' of Public Opinion in the English Revolution, *American Journal of Sociology*, Vol. 101/6 (1996), p. 1508.

4. Davison, Roderic H., "The Advent of the Electric Telegraph in the Ottoman Empire: How Morse's Invention was Introduced at the Time of the Crimean War," *Essays in Ottoman and Turkish History, 1774–1923: The Impact of the West* (London, 1990), p. 155.

5. Faroqhi, Suraiya, "Political Initiatives 'From the Bottom Up' in the Sixteenth and Seventeenth Century Ottoman Empire: Some Evidence for Their Existence," in Faroqhi, Suraiya (ed.), *Coping with the State: Political Conflict and Crime in the Ottoman Empire, 1550–1720* (Istanbul, 1995), p. 2.

6. Faroqhi, "Political Initiatives 'From the Bottom Up'," p. 2 (after İlber Ortaylı).

7. Tahsin Paşa, *Abdülhamit Yıldız Hatıraları* (Abdülhamid's Yıldız Palace Memoirs) (Istanbul, 1931), p. 31 [in Turkish]; Karateke, Hakan T., *Padişahım Cok Yaşa! Osmanlı Devletinin Son Yuzyılında Merasimler* (Long Live the Sultan! Ceremonies in the Ottoman Empire during its Last Century) (Istanbul, 2004), pp. 119–21 [in Turkish].

8. Haslip, Joan, *The Sultan: The Life of Abdul Hamid II* (London, 1973), pp. 150–1; Pears, Edwin, *Forty Years in Constantinople: The Recollections of Sir Edwin Pears 1873–1915* (London, 1916), p. 115; interestingly, due to Abdülhamid's fears of assassination, direct contact with the sultan during the *selamlık* procession was forbidden and subjects were not allowed to hand their petitions directly to the sultan as before. See Georgeon, François, "Le sultan caché: réclusion du souverain et mise en scène du pouvoir à l'époque de Abdülhamid II (1876–1909)," *Turcica*, Vol. 29 (1997), pp. 103–4.

9. Chalcraft, John, "Engaging the State: Peasants and Petitions in Egypt on the Eve of Colonial Rule," *International Journal of Middle Eastern Studies*, Vol. 37/3 (2005), p. 309.

10. In this context, Irene Schneider's description of petitioners' expectations from the Shah of Iran (and vice versa) at about the same period is illuminating: "Whereas the Shāh connected political control to enforce his autocratic position with a social acceptance that relied on the traditional ideal type of a just ruler, the petitioners expected the implementation of justice and a life in peace and safety [. . .]. The petitioners not only perceived the Shāh as being omnipotent and the only person able to implement justice, but also as being obliged to respond to the petitions and to implement justice. Whenever their disappointment was triggered and exacerbated, for example when petitions were unanswered or officials flouted the Shāh's orders etc., this second perception grew stronger and embraced both an implicit criticism of the system and a demand for action." See Schneider, Irene, *The Petitioning System in Iran: State, Society, and Power Relations in the Late 19th Century* (Wiesbaden, 2006), pp. 103–4.

11. On this crisis at the end of the nineteenth century and the various means the Empire used in order to confront it, see Deringil, Selim, *The Well Protected Domains: Ideology and the Legitimation of Power in the Ottoman Empire, 1876–1909* (London, 1999), pp. 8–11; Karpat, Kemal H., *The Politicization of Islam: Reconstructing Identity, State, Faith, and Community in the Late Ottoman State* (New York and Oxford, 2001), pp. 166–7; Özbek, Nadir, "Philanthropic Activity, Ottoman Patriotism, and the Hamidian Regime, 1876–1909," *International Journal of Middle Eastern Studies*, Vol. 37 (2005), p. 62.

12. For comparison, Cecilia Nubola, when discussing supplications in the Italian states in the early modern period, writes the following about the state's growing intervention in its subjects' lives: "The state's growing invasive and bureaucratic presence accelerated the process of centralization, which had as long-term consequences the loss of "freedom" and the autonomies and traditional rights of communities. Not only did the supplications of communities and groups call for a "weightier" presence of the state. Single persons turned to princes and magistracies in the hope that these might take on their personal problems." See Nubola, Cecilia, *"Supplications between Politics and Justice: The Northern and Central Italian States in the Early Modern Age,"* in van Voss, Lex Heerma (ed.), *Petitions in Social History, International Review of Social History,* Vol. 46/Supplement 9 (2001), p. 55.

13. *Başbakanlık Osmanlı Arşivi* (henceforth BOA), HR. TO., 396/79, 18 Rebiyülâhır 1309 [21 November 1891, in the translation to Ottoman Turkish of the letter in Arabic it is erroneously written that the letter has no date].

14. Following several rounds of administrative reorganization, the area which later became known as Mandatory Palestine consisted at the time of the *Sancak*s (districts) of Nablus and Acre in the center and north (both part of the *vilayet* of Beirut as of 1888 whereas beforehand they belonged to the *vilayet* of Şam, Syria), and the *mutasarrıflık* (independent district) of Jerusalem in the center and south, which was established in 1872 and was directly governed from Istanbul (before 1872 Jerusalem also belonged to the *vilayet* of Şam). In the Ottoman administrative system, a *mutasarrıflık* was one level below a province (*vilayet*). The Ottomans, who wanted to reflect the increasing importance of Palestine and Jerusalem in its center, apparently decided to use this framework and not to constitute a new *vilayet*, given the small size of the area and the existence in the Levant of the provinces of Beirut and Damascus. See Abu-Manneh: "The Rise of the Sanjak of Jerusalem," pp. 41–51.

15. See Reinkowski, Maurus, "Late Ottoman Rule over Palestine: Its Evaluation in Arab, Turkish and Israeli Histories, 1970–90," *Middle Eastern Studies,* Vol. 35/1 (1999), pp. 90–1.

16. For several key examples, see Kayyali, A.W., *Palestine: A Modern History* (London, 1978); Tibawi, A. L., *A Modern History of Syria, including Lebanon and Palestine* (London, 1969); Gorny, Yosef, *Zionism and the Arabs, 1882–1948: A Study of Ideology* (Oxford, 1987); Shapira, Anita, *Land and Power: The Zionist Resort to Force, 1881–1948* (New York, 1992).

17. Reinkowski, "Late Ottoman Rule over Palestine: Its Evaluation," pp. 77–81.

18. Doumani, Beshara, "Rediscovering Ottoman Palestine: Writing Palestinians into History," *Journal of Palestine Studies,* Vol. XXI/2 (winter 1992), pp. 10–13 (what Doumani calls the "Affirmation of Identity" genre).

19. In recent years, more emphasis has been placed on intellectual and social history. For several such prominent works, see Campos, Michelle U., *Ottoman Brothers: Muslims, Christians, and Jews in Early Twentieth-Century Palestine* (Stanford, 2011); Jacobson, Abigail, *From Empire to Empire: Jerusalem between Ottoman and British Rule* (Syracuse, 2011); Tamari, Salim, *Mountain against the Sea: Essays on Palestinian Society and Culture* (Berkley, 2009); for several key sources discussing the voices of Palestine's Arab educated elite at the time which were published in recent years, see al-Jawhariyya, Wasif, *al-Quds al-'uthmaniyya fil-mudhakkirat al-Jawhariyya* (Ottoman Jerusalem in al-Jawhariyya Memoirs), Vol. I, edited by Tamari, Salim and Issam Nassar (Jerusalem, 2003) [in Arabic]; al-Sakakini, Khalil, *The Diaries of Khalil Sakakini*, Vol. I–II, edited by Musallam, Akram (Ramallah, 2003–4) [in Arabic]; Tamari, Salim (ed.), *The Year of the Locust: A Soldier's Diary and the Erasure of Palestine's Ottoman Past* (Berkley, 2011).

20. For instance, see Shafir, Gershon, *Land, Labor and the Origins of the Israeli-Palestinian Conflict, 1882–1914* (Cambridge, 1989); Lockman, Zachary, *Comrades and Enemies: Arab and Jewish Workers in Palestine, 1906–1948* (Berkley, 1996).

21. For instance, see Muslih, Muhammad Y., *The Origins of Palestinian Nationalism* (New York, 1988); Porath, Yehoshua, *The Emergence of the Palestinian-Arab National Movement, 1918–1929* (London, 1974); Kayyali: *Palestine*; Tibawi: *A Modern History of Syria*; Gorny: *Zionism and the Arabs*; Shapira, *Land and Power*; Morris, Benny, *Righteous Victims: A History of the Zionist-Arab Conflict, 1881–2001* (New York, 2001); the one exception is the period after the Young Turk Revolution of 1908 which has received more attention in research because it is perceived as the seedbed for the bi-national political conflict in Palestine. For instance, see Mandel, Neville J., *The Arabs and Zionism before World War I* (Berkley, 1976). Most of this seminal book, which is still considered authoritative today, focuses on the period between 1908 and 1914, although it deals with the period between 1882 and 1914; for an interesting attempt to link the Jewish–Arab conflict to deeper historical roots see Kimmerling, Barukh and Joel Migdal, *Palestinians: The Making of a People* (New York, 1993); Alexander Schölch decided to focus on the period preceding 1882 and did not continue into the period of the proto-Zionist–Arab encounters because in his opinion the situation in Palestine completely changed after this year. See Schölch, Alexander, *Palestine in Transformation 1856–1882: Studies in Social, Economic and Political Development* (Washington, DC, 1993).

22. In using this term I refer to the Jewish national activity in Palestine between the early 1880s and 1897, the year in which the Zionist Congress met for the first time and the Zionist Movement was officially established.

23. For instance, consular reports, travelers' accounts, diaries and memoirs and, in general, a plethora of Jewish and Zionist sources portraying nineteenth-century Palestine.

24. Khalidi, Rashid, *Palestinian Identity: The Construction of Modern National Consciousness* (New York, 1997), pp. 88–91; for several key works based on Ottoman archival material that deal with Palestine during the last decades of Ottoman rule, see Abu-Manneh, Butrus, "The Rise of the Sanjak of Jerusalem in the Late Nineteenth Century," in Pappé, Ilan (ed.), *The Israel/Palestine Question* (London, 1999), pp. 41–51; Gerber: *Ottoman Rule*; idem, "A New Look at the Tanzīmāt: The Case of the Province of Jerusalem," in Kushner, David (ed.), *Palestine in the Late Ottoman Period: Political, Social, and Economic Transformation* (Leiden, 1986), pp. 30–45; Fischel, Roy and Ruth Kark, "Sultan Abdülhamid II and Palestine: Private lands and Imperial Policy," *New Perspectives on Turkey*, Vol. 39 (Fall 2008), pp. 126–66; Kushner, David, "The Last Generation of Ottoman Rule in Eretz Israel, 1882–1914," in Kolatt, Israel (ed.), *The History of the Jewish Community in Eretz Israel since 1882: The Ottoman Period*, Vol. I (Jerusalem, 1989), pp. 1–74 [in Hebrew]; idem, *To be Governor of Jerusalem: The City and District during the Time of Ali Ekrem Bey, 1906–1908* (Istanbul, 2005); Avcı, Yasemin, *Değişim Sürecinde Bir Osmanlı Kenti: Kudüs 1890–1914* (An Ottoman City in Transition: Jerusalem 1890–1914) (Ankara, 2004) [in Turkish].

25. On the literacy rate of the population of Palestine at the end of the nineteenth century, see Ayalon, Ami, *Reading Palestine: Printing and Literacy, 1900–1948* (Austin, TX, 2004), chapter 1.

26. For further details, see Khalidi: *Palestinian Identity*, pp. 89–93.

27. For a unique study of the rural population in the District of Jerusalem in the sixteenth century based on *shari'a* court records, see Singer, Amy, *Palestinian Peasants and Ottoman Officials: Rural Administration around Sixteenth-Century Jerusalem* (Cambridge, 1994).

28. Cohen, Amnon, "A Tale of Two Women: Facets of Jewish Life in Nineteenth-Century Jerusalem as Seen through the Muslim Court Records," in Levy, Avigdor (ed.), *Jews, Turks, Ottomans: A Shared History, Fifteenth Through Twentieth Century* (Syracuse, 2002), p. 119.

29. Rubin, Avi, "Legal Borrowing and its Impact on Ottoman Legal Culture in the Late Nineteenth Century," *Continuity and Change*, Vol. 22/2 (2007), p. 279; to date, there is still no study devoted to the *nazamiye* courts in Palestine.

30. Gerber: *Ottoman Rule in Jerusalem*, chapter 5.

31. For several major works based on *shari'a* court records, see Tucker, Judith E., *In the House of the Law: Gender and Islamic Law in Ottoman Syria and Palestine* (Berkeley, 1998); Yazbak, Mahmoud, *Haifa in the Late Ottoman Period,*

1864–1914: A Muslim Town in Transition (Leiden, 1998); Cohen, Amnon, Elisheva Ben-Shimon-Pikali and Eyal Ginio, *Jews in the Moslem Religious Court: Society, Economy and Communal Organization in the XIX Century: Documents from Ottoman Jerusalem* (Jerusalem, 2003) [in Hebrew]; Agmon, Iris, *Family & Court: Legal Culture and Modernity in Late Ottoman Palestine* (Syracuse, NY, 2006).

32. For several works on late Ottoman Palestine from recent years which are based in part on sources from the central Ottoman archives, see Fishman, Louis, *Palestine Revisited: Reassessing the Jewish and Arab National Movements, 1908–1914* (Ph.D. Dissertation, University of Chicago, 2007); Büssow, Johann, *Hamidian Palestine: Politics and Society in the District of Jerusalem, 1872–1908* (Leiden, 2011); Avcı: *Değişim Sürecinde Bir Osmanlı Kenti: Kudüs 1890–1914*; Der Matossian, *Ethnic Politics in Post-Revolutionary Ottoman Empire.*

33. To assess the potential of Ottoman sources from the collections of the main Ottoman archive in Istanbul for historians who study Palestine at the end of the nineteenth century, see a recently published collection of documents by the *Başbakanlık Osmanlı Arşivi*, part of a series dealing with various provinces of the Ottoman Empire, entitled *Osmanlı Belgelerinde Filistin* (Istanbul, 2009) [in Turkish].

34. The most comprehensive work in recent years on the rural population of Palestine during the late Ottoman period was written by the historical geographer David Grossman. See Grossman, David, *Arab Demography and Early Jewish Settlement in Palestine: Distribution and Population Density during the Late Ottoman and Early Mandate Periods* (Jerusalem, 2004) [in Hebrew].

35. For the most updated catalogue of the archive, see *Başbakanlık Osmanlı Arşivi Rehberi* (Catalogue of the Ottoman Archive at the Prime Minister's Office) (Ankara, 2010) [in Turkish].

36. For more on the large volume of telegraphs sent from the District of Jerusalem to Istanbul at the end of the nineteenth century, the logbooks registering the traffic of telegraphs between Istanbul and Jerusalem can be consulted. See BOA. VGG.d 312, 314, 315, 316, 317, 974.

37. For more on this process, see Abu-Manneh, Butrus, "Jerusalem in the Tanzimat Period: The New Ottoman Administration and the Notables," *Die Welt des Islams*, Vol. 30/1 (1990), pp. 1–44.

38. Abu-Manneh: "The Rise of the Sanjak of Jerusalem," pp. 41–51; Büssow: *Hamidian Palestine*, chapter 1.

39. Ben-Arieh, Yehoshua, "ha-Nof ha-yishuvi shel Eretz-Yisrael 'erev ha-hityashvut ha-tsiyonit" (The Settlement Landscape of Eretz-Yisrael on the Eve of Zionist Colonization), in Kolatt, Israel (ed.). *The History of the Jewish Community in Eretz Israel since 1882*, Vol. I (Jerusalem, 1989), p. 77 [in Hebrew] (the numbers are approximations).

40. Among these projects were the construction of a carriage road to Jerusalem in 1867, the opening of a train line to Jerusalem in 1892, a telegraph network in the mid-1860s, renovation of the port and the arrival of steam boats, establishment of new neighborhoods outside the Old City wall, building projects and the like.

41. Ben-Arieh: "ha-Nof ha-yishuvi," pp. 88–90; Kark, Ruth, "The Rise and Decline of Coastal Towns in Palestine," in Gilbar, Gad (ed.), *Ottoman Palestine, 1800–1914: Studies in Social and Economic History* (Leiden, 1990), pp. 74–80; Büssow: *Hamidian Palestine*, pp. 272–73.

42. For a recent study of Gaza politics and society at the end of the nineteenth century, see Büssow: Hamidian Palestine, pp. 258–305.

43. Grossman: *Arab Demography and Early Jewish Settlement in Palestine*, pp. 144–81.

44. Ibid., pp. 163–5, 178–9; see also al-Dabbagh, Mustafa Murad, *Biladuna Filastin* (Our Country Palestine), Vol. I, part 2, pp. 215–73 (Beirut, 1974) [in Arabic].

45. See Hütteroth, Wolf-Dieter and Kamal Abdulfattah, *Historical Geography of Palestine, Transjordan and Southern Syria in the Late 16th Century* (Erlangen, 1977), pp. 142–56.

46. Grossman: "Rural Settlement," pp. 65–8, 75, 85–6; Kressel, Gidon and R. Aharoni, "Egyptian Immigrants in the Bilad Esh-Sham," *Jama'a*, Vol. 12 (2004), pp. 201–45 [in Hebrew]; Baldensperger wrote in 1906 that "in Philistia [the southern Palestine coast] the smaller villages have hardly been in peaceful possession for more than thirty years, and bloody contests have occurred yearly, even since the establishment of the legal deeds, merely on account of the illegal action, real or presumed of the new possessors [. . .]. Naturally, the further the villages are away from the centers of government, the fiercer the contests." See Baldensperger, Philip, "The Immovable East," *Palestine Exploration Fund: Quarterly Statement for 1906*, p. 196.

47. Baldensperger, Philip, *The Immovable East – Studies of the People and Customs of Palestine* (Tel-Aviv, 1982), p. 115 [in Hebrew]; idem, "The Immovable East," *Palestine Exploration Fund: Quarterly Statement for 1917*, p. 161.

48. About the settlement of various immigrant groups in the outskirts of Jaffa, from Palestine, as from other places in the Empire, and at times even from places outside its borders, see Sa'id, Ibrahim Hasan, *Yafa: Min al-ghazw al-Nabolyonni ila hamlat Ibrahim Basha, 1799–1831* (Jaffa: From the Raid of Napoleon to the Campaign of Ibrahim Pasha) (Beirut, 2006), pp. 207–10 [in Arabic].

49. See von Oppenheim, Max Freiherr, *Die Beduinen*, Vol. II (Hildeshein, 1983), pp. 55–64.

50. Muslih: *The Origins of Palestinian Identity*, p. 31.
51. Such mansions existed, for example, in the valley where the small colony of Nes-Ziona was situated, some 15 kilometers south-east of Jaffa. See Granott (Granovsky), Abraham, *ha-Mishtar ha-qarqaʻi be-Eretz-Yisra'el* (The Land Regime in Eretz-Israel) (Tel-Aviv, 1949), p. 76 [in Hebrew].
52. Grossman, David, *Expansion and Desertion: The Arab Village and its Offshoots in Ottoman Palestine* (Jerusalem, 1994), p. 35 [in Hebrew]; idem, *Arab Demography*, p. 34.

Chapter 1: The Ottoman Institution of Petitions to the Ruler in Global and Islamic Perspectives

1. For example, on petitions sent by native populations in the British Commonwealth, see de Costa, Ravi, "Identity, Authority, and the Moral Worlds of Indigenous Petitions," *Comparative Studies in Society and History*, Vol. 48/3 (2006), pp. 669–98.
2. van Voss, Lex Heerma, "Introduction," *Petitions in Social History*, p. 1.
3. For instance, see Kracke, Edward A., "Early Visions of Justice for the Humble in East and West," *Journal of the American Oriental Society*, Vol. 96/4, (1976), pp. 492–8.
4. Mesad Hashvyahu is a site on the Mediterranean coast, some 15 kilometers south of the modern-day city of Tel-Aviv – Jaffa in Israel, where the ruins of an ancient fortress were found. It was located on the Biblical border between Judea and the Philistines.
5. In Smelik, Klaas A.D., *Writings from Ancient Israel: A Handbook of Historical and Religious Sources* (Louisville, Kentucky, 1991), p. 96 (translated by G.I. Davis); see also "Mikhtav tluna mi-Metsad Hashavyahu" (a complaint letter from Mesad Hashvyahu) in Ahituv, Shmuel, *HaKetav VeHaMiktav* (Jerusalem, 2005), pp. 143–9 [in Hebrew].
6. On the criteria determining what constitutes a "petition," see van Voss: "Introduction," p. 2; Würgler, Andreas, "Voices from among the "Silent Masses": Humble Petitions and Social Conflicts in Early Modern Central Europe," *Petitions in Social History*, pp. 11–34. Würgler writes that "Petitions, grievances, and supplications, *Gravamina, Suppliken,* and *Beschwerden, doléances, requêtes,* and *représentations, gravami, petizioni,* and *querele, clamores, greuges* and *griefs* – or whatever they have been called in changing times and regions – were produced by individuals or groups, regardless of their age, status, class, ethnicity, religion, or sex. As they were composed in the most varied situations of life they document needs and interests, hopes and experiences, attitudes and activities". See p. 12.

7. Davis, Natalie Zemon, *Fiction in the Archives: Pardon Tales and their Tellers in Sixteenth-Century France* (Stanford, 1987), pp. 3–5.

8. Ibid., pp. 3–5, 7–8, 111–14.

9. Shaw, J. E., "Writing to the Prince: Supplications, Equity, and Absolutism in Sixteenth-Century Tuscany," *Past and Present*, Vol. 215 (2012), p. 65.

10. Würgler: "Voices from among the "Silent Masses"," p. 32.

11. Nielsen, Jørgen S., *Secular Justice in an Islamic State: Mazālim under the Baḥrī Mamlūks, 662/1294–789/1387* (Istanbul, 1985), pp. 1–2. Nielsen writes about petitions to the Sasanid king that "the appeal to the king constituted an extraordinary judicial system which worked parallel to the ordinary system and which heard cases of all kinds – not only those involving official abuse of power." Nielsen notes that the Muslims also inherited the notion of the ruler as the source of justice and the address for subjects' appeals from the Byzantines (p. 3); see also Schacht, Joseph, "The Schools of Law and Later Developments of Jurisprudence," in Khadduri, Majid and Herbert J. Liebesny (eds.), *Law in the Middle East: Origin and Development of Islamic Law*, Vol. I (Washington, DC, 1955), p. 59.

12. Nielsen, J. S., "Mazālim," *Encyclopaedia of Islam*, second edition. Nielsen also suggests that the *mazalim* represented "the ideal of open access to tribal leaders in pre-Islamic Arabia."

13. Long, David E., "The Board of Grievances in Saudi Arabia," *Middle East Journal*, Vol. 27/1 (1973), p. 71.

14. Nielsen: *Secular Justice in an Islamic State*, p. 3.

15. al-Mawardi, *The Ordinances of Government: A Translation of Al-Aḥkām al-Sulṭ aniyya w' al-Wilāyāt al-Dīniyya*, translated by Wahaba, Wafaa H. (London, 1996); Nimrod Hurvitz remarks that Islamic legal experts during the first centuries of Islam refrained from formulating aspects pertaining to public law and preferred to leave this field to the conduct of rulers and political elites. In this sense, al-Mawardi's work in the eleventh century is unique. See Hurvitz, Nimrod, "The Contribution of Early Islamic Rulers to Adjudication and Legislation: The Case of Mazalim Tribunals," *The New East*, Vol. 49 (2010), pp. 12–13, 27–8 [in Hebrew].

16. al-Mawardi: *The Ordinances of Government*, pp. 90–3.

17. Ibid.

18. Lambton, Ann, *State and Government in Medieval Islam: An Introduction to the Study of Islamic Political Theory* (Oxford, 1981), p. 88.

19. Lambton, Ann, *State and Government in Medieval Islam*, p. 84.

20. See Nielsen: *Secular Justice in an Islamic State*, p.17.

21. Ibid., p. 2.

22. Nielsen: "Mazālim."

23. Nielsen: "Maẓālim"; Hurvitz argues that the separation between the rulers who implemented *siyasa shar'iyya* and actual practices of ruling, and the jurists who dealt with *fiqh* and the legal doctrines, served both sides and did not necessarily lead to tension between them. See Hurvitz: "The Contribution of Early Islamic Rulers to Adjudication and Legislation," pp. 11–15, 27–8; about the absence of *mazalim* from the system of *fiqh*, see also Tyan, Emile, "Judicial Organization," *Law in the Middle East: Origin and Development of Islamic Law*, p. 268.

24. Tillier, Mathieu, "*Qāḍīs* and the Political Use of the *Maẓālim* Jurisdiction under the 'Abbāsids," in Lange, C. C. and M. Fierro (eds.), *Public Violence in Islamic Societies: Power, Discipline, and the Construction of the Public Sphere, 7th-19th Centuries CE* (Edinburgh, 2009), pp. 47–9, 54–5.

25. Ibid., p. 42; Nielsen: "Maẓālim"; see also Hurvitz: "The Contribution of Early Islamic Rulers to Adjudication and Legislation," pp. 11–29.

26. For information about researchers who support the latter point, see Tillier, "*Qāḍīs* and the Political Use of the *Maẓālim*," p. 42 fn. 1; Ursinus: *Grievance Administration*, p. 3; David Powers discusses other forms of appeal in the Islamic legal system which he defines as "Islamic successor review" and criticizes the previously prevailing notion among Islamicists that "there are no appellate structures in Islamic law, that the decision of a kadı is final and irrevocable, that a judge may not change his mind once he has rendered his decision, and that a judgment may not be reversed under *any* circumstances." See Powers, David S., "On Judicial Review in Islamic Law," *Law and Society Review*, Vol. 26/2 (1992), p. 316; Nielsen also writes that occasionally *mazalim* served as courts of appeal against decisions taken by *kadı*s. See Nielsen: "Maẓālim."

27. Ibid; see also Irwin, Robert, "The Privatization of "Justice" under the Circassian Mamluks," *Mamluk Studies Review*, Vol. IV (2002), pp. 63–4.

28. Nielsen: "Maẓālim."

29. Tillier: "*Qāḍīs* and the Political Use of the *Maẓālim* Jurisdiction under the 'Abbāsids," pp. 57, 59 ("To consider *maẓālim* justice as 'secular' as opposed to the 'religious' justice of the *qāḍī*s would be inconsistent with that time [the Abbasid]").

30. Nielsen: *Secular Justice in an Islamic State*, pp. 32–3. Double sales was a way to collect "interest" while avoiding usufruct, which is forbidden according to Islamic law.

31. Tyan: "Judicial Organization," pp. 266–7.

32. Nielsen: *Secular Justice in an Islamic State*, pp. 31–3; Long writes that "the only limitations on *maẓālim* courts were those legal provisions in *sharī'ah* law which established express prohibitions." See Long: "The Board of Grievances," p. 72.

33. Schacht: "The Schools of Law," p. 59; Schacht also adds that, in addition to wrongdoings and injustices, *mazalim* during the Abbasid period also dealt with "the more important lawsuits concerning property, which would in theory come within the jurisdiction of the qāḍīs.

34. Nizam al-Mulk, *The Book of Government or Rules for Kings*, translated by H. Darke (London, 1978), pp. 13–14.

35. Nielsen: *Secular Justice in an Islamic State*, pp. 7, 26; about Seljukid influence on petitions during the Ayyubid period, see Stern, S.M., "Petitions from the Ayyūbid Period," *Bulletin of the School of Oriental and African Studies University of London*, Vol. 27/1 (1964), pp. 15–16.

36. Albrecht Fuess argues that the *mazalim* courts ceased to exist when the Ottomans conquered Egypt and took it from the Mamluks. See Fuess, Albrecht, "Ẓulm by Maẓālim? The Political Implications of the Use of Maẓālim Jurisdiction by the Mamluk Sultans," *Mamluk Studies Review*, Vol. XIII/1 (2009), p. 142; Ursinus, however, discusses the system of complaints (*şikâyet*) at the Ottoman provincial level in the late eighteenth century as a form of a *mazalim* court. See Ursinus: *Grievance Administration (şikâyet) in an Ottoman Province*, p. 2.

37. Nielsen: "Maẓālim."

38. See also Irwin: "The Privatization of 'Justice' under the Circassian Mamluks," pp. 69–70.

39. The question whether on not the Mongol *yasa* played a role in the Mamluk state remains open to discussion. David Ayalon argued that the Mongol *yasa* played an important role in the Mamluk Justice system. Nielsen rebutted Ayalon's claim although it seems that the more important issue was that the Mamluk sultans were highly autonomous as leaders of the justice system, even when their acts did not adhere to the *shari'a*. See Irwin, ibid., p. 64; see also Fuess: "Ẓulm by Maẓālim?," p. 132.

40. Nielsen: *Secular Justice in an Islamic State*, pp. 51–3.

41. Ibid., pp. 43–7; see also chapter 7.

42. Göçek, Fatma M., *Rise of the Bourgeoisie, Demise of Empire* (New York, 1996), pp. 20–3; Hallaq, Wael B., *An Introduction to Islamic Law* (Cambridge, UK and New York, 2009), pp. 75–6.

43. Ibid., p. 77.

44. Mardin, Şerif, "Power, Civil Society, and Culture in the Ottoman Empire," *Comparative Studies in Society and History*, Vol. 11 (1969), p. 260.

45. According to this notion, all the components of the cycle (the ruler, the army, the bureaucracy, the tax-paying peasants, the rule of law, the *shari'a*, the state) were dependent on each other and could not operate or sustain themselves if one of the components of the cycle malfunctioned. For further details, see Hallaq: *An Introduction to Islamic Law*, pp. 73–4; see also Darling, Linda T.,

A History of Social Justuce and Political Power in the Middle East: The Circle of Justice from Mesopotamia to Globalization (London and New York, 2013).

46. See Ginio, Eyal, "Coping with the State's Agents 'from Below:' Petitions, Legal Appeal and the Sultan's Justice in Ottoman Legal Practice," in Gara, Eleni, M. Erdem Kabadayı and Christoph K. Neumann (eds.), *Popular Protest and Political Participation in the Ottoman Empire: Collective Volume in Honor of Prof. Suraiya Faroqhi* (Istanbul, 2011), pp. 41–56.

47. Most studies on the Ottoman institution of petitioning the ruler begin in the sixteenth century. However, it is more than likely that a form of petitioning system was in place much earlier in Ottoman history although few sources are available today.

48. Faroqhi, Suraiya, "Introduction," *Coping with the State*, p. XV; idem, "Political Initiatives," pp. 2–3; idem, "Political Activity among Ottoman Taxpayers and the Problem of Sultanic Legitimation (1570–1650)," *Coping with the State*," p. 13; Würgler writes that "By supplications, *gravamina*, and petitions, ordinary people forced their rulers to react to specific problems. They thus played a part in the setting of political agendas." See Würgler: "Voices from among the "Silent Masses"," p. 31.

49. Hagen, Gottfried, "Legitimacy and World Order," *Legitimizing the Order: The Ottoman Rhetoric of State Power*, p. 68.

50. The sensitivity of the Ottoman government to abandonment of the land by peasants is clear from the petitions, and was deliberately included by petition-writers to play on this sore point.

51. About revolts and acts of protest by the rural population in the Ottoman Empire during the nineteenth century and the reasons behind them, see Quataert, Donald, "Rural Unrest in the Ottoman Empire, 1830–1914," in Kazemi, Farhad and John Waterbury (eds.), *Peasants and Politics in the Modern Middle East* (Miami, 1991), pp. 38–49; in the period discussed here, there were no rebellions in Palestine similar to those that broke out there even as late as 1834. Interestingly, however, such revolts did take place in nearby regions such as the Hawran in Syria which witnessed considerable unrest and violence at the end of the nineteenth century. See Schatkowski, Linda S., "Violence in Rural Syria in the 1880s and 1890s: State Centralization, Rural Integration, and the World Market," *Peasants and Politics in the Modern Middle East*, pp. 50–84.

52. İnalcık, Halil, *The Ottoman Empire: The Classical Age 1300–1600* (London, 2002), p. 91; Papastamatiou, Demetrios, "The Right of Appeal to State Intervention as a Means of Political Mobilisation of the *Reaya* in the Ottoman Provinces: Some Preliminary Remarks on the Eighteenth-Century Morea (Peloponnese)," *Political Initiatives 'From the Bottom Up:' Halcyon Days in Crete VII, A Symposium held in Rathymno, 9–11 January 2009* (Rathymno, 2012), p. 171.

53. For instance, see Ursinus: *Grievance Administration*, p. 37.

54. For activities such as these in the period preceding the Young Turk Revolution in 1908, see Kansu, Aykut, *The Revolution of 1908 in Turkey* (Leiden, 1997), chapter 2; see also Hanioğlu, Şükrü M., *Preparation for a Revolution: The Young Turks, 1902–1908* (Oxford, 2001), chapter 5.

55. For instance, see Faroqhi: "Political Initiatives," pp. 1–11; Ginio, Eyal, "Patronage, Intervention and Violence in the Legal Process in Eighteenth-Century Salonica and Its Province," in Shaham, Ron (ed.), *Law, Custom, and Statute in the Muslim World* (Leiden, 2007), pp. 111–30.

56. Heyd, Uriel, *Ottoman Documents on Palestine, 1552–1615: A Study of the Firman According to the Mühimme Defteri* (Oxford, 1960), p. 14; İnalcık writes that the Ottoman Imperial Council simultaneously served as a high court as well as a cabinet. See İnalcık: *The Ottoman Empire: The Classical Age 1300–1600*, p. 93.

57. Heyd: *Ottoman Documents on Palestine*, p. 14.

58. Ursinus: *Grievance Administration*, pp. 8–9; see also Heyd, Uriel, *Studies in Old Ottoman Criminal Law* (Oxford, 1973), p. 226.

59. On *arz-i mahzar*, see İnalcık, Halil, "Şikâyet Hakkı: 'Arż-i Ḥâl ve 'Arż-i Maḥ żar'lar," *Osmanlı Araştırmaları*, VII–VIII (1988), pp. 33–54 [in Turkish]; for one interesting case of collective petitioning from Palestine during the late Ottoman period by both Muslims and Christians who protested against archeological excavations in Haram al-Sharif in Jerusalem, see Fishman, Louis, "The 1911 Haram al-Sharif Incident: Palestinian Notables versus the Ottoman Administration," *Journal of Palestine Studies*, Vol. XXXIV/3 (2005), pp. 6–22.

60. Chalcraft: "Engaging the State," p. 307 ("Petition writing against inter-mediaries was risky. Notables had significant local powers").

61. For more details on the subject of appeals in the Ottoman legal system in which the Imperial Council in Istanbul served to a certain degree as a court of appeal for the *kadıs*' courts in the provinces, see Ginio, Eyal, "The Administration of Criminal Justice in Ottoman Selânik (Salonica) during the Eighteenth Century," *Turcica* 30 (1998), pp. 197–200; İnalcık, Halil, "Istanbul: An Islamic City," *Journal of Islamic Studies*, Vol. I (1990), p. 16.

62. For instance, see Minkov, Anton, *Conversions to Islam in the Balkans: Kisve Bahası Petitions and Ottoman Social Life, 1670–1730* (Leiden and Boston, 2004).

63. Darling, Linda T., *Revenue-Raising and Legitimacy: Tax Collection and Finance Administration in the Ottoman Empire, 1560–1660* (Leiden, 1996), chapter 8.

64. Gradeva, Rossitsa, "From the Bottom Up and Back Again until Who Knows When: Church Restoration Procedures in the Ottoman Empire,

Seventeenth-Eighteenth Centuries (Preliminary Notes)," *Political Initiatives "From the Bottom Up"*, pp. 135–63.

65. Faroqhi: "Political Initiatives," pp. 8–9; about the process of issuing a *ferman*, see Heyd: *Ottoman Documents on Palestine, 1552–1615*, pp. 13–18.

66. On the registration of imperial *ferman*s sent from Istanbul to the *shariʿa* court, for instance in Jerusalem, see Cohen, Amnon, *Ottoman Documents on the Jewish Community of Jerusalem in the Sixteenth Century* (Jerusalem, 1976), pp. 9–13 [in Hebrew].

67. Heyd: *Ottoman Documents on Palestine, 1552–1615*, p. 14.

68. Ibid., p. 19; Cohen: *Ottoman Documents on the Jewish Community of Jerusalem in the Sixteenth Century*, pp. 52–3.

69. Ibid; Faroqhi: "Political Activity," p. 14.

70. Heyd: *Ottoman Documents on Palestine, 1552–1615*, pp. XV–XVII, 6.

71. Ursinus: *Grievance Administration*, p. 7 fn. 38 (*Şikâyet* registers are found for the years 1649–1813); at a certain point, internal division was created within the registers of complaints which were organized geographically/administratively. See Faroqhi, Suraiya, "Guildsmen Complain to the Sultan: Artisans' Disputes and the Ottoman Administration in the 18th Century," in Karateke, Hakan T. and Maurus Reinkowski (eds.), *Legitimizing the Order: The Ottoman Rhetoric of State Power* (Leiden and Boston, 2005), p. 183; as of the mid-eighteenth century the important provinces had separate registers of complaints known as *Vilayet Ahkâm Defterleri*. See Faroqhi, Suraiya, *Approaching Ottoman History: An Introduction to the Sources* (Cambridge, 1999), p. 51; for a study analyzing *Ahkâm Defterleri* concerning Morea (The Peloponnese), see Papastamatiou, "The Right of Appeal to State Intervention," pp. 165–90; for an analysis of the registers of complaints and center-periphery relationships, see Gerber, Haim, *State, Society, and Law in Islam: Ottoman Law in Comparative Perspective* (Albany. N.Y., 1994), chapter 5.

72. Rubin, Avi, *Ottoman Nizamiye Courts: Law and Modernity* (New York, 2011), p. 83.

73. Davison: "The Advent of the Electric Telegraph," pp. 133–65; see also Feener, Michael. R., "New Networks and New Knowledge: Migrations, Communications, and the Refiguration of the Muslim Community in the Nineteenth and Early Twentieth Centuries," in Hefner, Robert W. (ed.), *The New Cambridge History of Islam: Muslims and Modernity Culture and Society since 1800*, Vol. VI (Cambridge, 2010), pp. 50–1.

74. Bektas, Yakup, "The Sultan's Messenger: Cultural Constructions of Ottoman Telegraphy, 1847–1880," *Technology and Culture*, Vol. 41/4 (2000), pp. 694–5.

75. Davison: "The Advent of the Electric Telegraph," p. 148. Similarly, Bektas writes (p. 672) that "with the telegraph, the sultan's orders could now be quickly conveyed to the governors and officials, who could be summoned to Istanbul or be replaced without warning. Furthermore, public complaints and petitions about pashas and other matters could be communicated to the sultan directly."

76. For the influence of the telegraph in Ottoman Syria, see Rogan, Eugene, "Instant Communication: The Impact of the Telegraph in Ottoman Syria," in Philipp, Thomas and Brigit Schaebler (eds.), *The Syrian Land: Processes of Integration and Fragmentation, Bilād al-Shām from the 18th to the 20th Century* (Stutgart, 1998), pp. 113–28; for the telegraph's influence in Iran, see Shahvar, Soli, "Iron Poles, Wooden Poles: The Electric Telegraph and the Ottoman–Iranian Boundary Conflict, 1863–1865," *British Journal of Middle Eastern Studies*, Vol. 34/1, 2007, pp. 23–42; apparently, there were difficulties at times in sending telegraphs from Ottoman post offices and the clerks censored some issues they considered delicate. Moreover, sometimes it took a few days for a telegraph to arrive. See Grant, Elihu, *The People of Palestine: An Enlarged Edition of "The Peasantry of Palestine, Life, Manners and Customs of the Village"* (Westport, Connecticut, 1976), p. 231.

77. Bektas, "The Sultan's Messenger," p. 694–5.

78. Pamuk, Şevket, *İstanbul ve Diğer Kentlerde 500 Yıllık Fiyatlar ve Ücretler 1469–1998* (Prices and Fees in Istanbul and Other Cities during a Period of 500 Years) (Ankara: 2000), pp. 17–18 [in Turkish].

79. Faroqhi: "Political Initiatives," p. 2; Shaw, when writing on sixteenth-century Tuscany, argues that absolutist regimes tended to lead to increased petitioning compared with republican eras. See Shaw: "Writing to the Prince," p. 56.

80. Similar processes took place in the emerging early modern central European states. Würgler, for example, writes that "[T]he emerging territorial state *sought* the role of mediator by expanding into formerly autonomous local or corporate spheres. But, on the other hand, the state *was sought* by individuals and collectives who trusted in its mediating capacities." Würgler: "Voices from among the "Silent Masses"," p. 31.

81. Translated in Landen, R.G., *The Emergence of the Modern Middle East* (New York, 1970), p. 100.

82. Karateke, Hakan T., "Legitimizing the Ottoman Sultanate: A Framework for Historical Analysis," *Legitimizing the Order: The Ottoman Rhetoric of State Power*, p. 49.

83. Chalcraft: "Engaging the State," p. 306.

84. Hiroshi Kato claims that the system of petitioning the Khedive in Egypt continued to be effective until the judicial reforms at the end of the nineteenth

century. See Kato, Hiroshi, "The Egyptian Rural Society in the Mid-Nineteenth Century as Reflected in the Documents on Petition for the Exemption from Military Service," *Mediterranean World*, Vol. XIV (1995), p. 61.

85. Chalcraft, John, *The Striking Cabbies of Cairo and Other Stories: Crafts and Guilds in Egypt, 1863–1914* (Albany, New York, 2004), p. 67.

86. Schneider: *The Petitioning System in Iran*, p. 86.

87. Faroqhi demonstrates how even in the period of decentralization which characterized the eighteenth-century Ottoman Empire, when the sultans were hardly in a position to impose their will in the Empire's provinces, petitions were still being sent to the imperial center, in fact in larger numbers, and the opinion/approval of the sultan was sought for and perceived as very important. See Faroqhi: "Guildsmen Complain to the Sultan," pp. 183–4.

88. Schneider: *The Petitioning System in Iran*, p. 104.

89. Shaw: "Writing to the Prince," p. 55 ("Princely interference in justice needs to be considered in parallel to the development of an absolutist conception of justice, moving away from an autonomous corpus of 'scientific' rules and towards an emphasis on sovereign will").

90. Petitions from Palestine referred to the local authorities are occasionally mentioned in the literature but no thorough research has been dedicated to them to date. For instance, see Gerber: *Ottoman Rule in Jerusalem*; Doumani, Beshara, *Rediscovering Palestine: Merchants and Peasants in Jabal Nablus, 1700– 1900* (Berkeley, 1995); LeVine, Mark, *Overthrowing Geography: Jaffa, Tel Aviv, and the Struggle for Palestine, 1880–1948* (Berkley, 2005); Hanssen, Jens, *Fin de Siècle Beirut: The Making of a Provincial Capital* (Oxford and New York, 2005); Campos: *Ottoman Brothers*.

91. Rogan: "Instant Communication," p. 114; about the importance the central government attributed the telegraph offices we can learn from the fact that its directors in Jerusalem were not locals. See al-Madani, Ziad 'Abdel 'Aziz, *The Waqfs (Endowments) in Jerusalem and within the Vicinity in the Nineteenth Century* (Amman, 2004), p. 64 [in Arabic].

92. Gerber: *Ottoman Rule in Jerusalem, 1890–1914*, chapters 7–9.

93. Ibid., pp. 168–9 (particularly as regards the Gaza region).

Chapter 2: General Features of the Petitions

1. http://www.devletarsivleri.gov.tr/katalog (registration is required to use the website).

2. For some regions, there were separate *Vilayet Ahkâm Defterleri* which compensate for this problem and make it possible to examine petitions from specific

regions. However, the *Ahkâm Defterleri* of Şam (Syria) which exists in the Archive (BOA. A.{DVNS.ŞM.D) has little information directly applicable to the topic of this book.

3. On the functions of the Foreign Ministry, see Shaw, Stanford J. and Ezel Kural Shaw, *History of the Ottoman Empire and Modern Turkey: Reform, Revolution, and Republic – The Rise of Modern Turkey, 1808–1975*, Vol. II (New York, 1976), pp. 72–3.

4. BOA. HR. TO., 387/61.

5. James Baldwin claims that in seventeenth- and eighteenth-century Ottoman Egypt, subjects preferred to send petitions to the sultan in Istanbul instead of going first to the local *shari'a* court, to ensure that the decision taken later by this court (when the matter was referred back to it from Istanbul) would be implemented, and as a means of deterrence vis-à-vis the people with whom they were litigating in court. See Baldwin, James E., "Petitioning the Sultan in Ottoman Egypt," *Bulletin of the School of Oriental and African Studies*, 75/3 (2012), pp. 499–525.

6. For instance, see BOA. HR. TO., 388/68, 17 Haziran 1297 [29 June 1881] (a petition sent from [the district of] Beirut to the Council of State by two representatives of farmers – most probably from the tribal group of Abu-Kishk – who cultivated land near al-'Awja River [in Hebrew: ha-Yarkon] in the sub-district of Jaffa, concerning the *vergi* tax, the status of their land and an allegedly excessive levy of taxes by the tax collector; HR. TO., 388/54, 14 Mart 1297 [26 March 1881] (a petition by an agent [*vekil*] of the village of Sarafand al-'Amar named Muhammad al-'Attar to the Ministry of Interior concerning the collection of the *vergi* tax from this village).

7. For instance, see BOA. HR. TO., 389/20, 4 Mayıs 1298 [16 May 1882] (a translation from Arabic into Ottoman of a petition addressed to the *Şûra-yı Devlet, Dahiliye* and *Baş Vekâleti* [Grand Vizier], submitted by the farmers of "Qula and Za'faraniyya [?]" headed by Faris al-Ikşik [Kişk]. These were two tax-farms, *mukataalar*, north of the al-'Awja River, where the semi-sedentary Bedouin group of Arab Abu-Kishk, known also as Arab al-'Awja, resided).

8. For instance, see BOA. HR. TO., 389/104, 12 Şaban 1301 [7 June 1884] (a translation into Ottoman from Arabic of a petition by the same Abu-Kishk group concerning the inclusion of its land in *waqf* land. According to the header added at the Translation Bureau, the petition was submitted by the sheikh of the group, Muhammad Yusuf Abu-Kishk, and two of his companions, whose names are not mentioned); see also 389/100 (a similar petition submitted that day).

9. For instance, see BOA. HR. TO., 387/61.

10. About the term *ahali*, see Faroqhi: "Political Initiatives," p. 6.

11. For instance, see BOA. HR. TO., 396/79 (a complaint submitted jointly by the *muhtar*s of eight villages in the area of Masmiyya about the collection of the *vergi* tax from their villages); about the role of the *muhtar*s, see Büssow: *Hamidian Palestine*, pp. 73–5.

12. For instance, see BOA. HR. TO., 396/79. On the importance of seals and their meaning in the context of the *shariʻa* courts, see Agmon, Iris, "Recording Procedures and Legal Culture in the Late Ottoman Shariʻa Court of Jaffa, 1865–1890," *Islamic Law and Society*, Vol. 11/3 (2004), pp. 360–4.

13. For instance, see BOA. DH. MKT., 1771/129, 1 Rebiyülevvel 1308 [15 October 1890] (telegraph to the *mutasarrıflık* of Jerusalem from the Ministry of Interior concerning a petition by sheikh Ibrahim Sutri from the *nahiya* of Ramle); HR. TO., 389/104.

14. See the four names and seals in BOA. HR. TO., 395/32, 3 Kânunuevvel 1306 [15 December 1890]. One of the seals belongs to the *muhtar* of the tribal group that resided in Khirbat Duran and is larger in size whereas the three other seals are smaller in size and include only the names of the petitioners. At the beginning of the petition, written in Arabic, it is stated that it was submitted by the "*mukhtar wa-ikhtiyariyyat ʻashirat ʻurban Abu-Hataba*."

15. BOA. HR. TO., 397/24, 24 Şaban 1308 [4 April 1892] (a petition by Jaffa's *Nakibüleşraf*, Mahmmud Kayyali, together with 38 people from the town to stop the inspector of *Defter-i Hakani* in Beirut, Zekati Efendi, from conducting a new land survey).

16. The one exception I found is from the period after the Young Turk Revolution. See BOA. DH. EUM. EMN., 30/5, 16 Temmuz 1329 [29 July 1913] (a collective petition from the sub-districts of Gaza signed by dozens of *muhtar*s, *imam*s and members of the tribal leadership (*ikhtiyariyya*) of the Abu-Kishk tribal group in the sub-district of Jaffa, against Jewish activity. This petition is analyzed in more detail in the following chapters).

17. For instance, see BOA. HR. TO., 396/16, 17 Temmuz 1307 [29 July 1891] (a petition in Arabic by dozens of landowners in Jaffa, both Muslim and Christian, against the inspector of *Defter-i Hakani* in Beirut, Zekati Efendi, who wanted to conduct a new land survey to revert lands which *de facto* were treated as *mülk* lands to their *de jure* status as *miri* lands).

18. BOA. DH. MUİ., 43–1/54, 11 Teşrinisani 1325 [24 November 1909] (a petition sent from Jaffa by the daughters of Ismaʻil al-Shakir concerning an argument with the local *waqf* official, who allegedly confiscated land they possessed).

19. For instance, see BOA. HR. TO., 553/46, 1 Temmuz 1296 [13 July 1876] (a petition by a person from Jaffa named ʻAbd al-Qadir al-Dabbagh [written in Ottoman: Abdülqadir], whose son was murdered, claiming that the local government did not do enough to investigate the crime).

20. The *arazi ve musakkafat vergisi* (better known as *vergi*, not to be confused with the modern Turkish word for "tax") was the annual tax introduced as part of the Tanzimat reforms (although it had Islamic roots) on all immovable goods, including agricultural land and buildings. One of the reasons the *vergi* was a burden was that it was paid in cash and not in kind. The *vergi* rate varied between 4 and 4.5 per thousand and was supposed to be re-evaluated every few years based on land surveys, although in practice such surveys were rather rare. The tithe supposedly stood at 10 percent of the crop yield but additional amounts were levied by the Ottoman state at the end of the nineteenth century to as much as 12.63 percent of the crop (and, in practice, usually much more). See Granott (Granovsky), Abraham, *Land Taxation in Palestine* (Tel-Aviv, 1927), pp. 18–23.

21. For instance, see BOA. BEO., 42/3111, 8 Muharrem 1310 [2 August 1892] (an order from the *Sadaret* to the Naval Ministry (*Bahriye Nazareti*) to finance boat fare for a poor person named Toplu Selim who could not afford to pay for a ticket to Jaffa. This order was probably issued in response to a petition this person submitted).

22. BOA. HR. TO., 400/8, 11 Temmuz 1325 [24 July 1909] (a collective petition from Gaza sent after the Revolution of 1908 to the *Sadaret* signed by Muslim, Christian and Jewish religious representatives and notables in favor of Mustafa Efendi, "the former clerk in charge of state lands in the town").

23. Salim Tamari calls them *katib adiliyyah* (in the singular, written elsewhere as *katib al-'adliyya*) and says they used to sit in cafés or next to public buildings, where they received the public, wrote petitions and filled in official forms for a fee. See Tamari: *Mountain against the Sea*, p. 177; other terms used to designate the public petition-writers were *köşebaşı* and *yazıcısı* (in the singular). See Akiba, Jun, "The Practice of Writing Curricula Vitae among the Lower Government Employees in the Late Ottoman Empire: Workers at the *Şeyhülislâm*'s Office," *European Journal of Turkish Studies*, Vol. 6 (2007), p. 14.

24. The Ottoman post and telegraph services were united in 1871 under one department after previously being separate. See Davison: "The Advent of the Electric Telegraph," pp. 141, 152.

25. On the illiteracy rate in Palestine at the end of the nineteenth century, see Ayalon: *Reading Palestine*, chapter 1; as regards the question of how the villagers dealt with the problem of reading and writing, the characterization by Eliyahu Zeev Levin-Epstein, the head of the colony of Rehovot during its early years, is instructive: "In every village there is only one person who knows how to write. He is called *katib*, that is to say the scribe of the village.

All the other dwellers of the village know neither how to read or write. And when the sheikhs had to sign their name on a certain document, they did so in one of the following two ways: either they had a copper seal, in which their name was inscribed, and they dipped the seal in ink and stamped it on a paper, or they would dip their fingers in ink and press them on the document, instead of a signature. And if one of the villagers had to write a document, he did not need to write, since he did not know how to write, but instead everything was done by a professional person, who made sure there were two witnesses present, who testified that they have heard in their own ears, that so and so the son of so and so ordered this document written." See Levin-Epstein, Eliyahu, *Zikhronotai* (My Memoirs) (Tel-Aviv, 1932), p. 239 [in Hebrew].

26. For example, the opening greetings, presentation of the case and the "facts," mentions of the law or other cases, specific requests, and concluding remarks and salutations.

27. For instance, the missionary George Robinson Lees (1860–1944) wrote the following about the scribes in Palestine at the end of the nineteenth century: "The[y] are known by their clothing, and the inkhorn in the girdle [. . .] not by plate on an office door [. . .]. They will be seen in the market-place looking for clients. They consider extreme politeness a part of their stock-in-trade, just as it is necessary in England for some men to "appear well" as they say "to create a favorable impression". The scribes in the modern market-place [. . .] are writers of petitions and letters, and not necessarily learned in the law, though a certain amount of legal knowledge is required to fulfill the conditions of the local government regarding contracts and matters relating to the sale of property. As soon as one is approached he draws from his inkhorn his reed pen, dips it into the sponge filled with ink at the other end, places the paper, which has been drawn from his bosom, on his hand, and writes whatever is required without even sitting – a "ready writer" indeed [. . .]. Neither office nor desk is required, everything being carried on the person. When the letter or petition is finished, the sand or dust in the street is scattered over it, then blown away; a handy substitute being near, no blotting-paper is ever used. Nor is there such a thing as a signature; the peasant cannot write, and even if he could, he would still seal the document with his ring like his betters [. . .]. Nearly every peasant wears a ring with his seal on it; if he does not own such a mark of distinction he dips his thumb in the ink and presses it on the paper instead. The Scribe is most frequently employed in writing petitions, as no suppliant can make a personal application to the Megliss (Council), or a Government official in the Seraglio (palace, YBB), he must present his case in writing, duly sealed and stamped, however trivial."

See Lees, Rev. George Robinson, *Village Life in Palestine: A Description of the Religion, Home Life, Manners, Customs, Characteristics and Superstitions of the Peasants of the Holy Land, with Reference to the Bible* (London, New York and Bombay, 1905), pp. 191–2.

28. Findley cites evidence that, at times, Ottoman officials wrote petitions in return for payment during their work hours, a phenomenon which was strongly opposed by their supervisors which was known derogatorily as *kağıt haffaflığı* (literally "making shoes out of paper"). See Findley, Carter V., *Ottoman Civil Officialdom: A Social History* (Princeton, NJ, 1989), p. 216. Rubin also quotes Judge Şehbaz who claimed the old trade of petition-writing as having a negative effect on Ottoman law. See Rubin: *Ottoman Nizamiye Courts*, p. 105.

29. Rubin argues that, at times, *arzuhalcis* also served as "legal representatives in courts" before the time when modern certified attorneys were required to appeal to the *nizamiye* courts. One of the reasons he cites for this occurrence is the fact the *arzuhalcis* needed a special permit to work in their occupation. See Rubin, Avi, "From Legal Representation to Advocacy: Attorneys and Clients in the Ottoman Nizamiye Courts," *International Journal of Middle Eastern Studies*, Vol. 44 (2012), p. 115.

30. For more details on the petition-writers, see Pakalın, Mehmed Z., *Osmanlı Tarih Deyimleri ve Terimleri Sözlüğü* (Dictionary of Ottoman Historical Idioms and Terms), Vol. I (Istanbul, 1983) [in Turkish], pp. 90–1; Refik, Ahmet, *Hicrî On İkinci Asırda İstanbul Hayatı (1100–1200)* (Life in Istanbul in the Twelfth *Hicri* Century) (Istanbul, 1930), p. 207 [in Turkish] (a *ferman* from 1764 concerning the occupation of the petition-writers); Lewis, G.L., "'Arż Ḥāl," *Encyclopaedia of Islam*, 2nd edition, Brill Online; Chalcraft: "Engaging the State," pp. 306–7. See also al-Qasimi, Jamal al-Din and Khalil al-'Azm, *Qamus al-sina'at al-shamiyya* (Dictionary of Crafts in Damascus), Vol. II (Paris, 1960), pp. 307–8 [in Arabic].

31. For instance, see Hayret, Mehmet Efendi, *Fihrest İnşa-yı Hayret Efendi* (Cairo, 1825) [in Ottoman Turkish] (this manual contains sample letters teaching scribes how to write to various officials, office holders and high ranking officers and bureaucrats); see also segments of the book by al-'Attar, Hasan, *Kitab insha al-'Attar* (al-Attar's Book of Correspondence) (Istanbul, 1299 [1881]) [in Arabic] (this book, which appeared in several editions, aimed at larger segments within the educated elite, and not merely the scribes, and it includes a wider variety of letters, including various social interactions and approaches to various professionals); manuals instructing how to write letters and petitions existed in many other societies in Europe and elsewhere. Christa Hämmerle notes that new manuals were written over the

course of the nineteenth century "in response to rapidly changing historical conditions." These manuals, however, still "adhered in part to the principles of ancient rhetoric." See Hämmerle, Christa, "Requests, Complaints, Demands. Preliminary Thoughts on the Petitioning Letters of Lower-Class Austrian Women, 1865–1918," in Bland, Caroline and Máire Cross (eds.), *Gender and Politics in the Age of Letter-Writing, 1750–2000* (Burlington, VT, 2004), p. 116.

32. For a manual instructing ordinary people how to write petitions and various letters (both personal and public) themselves without the help of a professional letter-writer, see al-Shalfun, Yusuf Efendi, *Turjuman al-mukataba* (Index of Writing/Compendium of Correspondence) (Beirut, 1887), 7th edition [in Arabic]. This booklet was published by several publishing houses in several editions starting in the late 1860s (see Document 1). It differs considerably from previous manuals such as the ones by Hayret and al-'Attar, reflecting the changing times.

33. Hämmerle: "Requests, Complaints, Demands," p. 116.

34. van Voss: "Introduction," pp. 8–9; Erdem Kabadayı (following Würgler) deliberates the extent to which petitions contained a variant of an ego-document. See Kabadayı, Erdem M., "Petitioning as Political Action: Petitioning Practices of Workers in Ottoman Factories," *Popular Protest and Political Participation in the Ottoman Empire*, pp. 62–3.

35. See BOA. DH. MKT., 359/26, 23 Recep 1312 [20 January 1895] (a petition in Arabic from Gaza to the Ministry of the Interior signed by *Mufti* Muhammad al-Hanafi Efendi against the local *kaymakam*, Hasan Bay, who, among other accusations, allegedly forced people to send petitions against his opponents and sent petitions which he faked himself.

36. For more on the discourse on constitutional rights in the aftermath of the 1908 Revolution, see Campos: *Ottoman Brothers*, p. 6. Campos writes that "Ottoman citizens studied and cited the constitution and other revolutionary 'sacred texts' that endowed them with political power, and they utilized a variety of tools to exercise and preserve that power." About the virulent criticism of the Abdülhamid period, Campos writes that "[i]n public addresses and on the pages of the newly free press, complaints of the sufferings of the past thirty-three years abounded. Father, brother, and son had feared each other, neighbors had informed on one another, and man had to hide his own thoughts from himself" (p. 45); among the accusations leveled was that the corruption during the former regime allowed Jews to take over Palestine and to set up a Zionist regime that would undermine the political integrity of the Empire. Petitions warned that a continuation of this policy would be damaging to the Empire, and the new era was compared with the rise of

the sun. For instance, see BOA. HR. TO., 401/58, 22 Kânunusani 1325 [2 February 1910]; BOA. DH. MUİ., 77–1/24, 9 Şubat 1325 [22 February 1910] (two petitions by the villagers of al-Masmiyya, some 25 kilometers northeast of Gaza against the Bedouin group of al-Wuhaydat, over the usage of the land of al-Mukhayzin. The conflict led to a trial and the submission of dozens of petitions to Istanbul by both parties. The villagers claimed that they had farmed the land for hundreds of years whereas the Bedouins took possession illegally during the reign of Abdülhamid II).

37. Watenpaugh, Keith David, *Being Modern in the Middle East: Revolution, Nationalism, Colonialism, and the Arab Middle Class* (Princeton, 2006), p. 4.

38. Kark, Ruth, *Jaffa: A City in Evolution, 1799–1917* (Jerusalem, 1990), pp. 217–20; Carmel, Alex, "Taharut, hadira ve nochehut: ha-Pe'ilut ha-notsrit ve-hashpa'ata be-Eretz Yisra'el" (Competition, Penetration, and Presence: Christian Activity and its Influence in the Land of Israel), in Bartal, Israel and Yehoshua Ben-Arieh (eds.), *The History of Eretz Israel: The Last Phase of Ottoman Rule (1799–1917)*, Vol. VIII (Jerusalem, 1983), p. 147 [in Hebrew].

39. Kark: "The Rise and Decline of Coastal Towns in Palestine," p. 80.

40. Ben-Arieh: "ha-Nof ha-yishuvi," p. 133; Kark: *Jaffa*, p. 217; Collins, Norman J. and Anton Steichele, *The Ottoman and Telegraph Offices in Palestine and Sinai* (London, 2000); Giray, Kemal (trans.), *Ottoman Post in Palestine, 1840–1914: Vol. I – Jerusalem* (Istanbul, 2004).

41. Sometimes there are also very long telegraphs with a very long list of petitioners. For instance, see BOA. Y. MTV., 77/140, 10 Nisan 1309 [22 April 1893] (a petition sent by telegraph from Gaza signed by dozens of people in support of the local *mufti*, al-Sayyid Muhammad al-Hanafi Efendi al-Husayni, who was allegedly slandered by several people).

42. Certain circles within the educated and commercial elite of Greater Syria were apparently aware of the telegraph and its importance well before it was available in the region. For instance, concerning awareness in the mid-1850s, see Bustrus, Salim, *al-Nuzha al-shahiyya fil-rihla al-Salimiyya 1855* (About the Magnificent Journey of Salim, 1855), edited by Wahab, Qasim (Beirut, 2003), pp. 88–9 [in Arabic].

43. See Collins: *The Ottoman Post and Telegraph Offices*, pp. 12–15.

44. About the use of French in the Ottoman telegraph, see Davison: "The Advent of the Electric Telegraph," pp. 150–1.

45. For instance, see BOA. HR. TO., 395/32 (the petition is addressed to "our exalted high esteemed master [the Grand Vizier]."

46. For an example of a sentence which includes exceptional flattery, see BOA. HR. TO., 391/42 (2), 10 Recep 1303 [14 April 1886] (a petition by the *imam* of the mosque in Jaffa to receive financial aid): "Your honorable minister

[. . .], the eye of the Sultanate, the crown of the Ottoman State, may God fulfill his joy and elevate his esteem."

47. BOA. HR. TO., 461/7 [archival given date: 6 April 1876] (an undated petition by the "poor people of Jaffa" against the *kaymakam* Ihsan Bay and his deputy, 'Abd al-Rahman Efendi, for mistreatment of the local population and for corruption).

48. For some of these reasons, see Appendix 1; for a very interesting linguistic analysis of petitions submitted to the sultan by converts to Islam at the end of the seventeenth century and the early eighteenth century, see Minkov: *Conversion to Islam in the Balkans*, chapter 4.

49. Maurus Reinkowski, when writing about Ottoman correspondence during the Tanzimat period, calls such referrals "secularized 'Islamic' vocabulary" which is used as figures of speech, a definition which applies here as well. See, Reinkowski, Maurus, "The State's Security and the Subjects' Prosperity: Notions of Order in Ottoman Bureaucratic Correspondence (19th Century)," *Legitimizing the Order: The Ottoman Rhetoric of State Power*, p. 199.

50. For instance, see BOA. DH. MUİ., 87–1/37, 12 Recep 1328 [archival given date: 20 July 1910] (a series of petitions sent to various bodies and functionaries in Istanbul by Rashid Abu-Khadra' from Gaza who claims he was illegally imprisoned due to the activity of corrupt officials in cahoots with members of his family who opposed him).

51. For an eloquent usage of all these reasons, see BOA. HR. TO., 390/74 (Appendix 6).

52. For instance, see BOA. HR. TO., 398/30, 21 Eylül 1308 [3 October 1892] (a petition sent by the former mayor of Jaffa demanding the transfer of the *kaymakam* of Jaffa, who was responsible for the petitioner's alleged illegal firing, and the appointment of another person to his post, in spite of an explicit order from the *mutasarrıf* of Jerusalem to reinstate the petitioner); HR. TO., 536/77, 18 January 1892 (a petition in French to the Grand Vizier by Yosef Moyal, a Maghrebi Jewish entrepreneur and businessman from Jaffa who was also the agent of Iran, against the *kaymakam* of Jaffa. As will be discussed below, Moyal was a constant submitter of petitions).

53. BOA. HR. TO., 396/16, 17 Temmuz 1307 [29 July 1891].

54. About the efforts by petitioners to create a shared moral world with the ruler, see de Costa: "Identity, Authority, and the Moral Worlds of Indigenous Petitions," p. 670.

55. About implied threats in petitions submitted to the shah of Iran, see Schneider: *The Petitioning System in Iran*, pp. 87–9.

56. Chalcraft: "Engaging the State," p. 318.

57. BOA. HR. TO., 396/79.

58. BOA. Y. MTV., 77/140.

Chapter 3: Petitions by the Urban Population of Gaza and Jaffa

1. For a conceptualization of the composition and social role of Palestine's elite at the time, see Büssow: *Hamidian Palestine*, chapters 5 and 6.

2. For more on these families, see Manna', 'Adil, *A'lam Filastin fi awakhir al-'ahd al-'uthmani* (The Notables of Palestine during the Late Ottoman Period), 2nd edition (Beirut, 1995), p. 19 [in Arabic]; Muslih: *The Origins of Palestinian Nationalism*, pp. 26–8; for a recent attempt to pin down the essence of these leading Jerusalemite households, based on several examples over time, see Büssow: *Hamidian Palestine*, pp. 325–6.

3. See Abu-Manneh: "Jerusalem in the Tanzimat Period," pp. 1–44.

4. Khalidi: *Palestinian Identity*, p. 38.

5. Gerber: *Ottoman Rule in Jerusalem*, particularly pp. 123–30, but elsewhere throughout the book as well.

6. Muslih: *The Origin of Palestinian Nationalism*, pp. 24, 36.

7. Ibid., p. 30.

8. Ibid., p. 31; see also Büssow: *Hamidian Palestine*, pp. 283–301.

9. Gerber, Haim, *The Social Origins of the Modern Middle East* (Boulder, CO, 1994), pp. 75–82.

10. See Stein, Kenneth W., *The Land Question in Palestine, 1917–1939* (Chapel Hill and London, 1984), pp. 24–8; and Kark, Ruth and Michal Oren-Nordheim, *Jerusalem and its Environs: Quarters, Neighborhoods, Villages, 1800–1948* (Detroit, 2001), pp. 219–25, 295.

11. Gerber: *Ottoman Rule in Jerusalem*, chapter 4.

12. Khalidi: *Palestinian Identity*, pp. 68–9.

13. Gerber: *Ottoman Rule in Jerusalem*, pp. 93–109.

14. Khalidi: *Palestinian Identity*, p. 95; Muslih: *The Origins of Palestinian Nationalism*, pp. 37–8.

15. In this regard, Hanssen showed how the people of Beirut tried for nearly two decades to separate the city from the Province of Şam and make it a new province, which finally took place in 1888. One of the means they deployed in the process was the submission of petitions to Istanbul. See Hanssen: *Fin de Siècle Beirut*, chapter 1.

16. BOA. DH. MKT., 2126/56, 15 Cemaziyülevvel 1316 [31 October 1898] (the Ministry of the Interior requests Jerusalem to deal with a petition by the "people and *muhtar*s of Ramle" who asked to revert to being a *kaymakamlık* as in the past, *kama fi sabık*, and stressed that a previous petition was not answered); for an earlier request by the people of Ramle to became a separate *kaymakam*, see ŞD. MLK., 2272/48, 20 Zilkade 1296 (5 November 1879) (Jerusalem is asked by *Şûra-yı Devlet* to provide more information about

Ramle's ability to sustain itself as a center of a *kaymakamlık* in terms of paying the salaries of the extra personnel required).

17. BOA. BEO., 590/44210, 28 Cemaziyülevvel 1312 [27 November 1894] (a petition in Arabic signed by four *muhtars*. The *Serasker*, Reza Paşa, when requested to respond to the petition, wrote to the *Sadaret* on 2 April 1895 that the decision had been made to move the center to Jaffa and was approved by all the authorities and authorized by the sultan. The Fifth Army was asked to notify the people of Ramle of this final decision).

18. BOA. DH. MKT., 2538/37, 17 Cemaziyülâhır 1319 [1 October 1901] (from the Ministry of Interior to the Ministry of Post and Telegraph).

19. BOA. HR. TO., 461/83, 13 September 1876 [archival given date; in the translation of the petition it states that the original had no date] (from Gaza to *Bab-ı Âli*); see also Büssow: *Hamidian Palestine*, p. 289.

20. BOA. HR. TO., 553/88, 7 Teşrinisani 1292 [19 November 1876].

21. BOA. HR. TO., 554/30, 28 January 1877 (archival given date; the translation of the letter bears no date); about this weekly newspaper, which first appeared in Istanbul in the early 1860s on the initiative of the Lebanese intellectual Ahmad Faris al-Shidyaq with the support of the Ottoman Empire, see di Tarrazi, Filib, *Ta'rikh al-sahafa al-'arabiyya* (The History of Arab Press), Vol. I (Beirut, 1913), pp. 61–4 [in Arabic].

22. About the division of the Bedouin tribes near Gaza and their relationship with this town, see, al-Mubayyid, Salim 'Arafat, *Ghazza wa-qita'iha: Dirasa fi khulud al-makan wa-hadarat al-sukkan min al-'asr al-hajari al-hadith hatta al-harb al-'alamiyya al-ula* (Gaza and Its Region: A Study of the Eternity of the Place and the Culture of Its People from the Modern Stone Age until World War I) (Cairo, 1987), p. 381 [in Arabic].

23. BOA. HR. TO., 554/80, 6 Nisan 1293 [18 April 1877] (a translation from Arabic into Ottoman of two petitions sent from Gaza to the *Mabeyn* and to the Ministry of the Interior with the signatures of five and ten people, respectively); see also HR. TO., 554/56, 9 Şubat 1292 [2 February 1877] (two petitions that were submitted separately to the *Sadaret* and to the Ministry of the Interior by tribal leaders in Gaza against the former *mufti* and his son 'Abd al-Hayy, who together with their tribal allies, a member of the administrative council, and the *kaymakam*, 'Umar 'Abd al-Salam stirred up unrest among the Bedouin tribes near Gaza).

24. For more on this figure, see Khalidi: *Palestinian Identity*, chapter 4; Manna': *A'lam Filastin*, p. 146.

25. About him, see Kushner, David, "The Ottoman Governors of Palestine, 1864–1914," *Middle Eastern Studies*, Vol. 23/3 (July 1987), pp. 276–7, 283, 287.

26. About him, see Manna': *A'lam Filastin*, p. 99.

27. About him, see al-Tabbaʿ, ʿUthman, *Ithaf al-aʿizza fi taʾrikh Ghazza* (Presenting the Notables in the History of Gaza), edited by Abu-Hashim, ʿAbdullatif (Gaza, 1999), Vol. IV, pp. 357–73 [in Arabic].

28. BOA. HR. TO., 390/56, 22 Zilkade 1302 [2 September 1885] (a petition to *Sadaret* signed by ʿAbd al-Rahman Shafiq al-Husayni, ʿAbd al-Hayy Faʾiq al-Husayni, Muhammd al-Hanafi al-Husayni, and Husayn al-Husayni); see also HR. TO., 390/70, 9 Muharrem 1303 [18 October 1885].

29. For more about this figure, see Mannaʿ: *Aʿlam Filastin*, p. 312; al-Tabbaʿ: *Ithaf al-aʿizza*, Vol. IV, p. 310.

30. BOA. HR. TO., 390/74, 7 Zilhicce1302 [17 September 1885] (a petition to Şakir Paşa, who is designated in the translation of the petition into Ottoman as "the brother of the Grand Vizier," signed by ʿAbd al-Rahman Shafiq al-Husayni, ʿAbd al-Faʾiq al-Husayni, Muhammd al-Hanafi al-Husayni, and Husayn al-Husayni).

31. About this figure, see Kushner: "The Ottoman Governors of Palestine," p. 277 (the governor was fired in 1877 due to allegations regarding oppression and corruption as well as the dismissal of his patron in Istanbul, the former Grand Vizier Mahmud Nedim Paşa [1818–83]).

32. BOA. DH. MKT., 2013/130, 10 Rebiyülâhır 1310 [1 November 1892] (a petition to the Ministry of the Interior signed by ʿAbd al-Hayy Faʾiq al-Husayni and Husayn Tawfiq al-Husayni).

33. BOA. HR. TO., 399/3, 9 Nisan 1309 [21 April 1893] (a petition to the *Sadaret* signed by 91 notables and religious scholars from Gaza); see also a similar petition sent on the same day to the Ministry of the Interior, DH. MKT., 28/17, 9 Nisan 1309 [21 April 1893].

34. BOA. HR. TO., 394/67, 2 Eylül 1306 [14 September 1890] (a petition to the *Sadaret* signed by 42 people from Gaza against the possible appointment of Muhammad al-Hanafi, the son of Ahmad Muhyi al-Din, as the *mufti* of Gaza and in favor of appointing Muhammad Saqallah as the *mufti*); see also HR. TO., 395/44, 23 Kânunuevvel 1306 [4 January 1891] (a petition to the *Sadaret* submitted by Bedouins in Gaza against the governor of Jerusalem, Reşat Paşa, and two notables from this town named Salim al-Husayni and ʿArif Bey who, together with Muhammad al-Hanafi and his brothers, the sons of the former *mufti* of Gaza, collaborated with their rivals among the Bedouins, and persecuted them); and HR. TO., 393/53, 26 Teşrinisani 1308 [8 December 1892] (a petition to the *Sadaret* signed by 64 people from Gaza in favor of Saqallah).

35. BOA. BEO., 144/10734, 12 Kânunusani 1308 [24 January 1893] (*Şeyhülislam* was asked to relate to complaints against Muhammad al-Hanafi Efendi. Saqallah is cited as saying he would not feel comfortable about being nominated to the position of Jaffa's *kadı*).

36. BOA. DH. MKT., 54/14, 15 Zilkade 1310 [31 May 1893] (the Ministry of the Interior refers the matter of the *mufti* to *Şeyhülislam* for its decision, including the related material).

37. BOA. DH. MKT., 359/26, 23 Recep 1312 [20 January 1895].

38. BOA. DH. MKT., 2193/104, 16 Zilhicce 1315 [27 April 1899] (the Ministry of the Interior to the *Sadaret* about a request by the former *mufti* Muhammad al-Hanafi and others to be sent to Jerusalem and be tried with the *kaymakam* of Gaza and his supporters who, it is claimed, persecuted them; an approval is needed for a decision by the Council of Ministers on this matter); Y. PRK. AZJ., 40/89, 22 Haziran 1316 [5 July 1900] (a petition to the *Mabeyn* submitted by Muhammad al-Hanafi Efendi, his brother and his son to be pardoned and, it is implied, allowed to go back to their home from exile in Ankara where they had resided for three years).

39. For instance, see BOA. HR. TO., 534/52, 25 Eylül 1306 [7 October 1890] (a petition from Jaffa sent by "an Ottoman" against Jaffa's *kaymakam* Musa Kazim al-Husayni. The petitioner expresses joy that he is about to be appointed to another position and asks that the *kaymakam* of Gaza 'Ali Efendi not be named to replace him. Possibly this petition reflects a local struggle among the elite of Jaffa and Jerusalem given that al-Husayni was from Jerusalem).

40. BOA. HR. TO., 396/83, 8 Kânunuevvel 1307 [20 December 1891] (a collective petition from Jaffa to the *Sadaret* against the *kaymakam* signed by 17 people in the name of "Jaffa's poor people").

41. BOA. HR.TO., 388/104, 19 Teşrinievvel 1297 [31 October 1881].

42. BOA. HR. TO., 554/12, 20 Kânunuevvel 1292 [11 January 1877]; the *kaymakam* of Gaza at the time was Mehmed Zuhdi Efendi. See Büssow: *Hamidian Palestine*, p. 550.

43. BOA. HR. TO., 461/54, 19 Cemaziyülâhıir 1293 [12 July 1876] (46 orchard owners from Jaffa to the *Sadaret*).

44. Perhaps Simsim, some 15 kilometers north-east of Gaza.

45. BOA. DH. MKT., 2313/135, 3 Zilkade 1315 [written by mistake as 1317 as the *hicri* and *mali* years were confused in the document; 15 January 1900] (the Ministry of the Interior to the *Sadaret*, transferring a report by Jerusalem on the case and asking for guidance).

46. BOA. DH. MKT., 2425/103, 13 Recep 1318 [6 November 1900] (the Ministry of the Interior transfers the decisions to Jerusalem and asks it to make an investigation in light of the prohibition).

47. BOA. HR. TO., 389/70, 19 Kânunusani 1299 [31 January 1884] (a translation into Ottoman of a petition sent from Jaffa in Arabic. The original petition bore no date).

48. BOA. BEO., 507/37962, 16 Teşrinievvel 1310 [28 October 1894] ('Abd al-Hayy al-Husayni to the *Sadaret*).

49. BOA. HR. TO., 461/7.

50. BOA. HR. TO., 459/68 (not dated or signed, archival date is 25 September 1875); 'Ali Bey apparently did serve in the end as the *kaymakam*. See list of Gaza's *kaymakam*s in Büssow: *Hamidian Palestine*, p. 550.

51. Petitions requesting official intervention in private matters were, in fact, not a new phenomenon in Ottoman history. See Faroqhi: "Political initiatives," p. 6.

52. About him, see al-Tabba': *Ithaf al-a'izza*, Vol. III, pp. 18–23 (including family tree).

53. See ibid; see also Büssow: *Hamidian Palestine*, p. 297.

54. BOA. HR. TO., 391/4, 25 Kânunuevvel 1301 [6 January 1886].

55. About the Abu-Khadra' family in Gaza, see al-Tabba': *Ithaf al-a'izza*, Vol. III, p. 163.

56. BOA. DH. MUİ., 87–1/37; for this specific petition, see 20 Mart 1326 [2 April 1910] (Abu-Khadra' to the Ministry of War).

57. BOA. ŞD., 2295/13, 16 Cemaziyülâhir 1320 [20 September 1902].

58. See Büssow: *Hamidian Palestine*, p. 553 (quoting Tabba').

59. Nubola describes a similar development of flooding the system with petitions, which were considered "intolerable abuse" in the Italian states in the early modern period. See Nubola: *"Supplications between Politics and Justice,"* p. 45.

60. BOA. DH. MUİ., 87–1/37.

61. BOA. ŞD., 2295/13 (the governor refers to the case of Abu-Khadra' as well as to a person named Ahmad 'Abbas from Gaza, but mentions that there are similar cases).

62. About Moyal, see "Yosef Bey Moyal," in Tidhar, David (ed.), *Encyclopedia of the Founders and Builders of Israel* (Tel-Aviv, 1949), Vol. III, p. 1184 [in Hebrew].

63. BOA. HR. TO., 536/77.

64. BOA. DH. MKT., 430/66, 9 Eylül 1311 [21 September 1895] (from the Ministry of the Interior to Jerusalem).

65. BOA. DH. MKT., 2269/61, 9 Recep 1317 [13 November 1899] (from the Ministry of the Interior to Şeyhülislam).

66. BOA. DH. MKT., 2298/91, 21 Ramazan 1317 [23 January 1900] (from the Ministry of the Interior to the Ministry of Justice).

67. BOA. MV., 101/15, 19 Cemaziyülâhir 1318 [14 October 1900] (a decision by *Meclis-i Vükelâ*).

68. About the Haykal family, see Agmon: *Family & Court*, pp. 222–7; Haykal, Yusuf, *Ayyam al-siba: Suwar min al-haya wa-safhat min al-tarikh* (The Days

of Adolescence: Pictures from Life and Pages of History) (Amman, 1988), pp. 216–18 [in Arabic].

69. BOA. HR. TO., 393/44, 27 Teşrinisani 1305 [9 Decmeber 1889]. The *mazbata* was issued on 29 August 1889; Asteriadis was a Greek Orthodox from Jerusalem who later served as the city's mayor.

70. BOA. DH. MKT., 2553/45, 25 Şaban 1319 [7 December 1901] (from the Ministry of the Interior to Jerusalem).

71. BOA. HR. TO., 553/46, 1 Temmuz 1292 [13 July 1876] (a translation of al-Dabbagh's petition from Arabic into Ottoman).

72. BOA. HR. TO., 391/95, 22 Zilhicce 1304 [21 September 1886].

73. About him, see Manna': *A'lam Filastin*, p. 199; al-Tabba': *Ithaf al-a'izza*, Vol. IV, pp. 275–285; see also http://www.almoajam.org/poet_details.php?id=6433

74. BOA. BEO., 110/8227, 1 Cemaziyülevvel 1310 [21 November 1892].

75. Ibid., 16 Teşrinisani 1308 [28 November 1892].

76. BOA. DH. MKT., 1959/56, 14 Zilkade 1309 [10 June 1892]; a similar petition by a Jewish pharmacist from Jaffa a few years later was rejected and he was told to attend medical school for three years. See BOA. BEO., 486/36419, 26 Ağustos 1310 [7 September 1894] (a petition by Ilyas Fridlib [?] to the *Sadaret* arguing that he had worked as a pharmacist for 15 years and requesting permission to take an exam in Istanbul to obtain a diploma, after his request was rejected by the Ministry of Health. The medical school within the military schools answered that the petitioner must do three years of coursework before taking the diploma exam).

77. BOA. DH. MKT., 1524/43, 11 Temmuz 1304 [23 July 1888].

78. BOA. ŞD., 2935/40, 21 Teşrinievvel 1306 [2 November 1890]; Mr. Lombardo himself applied to the *Sadaret* to complain about the handling of a contract for the irrigation of gardens in the region of Jaffa. He claimed that he represented Mr. Alexander de Girardin, a well-known developer, and the son of Emile de Girardin (1802–81), "a publicist who defended the Empire on every occasion." Moreover, a competing offer submitted by a person named Philippe Melhame was apparently not based on an actual survey of the terrain and was thus invalid. The petitioner wondered why it was decided to hold a tender between the two bidders, a process which was clearly ill-advised. See BOA. HR. TO., 535/28, 1 February 1891. On Emile de Girardin, see Geyikdagi, Necla "French Direct Investments in the Ottoman Empire before World War I," *Enterprise Soc*, Vol. XII/3 (2011), pp. 525–61.

Chapter 4: Petitions by the Rural Population and the Bedouins

1. Waterbury, John, "Peasants Defy Categorization (As Well as Landlords and the State)," *Peasants and Politics in the Modern Middle East*, p. 4.

2. About the problem of Bedouin representation in *shariʿa* courts, see Meier, Astrid, "Bedouins in the Ottoman Juridical: Field Select Cases from Syrian Court Records, Seventeenth to Nineteenth Centuries," *Euroasian Studies*, Vol. IX/1–2 (2011), pp. 189–91.

3. Waterbury writes in this regard that the peasants' "numbers and their aggregate weight in economic life have not been remotely reflected in their political influence." See Waterbury: "Peasants Defy Categorization," p. 1.

4. See Beinin, Joel, *Workers and Peasants in the Modern Middle East* (Cambridge, 2001), pp. 69–70.

5. For instance, about cooperation between peasants and Bedouins in revolting against the Egyptian invasion in the 1830s, see Safi, Khaled M., "Territorial Awareness in the 1834 Palestinian Revolt," in Heacock, Roger (ed.), *Temps et éspaces en Palestine* (Beirut, 2008), pp. 43–54; Manna', ʿAdil, *Taʾrikh Filastin fi awakhir al-ʿahd al-ʿuthmani, 1700–1918: Qiraʾa jadida* (History of Palestine at the End of the Ottoman Period: A New Reading) (Beirut, 1999), pp. 181–2 [in Arabic].

6. Grossman, David, "Rural Settlement in the Southern Coastal Plain and the Shefelah, 1835–1945," *Cathedra*, Vol. 45 (1987), pp. 57–9 [in Hebrew].

7. Ben-Arieh, Yehoshua, "Ukhlusiyat Eretz-Yisrael vi-yishuvah ʿerev mifʿal ha-hityashvut ha-tsiyoni" (The Population of Eretz-Yisrael and Its Settlements on the Eve of the Zionist Colonization), in Ben-Arieh, Yehoshua, Yossi Ben-Artzi and Haim Goren (eds.), *Historical Geographical Studies in the Settlement of Eretz Israel*, Vol. I (Jerusalem, 1987), pp. 12–13 [in Hebrew].

8. Reilly, James, "The Peasantry of Late Ottoman Palestine," *Journal of Palestine Studies*, Vol. 10/4 (1981), pp. 87–8. Many of the new settlements in the plains started as temporary seasonal dwellings for the hill people, who cultivated their lands in the plains during the high agricultural seasons. These places, called *khirba*s or *nazla*s, often developed later into permanent settlements.

9. To a certain extent, this group of landowners started to emerge even prior to 1858. See Doumani: "Rediscovering Ottoman Palestine," p. 12.

10. Interestingly, Sultan Abdülhamid II was also one of the major landowners in Palestine, if not the largest, and invested considerable funds from the Privy Treasury to that end. See Fischel and Kark: "Sultan Abdülhamid II and Palestine: Private lands and Imperial Policy," pp. 126–66; see also Büssow: *Hamidian Palestine*, pp. 92–3.

11. Muslih: *The Origins of Palestinian Nationalism*, p. 22.
12. Ben-Arieh: "ha-Nof ha-yishuvi," p. 77 (all figures are approximations); Justin McCarthy's figures, which are mainly based on the Ottoman censuses, are about 25 percent higher. He reaches the conclusion that in 1881/2 there were 403,795 Muslims in Palestine, 43,659 Christians and 15,011 Jews; he considers that the total population was 462,465. See McCarthy, Justin, *The Population of Palestine: Population History and Statistics of the Late Ottoman Period and the Mandate* (New York, 1990), p. 10; Beshara Doumani also concludes, based on the minutes of the Nablus advisory council and on the Ottoman population count, that Ben-Arieh's figures considerably underestimate the actual population. See Doumani, Beshara, "The Political Economy of Population Counts in Ottoman Palestine, circa 1850," *International Journal of Middle Eastern Studies*, Vol. 26/1 (1994), pp. 1–17.
13. Ben-Arieh, Yehoshua, "The Villages in Sancak Gaza (including Jaffa and Ramla) in the Eighteen-Seventies," *Shalem*, Vol. 5 (1987), p. 173 [in Hebrew] (the administrative units used by Ben-Arieh are idiosyncratic; for instance, "Sancak of Gaza").
14. For instance, see Grant: *The People of Palestine*, pp. 226–27.
15. Ehud Toledano cites a vivid example of the importance of written documents among illiterate populations, in this case manumitted slaves, who used others to write documents which they could not even read. See Toledano, Ehud R., *As if Silent and Absent* (New Haven & London, 2007), p. 119.
16. Chalcraft: "Engaging the State," pp. 308–9.
17. Ibid., p. 304.
18. On this eventuality, see ibid., p. 308.
19. The collection of the tithe also applied to the Jewish colonies which complained that it could reach up to 50 percent of the yields. About the difficulties of the Jewish colonists in Qastina (Beer-Tuvia) concerning the tithe payments and their efforts to find intermediaries to influence the authorities to remedy the situation, see Ets-Hadar, Avraham, *Ilanot le-Toldot ha-Yishuv be-Eretz-Yisrael, 1830–1920* (Documents about the Yishuv in Eretz-Yisrael, 1830–1920) (Tel-Aviv, 1967), pp. 216–36 [in Hebrew].
20. BOA. HR. TO., 396/79.
21. See Granott: *ha-Mishtar ha-qarqa'i be-Eretz-Yisra'el*, p. 140.
22. About Rabah al-Husayni, who served as Jerusalem's *Nakibüleşraf* like his father and his grandfather, see Pappe, Ilan, *Aristocracy of the Land: The Husayni Family, Political Biography* (Jerusalem, 2002), pp. 110, 123, 125, 127, 143 [in Hebrew].
23. Koca Sinan Paşa, 1506–96, was an Ottoman statesman who served five times as Grand Vizier. He established a considerable number of endowments

in various places in the Empire. About the *waqf*s of Sinan Paşa Empire-wide, see Meier, Astrid, "The Charities of a Grand Vizier: Towards a Comparative Approach to Koca Sinân Pasha's Endowment Deeds (989–1004/1581–1596)," *Turcica*, Vol. 43 (2011), pp. 303–37.

24. BOA. HR. TO., 387/61.

25. Baer, Gabriel, *Fellah and Townsman in the Middle East: Studies in Social History* (London, 1982), pp. 88–9.

26. Campos: *Ottoman Brothers*, pp. 11–12.

27. About this division, see Schölch: *Palestine in Transformation 1856–1882*, pp. 191–2; Hoexter, Miriam, "The Role of the Qays and Yaman Factions in Local Political Divisions: Jabal Nāblus Compared with the Judean Hills in the First Half of the Nineteenth Century," *African and Asian Studies*, Vol. 9 (1973), pp. 249–311.

28. Schölch, *Palestine in Transformation, 1856–1882*, p. 192.

29. Reilly: "The Peasantry of Late Ottoman Palestine," p. 89.

30. Doumani: "Rediscovering Ottoman Palestine," pp. 9–10; Khalidi: *Palestinian Identity*, pp. 65, 84.

31. Khalidi: ibid.

32. On these unofficial meetings of the *muhtar*s from the villages in the region of Jaffa in this town, see the memoirs of the David Niman, a Jewish colonist from Eqron, *Be-Reshit baroh {. . .}: Zikhronotav shel David Niman* (In the Beginning [. . .]: The Memoirs of David Niman) (Tel-Aviv, 1962/3), p. 46 [in Hebrew].

33. For example, see BOA. HR. TO., 390/2, 1 Safer 1302 [20 November 1884] (a translation from Arabic into Ottoman of a collective petition signed by 47 *muhtar*s of villages in the sub-district of Gaza with a request to reduce the amount of *vergi* tax they were instructed to pay; see also HR. TO., 395/60 [10 February 1891] (a joint petition by the *muhtar*s of several villages in the region of Qastina-Masmiyya to reduce the amount of the *vergi* tax levied on them); for similar petitions with variations, including in the signatures, see 395/61, 5 Şubat 1306 [17 February 1891]; 395/104, 1 Zilhicce 1308 [8 July 1891]; 396/79.

34. Vilnay, for instance, has written about the importance of Nabi Ganda (in Arabic: Qanda) north of Yibna near the village of al-Qubeiba for the Arab population in the area, a place where according to the tradition Gad, the son of Jacob, is buried. See Vilnay, Zeev, *Toldot ha-ʿaravim veha-muslemim be-Eretz-Yisraʾel* (The History of Arabs and Muslims in *Eretz-Israel*), Vol. II, p. 346 [in Hebrew]; see also Shimʿoni, Yaʿaqov, *ʿArviye Eretz-Yisrael* (The Arabs of Eretz-Yisrael) (Tel-Aviv, 1947), p. 71 [in Hebrew] (about attendance at a grave of the Prophet's companion Abu-Huraira in Yibna).

35. al-Tabbaʿ: *Ithaf al-aʿizza*, Vol. II, pp. 160–3; see also BOA. HR. TO., 390/70.

36. In this context, Baldensperger writes that the *efendi*s of Ramle were "in charge of the standard of Rubin with all the incomes and expenses depending on the shrine and the yearly fair held on the borders of Rubin in September," which shows the regional nature of this celebration. See Baldensperger, Philip, "The Immovable East," *Palestine Exploration Fund: Quarterly Statement for 1917*, p. 160; see also Rantisi, Ilyas, "Mawsim Rubin" (The Festival of Rubin), in *'Itr Madinat Yafa* (The Perfume of the City of Jaffa) (Nazareth, 1991), pp. 71–3 [in Arabic].

37. Vilnay writes that the celebrations in Nabi-Rubin attracted both urban and rural population from all over the "land of Judea." See Vilnay: *Toldot*, Vol. II, pp. 342–4 [in Hebrew].

38. See ibid., p. 346.

39. Shim'oni: *'Arviye Eretz-Yisrael*, pp. 223–5.

40. The connections between leading Gazan families and elements in the town's rural periphery are also found in petitions submitted by rival Gazan families and their allies. For instance, see BOA. HR. TO., 554/56 (tribal leaders in Gaza complain that the former *mufti* from the al-Husayni family and his son 'Abd al-Hayy, together with their tribal allies, a member of the administrative council and the *kaymakam* 'Umar 'Abd al-Salam, stirred up unrest among the Bedouin tribes near Gaza); HR. TO., 554/80 (two collective petitions to complain about the son of *mufti* Ahmad Muhyi al-Din al-Husayni, named Husayn, who collaborated with the Bedouin tribes in the region of Gaza and with the *kaymakam* 'Umar, who was their relative. The Bedouins, it is argued, were encouraged to attack the farmers in the region and harass them as well as the people of Gaza, who thus lived in fear; HR. TO., 395/44 (Bedouins in the *kaza* of Gaza complain about the governor of Jerusalem, two notables from this town and the sons of the former *mufti* of Gaza, who all collaborated with their rivals among the Bedouins and persecuted them).

41. Büssow points out that this "administrative regionalization might have helped consolidate the domination of urban overlords over the countryside." See Büssow: *Hamidian Palestine*, p. 266.

42. Büssow notes that "according to numerous outside observers, among them Ottoman officials, Christian missionaries, social scientists and Zionist settlers, the peasants of the Gaza region were victims of exploitation by the urban notables from Gaza city." See Büssow, ibid; for an analysis of the ways in which the leading urban notables acquired influence, positions and prestige, see Gerber, Haim, *Remembering and Imagining Palestine: Identity and Nationalism from the Crusades to the Present* (New York, 2008), pp. 46–7; and

Tamari: *Mountain against the Sea*, pp. 4–7. Tamari writes about the urban–rural relationships that "[t]he social basis of clan power seems to have been associated with two interrelated features. The first was the number of men that clan notables could mobilize on their side in factional struggles – a factor that was dependent, as far as peasants were concerned, on the amount of land under control by the clan head and the intricate system of patronage he maintained with his sharecroppers and semiautonomous peasants, which in turn was influenced by his ability to act as their creditor in an increasingly monetized economy. The second feature was the access that the clan head and his relatives and aides had to public office, and thus his ability to extend services to his clients in return for their support in factional conflicts."

43. Doumani: *Rediscovering Palestine*.

44. About the grave of sheikh al-Qatrawi, see al-Qatrawi, Jamal 'Abd al-Rahim, *Qatra: al-Huwiyya wal-ta'rikh* (Qatra: Its Characteristics and History) (Gaza, 2000), p. 52 [in Arabic]; al-Tabba': *Ithaf al-a'izza*, Vol. II, p. 427.

45. Hissin, Haim, *Memoirs and Letters of an Early Pioneer* (Jerusalem, 1990), pp. 139–40 [in Hebrew]; on the presence of Sufis in the rural area in Palestine, see *Shim'oni: The Arabs of Eretz-Yisrael*, p. 73; and de Jong, Frederick, "The Sufi Orders in Nineteenth- and Twentieth-Century Palestine: A Preliminary Survey Concerning their Identity, Organization, Characteristics and Continuity," in idem, *Sufi Orders in Ottoman and Post-Ottoman Egypt and the Middle East* (Istanbul, 1999), pp. 99–122.

46. For instance, see *Mikhtavim mi-Eretz-Yisrael* (Letters from the Land of Israel), Vol. I/1 (1893), 26 March 1893 (mediation between Rehovot and the Bedouins of Arab Abu al-Fadl by an Arab notable from the region after a severe clash between the two parties in 1893).

47. For instance, see al-Qatrawi: *Qatra: al-Huwiyya wal-ta'rikh*, pp. 135–6 (on marriage relationships between Qatra and adjacent villages).

48. Avitsur: *Daily Life in Iretz Israel in the XIX Century*, p. 176.

49. Büssow: *Hamidian Palestine*, p. 263.

50. For more details, see Ben-Bassat, Yuval, "Proto-Zionist–Arab Encounters in Late Nineteenth Century Palestine: Socioregional Dimensions," *Journal of Palestine Studies*, Vol. XXXVIII/2 (Winter 2009), pp. 42–63.

51. For more details, see ibid; on the agency of the peasants, see Khalidi, Rashid, "Palestinian Peasant Resistance to Zionism before World War I," in Said, Edward and Christopher Hitchens (eds.), *Blaming the Victims: Spurious Scholarship and the Palestinian Question* (London and New York, 2001), pp. 207–33.

52. BOA. HR. TO., 396/79.

53. Zarnuqa was located in the northern part of the *kaza* of Gaza, whereas the adjacent colony of Rehovot was located in the southern part of the *kaza* of Jaffa.

54. BOA. DH. EUM. EMN., 30/5.

55. On the Ottoman effort to settle the tribes of Transjordan, see Rogan, Eugene L., *Frontiers of State in the Late Ottoman Empire: Transjordan, 1850– 1921* (Cambridge, 1999), pp. 82–94; see also BOA. DH. MKT., 1905/48, 24 Cemaziyülevvel 1309 [26 December 1891] (the Ministry of the Interior orders the District of Jerusalem to act swiftly to implement previous decisions to end the land disputes between the Bedouin tribes in Gaza and incorporate the land into the *tapu* regime. The current situation had to be resolved as it lead to endless bloody quarrels. The order followed a complaint by the Commander of the Fifth Army); DH. MKT., 1983/109, 13 Muharrem 1310 [7 August 1892] (the Ministry of the Interior writes to the District of Jerusalem about the need to complete the *yoklama* survey in Gaza and act to settle the Bedouins in the region to protect the state's revenues).

56. On the Ottoman policies concerning the Bedouins in nineteenth-century Palestine, see Frantzman, Seth J. and Ruth Kark, "Bedouin Settlement in Late Ottoman and British Mandatory Palestine: Influence on Cultural and Environmental Landscape, 1870–1948," *New Middle Eastern Studies*, Vol. 1 (2011), pp. 4–9; see also BOA. İ. ŞD., 41/2144, 12 Ramazan 1295 [9 September 1878] (a decision by the *Şûra-yı Devlet* concerning the payment of salaries of soldiers who were sent to the region of Gaza to subdue Bedouin activity which caused damage to agricultural fields and trade. The Bedouins, it is claimed, were so busy with their internal strife that there was no time left for them to cultivate the fields); DH. MKT., 1897/17, 1 Cemaziyülevvel 1309 [3 December 1891] (an order from the Ministry of the Interior to the District of Jerusalem to investigate complaints about Bedouin attacks on travelers between Gaza and al-Majdal. The local authorities were accused of failing to give redress to the victims who complained and, to the contrary, even supported the accused. The order from Istanbul came following a complaint by the commander of the Fifth Army and the *komandan* of Jerusalem whom, we can assume, were probably approached by the victims and transferred their petition to the *Serasker* in Istanbul).

57. About the Ottoman perceptions of the desert and the Bedouins, see Ginio, Eyal, "Presenting the Desert to the Ottomans during WWI: The Perspective of the *Harb Mecmuasi*," *New Perspectives on Turkey*, Vol. 33 (2005), pp. 43–62; about the Ottoman "civilizing mission," see Deringil, Selim, "'They Live in a State of Nomadism and Savagery': The Late Ottoman Empire and the

Post-Colonial Debate," *Comparative Studies of Society and History*, Vol. 45/2 (2003), pp. 311–42; Meier writes that, customarily, Bedouins were suspected by the Ottoman authorities "not only as a security risk, particularly in their dealings with peasants and travelers, but also on a more moral level, as their doubtful adherence to the precepts of Islam was seen to undermine the ethical base and the social order of the empire." See Meier: "Bedouins in the Ottoman Juridical Field," p. 193.

58. Gerber: "A New Look at the Tanzīmāt," p. 31; Maoz, Moshe, *Ottoman Reform in Syria and Palestine, 1840–1861: The Impact of the Tanzimat on Politics and Society* (Oxford, 1968), chapter 9 ("The Struggle against the Bedouins").

59. Karmon, Yehuda, Geographical Conditions in the Sharon Plain and their Impact on its Settlement," *Bulletin of the Israel Exploration Society*, Vol. XXIII/3–4 (1959), p. 118 [in Hebrew]; Grossman: *Arab Demography and Early Jewish Settlement in Palestine*, pp. 160–4; Ben-Arieh: "Geographic Aspects of the Development of the First Jewish Settlements in Palestine," p. 88.

60. For instance see, Ze'evi, Dror, *An Ottoman Century: The District of Jerusalem in the 1600's* (Albany, 1996), pp. 87–114; Singer: *Palestinian Peasants and Ottoman Officials*, p. 114.

61. About the process of sedentarization experienced by the Bedouins of Palestine at the end of the nineteenth century, see Meir, Avinoam, "Contemporary State Discourse and Historical Pastoral Spatiality: Contradictions in the Land Conflict between the Israeli Bedouin and the State," *Ethnic and Racial Studies*, Vol. 32/5 (2009), pp. 828–34; and Frantzman and Kark: "Bedouin Settlement in Late Ottoman and British Mandatory Palestine," pp. 9–12.

62. For instance, see BOA. HR. TO., 395/44; 554/56; 554/80.

63. For instance, see BOA. DH. MKT., 1750/62, 26 Zilhicce 1307 [13 August 1890] (the Ministry of the Interior asks the District of Jerusalem to explain why tribal leaders who were arrested in Gaza following fights between the tribes were released from jail. The request came following a complaint by the *Serasker*).

64. BOA. HR. TO., 394/59, 8 Ağustos 1306 [20 August 1890] (a petition sent by telegraph to the Grand Vizier by the *muhtar*s of two villages in the *kaza* of Gaza about the damage caused by Bedouin raids and their loss of security).

65. This term might be an indicator of an entrenched stereotype vis-à-vis the Bedouins.

66. BOA. İ. ŞD., 41/2144; see also DH. MKT., 1905/48; 1983/109; 1897/17.

67. On the government's policy regarding the Bedouins in the northern Negev and the measures to win over the support and loyalty of the Bedouins, see Kushner: *To be Governor of Jerusalem*, chapter 7; on the effort by the Empire

to obtain the support of tribal leaders in the Empire by establishing a special school in Istanbul for their children, see Rogan, Eugene, "'Aşiret Mektebi: Abdülhamid IIs school for tribes, 1892–1907," *International Journal of Middle East Studies*, Vol. 28 (1996), pp. 83–107.

68. See Rogan: *Frontiers of the State*, chapters 2 and 3.

69. BOA. A. MKT., 04, 78/29 (undated letter with no addressee signed by "all the people of the village of Yahudiyya" as well as by Mustafa al-Halil, sheikh Ibrahim al-Hajj, sheikh Hasan Bakir, and sheikh 'Abdalla al-Khatib); an order was sent to Jerusalem from Istanbul to investigate the case on 8 Cemaziyülevvel 1271 [27 January 1855].

70. *Palestine Exploration Fund* (PEF), maps 13 and 16 (prepared between 1872 and 1877). According to the maps, the area between Jaffa in the north and Nahr al-Rubin in the south was occupied by the Bedouin groups of "Arab es-Suteriyeh and et-Tiuriyeh," and that between Nahr al-Rubin in the north and Nahr al-Sukereir in the south was occupied by the Bedouin groups of "Arab es-Suarki, er-Rumeilat, and Melalhah."

71. About this group see, Khalidi, Walid, *All that Remains: The Palestinian Villages Occupied and Depopulated by Israel in 1948* (Washington, 1992), p. 356; Grossman, *Expansion and Desertion*, p. 35; Abu-Hajr, Amina Ibrahim, *Mawsu'at al-mudun wal-qura al-filastiniyya* (Encyclopedia of Palestinian Towns and Villages), Vol. I (Amman, 2003), p. 446 [in Arabic]; see also von-Oppenheim: *Die Beduinen*, Vol. II, pp. 63–4.

72. Levin-Epstein: *Zikhronotai*, p. 240; *Mikhtavim mi-Eretz-Yisrael*, 19 March 1893, pp. 3–4; see also BOA. DH. MKT., 1771/129; 1795/85, 15 Cemaziyülevvel, 1308 [27 December 1890] (a telegraph to the *mutasarrıflık* of Jerusalem from the Ministry of the Interior about a petition by the Abu-Hataba tribe from Khirbat Duran, signed by Hamdan Abu-Hataba and his friends); for the petition itself, see Appendix 3.

73. This expression, the Arabic origin of which is clear, appears as it is in the Ottoman translation of the petition which originally was written in Arabic.

74. BOA. HR. TO., 395/32.

75. This group is indicated in the PEF map in the sand dunes south of Jaffa (see Map 2). See also fn. 70 in this chapter.

76. See BOA. DH. MKT., 2729/89, 13 Muharrem 1327 [2 February 1909] (the Ministry of the Interior sends Nazim Paşa information about a complaint by the Bedouins near Ramle against the former *mutasarrıf* of Jerusalem Reşid Bey and asks him to investigate the case. The Bedouins claimed that the *mutasarrıf* authorized the sale of their land illegally at a very low price. They demand their land back or to receive compensation. They add that previous complaints went unanswered and that pressure was put on them to declare

that they had no connection to the land); DH. MKT., 2778/12, 17 Şubat 1324 [2 March 1909] (Nazim Paşa reports to the Ministry of the Interior about the investigation he carried out on the ground. His report is informative and includes the basic details of the argument which revolves around two plots of land, one composed of 6,000 *dönüm*s and the other of 3,000, which the municipality sold, whereas the Bedouins claimed they cultivated the second plot and thus demanded compensation); DH. MKT., 2753/71, 8 Şaban 1327 [25 August 1909] (the Ministry of the Interior asks Nazim Paşa who is in Jerusalem to investigate the Bedouins' complaint, most probably as a result of another petition about the same topic by the same group).

77. See BOA. HR. TO 389/104 (a petition by Muhammad Yusuf Abu-Kishk and his companions against the classification of their land as *waqf*); see also HR. TO., 389/100; for similar claims by the village of Shaykh Muwannis (often written and pronounced as Munnis), which also involved an argument about the inclusion of their land in the same *waqf* endowment (*waqf* 'Ali Bin 'Alil), the taxes due from it, and the behavior of the *waqf*'s *mütevelli*s, see BOA. HR. TO., 463/10, 3 July 1877 (archival given date).

78. BOA. HR. TO., 552/11, 19 Haziran 1291 [1 July 1875] (a translation into Ottoman of a petition in Arabic addressed to *Şeyhülislam* signed by the *müdür* of the tribe of Tarabin, Mansur and sheikh Hammad al-Sufi)

79. About him, see Büssow: *Hamidian Palestine*, pp. 370–2.

80. BOA. DH. MKT., 2242/27, 26 Rebiyülâhır 1317 [3 September 1899] (from the Ministry of the Interior to the District of Jerusalem concerning a petition signed by two persons named Ahmad Hamdy and Muhammad Rafiq to protest the activities of Ibrahim Abu-Rabah (al-Dajani), who pretended to be a holy man, attracted many followers from amongst the villagers and Bedouins, and was allegedly involved in seditious political activity); see also DH.MKT. 2303/54, 8 Şevval 1317 [9 February 1900] (a request by the Ministry of Interior from the Ministry of Justice to receive permission to take legal action against Abu-Rabah following information about his activities provided by the District of Jerusalem, including instigating false trials and bringing false witnesses to court. This letter probably follows an investigation ordered by Istanbul after the above petition was submitted. We do not possess the full correspondence concerning Abu-Rabah's activity).

81. Büssow: *Hamidian Palestine*, pp. 370–2; in 1899 the *kaymakam* of Jaffa tried to fire Abu-Rabah from the post of the Director of Education and this petition possibly also had to do with this event. Three years later, however, Abu-Rabah managed to buy his post back.

82. For similar claims about the 1830s, see Safi: "Territorial Awareness in the 1834 Palestinian Revolt," p. 53.

83. For more on aspects of regional cooperation and regional identity in the Gaza region, see Ben-Bassat, Yuval, "Regional Cooperation among the Rural Population of Palestine's Southern Coast as Reflected in Joint Petitions to İstanbul at the End of the Nineteenth Century," *New Perspectives on Turkey*, Vol. 46 (2012), pp. 213–38.

Chapter 5: Requests by Ottoman Officials Serving in Palestine

1. Erdoğdu, Teyfur, "Civil Officialdom and the Problem of Legitimacy in the Ottoman Empire (1876–1922)," *Legitimizing the Order: The Ottoman Rhetoric of State Power*, p. 227.
2. Kushner: "The Last Generation," pp. 12–13; interestingly, several of the governors of Jerusalem during the Hamidian era were trained in the Palace Secretariat and were appointed to Jerusalem as their first governing post, which indicates the region's growing importance in Ottoman eyes. See Kushner, David, "The District of Jerusalem in the Eyes of Three Ottoman Governors at the End of the Hamidian Period," *Middle Eastern Studies*, Vol. 35/2 (1999), pp. 83–4.
3. Kushner: "The Last Generation," pp. 15–16; for the power struggle between the governor and various officials whom he thought were corrupt and incompetent, see also throughout Kushner: *To be Governor of Jerusalem*.
4. Kushner: "The Last Generation," pp. 18–20.
5. About these problems in the Ottoman bureaucracy, see Erdoğdu: "Civil Officialdom and the Problem of Legitimacy," pp. 213–32.
6. Ibid., p. 219.
7. BOA. BEO., 809/60670, 25 Haziran 1312 [7 July 1896]; 3 Safar 1314 [14 July 1896].
8. BOA. Y. PRK. DH., 5/53, 25 Muharrem 1308 [19 August 1892] (petition to the Ministry of the Interior. The petitioner claims that a previous approach to the Ministry of Post and Telegraph went unanswered).
9. BOA. HR. TO., 391/42, 10 Recep 1303 [14 April 1886]; 3 Şaban 1313 [7 May 1886].
10. BOA. BEO., 1604/120265, 7 Ramazan 1318 [29 December 1900] (*Sadaret* orders *Maliye* to look into the petition).
11. BOA. Y. PRK. AZJ., 54/16, 3 Nisan 1324 [16 April 1908] (a petition by Muhammad Asif Bey, the addressee is missing); for a similar petition to the *Mabeyn* which is not signed (the second page is missing in the archive), but the content suggests it was probably written by the same Asif Bey, see Y. PRK. BŞK., 80/55, 29 Zilhicce 1327 (archival given date, there

is no date on the letter) [9 January 1910]; an order by the Sultan with regard to Asif Bey's petitions can be found at İ. HUS., 165/1326.Ra.69, 28 Rebiyülevvel 1326 [30 April 1908] (the Sultan orders the *Sadaret* to take a decision in the *Meclis-i Vükela* in the spirit of his former decision regarding Jewish immigration, after being told by the Ministry of the Interior about the approach of Asif Bey); the *Meclis-i Vükela* indeed decided to establish a committee to investigate the matter. See MV. 119/8, 2 Rebiyülâhır 1326 [4 May 1908].

12. BOA. HR. TO., 398/30.

13. Such cases refer to the administrative courts that operated in parallel to the *nizamiye* courts and dealt with administrative-bureaucratic matters involving state officials. See Brun, Nathan, *Judges and Lawyers in Eretz-Israel* (Jerusalem, 2008), p. 22 [in Hebrew].

14. BOA. BEO., 736/55140, 13 Şaban 1313 [29 January 1896] (from the *Sadaret* to the Ministry of the Interior).

15. BOA. ŞD., 3046/54, 11 Cemaziyülâhır 1325 [22 July 1907]; 15 Recep 1325 [24 August 1907].

16. BOA. ZB., 427/43, 21 Mart 1325 [3 April 1909] (from the Ministry of the Interior to Halab and Jerusalem).

17. BOA. DH. MKT., 2889/61, 15 Recep 1327 [2 August 1909] (from the Ministry of the Interior to Jerusalem, the response from Jerusalem was sent three weeks later).

18. BOA. ŞD., 2595/10, 10 Şevval 1309 [8 May 1892] (we do not possess the petition by the official himself but we can assume that he approached Istanbul, probably the Ministry of Education. The latter says that he was fired by an order of the Ministry of the Interior and the *Sadaret* after complaints were filed against him, but the court found him innocent. The Ministry of Education blamed the Ministry of the Interior for failing to notify it regarding the firing and says that it was against the law not to reinstate him. It specified the laws and its interpretation as proper grounds for its claims. The Ministry of the Interior wrote to the *Sadaret* that it did not order the dismissal of the official and that the problem was the ongoing investigation against him).

19. BOA. Y. PRK. AZJ., 40/89, 22 Haziran 1316 [5 July 1900]; for a previous request for pardon by the three, see DH. MKT. 2193/104, 16 Zilhicce 1316 [27 April 1899] (the Ministry of Interior informs the *Sadaret* that the *Meclis-i Vükela* decided to send the three back to Jerusalem to be tried there as they requested in their petition, where they complained about their mistreatment by the *kaymakam* of Gaza. The *Sadaret* needed to approve the decision, which we can assume was rejected, since two years later the three reapplied).

20. See Heyd: *Ottoman Documents on Palestine*, p. 13.

21. BOA. DH. MKT., 236/41, 10 Zilkade 1311 [15 May 1894] (the Ministry of the Interior asks *Maliye* to examine a petition by the first officer of the tax authority in Jaffa, Ömer Faiz Efendi, whose original petition we do not possess).

22. BOA. Y. PRK. DH., 7/29, 29 Kânunuevvel 1309 [10 January 1894].

23. Ahmet Cevat Paşa (known as Şakir Paşa, 1851–1900), an Ottoman statesman, who served as a Grand Vizier between 1891–95.

24. Probably referring here to Kıbrıslı Mehmet Kamil Paşa (1833–1914), an Ottoman statesman from Cyprus who served four times as Grand Vizier, including between 1885 and 1891.

25. BOA. Y. PRK. AZJ., 30/37, 24 Cemaziyülâhır 1312 [23 December 1894].

26. BOA. DH. MKT., 53/11, 14 Zilkade 1310 [30 May 1893] (from the Ministry of the Interior to Jerusalem).

27. Ahmet İzzet Paşa (1864–1937), the Ottoman chief of staff after the Young Turk Revolution, served as one of the Empire's last Grand Viziers.

28. BOA. DH. MKT., 2633/66, 20 Temmuz 1324 [2 August 1908].

29. BOA. Y. PRK. AZJ., 54/16; Y. PRK. BŞK., 80/55.

30. For one such example, see BOA. DH. MKT., 1620/123, 10 Ramazan 1306 [10 May 1889] (Istanbul asks Jerusalem to investigate a complaint by the population registrar in Gaza against the *kaymakam* who stirs up Muslim–Christian tensions).

31. BOA. PRK. AZJ., 30/45, 21 Kânunuevvel 1310 [2 January 1895] (to the *Sadaret*, versions of the same letter were sent to other offices as well).

32. BOA. DH. MKT., 2116/8, 26 Cemaziyülevvel 1316 [12 October 1898].

33. BOA. ŞD., 2984/86, 27 Teşrinievvel 1313 [8 November 1897] (the official whose name is Yusuf to *Şura-yı Devlet Mahkeme-yi Temyiz,* the high court of appeal for administrative matters for state officials). On this function of the *Şura-yı Devlet,* see Findley, Carter V., *Bureaucratic Reform in the Ottoman Empire: The Sublime Porte, 1789–1922* (Princeton, 1980), pp. 247–50.

Chapter 6: Social and Economic Matters

1. In this regard, Edmond Burke III writes that the Tanzimat reforms "inevitably led to a collision between reform-minded state bureaucrats and local elites, eager to defend their traditional rights and liberties. The Tanzimat also stimulated conflict with peasants and artisans, who experienced the state's encroachment primarily in the forms of military conscription and increased taxation." See Burke, Edmond III, "Changing Patterns of Peasant Protest," *Peasants and Politics in the Modern Middle East*, pp. 24–37.

2. In this regard, Ariel Salzmann defines the pre-reform practices in the provinces as "vernacular practices," which "subsumed diverse social, economic,

and cultural relationships that spanned the gap between provincial practices and the official order. Merchants, peasants, guildsmen, and tribes, individually and in groups, defended themselves in vernacular terms against exploitation and abuse at the hands of both Istanbul and local officials; they employed vernacular means to carve and maintain a protective niche within local sociopolitical hierarchies and organizational arrangements." The nineteenth-century Ottoman reforms attempted to eliminate these practices, a move which was opposed by various groups within the society. See Salzmann, Ariel, "Citizens in Search of a State: The Limits of Political Participation in the Late Ottoman Empire," in Hanagan, Michael and Charles Tilly (eds.), *Extending Citizenship, Reconfiguring States* (Lanham, Maryland, 1999), p. 40.

3. For instance, see the villagers' complaints on conflicting orders and fluctuations in decisions concerning the payment of *vergi* tax, in BOA. HR. TO., 396/79 (see Appendix 4). As noted, variants of this petition were sent several times by the villagers, who manifested growing impatience.

4. For a comprehensive review of the problems involving the implementation of the Ottoman land reforms, in particular the registration of land, see Zandberg, Haim, *Land Title Settlement in Eretz-Israel and in the State of Israel* (Ph.D. Dissertation: Hebrew University of Jerusalem, 1999), pp. 79–132 [in Hebrew].

5. Gerber: *Ottoman Rule in Jerusalem*, p. 199.

6. Ibid.

7. BOA. HR. TO., 396/16, 17 Temmuz 1307 [29 July 1891]; it is interesting that the *mutasarrıflık* of Jerusalem was subordinated to the District of Beirut in several areas, such as in the issue of land registration (*Defter-i Hakanî*), the second instance of appeal in the *nizamiye* courts and so on.

8. BOA. HR. TO., 397/24, 24 Nisan 1308 [6 May 1892].

9. BOA. HR. TO., 397/86, 24 Temmuz 1308 [5 August 1892].

10. BOA. İ. DFE., 3/1312, 27 Cemaziyülâhır 1312 [25 December 1894] (*Defter-i Hakani* to *Sadaret*). The Sultan approved the request that was transferred to him by the Grand Vizier but it was decided that Zekati Efendi would only prepare the map but not the *yoklama* (survey prior to land registration); for more on the preparation for implementing the decision to prepare a new map, see I. DFE., 3/1312-Za-05, 13 Şevval 1312 [9 April 1895] (a decision by *Şûra-yı Devlet* about the rationale for preparing the map, expenses, and the equipment needed, which was approved by the Sultan after the Grand Vizier submitted it to him).

11. BOA. MV., 84/89, 5 Zilhicce 1312 [30 May 1895] (the issue of the map is not mentioned here and it is stated that the role of the committee is to examine and determine the value of the orchards in Jaffa and provide details).

12. BOA. İ. ŞD. 115/6885, 21 Kânunuevvel 1307 [2 January 1892] (a draft of a decision by *Şûra-yı Devlet* regarding land in Jaffa).

13. Land on which land tax was paid. Originally these were lands that were held by non-Muslims during the Islamic conquests. Later on, such lands retained their status even when they shifted to Muslim hands, unlike lands on which only tithe was paid. Over the course of the nineteenth century, the Ottoman state started levying both the tithe tax and land tax on both types of land without taking the previous distinctions between them into account. See Granott (Granovsky), Abraham, *The Tax System in Palestine* (Tel-Aviv, 1933), pp. 150–4 [in Hebrew]; with regard to the term *kharaji* in the context used here, Beinin writes that in Egypt "in 1854 the government differentiated peasant lands (*kharajiyya*) from the privileged estates ('*ushuriyya*)" and that "the 1858 land law recognized these privileged estates as private property." See Beinin: *Workers and Peasants in the Modern Middle East*, p. 52.

14. BOA. İ. ŞD., 115/6885, 23 Kânunusani 1307 [4 February 1892]; see also DH. MKT., 1994/96, 7 Safar 1310 [31 August 1892] (the Ministry of the Interior orders the District of Jerusalem again to treat the land issue in Jaffa as it was previously ordered by a sultanic decree that was issued in response to petitions submitted by the local population. It is not clear why there was a need to send the order again to Jerusalem).

15. *Mukataa* is an area defined either for tax purposes or for rent paid to the *waqf* for cultivated land turned into gardens or building plots.

16. BOA. HR. TO., 557/83, 25 Teşrinievvel 1296 [6 November 1880] (the petition, written originally in Arabic, was sent to the *Sadaret* by Husayn al-Banna, a businessman from Jaffa and four of his companions). See also, HR. TO., 551/81, 14 Temmuz 1290 [26 July 1874] (a claim that previously, the tithe remained in the hands of the *waqf* supervisors); HR. TO., 461/54 (a petition by 46 orchard owners in the vicinity of Jaffa against the decision to start collecting tithe from them in addition to the *vergi* tax, a decision which they argued had brought them to the brink of bankruptcy).

17. BOA. HR. TO., 557/83. About this generic term used in the Arab provinces of the Ottoman Empire to refer to any kind of title deed. See Fischbach, Michael R., *State, Society and Land in Jordan* (Leiden, 2000), p. 28.

18. BOA. HR. TO., 557/83.

19. BOA. HR. TO., 553/40, 16 Haziran 1292 [28 June 1876].

20. BOA. DH. MKT., 2142/13, 16 Recep 1316 [30 November 1898].

21. BOA. DH. MKT., 1189/20, 2 Recep 1325 [11 August 1907] (the Ministry of the Interior sent Jerusalem's request to the *Sadaret*): about the scandals surrounding the foreign guards in Jaffa, see Büssow: *Hamidian Palestine*, pp. 237–8.

22. For more on Anton Ayyub, see Gidoni, David and Nir Carmi, "Mutagenesis for Seedlessness in Citrus," *Israel Journal of Plant Sciences*, Vol. 55 (2007), p. 133 (about a citrus fruit Ayyub developed); and http://antonayub. blogspot.com (about Ayyub's mansion near Jaffa).

23. BOA. HR. TO., 447/92, 12 December 1865 [archival given date, the translation of the petition into Ottoman says it was submitted without a date].

24. BOA. DH. MKT., 1757/26, 17 Muharrem 1308 [2 September 1890] (the Ministry of the Interior to *Rüsumat* (customs) asking to refer to a petition by several merchants from Beirut); about Beirutis involved in the profitable grain trade with Gaza, see Büssow: *Hamidian Palestine*, p. 273.

25. Barnes, John Robert, *An Introduction to Religious Foundations in the Ottoman Empire* (Leiden, 1986), pp. 102–4.

26. Gerber: *Ottoman Rule in Jerusalem*, chapter 8; Granott: *ha-Mishtar ha-qarqaʿi be-Eretz-Yisraʾel*, p. 140.

27. BOA. BEO., 1271/95317, 15 Şevval 1316 [26 February 1899] (from the *Sadaret* to the Ministry of Endowments).

28. BOA. BEO., 127/9522, 12 Kânunuevvel 1308 [24 December 1892] (from the *Sadaret* to the Ministry of Endowments); see also DH. MKT., 2047/93, 13 Recep 1310 [31 January 1893]; and DH. MKT., 2025/48, 10 Teşrinisani 1310 [22 November 1892] (from the Ministry of the Interior to Jerusalem with a request to investigate the complaint, which indicates that there were earlier complaints by Mustafa than those discussed above).

29. BOA. HR. TO., 390/70; see also Büssow: *Hamidian Palestine*, pp. 291–2.

30. BOA. HR. TO., 551/34, 26 Teşrinisani 1289 [8 December 1873] (a translation from Arabic into Ottoman of Ayyub's petition which was submitted to the *Sadaret*. The name of the farm involved was most probably distorted in the process of transmitting the telegraph or the translation).

31. BOA. DH. MKT., 1459/104, 6 Ağustos 1303 [18 August 1887] (from the Ministry of Justice to the Ministry of the Interior. The latter's reply after making the necessary investigations with Jerusalem was sent on 15 Safar 1305 [2 November 1887]).

32. BOA. DH. MUİ., 43–1/54, 5 Teşrinisani 1325 [18 November 1909]; 11 Teşrinisani 1325 [24 November 1909].

33. BOA. DH. MUİ., 43–1/54, 29 Zilkade 1327 [12 December 1909].

34. About this *waqf*, see Yazbak, Mahmoud, "The Islamic Waqf in Yaffa and the Urban Space: From the Ottoman State to the State of Israel," *Makan*, Vol. 2 (2010), p. 26.

35. BOA. ŞD., 2301/18, 18 Muharrem 1324 [14 March 1906].

36. BOA. DH. MUİ., 15–1/15, 17 Eylül 1325 [30 September 1909].

37. BOA. DH. MUİ., 15–1/15, 21 Ramazan 1327 [6 October 1909] (the representative of the *mutasarrıf* of Jerusalem to the Ministry of the Interior).

38. BOA. ŞD., 2980/15, a letter with an unclear date, the archival date assigned is 3 Şevval 1314 (7 March 1897); about the problematic nature of the port in Jaffa and the plans to upgrade it, see Kark: *Jaffa*, pp. 230–8.

39. For more on Navon Bey, see Glass, Joseph B., "The Biography in Historical-Geographical Research – Navon Bey: A Case Study," in Kark, Ruth (ed.), *The Land that became Israel: Studies in Historical Geography* (New-Haven, 1989), pp. 77–89; and idem, "Yosef Navon Bey and his Involvement in Late 19th Century Palestine's Development," *Cathedra*, Vol. 62 (1992), pp. 87–110 [in Hebrew].

40. BOA. BEO., 228/17026, 17 Haziran 1309 [29 June 1893] (a request by *Sadaret* from the Ministry of Commerce and Public Works, *Ticaret ve Nafia Nezareti*, to look into a petition from Yosef Navon about a concession for an irrigation project in the region of Jaffa which was submitted in French through two of his representatives).

41. BOA. ŞD., 2963/14, 11 December 1893 (from Navon's representative to Saʿid Paşa).

42. BOA. BEO., 1164/87278, 7 Rebiyülevvel 1316 [26 July 1898] (*Sadaret* to the Ministry of Commerce and Public Works).

43. BOA. HR. TO., 551/129, 8 Mayıs 1291 [20 May 1875] (a translation from Arabic into Ottoman of a collective petition by ten residents. The name of the neighborhood was most probably misspelled in the translation or in the process of sending the telegraph).

44. About him, see Mannaʿ: *Aʿlam Filastin*, p. 357; Büssow: *Hamidian Palestine*, p. 356, 384, 473–4.

45. BOA. BEO., 26/1891, 2 Zilhicce 1309 [28 June 1892] (correspondence about the petition between the Grand Vizier and the Ministry of Commerce).

46. For instance, see BOA. DH. MKT., 2017/23, 12 Rebiyülâhir 1310 [3 November 1892] (the Ministry of the Interior to the *Sadaret* about two candidates for the post of *kaymakam* of Jaffa. The governor of Jerusalem wanted a person who spoke foreign languages to be appointed due to the region's growing importance and the massive presence of foreigners there).

47. BOA. HR. TO., 533/19, 19 Ağustos 1305 [31 August 1889].

48. BOA. BEO., 404/3039, 9 Mayıs 1311 [21 May 1895] (from the *Sadaret* to the Ministry of Commerce and Public Works requesting information on whether the issue of oil and gas concessions was handled by this ministry).

49. BOA. HR. TO., 551/44, 17 Şubat 1289 [1 March 1874] (in Arabic, later translated to Ottoman).

50. BOA. HR. TO., 554/35, 20 Kânunusani 1293 [7 December 1876]; about al-Khalidi's close ties with the Greek Orthodox, see Büssow: *Hamidian Palestine*, p. 359.

51. BOA. DH. MKT., 2453/104, 2 Zilkade 1318 [21 February 1901] (Jerusalem is asked to investigate the petition which was submitted after the local authorities apparently did not address the concerns raised by the petitioners).

52. de Costa: "Identity, Authority, and the Moral Worlds of Indigenous Petitions," p. 670.

53. For instance, see Document 11.

54. For a discussion of the illusive term "corruption" in its Ottoman context, see Ergene, Boğaç A., *Local Court, Provincial Society, and Justice in the Ottoman Empire: Legal Practice and Dispute Resolution in Çankırı and Kastamonu (1652–1744)* (Leiden and Boston, 2003), pp. 108–15.

55. See Erdoğdu: "Civil Officialdom and the Problem of Legitimacy in the Ottoman Empire (1876–1922)," pp. 219–20.

56. BOA. HR. TO., 395/32 (see Appendix 3).

57. BOA. HR. TO., 554/35.

Chapter 7: The Ottoman Bureaucracy and Administration as Reflected in Petitions

1. Ursinus: *Grievance Administration*, pp. 37–8.

2. See examples of ways in which the administrative council in the District of Jerusalem discussed petitions throughout Gerber's *Ottoman Rule in Jerusalem*.

3. See BOA. HR. TO., 393/44.

4. For a similar pattern of behavior, see Baldwin: "Petitioning the Sultan in Ottoman Egypt," pp. 1–26.

5. Findley: *Ottoman Civil Officialdom*, pp. 219–20.

6. Rubin: *Ottoman Nizamiye Courts*, p. 106.

7. For comparison, writing about sixteenth-century Tuscany, Shaw writes that "supplications were typically used alongside other types of legal action. Supplications were a tactic embedded within a wider strategy: litigation at one or more magistracies, formal or informal arbitration, and extraordinary action via supplication." See Shaw: "Writing to the Prince," p. 73.

8. For comparison, about the importance of the *örf* in the petitioning system in Iran in the nineteenth century, see Schneider: *The Petitioning System in Iran*, pp. 21–4.

9. The shift from pre-modern petitions, where the grievances were more often about "real" abuse of power, to late nineteenth-century petitions, which frequently concerned the preservation of various rights and the fulfillment of various political goals, can be seen, for example, by comparing the petitions surveyed in this study to those from the eighteenth century as discussed in Cohen, Amnon Elisheva Simon-Pikali and Ovadia Salama, *Jews in the Moslem Religious Court: Society, Economy and Communal Organization in the XVIIIth Century: Documents from Ottoman Jerusalem* (Jerusalem, 1996) [in Hebrew].

10. On the rigidity of the practices at the *nizamiye* courts and the strict adherence to legal practices, regulations and procedures, see Rubin: "Legal Borrowing," pp. 279–303.

11. For a similar process which took place in Iran, see Mottahedeh, Roy, *The Mantle of the Prophet: Religion and Politics in Iran* (New York, 1985), p. 217.

12. For instance, see BOA. Y. PRK. BŞK., 42/55, 16 Safar 1313 [8 August 1895] (a petition by ten people from Gaza against the *mufti* which was sent to the Ministry of the Interior and from there referred to the Palace, which ordered the office of the *Şeyhülislam* to look into the matter).

13. See Findley: *Bureaucratic Reform*, pp. 245–7.

14. The major matters at the end of the nineteenth century were the civil affairs, finance and reform legislation. Previously, there were slightly different divisions and names to the sub-units within the council. Until 1880, for instance, there were five units: civil affairs, reform legislation, public works, finance and adjudication. Between 1880 and 1897, the council consisted of internal affairs, reforms legislation and adjudication units. See Findley, ibid., pp. 248–9.

15. BOA. MV., 119/8 (a decision by the *Meclis-i Vükela* to establish an investigative committee concerning the illegal stay in Palestine by Jewish visitors, in response to a petition by the former *kaymakam* of Jaffa, Asif Bey).

16. For instance, see BOA. DH. MKT., 1716/93, 28 Mart 1306 [9 April 1890] (the Ministry of the Interior notifies the sultan's decision to *Defter-i Hakani* and Jerusalem with regard to Sinan Paşa's lands in the colony of Rishon le-Zion, here called by its Arabic name 'Uyun Qara).

17. One such case was the issue of the status of Jaffa's lands discussed above, where the whole process can be traced from the petitions themselves, through the entire correspondence and investigation up to the imperial decision (see Documents 13.1 and 13.2; see also Appendices 2, 7.1 and 7.2). Apparently, a while later landowners in Jaffa petitioned again about the same problem but Jerusalem was ordered by Istanbul to refer them to the previous decision on the matter. See BOA. DH. MKT., 1994/96, 7 Safar 1310 [31 August 1892].

18. Heyd: *Ottoman Documents on Palestine, 1552–1615*, pp. 14–15.

19. Heyd, *Ottoman Documents on Palestine, 1552–1615*, p. 20.
20. Faroqhi: "Political Activity," p. 14.
21. See BOA. DH. MKT., 2778/12.
22. BOA. HR. TO., 390/74; for a similar approach to an intermediary by the Husaynis in Gaza, see also BOA. Y. MTV., 77/140 (Appendix 5).
23. BOA. BEO., 829/62126, 28 August 1896 (a telegraph from Rabbi Eliachar to the office of the Empire's acting Chief Rabbi in Istanbul about the need to prevent the expulsion of ʿArtuf's colonists [in French]).
24. BOA. DH. MKT., 1484/77, 28 Kânunusani 1303 [9 February 1888] (from the Ministry of the Interior to the Ministry of Endowments and the Ministry of Justice).
25. Agmon: "Recording Procedures and Legal Culture," pp. 334, 341.
26. About the definition of the *nizamiye* courts and why they should not be viewed as secular courts, see Rubin: *Ottoman Nizamiye Courts*, pp. 1–2. One of the main reasons was the introduction of the *Mecelle*, the codification of the *shariʿa* law which took place in the 1870s and served as the civil code of these courts.
27. Agmon: "Recording Procedures and Legal Culture," pp. 341–2.
28. Kushner: "The Last Generation," pp. 24–5.
29. BOA. DH. MUİ., 43–1/54.
30. Ibid., 29 Zilkade 1327 [12 December 1909].
31. For instance, see BOA. DH. MKT., 1670/9, 3 Rebiyülevvel 1305 [19 November 1887] (the Ministry of the Interior transfers to *Defter-i Hakani* information received from Jerusalem, including a decisions by a lower court and a court of appeal, about a demolition order for houses which were illegally built by Musa Bin Mordekhay Satun [?] and his friends in the Jewish colony of Yahudiyya some 15 kilometers east of Jaffa. We can assume that the correspondence followed a petition by the Jews to try to reverse the court order).
32. Included in this category are petitions which Jerusalem classified as aiming to harass the administration by petitioners who complained at every opportunity. The governor even added that there should be a law against such acts. See BOA. ŞD., 2295/13 (the governor of Jerusalem to *Şûra-yı Devlet*).
33. For one of these petitions, see BOA. DH. MUİ., 15–1/15.
34. Ibid., 21 Ramazan 1327 [6 October 1909] (from the representative of the governor of the District of Jerusalem to the Ministry of the Interior in Istanbul).
35. BOA. DH. MKT., 2729/89 (from the Ministry of the Interior to Nazim Paşa).
36. For instance, a representative of the Jewish hospital Misgav Ladach in Jerusalem, named Ishaq Vaza, asked the *Sadaret* to annul a decision by the administrative council of the *mutasarrıflık* to demolish the institute to

erect a mosque. The petitioner claimed that since it was *waqf* land only the *shari'a* court could approve such an act (which he was convinced it would reject). Istanbul ordered Jerusalem to look into the matter. See BOA. BEO., 3468/260052, 21 Kânunuevvel 1324 [3 January 1909].

37. For instance, see BOA. HR. TO., 512/78, 23 September 1879 [archival given date] (a collective petition by the *ulema* of Jerusalem to the *Sadaret* against plans to extend the term of office of Hasan Sadr al-Din Efendi, who served both as the head of the court of appeal in the *nizamiye* court as well as the head of the *shari'a* court. The petitioners cite his bad temper as the reason for their request); see also HR. TO., 395/79, 26 Mart 1307 [7 April 1891] (a petition by the sons of Khalil Abu-Khadra' from Gaza against the *naib* and the scribe of the *shari'a* court in Gaza who, together with a cousin of the petitioners named Sulayman, were misappropriating funds that belonged to a relative who needed a guardian, since he was still a minor and his father had died).

38. BOA. HR. TO., 391/4.

39. For instance, see BOA. DH. MKT., 2531/56, 29 Cemaziyülâhır 1319 [13 October 1901] (the Ministry of the Interior asks Jerusalem once more to refer to a second petition by Beshara Tasu [?] from Jaffa who complains he has a court order against Yosef Moyal and the local government to evacuate an orchard he owns but they refuse to do so).

40. Erdoğdu: "Civil Officialdom and the Problem of Legitimacy in the Ottoman Empire," p. 213.

41. Ibid., p. 214.

42. In this regard, Würgler writes that in Europe "[t]he growth of bureaucracy increased the occasions to petition, because petitioning became part of ordinary administrative procedure regarding application for public positions, membership of a corporation or community, safe conduct of Jews, permits of residence, marriage licences etc." See Würgler: "Voices from among the Silent Masses'," pp. 26–7.

43. Rubin: "Legal Borrowing," pp. 290–1.

44. For instance, see BOA. HR. TO., 396/16 (Appendix 2).

45. Consider, for example, the petition by the residents of Ramle to build barracks (*kışla*) in their town so its people would not have to be drafted in Jaffa. The correspondence between Ottoman ministries regarding the petition revealed that the issue was discussed with military commanders and with the General Staff (*Erkân-ı Harbiye*) and after long deliberations it was decided that Jaffa was a better location for the barracks. See BOA. BEO., 590/44210.

46. Shaw: *History of the Ottoman Empire and Modern Turkey*, Vol. II, pp. 246–7.

47. Rubin: *Ottoman Nizamiye Courts*, p. 84.

48. *Ibid.*, pp. 84–5.

Chapter 8: Templer and Zionist Activity as Reflected in Petitions to Istanbul

• *Earlier versions of the section in this chapter dealing with Zionist activity were published in MES, BJMES and Cathedra*

1. The Ottoman Empire was well aware of the rising importance of the Holy Land in European eyes and mounting European involvement. The Empire thus took deliberate steps to strengthen its hold over this region and subdue local rivals who could potentially cooperate with foreign powers. In fact, the establishment of the *mutasarrıflık* of Jerusalem in 1872, which was directly controlled from Istanbul, was part of the Ottoman response. The Empire, however, refrained from establishing one administrative umbrella unit that would combine the different parts of Palestine, because it wanted to avoid creating a pretext for further European intervention in the affairs of the Holy Land.

2. Carmel, Alex, "The German Settlers in Palestine and their Relations with the Local Arab Population and the Jewish Community," *Studies on Palestine during the Ottoman Period*, pp. 445–6.

3. Ben-Artzi, Yossi, "Religious Ideology and Landscape Formation: The Case of the German Templars in Eretz-Yisrael," in Baker, Alan and Gideon Biger (eds.), *Ideology and Landscape in Historical Perspective* (Cambridge, 1992), p. 101.

4. For details on such plans, see Katz, Yossef, "Paths of Zionist political Action in Turkey, 1882–1914: The Plan for Jewish Settlement in Turkey in the Young Turk Era," *International Journal of Turkish Studies*, Vol. 4 (1987), pp. 115–35.

5. Carmel: "The German Settlers in Palestine," p. 443.

6. Thalmann, Naftali, *The Character and Development of the Farm Economy in the Templer Colonies in Palestine, 1869–1939* (Jerusalem: Dissertation Submitted to the Hebrew University, 1991), pp. 1–6 [in Hebrew].

7. Carmel: "The German Settlers in Palestine," pp. 443–6.

8. Goren, Haim, "The Earliest Templar Settlement in the Holy Land," in Schiller, Ely (ed.), *Zev Vilnay's Jubilee Volume*, Vol. II (Jerusalem, 1987), p. 270 [in Hebrew].

9. Ben-Artzi, Yossi, *From Germany to the Holy Land: Templer Settlement in Palestine* (Jerusalem, 1996), pp. 106–07 [in Hebrew].

10. Carmel: "The German Settlers in Palestine," pp. 446–7.

11. Yazbak also claims that the Templers came to Palestine with built-in prejudices against its population. See Yazbak, Mahmoud, "Templars as Proto-Zionists? The 'German Colony' in Late Ottoman Haifa," *Journal of Palestine Studies*, Vol. XXVIII/4 (Summer 1999), p. 46.

12. Ibid., p. 45.

13. Carmel, Alex, *Hityashvut ha-Germanim be-Eretz-Yisrael be-shalhei ha-tekufa ha-'otmanit: Ba'ayoteiha ha-mediniyot veha-bein-Le'umiyot* (The Settlement of the German Templers in Eretz-Yisrael at the End of the Ottoman Period: Its Political and International Challenges) (Jerusalem, 1973), pp. 135–6, 234 [in Hebrew].

14. Ibid., pp. 24, 29, 43–5, 53, 60–1.

15. Carmel: "The German Settlers in Palestine," pp. 450–2.

16. Ibid., pp. 446–7, 453.

17. Yazbak: "Templars as Proto-Zionists?," pp. 44–5.

18. Carmel: "The German Settlers in Palestine," p. 453.

19. Ibid., p. 451.

20. Carmel: *Hityashvut*, p. 53.

21. Thalmann: *The Character and Development*, p. 236.

22. The Templers apparently often used the Arab agricultural system as a basis for comparison and improvement, while introducing innovations based on scientific experiments they conducted. For instance, they took various crops grown by the Arabs and improved the yields by using fertilizers; they also examined substitutes for the manure they took from the Arab villages, since they reached the conclusion that its value was low and that chemical fertilizers were much more beneficial. See Thalmann, Naftali, "Fritz Keller – A Pioneer of Modern Agriculture in Eretz-Israel: The Man and His Work," in Ben-Artzi, Yossi, Israel Bartal and Elchanan Reiner (eds.), *Studies in Geography and History in Honour of Yehoshua Ben-Arieh* (Jerusalem, 1999)," pp. 338–9 [in Hebrew].

23. BOA. HR. TO., 391/13, 16 Kânunusani 1301 [28 and 29 January 1886] (the same petition in several variations, two of them were sent to the *Sadaret* one day apart).

24. BOA. HR. TO., 391/30, 25 May 1886 (a telegraph to the *Sadaret* signed by "your slave the head of the Maronite Covenant in Jaffa and his partners").

25. In one possible case, "Nathan the German" complained that the *kaymakam* of Gaza had insulted him and besmirched his reputation. He asked for a trial to be held where he would be present with this official. BOA. HR. TO., 388/104.

26. BOA. HR. SYS., 16/22, 16 May 1885 (a translation into Ottoman of a letter to the Ministry of Foreign Affairs from the German Embassy about an

attack by 30 people on 13 Germans from Haifa traveling on the Haifa–Nazareth road).

27. BOA. HR. SYS., 18/48, 22 April 1891 (a memorandum in French sent from the German Embassy in Istanbul to the Ottoman Grand Vizier about a series of attacks in various places in the vicinity of Jaffa against German settlers and the failure of the local authorities there to handle the situation. The letter stresses the German settlers' contribution to the development of Palestine and Syria and to the Empire's coffers, and argues that they maintain good relationships with the local population and the authorities. However, the *kaymakam* of Jaffa does not help the settlers and is very hostile to them. Reinforcements should be sent to Jaffa and orders be given to the governor).

28. BOA. HR. SYS., 40/24, 21 July 1900.

29. BOA. HR. SYS., 84/84, 28 December 1913; see also BOA. HR. SYS., 84/86, 22 January 1914 (an update letter from the Sublime Porte to the German Embassy about a German woman in Haifa who was attacked by a gang of 40 people led by Fahri Abdulhadi. This individual, according to the update, turned himself in to the local authorities, as apprised from an update the Ministry of the Interior sent the Ministry of Foreign Affairs upon receiving an update from the District of Beirut); see also DH. EUM. EMN., 51/10, archival given date: 7 Rebiyülevvel 1332 (3 February 1914) (the Ministry of Foreign Affairs sends a translation of an undated report from the German Embassy to the Ministry of Interior. The Embassy complains about attacks on Germans in Haifa and Jaffa and about the general security situation in these regions. Beirut sent clarifications about two cases of attempted rape of German women in Haifa following a request by the Ministry of the Interior).

30. See the approval by the Sultan of a draft decision presented to him by the Grand Vizier in BOA. İ. DFE., 6/1315.B.05, 2 Kânunuevvel 1313 [14 December 1897]; see also Kark: *Jaffa*, p. 248.

31. A metric *dunam* equals 1,000 square meters, whereas the size of an Ottoman *dönüm* was 0.9193 metric *dunam*s (1/11 hectare, 0.227 acre).

32. Of all the immigrants from Europe, only several small groups from Bulgaria and Romania were considered Ottoman citizens, as they came from areas which were previously under Ottoman rule. Another group of immigrants came from Yemen – also an Ottoman territory – but most of them did not settle in the colonies. In several cases, Jews from Palestine itself participated in the establishment of the colonies.

33. Aaronsohn, Ran, "Cultural Landscape of Pre-Zionist Settlements," *The Land that became Israel: Studies in Historical Geography*, p. 147; for a conceptualization

of the issue of Jewish immigration in the Ottoman Empire at the time, see Karpat, Kemal H., "Jewish Population Movements in the Ottoman Empire, 1862–1914," in Levy, Avigdor (ed.), *The Jews of the Ottoman Empire* (Princeton, 1994), pp. 399–421.

34. Shapira: *Land and Power*, p. 53.

35. The whole ethos of the "second *'aliya*" was contrary to both the "old *yishuv*" and the "first *'aliya*" in that it was far more nationalistic and anti-colonial. The ethos of the "new Jew" was related to labor, especially manual work, puritanism, socialism, a new Jewish culture and above all the return of the Jew to *Eretz Yisra'el* which would be achieved by "the conquest of labor." Unlike the members of the "first *'aliya*," the "second *'aliya*" people maintained no ties with their countries of origin. Their main goal was the negation and eradication of the recent Jewish past.

36. Shapira: *Land and Power*, p. 53.

37. For instance, the Arab village of Qatra and the Jewish colony of Gedera clashed several times in the years following the colony's establishment in 1884. The immediate cause of these clashes was damage to the colony's fields by herdsmen from the village. However, an examination of the history of the land on which the colony was established reveals that, a few years earlier, the village had lost around 3,000 *dönüm*s due to debts. These ended up in the hands of a Frenchman named Philbert, who later sold land to the Jews. Until the arrival of the colonists, the villagers continued to cultivate their former land as tenants and, for every intent and purpose, still viewed it as theirs. This fact largely explains their opposition to the arrival of the Jews and the underlying reason behind the clashes between the two groups.

38. For instance, see records of daily clashes at the beginning of the twentieth century in the local archive of Rishon le-Zion. The records of the colony testify that even twenty years after this colony was established theft, trespassing and damage to property were still routine in the colony's relationships with the Arab villages around it. See Rishon le-Zion Archive: Outgoing letters, 1900–1902; Incoming letters, 1902–1903; Protocols 1899–1905.

39. See Ben-Bassat, Yuval, "Local Feuds or Premonitions of a Bi-National Conflict: A Reexamination of the Early Jewish – Arab Encounter in Palestine at the End of the 19th Century" (Unpublished Ph.D. Dissertation: University of Chicago, 2007), p. 70.

40. Ibid., chapter 4.

41. BOA. HR. TO., 395/32; see also DH. MKT., 1771/129; 1795/85.

42. See *Central Zionist Archive*, A 216/1, 29 February 1892, letter n. 19, pp. 45–8 (a letter from Eliyahu Levin-Epstein to the *Menuha ve-Nahla* society in

Warsaw which was behind the establishment of this colony); see also Levin-Epstein: *Zikhronotai*, pp. 240–4.

43. It is not entirely clear whether Levin-Epstein is referring to the metric *dunam* or the Ottoman *dönüm*.

44. Yehoshua Hankin (1864–1945), a leading Jewish land dealer in Palestine.

45. Levin-Epstein: *Zikhronotai*, p. 240.

46. BOA. HR. TO., 395/32.

47. Smilansky, Moshe, *Rehovot: Shishim shenot hayeha* (Rehovot: Sixty Years since its Establishment) (Rehovot, 1949/1950), pp. 31–2 [in Hebrew]. Smilansky adds another interesting point to his description of the clash between Rehovot and the Bedouins; namely, the aid extended to Rehovot by the other Jewish colonies in the region which sent reinforcements once the news of the events reached them. Eventually, in this case the two sides learned to get along with each other despite thorny relationships which lasted for a few more years.

48. Gerber: *Ottoman Rule in Jerusalem*, p. 199.

49. For a similar case, see HR. TO 389/100; 389/104.

50. BOA. HR. TO., 395/32.

51. A set of four petitions that are clearly related to each other although there are differences in the number of villages submitting each petition. See BOA. HR. TO., 395/60; 395/61; 395/104; 396/79.

52. BOA. HR. TO 396/79.

53. Zarnuqa was located south-west of the colony of Rehovot, some 25 kilometers south-east of Jaffa.

54. Gedera was a small colony in the northern Gaza sub-district established in 1884 by the young, single, secular-minded members of the *BILU* movement who immigrated to Palestine from Russia and initially supported a socialist and Jewish nationalist agenda.

55. BOA. HR. TO., 396/79.

56. BOA. HR. TO., 395/104.

57. On the al-Fula incident and its importance, see Khalidi: "Palestinian Peasant Resistance to Zionism before World War I," pp. 219–24; idem, *Palestinian Identity*, pp. 100–1, 106–10; Mandel: *The Arabs and Zionism*, pp. 106–7.

58. al-'Asali (1868–1916) came from a noble family in Damascus. He became a member of the Ottoman Parliament as a representative of his hometown. He was known as a very vocal opponent of Zionist activity and used this card in his campaign and later in Parliament.

59. Khalidi: *Palestinian Identity*, pp. 107–9; Khalidi: "Palestinian Peasant Resistance to Zionism," pp. 219–24.

60. BOA. DH. MUİ., 93/41, 24 Nisan 1326 [7 May 1910]; see also DH. MUİ., 98–2/1, 26 Mayıs 1326 [8 June 1910] (from the Ministry of the Interior to the

Ministry of Finance, regarding an investigation about illegal sales of lands in northern Palestine by Sursuk and Twayni to foreigners. The Ministry of the Interior transferred letters which were received from Beirut and Jerusalem about the matter. Beirut said the registration of the land transaction was a deliberate falsification by foreign consuls and the official in charge of the registration of contracts.

61. We cannot exclude the possibility that the petition by the villagers of al-Fula was initiated by al-ʿAsali himself who forced them to remain on their land despite its sale and did everything he could to prevent the transaction from being completed.

62. BOA. DH. EUM. EMN., 30/5; Mandel presents evidence that the villagers first sent a petition to the governor of Jerusalem before approaching Istanbul, which he learned about from correspondence between Jewish activists. According to the activists' correspondence cited by Mandel, this petition was organized by sheikh Sulayman al-Taji from Jaffa, who founded the Ottoman Patriotic Party in this town. See Mandel: *The Arabs and Zionism*, pp. 174–5.

63. Alroey, Gur, "The Servants of the Settlement or Vulgar Tyrants? A Hundred Years of the Hashomer Association: A Historical Perspective," *Cathedra*, Vol. 133 (2009), pp. 84–94 [in Hebrew]; see also Shafir: *Land, Labor*, p. 141 (cites examples of contemporary criticism in the colonies of *ha-Shomer*'s harsh attitude towards the Arab rural population).

64. Alroey: "The Servants of the Settlement or Vulgar Tyrants?," pp. 84–94; see also http://www.haaretz.co.il/misc/1.1282345

65. Smilansky: *Rehovot*, pp. 73–6.

66. Numerous examples of such approaches to consuls by foreign nationals can be found in Eliav, Mordechai, *Britain and the Holy Land, 1838–1914: Selected Documents from the British Consulate in Jerusalem* (Jerusalem, 1997); idem, *Under Imperial Austrian Protection: Selected Documents from the Archives of the Austrian Consulate in Jerusalem, 1849–1917* (Jerusalem, 1985) [in Hebrew].

67. Levin-Epstein: *Zikhronotai*, pp. 246–51.

68. Kushner: "The District of Jerusalem in the Eyes of Three Ottoman Governors," pp. 87–93.

69. BOA. Y. PRK. AZJ., 40/37, 21 Nisan 1316 [4 May 1900].

70. BOA. DH. MKT., 2084/37, 18 Rebiyülâhır 1318 [16 September 1897] (a letter from the Ministry of the Interior to the *mutasarrıflık* of Jerusalem about a petition by the villagers of Malabes which is said to be attached).

71. For instance, see BOA. HR. TO., 531/40, 20 October 1887 (a letter in French from Elie Scheid to the Grand Vizier, asking him to order the governors of Syria and Jerusalem to let Jewish colonists who became Ottoman citizens and who were loyal subjects of the Empire buy land and build houses and to stop creating obstacles, in accordance with the Sultan's promises that all the

subjects of the Empire deserve equal rights. Scheid enumerates the benefits the Empire would derive from their settlement); DH.MKT., 1530/17, 29 Zilhicce 1305 [7 August 1888] (an order from Istanbul to the *mutasarrıf* of Jerusalem, following a petition made by Scheid, to let Jews who settled before the prohibition on settlement activity came into effect and who accepted Ottoman citizenship, to build their houses, in accordance with the orders of the sultan); See also DH. MKT, 1475/47, 21 Rebiyülâhır 1305 [6 January 1888] (a letter sent from the Ministry of Interior to the Grand Vizier about building permission for local and foreign Jews who settled in the "regions of Syria and Jerusalem" as part of a long correspondence following a petition by Scheid).

72. For instance, see BOA. DH. MKT., 1471/65, 20 November 1888 (a request written in French by Scheid to the Minister of the Interior to be awarded an imperial medal).

73. Ibid.

74. For instance, see BOA. BEO., 507/37969, 12 Teşrinievvel 1310 [24 October 1894] (two petitions by Scheid to *Sadaret* against the *mutasarrıflık* of Jerusalem which did not let Baron de Rothschild complete a land transaction in Rishon le-Zion and did not put forward a valid explanation for its refusal, and about a construction permit in Rishon le-Zion and Petah-Tiqva).

75. Scheid, Elie, *Zikhronot* (Memoirs) (Jerusalem, 1983), pp. 89, 185–6, 202 [in Hebrew].

76. For instance, see BOA. Y.PRK. AZJ., 30/37 (a letter sent to the Sultan by an unknown official who "served seven years in the regions of Syria and Palestine" complaining about Rothschild's meeting with the Grand Vizier Cevat Paşa, during which they allegedly discussed the Jewish colonization effort in Palestine. In addition, it is argued in the letter that the aides of Cevat Paşa assisted Rothschild. The letter warns the Sultan about the deleterious effects of Jewish activity in Palestine on the Empire's interests and predicts that it will create a problem similar to that of the Armenians).

77. For example, see BOA. Y. A. HUS., 302/45, 5 Muharrem 1312 [9 July 1894] (the Sultan awards Lord Rothschild, whose bank secured a loan for the Empire, a medal and a present and congratulates him on receiving the title of Lord); 323/74, 8 Şevval 1312 [4 April 1895] (the Grand Vizier writes to the Sultan that Rothschild is worried about a delay in the Empire's repayment of a loan and that the issue must be taken care of soon); 319/21, 11 Şaban 1312 [7 February 1895] (the Grand Vizier writes to the Sultan about the loan conditions offered by Rothschild and receives sultanic approval).

78. For instance, see BOA. İ. HUS., 31/1312-Ca-084, 21 Cemaziyülevvel 1312 [20 November 1894] (the Sultan heard about Elie Scheid's donation of

500 francs to a hospital, and called it a noble act which gave him great satisfaction).

79. The colonies maintained internal land registrars, *Sifrei Ahuzot*, where they recorded the land transactions between themselves, as well as those conducted with the various colonization agencies. During the Mandate period, these registrars were recognized by the authorities as official documents, testifying to individuals' ownership of land in the colonies.

80. For instance, see Scheid: *Zikhronot*, p. 220 (about the arrest by the police of four colonists in Eqron following a request by Alphonse Bloch, the head of the Rothschild administration in the Judean colonies, whose headquarters were in the colony of Rishon le-Zion.

81. BOA. DH. MKT., 1484/77.

82. On Tiomkin, see Kark, Ruth, "Land Acquisition and New Agricultural Settlements in Palestine during the Tyomkin Period, 1890–1892," *ha-Tsiyonut*, Vol. 9 (1984), pp. 179–94 [in Hebrew].

83. BOA. HR. TO., 396/5, 26 Haziran 1307 [8 July 1891].

84. BOA. Y. MTV., 69/17, 23 Rebiyülevvel 1310 [15 October 1892] (a petition to the Sultan signed by R. Moncrieft [?] in the name of 500 Jewish families who lived in the *vilayet* of Şam).

85. BOA. DH. MUİ., 26–2/29 22 Haziran 1325 [5 July 1909]; 14 Temmuz 1325 [27 July 1909].

86. For instance, see BOA. İ. DH., 1465/1326-R-3, 6 Rebiyülâhır 1326 [7 May 1908] (a decision to establish a committee to examine the existing situation and suggest measures to prevent Jews who come to visit Palestine and remain despite the prohibitions. Measures taken have not been sufficient to prevent Jewish immigration).

87. For instance, see BOA. DH. MKT., 53/11, 14 Zilkade 1310 [30 May 1893] (an order from the Ministry of the Interior to the *mutasarrıf* of Jerusalem to investigate a petition by the *tapu* official in Jerusalem, 'Abd al-Razak Efendi, who claims he reported Jewish settlement activity in the *kaza* of Jaffa and was fired for allegedly enabling this activity); DH. MKT., 2633/66, 20 Temmuz 1324 [2 August 1908] (a petition submitted to the Grand Vizier immediately after the Revolution of 1908, perhaps in connection with this event, by the former mayor of Jaffa sheikh 'Ali, in request to return him to office and to fire the *kaymakam* of Jaffa. The latter, it is claimed, who worked hand in glove with foreign Jews and sold them lands, caused the former mayor to be dismissed when he reported the *kaymakam*'s illegal activity).

88. For more on the Ottoman policy vis-à-vis the question of Jewish immigration and settlement activity, see Mandel, Neville J., "Ottoman Policy and Restrictions on Jewish Settlement in Palestine, 1881–1908, *Middle Eastern*

Studies, 10/3 (1974), pp. 312–32; idem, "Ottoman Practices as Regards Jewish Settlement in Palestine, 1881–1908," *Middle Eastern Studies*, 11/1 (1975), pp. 33–46.

89. For instance, see BOA. İ. DH., 1237/96881, 17 Zilhicce 1308 [24 July 1891] (a decision by the Sultan, following an approach by the Grand Vizier regarding Jewish immigration to the Empire. The issue was discussed previously but no decision was made. Upon a request by the District of Beirut for instructions it was decided not to let Jews enter the Empire. The decision is general although the question mainly concerned Russian and Greek [sic!] Jews who immigrated to the region of Jerusalem).

90. For instance, see BOA. DH. MKT., 1890/25, 14 Rebiyülevvel 1309 [17 November 1891] (the Ministry of the Interior to the Grand Vizier about the need to take action against the activities of Rothschild and various Jewish societies which buy land in Palestine and Syria and whose activities might eventually lead to the creation of a new political problem for the Empire).

91. For instance, see BOA. İ. DH., 1237/96881.

92. For instance, see BOA. İ. DH., 97030, 11 Muharrem 1309 [17 August 1891] (the Sultan orders the Grand Vizier to prepare a decision regarding Jewish immigration from Russia to the Empire as there is still no definitive decision on this matter).

93. For instance, see BOA. İ. DH., 1237/96881.

94. For instance, see BOA. DH. MKT., 1981/45, 8 Muharrem 1310 [2 August 1892] (the Ministry of the Interior clarifies the policy regarding Jewish immigration to the Empire in a letter to various bureaus. They should not be given permission to enter; those who have already arrived should be prevented from going to Palestine and can settle only in places where there is already a massive Jewish presence such as Salonika. The correspondence was prompted by the arrival of a group of Jews from Odessa).

95. For instance, see BOA. Y. PRK. DH., 7/29, 29 Kânunuevvel 1309 [10 January 1894] (an anonymous complaint to the Ministry of the Interior by an Ottoman official who served in Jerusalem against illegal Jewish immigration and settlement activity with the help of local Jews and the cooperation of local Ottoman authorities in return for bribes); DH. MKT., 1953/87, 29 Şevval 1309 [27 May 1892] (from the Ministry of the Interior to the *mutasarrıflık* of Jerusalem regarding a complaint against the *kaymakam* of Jaffa, Mustafa Hikmet Efendi, who among other accusations, let Jews settle in violation of Imperial orders. Jerusalem wanted the person to be fired but was told that the Committee of Officials decided that there was not enough proof to take action. Jerusalem was asked to provide additional evidence against the official, if it wanted to continue the process).

Conclusion: Old Institutions, New Conditions, a New Meaning of Justice?

1. In this regard, the state's search for legitimacy must be kept in mind. Hagen writes that legitimacy is "the result of continuous negotiation between ruler and ruled," a remark which might explain the importance of the petitioning system to both the urban elite and the Empire in the period discussed here. See Hagan: "Legitimacy and World Order," p. 55.

2. About a similar phenomenon of flooding the system with petitions in the central and northern Italian states in the early modern period to the extent that this practice was defined as "intolerable abuse" and actions were taken to limit the submission of petitions, see Nubola: "Supplications between Politics and Justice," p. 47.

3. Campos, Michelle U., "Making Citizens, Contesting Citizenship in Late Ottoman Palestine," in Ben-Bassat, Yuval and Eyal Ginio (eds.), *Late Ottoman Palestine: The Period of Young Turk Rule* (London, 2011), p. 20; see also Rogan: "Instant Communication," p. 124 (about the influence of the telegraph on helping Ottoman subjects acquire a status more similar to that of citizens).

4. Darling: *Revenue Raising and Legitimacy*, pp. 283–99.

5. Zaret argues that mass petitions, under certain conditions, can be perceived as indicators of public opinion. See Zaret: "Petitions and the 'Invention' of Public Opinion," pp. 1541–2; recent research has demonstrated how printed petitions were used to mobilize public opinion in regions which had just gained independence from Ottoman tutelage, and how these affected Greek populations remaining within Ottoman borders during the early Tanzimat period. See Papataxiarchis, Evthymios, "Reconfiguring the Ottoman Political Imagination: Petitioning and Print Culture in the Early Tanzimat," *Political Initiatives "From the Bottom Up:" Halcyon Days in Crete*, pp. 191–226.

6. "Report of the King-Crane Commission," *Editor & Publisher*, 2 December 1922, pp. 1–26. In http://dcollections.oberlin.edu/cdm4/document.php?CISOROOT=/kingcrane&CISOPTR=1239&REC=1

7. Gelvin, James, "Demonstrating Communities in Post-Ottoman Syria," *The Journal of Interdisciplinary History*, Vol. 25/1 (1994), pp. 32–3; Reimer, Michael, "The King–Crane Commission at the Juncture of Politics and Historiography," *Critique: Critical Middle Eastern Studies*, Vol. 15/2 (2006), pp. 135–8.

8. Forman, Geremy and Alexandre Kedar, "Colonialism, Colonization, and Land Law in Mandate Palestine: The Zor al-Zarqa and Barrat Qisarya Land Disputes in Historical Perspective," *Theoretical Inquiries in Law*, Vol. 4/2 (2003), pp. 528, 535; Falah, Ghazi," Pre-State Jewish Colonization in Northern Palestine and its Impact on Local Bedouin Sedentarization 1914–1948," *Journal of Historical Geography*, Vol. XVII/3 (1991), pp. 304–5.

9. Forman and Kedar: "Colonialism, Colonization," p. 535.
10. Adler, Selig, "The Palestine Question in the Wilson Era," *Jewish Social Studies*, Vol. 10/4 (1948), p. 321.
11. For instance, see Segev, Tom, *One Palestine, Complete: Jews and Arabs under the British Mandate* (New York, 2001), p. 276.
12. For instance, about petitions in early republican Turkey, see Akın, Yiğit, "Reconsidering State, Party, and Society in Early Republican Turkey: Politics of Petitioning," *International Journal of Middle East Studies*, Vol. 39 (2007), pp. 435–57.

Appendices

1. Baer argues that the Husaynis rented the collection of this *waqf*'s revenues for an extended period of time (*khulu*). See Baer, Gabriel, "The Dismemberment of Awqāf in Early Nineteenth-Century Jerusalem," in Gilbar, Gad (ed.), *Ottoman Palestine, 1800–1914: Studies in Social and Economic History* (Leiden, 1990), pp. 309–10.
2. About the motive of migration in petitions, see Faroqhi: "Political Activity," pp. 31–3; Burke claims that avoidance and not open rebellion was the most typical reaction among the rural population in the Middle East as a means of dealing with hardships inflicted upon it. See Burke: "Changing Patterns of Peasant Protest," p. 24.
3. Levin-Epstein describes Haykal in his memoirs, when referring to the purchase of Rehovot's land, as a Muslim middleman (*sarsur* in Hebrew, not to be confused with the Arabic meaning of this word) who helped buy the land from its previous Christian landowner "an Efendi from Jaffa." See Levin-Epstein: *Zikhronotai*, p. 126.
4. About the *temettü* tax, see Vefiq Bay, Abdülrahman, *Tekâlif Kavaidi* (Tax Rules), Vol. II (Istanbul, 1330 [1911/1912]), pp. 163–79 [in Ottoman]. This tax was an annual graduated tax on business profits which was introduced during the Tanzimat and was paid mainly by artisans and merchants, whereas attempts to levy it on farmers were temporary and inconsistent.
5. The villagers refer here to the small colony of Gedera which was established in 1884 by members of the *BILU* movement, with the help of the *Hovevei Zion* movement.
6. The Husaynis in Gaza had close ties with the Khedive 'Abbas in Egypt which prompted Sultan Abdülhamid II to attempt to undermine their status and sources of influence. At that time, Yusuf Diya' al-Khalidi was still on good terms with Istanbul, a situation which changed later, and possibly

this is the background for his activity here. See Pappe: *Aristocracy of the Land*, pp. 118, 148.

7. For more on the Abu-Kishk tribal group, see al-Nimr, Ihsan, *Ta'rikh Jabal Nablus wal-Balqa* (The History of Jabal Nablus and al-Balqa), Vols. II (Nablus, 1961), pp. 412–13 [in Arabic]; Ashkenazi, Tuvia, *ha-Bedu'im be-Eretz-Yisra'el* (The Bedouins in Eretz-Israel) (Jerusalem, 2000), pp. 230–3, 247–54 [in Hebrew]; al-Dabbagh: *Biladuna Filastin*, pp. 345–6 [in Arabic].

BIBLIOGRAPHY

Archival Materials

Başbakanlık Devlet Osmanlı Arşivleri (BOA)

Sadaret Mektubi Kalemi (Grand Vizirate Correspondence Bureau), A. MKT

Bab-ı Âli Asafi Divan-ı Hümayun Sicilleri Şam-ı Şerif Ahkam Defterleri, A. {DVNS.ŞM.d}

Bab-ı Âli Evrak Odası (Sublime Porte, Secretariat), BEO

Collections of the Ministry of the Interior

- *Dahiliye Nezareti, Emniyet-i Umumiye Emniyet Şubesi Evrakı (Ministry of the Interior, General Security, Record Office), DH. EUM. EMN*
- *Dahiliye Nezareti, Mektubi Kalemi (Ministry of the Interior, Bureau of Correspondence), DH. MKT*
- *Dahiliye Nezareti, Muhaberat-ı Umumiye İdaresi Belgeleri, DH. MUİ*

Collections of the Foreign Ministry

- *Hariciye Nezareti, Siyasî Kısım (Foreign Office, Political Bureau), HR. SYS*
- *Hariciye Nezareti, Tercüme Odası (Foreign Office, Translation Bureau), HR. TO*

İrade (Sultanic Decrees)

- *İrade Defter-i Hakani, İ. DFE*
- *İrade Dahiliye, İ. DH*
- *İrade Hususi, İ. HUS*
- *İrade Şûra-yı Devlet, İ. ŞD*

Kudüs Gelen-Giden, (Jerusalem's incoming-outgoing telegraphs) VGG.L 312, 314, 315, 316, 317, 974

Meclis-i Vükela Mazbataları (Decisions of the Council of Ministers), MV

Şûra-yı Devlet (Council of State), ŞD

- *Şûra-yı Devlet (Council of State), ŞD*
- *Şûra-yı Devlet Mülkiye (Council of State, Administrative Unit), ŞD. MLK*

Yıldız Palace Collections

- *Yıldız Sadaret Hususi Maruzat Evrakı, Y. A. HUS*
- *Yıldız Mütenevvi Maruzat Evrakı, Y. MTV*
- *Yıldız Perakende Evrakı Arzuhal ve Jurnal, Y. PRK. AZJ*
- *Yıldız Perakende Evrakı Başkitabet Dairesi Maruzatı, Y. PRK. BŞK*
- *Yıldız Perakende Evrakı Dahiliye, Y. PRK. DH*

Zabtiye Nezareti Belgeleri (Gendarmerie), ZB

Central Zionist Archive (CZA)

- A 216/1

The Archive of Rishon le-Zion

- Outgoing letters, 1900–02
- Incoming letters, 1902–03
- Protocols 1899–1905

Maps

Palestine Exploration Fund (PEF)

Collections of Primary Sources

Başbakanlık Osmanlı Arşivi Rehberi (Catalogue of the Ottoman Archive at the Prime Minister's Office) (Ankara, 2010) [in Turkish].
Osmanlı Belgelerinde Filistin (Palestine in Ottoman Documents) (Istanbul, 2009) [in Turkish].

Memoirs, Diaries, Manuals

al-'Attar, Hasan, *Kitab insha al-'Attar* (al-Attar's Book of Correspondence) (Istanbul, 1299 [1881]) [in Arabic].
Baldensperger, Philip, "The Immovable East," *Palestine Exploration Fund: Quarterly Statement for 1906*, pp. 13–23, 97–102, 190–7.
——. "The Immovable East," *Palestine Exploration Fund: Quarterly Statement for 1917*, pp. 12–17, pp. 159–65.
——. *The Immovable East – Studies of the People and Customs of Palestine* (Tel-Aviv, 1982) [in Hebrew].
al-Bustani, Butrus, *Kitab da'irat al-ma'arif: Encyclopedie Arabe* (The Encyclopedia of Knowledge). Vol. VI (Beirut, 1876) [in Arabic].
Bustrus, Salim, *al-Nuzha al-shahiyya fil-rihla al-salimiyya 1855* (About the Magnificent Journey of Salim, 1855), edited by Wahab, Qasim (Beirut, 2003) [in Arabic].

Ets-Hadar, Avraham, *Ilanot le-toldot ha-yishuv be-Eretz-Yisrael, 1830–1920* (Documents about the Yishuv in Eretz-Yisrael, 1830–1920) (Tel-Aviv, 1967) [in Hebrew].

Grant, Elihu, *The People of Palestine: An Enlarged Edition of "The Peasantry of Palestine, Life, Manners and Customs of the Village"* (Westport, CT, 1976).

Haykal, Yusuf, *Ayyam al-siba: Suwar min al-haya wa-safhat min al-tarikh* (The Days of Adolescence: Pictures from Life and Pages of History) (Amman, 1988) [in Arabic].

Hayret, Mehmet Efendi, *Fihrest İnşa-yı Hayret Efendi* (Cairo, 1825) [in Ottoman Turkish].

Hissin, Haim, *Memoirs and Letters of an Early Pioneer* (Jerusalem, 1990) [in Hebrew].

al-Jawhariyya, Wasif, *al-Quds al-ʿuthmaniyya fil-mudhakkirat al-Jawhariyya* (Ottoman Jerusalem in al-Jawhariyya Memoirs), Vol. I, edited by Tamari, Salim and Issam Nassar (Jerusalem, 2003) [in Arabic].

Lees, Rev. George Robinson, *Village Life in Palestine: A Description of the Religion, Home Life, Manners, Customs, Characteristics and Superstitions of the Peasants of the Holy Land, with Reference to the Bible* (London, New York and Bombay, 1905).

Levin-Epstein, Eliyahu, *Zikhronotai* (My Memoirs) (Tel-Aviv, 1932) [in Hebrew].

Luncz, Abraham Moshe, *Luah Eretz-Yisra'el li-shnat hatarnav, shana rishona* (Eretz-Israel Almanac for 5656, the First Year) (Jerusalem, 1895/6) [in Hebrew].

al-Mawardi, ʿAli ibn Muhammad, *The Ordinances of Government: A Translation of Al-Ahkām al-Sulṭaniyya w' al-Wilāyāt al-Dīniyya*, translated by Wafaa H. Wahaba (London, 1996).

Niman, David, *Be-Reshit baroh {...}: Zikhronotav shel David Niman* (In the Beginning [...]: The Memoirs of David Niman) (Tel-Aviv, 1962/3) [in Hebrew].

Nizam al-Mulk, *The Book of Government or Rules for Kings*, translated by H. Darke (London, 1978).

Pears, Edwin, *Forty Years in Constantinople: The Recollections of Sir Edwin Pears 1873–1915* (London, 1916).

al-Qasimi, Jamal al-Din and Khalil al-ʿAzm, *Qamus al-sinaʿat al-Shamiyya* (Dictionary of Crafts in Damascus), Vol. II (Paris, 1960) [in Arabic].

al-Qatrawi, Jamal ʿAbd al-Rahim, *Qatra: al-Huwiyya wal-ta'rikh* (Qatra: Its Characteristics and History) (Gaza, 2000) [in Arabic].

Refik, Ahmet, *Hicrî On Ikinci Asırda Istanbul Hayatı (1100–1200)* (Life in Istanbul in the Twelfth *Hicri* Century) (Istanbul, 1930) [in Turkish].

al-Sakakini, Khalil, *The Diaries of Khalil Sakakini*, Vol. I–II, in Musallam, Akram (ed.) (Ramallah, 2003–4) [in Arabic].

Scheid, Elie, *Zikhronot* (Memoirs) (Jerusalem, 1983) [in Hebrew].

al-Shalfun, Yusuf Efendi, *Turjuman al-mukataba* (Index of Writing/Compendium of Correspondence), 7th edition (Beirut, 1887) [in Arabic].

Tahsin Paşa, *Abdulhamit: Yıldız Hatıraları* (Abdülhamid: Yıldız Palace Memoirs) (Istanbul, 1931) [in Turkish].

Tamari, Salim (ed.), *The Year of the Locust: A Soldier's Diary and the Erasure of Palestine's Ottoman Past* (Berkeley, 2011).

Thornbury, Walter, *Turkish Life and Character*, Vol. I (London, 1860).

Wright, George Newenham and Charles Henry Timperley, *The Gallery of Engravings*, Vol. III (London, 1844).

Vefiq Bay, Abdülrahman, *Tekâlif Kavaidi* (Tax Rules), Vol. II (Istanbul, 1330 [1911/1912]) [in Ottoman Turkish].

Newspapers

Mikhtavim mi-Eretz-Yisrael (Letters from the Land of Israel)

Reports

"Report of the King–Crane Commission," *Editor & Publisher*, 2 December 1922, pp. 1–26

http://dcollections.oberlin.edu/cdm4/document.php?CISOROOT=/kingcrane&CISOPTR=1239&REC=1

Internet Sites

http://www.devletarsivleri.gov.tr/katalog

http://www.almoajam.org/poet_details.php?id=6433

http://www.antonayub.blogspot.com

http://www.haaretz.co.il/misc/1.1282345

Secondary Sources

Aaronsohn, Ran, "Cultural Landscape of Pre-Zionist Settlements," in Kark, Ruth (ed.), *The Land that became Israel: Studies in Historical Geography* (New Haven, 1990), pp. 147–63.

Abu-Hajr, Amina Ibrahim, *Mawsu'at al-mudun wal-qura al-filastiniyya* (Encyclopedia of the Palestinian Towns and Villages), Vol. I (Amman, 2003) [in Arabic].

Abu-Manneh, Butrus, "Jerusalem in the Tanzimat Period: The New Ottoman Administration and the Notables," *Die Welt des Islams*, Vol. 30/1 (1990), pp. 1–44.

———. "The Rise of the Sanjak of Jerusalem in the Late Nineteenth Century," in Pappé, Ilan (ed.), *The Israel/Palestine Question* (London, 1999), pp. 41–51.

Adler, Selig, "The Palestine Question in the Wilson Era," *Jewish Social Studies*, Vol. 10/4 (1948), pp. 303–34.

Agmon, Iris, "Recording Procedures and Legal Culture in the Late Ottoman Shari'a Court of Jaffa, 1865–1890," *Islamic Law and Society*, Vol. 11/3 (2004), pp. 333–77.

———. *Family & Court: Legal Culture and Modernity in Late Ottoman Palestine* (Syracuse, 2006).

Ahituv, Shmuel, *HaKetav VeHaMiktav* (Jerusalem, 2005) [in Hebrew].

Akiba, Jun, "The Practice of Writing Curricula Vitae among the Lower Government Employees in the Late Ottoman Empire: Workers at the *Şeyhülislâm*'s Office," *European Journal of Turkish Studies*, Vol. 6 (2007), pp. 1–26.

Akın, Yiğit, "Reconsidering State, Party, and Society in Early Republican Turkey: Politics of Petitioning," *International Journal of Middle East Studies*, Vol. 39 (2007), pp. 435–57.

Alroey, Gur, "The Servants of the Settlement or Vulgar Tyrants? A Hundred Years of the Hashomer Association: A Historical Perspective," *Cathedra*, Vol. 133 (2009), pp. 77–104 [in Hebrew].

Ashkenazi, Tuvia, *ha-Bedu'im be-Eretz-Yisra'el* (The Bedouins in Eretz-Israel) (Jerusalem, 2000) [in Hebrew].

Avcı, Yasemin, *Değişim Sürecinde Bir Osmanlı Kenti: Kudüs 1890–1914* (An Ottoman City in Transition: Jerusalem 1890–1914) (Ankara, 2004) [in Turkish].

Avitsur, Shmu'el, *Daily Life in Iretz Israel in the XIX Century* (Tel-Aviv, 1972) [in Hebrew].

Ayalon, Ami, *Reading Palestine: Printing and Literacy, 1900–1948* (Austin, TX, 2004).

Baer, Gabriel, *Fellah and Townsman in the Middle East: Studies in Social History* (London, 1982).

———. "The Dismemberment of Awqāf in Early Nineteenth-Century Jerusalem," in Gilbar, Gad (ed.), *Ottoman Palestine, 1800–1914: Studies in Social and Economic History* (Leiden, 1990), pp. 299–319.

Baldwin, James E., "Petitioning the Sultan in Ottoman Egypt," *Bulletin of the School of Oriental and African Studies*, 75/3 (2012), pp. 499–524.

Barnes, John Robert, *An Introduction to Religious Foundations in the Ottoman Empire* (Leiden, 1986).

Beinin, Joel, *Workers and Peasants in the Modern Middle East* (Cambridge, 2001).

Bektas, Yakup, "The Sultan's Messenger: Cultural Constructions of Ottoman Telegraphy, 1847–1880," *Technology and Culture*, Vol. 41/4 (2000), pp. 669–96.

Ben-Arieh, Yehoshua, "Geographic Aspects of the Development of the First Jewish Settlements in Palestine," in Eliav, Mordechai (ed.), *The First Aliyah*, Vol. I (Jerusalem, 1981), pp. 85–96 [in Hebrew].

———. "Ukhlusiyat Eretz-Yisra'el vi-yshuvah 'erev mif'al ha-hityashvut ha-tsiyoni" (The Population of Eretz-Israel and its Settlements on the Eve of the Zionist Colonization), in Ben-Arieh, Yehoshua, Yossi Ben-Artzi and Haim Goren (eds.), *Historical-Geographical Studies in the Settlement of Eretz-Israel*, Vol. I (Jerusalem, 1987), pp. 4–13 [in Hebrew].

———. "The Villages in Sancak Gaza (including Jaffa and Ramla) in the Eighteen-Seventies," *Shalem*, Vol. 5 (1987), pp. 139–87 [in Hebrew].

——. "ha-Nof ha-yishuvi shel Eretz-Yisra'el 'erev ha-hityashvut ha-tsiyonit" (The Settlement Landscape of the Land of Israel on the Eve of Zionist Colonization), in Kolatt, Israel (ed.), *The History of the Jewish Community in Eretz Israel since 1882*, Vol. I (Jerusalem, 1989), pp. 75–141 [in Hebrew].

Ben-Artzi, Yossi, "Religious Ideology and Landscape Formation: The Case of the German Templars in Eretz-Yisrael," in Baker, Alan and Gideon Biger (eds.), *Ideology and Landscape in Historical Perspective* (Cambridge, 1992), pp. 83–106.

——. *From Germany to the Holy Land: Templer Settlement in Palestine* (Jerusalem, 1996) [in Hebrew].

Ben-Bassat, Yuval, *Local Feuds or Premonitions of a Bi-National Conflict: A Reexamination of the Early Jewish – Arab Encounter in Palestine at the End of the 19th Century* (Unpublished Ph.D. Dissertation: University of Chicago, 2007).

——. "Proto-Zionist – Arab Encounters in Late Nineteenth-Century Palestine: Socioregional Dimensions," *Journal of Palestine Studies*, Vol. XXXVIII/2 (2009), pp. 42–63.

——. "Regional Cooperation among the Rural Population of Palestine's Southern Coast as Reflected in Joint Petitions to İstanbul at the End of the Nineteenth Century," *New Perspectives on Turkey*, Vol. 46 (2012), pp. 213–38.

Brun, Nathan, *Judges and Lawyers in Eretz-Israel* (Jerusalem, 2008) [in Hebrew].

Burke, Edmond III, "Changing Patterns of Peasant Protest," in Kazemi, Farhad and John Waterbury (eds.), *Peasants and Politics in the Modern Middle East* (Miami, 1991), pp. 24–37.

Büssow, Johann, *Hamidian Palestine: Politics and Society in the District of Jerusalem, 1872–1908* (Leiden and Boston, 2011).

Campos, Michelle U., *Ottoman Brothers: Muslims, Christians, and Jews in Early Twentieth-Century Palestine* (Stanford, 2011).

——. "Making Citizens, Contesting Citizenship in Late Ottoman Palestine," in Ben-Bassat, Yuval and Eyal Ginio (eds.), *Late Ottoman Palestine: The Period of Young Turk Rule* (London, 2011).

Carmel, Alex, *Hityashvut ha-germanim be-Eretz-Yisrael be-shalhei ha-tekufa ha-'otmanit: Ba'ayoteiha ha-mediniyot veha-bein-le'umiyot* (The Settlement of the German Templers in Eretz-Yisrael at the End of the Ottoman Period: Its Political and International Challenges) (Jerusalem, 1973) [in Hebrew].

——. "The German Settlers in Palestine and their Relations with the Local Arab Population and the Jewish Community," in Ma'oz, Moshe (ed.), *Studies on Palestine during the Ottoman Period* (Jerusalem, 1975), pp. 443–65.

——. "Taharut, hadira ve nochehut: ha-Pe'ilut ha-notsrit ve-hashpa'ata be-Eretz Yisra'el" (Competition, Penetration, and Presence: The Christian Activity and its Influence in the Land of Israel), in Bartal, Israel and Yehoshua Ben-Arieh (eds.), *The History of Eretz Israel: The Last Phase of Ottoman Rule (1799–1917)*, Vol. VIII (Jerusalem, 1983), pp. 109–51[in Hebrew].

Chalcraft, John, *The Striking Cabbies of Cairo and Other Stories: Crafts and Guilds in Egypt, 1863–1914* (Albany, New York, 2004).

——. "Engaging the State: Peasants and Petitions in Egypt on the Eve of Colonial Rule," *International Journal of Middle Eastern Studies*, Vol. 37/3 (2005), pp. 303–25.

Cohen, Amnon, *Ottoman Documents on the Jewish Community of Jerusalem in the Sixteenth Century* (Jerusalem, 1976) [in Hebrew].

——. "A Tale of Two Women: Facets of Jewish Life in Nineteenth-Century Jerusalem as Seen through the Muslim Court Record," in Levy, Avigdor (ed.), *Jews, Turks, Ottomans: A Shared History, Fifteenth Through Twentieth Century* (Syracuse, 2002), pp. 119–26.

Cohen, Amnon and Elisheva Simon-Pikali, *Jews in the Moslem Religious Court: Society, Economy and Communal Organization in the XVIth Century: Documents from Ottoman Jerusalem* (Jerusalem, 1993) [in Hebrew].

Cohen, Amnon, Elisheva Simon-Pikali, and Ovadia Salama, *Jews in the Moslem Religious Court: Society, Economy and Communal Organization in the XVIIIth Century: Documents from Ottoman Jerusalem* (Jerusalem, 1996) [in Hebrew].

Cohen, Amnon, Elisheva Ben-Shimon-Pikali and Eyal Ginio, *Jews in the Moslem Religious Court: Society, Economy and Communal Organization in the XIX Century: Documents from Ottoman Jerusalem* (Jerusalem, 2003) [in Hebrew].

Collins, Norman. J. and Anton Steichele, *The Ottoman and Telegraph Offices in Palestine and Sinai* (London, 2000).

de Costa, Ravi, "Identity, Authority, and the Moral Worlds of Indigenous Petitions," *Comparative Studies in Society and History*, Vol. 48/3 (2006), pp. 669–98.

al-Dabbagh, Mustafa Murad, *Biladuna Filastin* (Our Country Palestine), Vol. I–IX (Beirut, 1974) [in Arabic].

Darling, Linda T., *Revenue-Raising and Legitimacy: Tax Collection and Finance Administration in the Ottoman Empire, 1560–1660* (Leiden, 1996).

——. *A History of Social Justice and Political Power in the Middle East: The Circle of Justice from Mesopotamia to Globalization*, (London and New York, 2013).

Davis, Natalie Zemon, *Fiction in the Archives: Pardon Tales and their Tellers in Sixteenth-Century France* (Cambridge, 1987).

Davison, Roderic H., "The Advent of the Electric Telegraph in the Ottoman Empire: How Morse's Invention was Introduced at the Time of the Crimean War," in idem, *Essays in Ottoman and Turkish History, 1774–1923: The Impact of the West* (London, 1990), pp. 133–65.

Deringil, Selim, *The Well Protected Domains: Ideology and the Legitimation of Power in the Ottoman Empire, 1876–1909* (London, 1999).

——. "'They Live in a State of Nomadism and Savagery': The Late Ottoman Empire and the Post-Colonial Debate," *Comparative Studies of Society and History*, Vol. 45/2 (2003), pp. 311–42.

Der Matossian, Bedross, *Ethnic Politics in Post-Revolutionary Ottoman Empire: Armenians, Arabs and Jews in the Second Constitutional Period (1908–1909)* (Unpublished Ph.D. Dissertation: Columbia University, 2008).

Doumani, Beshara, "Rediscovering Ottoman Palestine: Writing Palestinians into History," *Journal of Palestine Studies*, Vol. XXI/2 (Winter 1992), pp. 5–28.

——. "The Political Economy of Population Counts in Ottoman Palestine, circa 1850," *International Journal of Middle Eastern Studies*, Vol. 26/1 (1994), pp. 1–17.

——. *Rediscovering Palestine: Merchants and Peasants in Jabal Nablus, 1700–1900* (Berkeley, 1995).

Eliav, Mordechai, *Under Imperial Austrian Protection: Selected Documents from Archives of the Austrian Consulate in Jerusalem, 1849–1917* (Jerusalem, 1985) [in Hebrew].

——. *Britain and the Holy Land, 1838–1914: Selected Documents from the British Consulate in Jerusalem* (Jerusalem, 1997).

Erdoğdu, Teyfur, "Civil Officialdom and the Problem of Legitimacy in the Ottoman Empire (1876–1922)," in Karateke, Hakan T. and Maurus Reinkowski (eds.), *Legitimizing the Order: The Ottoman Rhetoric of State Power* (Leiden and Boston, 2005), pp. 213–32.

Ergene, Boğaç A., *Local Court, Provincial Society, and Justice in the Ottoman Empire: Legal Practice and Dispute Resolution in Çankırı and Kastamonu (1652–1744)* (Leiden and Boston, 2003).

Falah, Ghazi, "Pre-State Jewish Colonization in Northern Palestine and its Impact on Local Bedouin Sedentarization 1914–1948," *Journal of Historical Geography*, Vol. 17/3 (1991), pp. 289–309.

Faroqhi, Suraiya, "Introduction," in idem, *Coping with the State: Political Conflict and Crime in the Ottoman Empire, 1550–1720* (Istanbul, 1995), pp. VII–XXIII.

——. "Political Initiatives 'From the Bottom Up' in the Sixteenth and Seventeenth Century Ottoman Empire: Some Evidence for Their Existence," *Coping with the State: Political Conflict and Crime in the Ottoman Empire, 1550–1720*, pp. 1–11.

——. "Political Activity among Ottoman Taxpayers and the Problem of Sultanic Legitimation (1570–1650)," *Coping with the State: Political Conflict and Crime in the Ottoman Empire, 1550–1720*, pp. 13–41.

——. *Approaching Ottoman History: An Introduction to the Sources* (Cambridge, 1999).

——. "Guildsmen Complain to the Sultan: Artisans' Disputes and the Ottoman Administration in the 18th Century," *Legitimizing the Order: The Ottoman Rhetoric of State Power*, pp. 177–93.

Feener, Michael R., "New Networks and New Knowledge: Migrations, Communications, and the Refiguration of the Muslim Community in the Nineteenth and Early Twentieth Centuries," in Hefner, Robert W. (ed.), *The New Cambridge History of Islam: Muslims and Modernity Culture and Society since 1800*, Vol. VI (Cambridge, 2010), pp. 39–66.

Findley, C.V., *Bureaucratic Reform in the Ottoman Empire: The Sublime Porte, 1789–1922* (Princeton, 1980).

——. *Ottoman Civil Officialdom: A Social History* (Princeton, 1989)

Fischbach, Michael R., *State, Society and Land in Jordan* (Leiden, 2000).

Fischel, Roy and Ruth Kark, "Sultan Abdülhamid II and Palestine: Private Lands and Imperial Policy," *New Perspectives on Turkey*, Vol. 39 (Fall 2008), pp. 126–66.

Fishman, Louis, "The 1911 Haram al-Sharif Incident: Palestinian Notables versus the Ottoman Administration," *Journal of Palestine Studies*, Vol. XXXIV/3 (2005), pp. 6–22.

——. *Palestine Revisited: Reassessing the Jewish and Arab National Movements, 1908–1914* (Unpublished Ph. D. Dissertation, University of Chicago, 2007).

Forman, Geremy and Alexandre Kedar, "Colonialism, Colonization, and Land Law in Mandate Palestine: The Zor al-Zarqa and Barrat Qisarya Land Disputes in Historical Perspective," *Theoretical Inquiries in Law*, Vol. 4/2 (2003), pp. 491–540.

Frantzman, Seth J. and Ruth Kark, "Bedouin Settlement in Late Ottoman and British Mandatory Palestine: Influence on Cultural and Environmental Landscape, 1870–1948," *New Middle Eastern Studies*, Vol. 1 (2011), pp. 1–22.

Fuess, Albrecht, "Ẓulm by Maẓālim? The Political Implications of the Use of Maẓālim Jurisdiction by the Mamluk Sultans," *Mamluk Studies Review*, Vol. XIII/1 (2009), pp. 122–47.

Gelvin, James, "Demonstrating Communities in Post-Ottoman Syria," *Journal of Interdisciplinary History*, Vol. 25/1 (1994), pp. 23–44.

Georgeon, François, "Le Sultan Caché Réclusion du Souverain et Mise en Scène du Pouvoir à l'Époque de Abdülhamid II (1876–1909)," *Turcica*, Vol. 29 (1997), pp. 93–124.

Gerber, Haim, *Ottoman Rule in Jerusalem, 1890–1914* (Berlin, 1985).

——. "A New Look at the Tanzīmāt: The Case of the Province of Jerusalem," in Kushner, David (ed.), *Palestine in the Late Ottoman Period: Political, Social, and Economic Transformation* (Leiden, 1986), pp. 30–45.

——. *The Social Origins of the Modern Middle East* (Boulder, CO, 1994).

——. *State, Society, and Law in Islam: Ottoman Law in Comparative Perspective* (Albany. NY, 1994).

——. *Remembering and Imagining Palestine: Identity and Nationalism from the Crusades to the Present* (New York, 2008).

Geyikdagi, Necla, "French Direct Investments in the Ottoman Empire before World War I," *Enterprise and Society*, Vol. 12/3 (2011), pp. 525–61.

Gidoni, David and Nir Carmi, "Mutagenesis for Seedlessness in Citrus," *Israel Journal of Plant Sciences*, Vol. 55 (2007), pp. 133–35.

Ginio, Eyal, "The Administration of Criminal Justice in Ottoman Selânik (Salonica) during the Eighteenth Century," *Turcica*, Vol. 30 (1998), pp. 185–209.

——. "Presenting the Desert to the Ottomans during WWI: The Perspective of the *Harb Mecmuasi*," *New Perspectives on Turkey*, Vol. 33 (2005), pp. 43–62.

——. "Patronage, Intervention and Violence in the Legal Process in Eighteenth-Century Salonica and Its Province," in Shaham, Ron (ed.), *Law, Custom, and Statute in the Muslim World* (Leiden, 2007), pp. 111–30.

——. "Coping with the State's Agents 'from below': Petitions, Legal Appeal, and the Sultan's Justice in Ottoman Legal Practice," in Gara, Eleni, M. Erdem Kabadayı and Christoph K. Neumann (eds.), *Popular Protest and Political Participation in the Ottoman Empire: Studies in Honor of Suraiya Faroqhi* (Istanbul, 2011), pp. 41–56.

Giray, Kemal (translator), *Ottoman Post in Palestine, 1840–1914: Jerusalem*, Vol. I. (Istanbul, 2004).

Glass, Joseph B., "The Biography in Historical-Geographical Research – Navon Bey: A Case Study," *The Land that became Israel: Studies in Historical Geography*, pp. 77–89.

——. "Yosef Navon Bey and his Involvement in Late 19th Century Palestine's Development," *Cathedra*, Vol. 62 (1992), pp. 87–110 [in Hebrew].

Goren, Haim, "The Earliest Templar Settlement in the Holy Land," in Schiller, Ely (ed.), *Zev Vilnay's Jubilee Volume*, Vol. II (Jerusalem, 1987), pp. 269–76.

Gorny, Yosef, *Zionism and the Arabs, 1882–1948: A Study of Ideology* (Oxford, 1987).

Göçek, Fatma M., *Rise of the Bourgeoisie, Demise of Empire* (New York, 1996).

Gradeva, Rossitsa, "From the Bottom Up and Back Again until Who Knows When: Church Restoration Procedures in the Ottoman Empire, Seventeenth-Eighteenth Centuries (Preliminary Notes)," in Anastasopoulos, Antonis (ed.), *Political Initiatives 'From the Bottom Up:' Halcyon Days in Crete VII, A Symposium Held in Rathymno 9–11 January 2009* (Rethymno, 2012), pp. 135–63.

Granott (Granovsky), Abraham, *Land Taxation in Palestine* (Tel-Aviv, 1927).

——. *The Tax System in Palestine* (Tel-Aviv, 1933) [in Hebrew].

——. *ha-Mishtar ha-qarqaʻi be-Eretz-Yisraʼel* (The Land Regime in Eretz-Israel) (Tel-Aviv, 1949) [in Hebrew].

Grossman, David, "Rural Settlement in the Southern Coastal Plain and the Shefelah, 1835–1945," *Cathedra*, Vol. 45 (1987), pp. 57–86 [in Hebrew].

——. *Expansion and Desertion: The Arab Village and its Offshoots in Ottoman Palestine* (Jerusalem, 1994) [in Hebrew].

——. *Arab Demography and Early Jewish Settlement in Palestine: Distribution and Population Density during the Late Ottoman and Early Mandate Periods* (Jerusalem, 2004) [in Hebrew].

Hagen, Gottfried, "Legitimacy and World Order," *Legitimizing the Order: The Ottoman Rhetoric of State Power*, pp. 55–83.

Hallaq, Wael B., *An Introduction to Islamic Law* (Cambridge/UK and New York, 2009).

Hämmerle, Christa, "Requests, Complaints, Demands. Preliminary Thoughts on the Petitioning Letters of Lower-Class Austrian Women, 1865–1918," in Bland, Caroline and Máire Cross (eds.), *Gender and Politics in the Age of Letter-Writing, 1750–2000* (Burlington, VT, 2004), pp. 115–33.

Hanioğlu, Şükrü M., *Preparation for a Revolution: The Young Turks, 1902–1908* (Oxford, 2001).

Hanssen, Jens, *Fin de Siècle Beirut: The Making of a Provincial Capital* (Oxford and New York, 2005).

Haslip, Joan, *The Sultan: The Life of Abdul Hamid II* (London, 1973).

Heyd, Uriel, *Ottoman Documents on Palestine, 1552–1615: A Study of the Firman According to the Mühimme Defteri* (Oxford, 1960).

———. *Studies in Old Ottoman Criminal Law* (Oxford, 1973).

Hoexter, Miriam, "The Role of the Qays and Yaman Factions in Local Political Divisions: Jabal Nāblus Compared with the Judean Hills in the First Half of the Nineteenth Century," *African and Asian Studies*, Vol. 9 (1973), pp. 249–311.

Hurvitz, Nimrod, "The Contribution of Early Islamic Rulers to Adjudication and Legislation: The Case of Mazalim Tribunals," *New East*, Vol. 49 (2010), pp. 11–29 [in Hebrew]

Hütteroth, Wolf-Dieter and Kamal Abdulfattah, *Historical Geography of Palestine, Transjordan and Southern Syria in the Late 16th Century* (Erlangen, 1977).

İnalcık, Halil, "Şikâyet Hakkı: 'Arż-i Ḥâl ve 'Arż-i Maḥżar'lar," *Osmanlı Araştırmaları*, Vol. VII–VIII (1988), pp. 33–54 [in Turkish].

———. "Istanbul: An Islamic City," *Journal of Islamic Studies*, Vol. I (1990), pp. 1–23.

———. *The Ottoman Empire: The Classical Age 1300–1600* (London, 2002).

Irwin, Robert, "The Privatization of "Justice" under the Circassian Mamluks," *Mamluk Studies Review*, Vol. 4 (2002), pp. 63–70.

Jacobson, Abigail, *From Empire to Empire: Jerusalem between Ottoman and British Rule* (Syracuse, 2011).

de Jong, Frederick, "The Sufi Orders in Nineteenth and Twentieth-Century Palestine: A Preliminary Survey Concerning their Identity, Organization, Characteristics and Continuity," in idem, *Sufi Orders in Ottoman and Post-Ottoman Egypt and the Middle East* (Istanbul, 1999), pp. 99–122.

Kabadayı, Erdem M., "Petitioning as Political Action: Petitioning Practices of Workers in Ottoman Factories," *Popular Protest and Political Participation in the Ottoman Empire*, pp. 58–74.

Kansu, Aykut, *The Revolution of 1908 in Turkey* (Leiden, 1997).

Karateke, Hakan T., *Padişahım Çok Yaşa! Osmanlı Devletinin Son Yüzyılında Merasimler* (Long Live the Sultan: Official Ceremonies in the Last Century of the Ottoman Empire) (Istanbul, 2004) [in Turkish].

———. "Legitimizing the Ottoman Sultanate: A Framework for Historical Analysis," *Legitimizing the Order: The Ottoman Rhetoric of State Power*, pp. 13–52.

Kark, Ruth, "Land Acquisition and New Agricultural Settlements in Palestine during the Tyomkin Period, 1890–1892," *ha-Tsiyonut*, Vol. 9 (1984), pp. 179–94 [in Hebrew].

———. "The Rise and Decline of Coastal Towns in Palestine," in Gilbar, Gad (ed.), *Ottoman Palestine, 1800–1914: Studies in Social and Economic History* (Leiden, 1990), pp. 69–89.

——. *Jaffa: A City in Evolution, 1799–1917* (Jerusalem, 1990).

Kark, Ruth and Michal Oren-Nordheim, *Jerusalem and its Environs: Quarters, Neighborhoods, Villages, 1800–1948* (Detroit, 2001).

Karmon, Yehuda, "Geographical Conditions in the Sharon Plain and their Impact on its Settlement," *Bulletin of the Israel Exploration Society*, Vol. XXIII/3–4 (1959), pp. 111–33 [in Hebrew].

Karpat, Kemal H., "Jewish Population Movements in the Ottoman Empire, 1862–1914," in Levy, Avigdor (ed.), *The Jews of the Ottoman Empire* (Princeton, 1994), pp. 399–421.

——. *The Politicization of Islam: Reconstructing Identity, State, Faith, and Community in the Late Ottoman State* (New York and Oxford, 2001).

Kato, Hiroshi, "The Egyptian Rural Society in the Mid-Nineteenth Century as Reflected in the Documents on Petition for the Exemption from Military Service," *Mediterranean World*, Vol. XIV (1995), pp. 59–70.

Katz, Yossef, "Paths of Zionist Political Action in Turkey, 1882–1914: The Plan for Jewish Settlement in Turkey in the Young Turk Era," *International Journal of Turkish Studies*, Vol. 4 (1987), pp. 115–35.

Kayyali, A.W., *Palestine: A Modern History* (London, 1978).

Khalidi, Rashid, "Palestinian Peasant Resistance to Zionism before World War I," in Said, W. Edward and Christopher Hitchens (eds.), *Blaming the Victims: Spurious Scholarship and the Palestinian Question* (London and New York, 2001), pp. 207–33.

——. *Palestinian Identity: The Construction of Modern National Consciousness* (New York, 1997).

Khalidi, Walid, *All that Remains: The Palestinian Villages Occupied and Depopulated by Israel in 1948* (Washington, 1992).

Kimmerling, Barukh and Joel Migdal, *Palestinians: The Making of a People* (New York, 1993).

Kracke, Edward A., "Early Visions of Justice for the Humble in East and West," *Journal of the American Oriental Society*, Vol. 96/4 (1976), pp. 492–98.

Kressel, Gideon and R. Aharoni, "Egyptian Immigrants in the Bilad Esh-Sham," *Jama'a*, Vol. 12 (2004), pp. 201–45 [in Hebrew].

Kushner, David, "The Ottoman Governors of Palestine, 1864–1914," *Middle Eastern Studies*, Vol. 23/3 (July 1987), pp. 274–90.

——. "The Last Generation of Ottoman Rule in Eretz Israel, 1882–1914," in Kolatt, Israel (ed.), *The History of the Jewish Community in Eretz Israel since 1882: The Ottoman Period* (Vol. I) (Jerusalem, 1989), pp. 1–74 [in Hebrew].

——. "The District of Jerusalem in the Eyes of Three Ottoman Governors at the End of the Hamidian Period," *Middle Eastern Studies*, Vol. 35/2 (1999), pp. 83–102.

——. *To be Governor of Jerusalem: The City and District during the Time of Ali Ekrem Bey, 1906–1908* (Istanbul, 2005).

Lambton, Ann, *State and Government in Medieval Islam: An Introduction to the Study of Islamic Political Theory* (Oxford, 1981).

Landen, R.G. (translator), *The Emergence of the Modern Middle East* (New York, 1970).

LeVine, Mark, *Overthrowing Geography: Jaffa, Tel Aviv, and the Struggle for Palestine, 1880–1948* (Berkley, 2005).

Lewis, G.L., "'Arḍ Ḥāl," *Encyclopaedia of Islam*, 2nd edition, Brill Online.

Lockman, Zachary, *Comrades and Enemies: Arab and Jewish Workers in Palestine, 1906–1948* (Berkeley, 1996).

Long, David E., "The Board of Grievances in Saudi Arabia," *Middle East Journal*, Vol. 27/1 (1973), pp. 71–5.

al-Madani, Ziad ʿAbdel ʿAziz, *The Waqfs (Endowments) in Jerusalem and within the Vicinity in the Nineteenth Century* (Amman, 2004) [in Arabic].

Mandel, Neville J., "Ottoman Policy and Restrictions on Jewish Settlement in Palestine, 1881–1908, *Middle Eastern Studies*, 10/3 (1974), pp. 312–32.

———. "Ottoman Practices as Regards Jewish Settlement in Palestine, 1881–1908," *Middle Eastern Studies*, 11/1 (1975), pp. 33–46.

———. *The Arabs and Zionism before World War I* (Berkeley, 1976).

Mannaʿ, ʿAdil, *Aʿlam Filastin fi awakhir al-ʿahd al-ʿuthmani* (The Notables of Palestine during the Late Ottoman Period), 2nd edition (Beirut, 1995) [in Arabic].

———. *Taʾrikh Filastin fi awakhir al-ʿahd al-ʿuthmani, 1700–1918: Qiraʾa jadida* (History of Palestine at the End of the Ottoman Period: A New Reading) (Beirut, 1999) [in Arabic].

Maoz, Moshe, *Ottoman Reform in Syria and Palestine, 1840–1861: The Impact of the Tanzimat on Politics and Society* (Oxford, 1968).

Mardin, Şerif, "Power, Civil Society, and Culture in the Ottoman Empire," *Comparative Studies in Society and History*, Vol. 11/4 (1969), pp. 258–81.

McCarthy, Justin, *The Population of Palestine: Population History and Statistics of the Late Ottoman Period and the Mandate* (New York, 1990).

Meier, Astrid, "The Charities of a Grand Vizier: Towards a Comparative Approach to Koca Sinân Pasha's Endowment Deeds (989–1004/1581–1596)," *Turcica*, Vol. 43 (2011), pp. 303–37.

———. "Bedouins in the Ottoman Juridical Field: Select Cases from Syrian Court Records, Seventeenth to Nineteenth Centuries," *Euroasian Studies*, Vol. IX/1–2 (2011), pp. 187–211.

Meir, Avinoam, "Contemporary state Discourse and Historical Pastoral Spatiality: Contradictions in the Land Conflict between the Israeli Bedouin and the State," *Ethnic and Racial Studies*, Vol. 32/5 (2009), pp. 823–43.

Minkov, Anton, *Conversions to Islam in the Balkans: Kisve Bahası Petitions and Ottoman Social Life, 1670–1730* (Leiden and Boston, 2004).

Morris, Benny, *Righteous Victims: A History of the Zionist-Arab Conflict, 1881–2001* (New York, 2001).

Mottahedeh, Roy, *The Mantle of the Prophet: Religion and Politics in Iran* (New York, 1985).

al-Mubayyid, Salim 'Arafat, *Ghazza wa-qita'iha: Dirasa fi khulud al-makan wa-hadarat al-sukkan min al-'asr al-hajari al-hadith hatta al-harb al-'alamiyya al-ula* (Gaza and Its Region: A Study of the Eternity of the Place and the Culture of Its People from the Modern Stone Age until World War I) (Cairo, 1987) [in Arabic].

Muslih, Muhammad Y., *The Origins of Palestinian Nationalism* (New York, 1988).

Nielsen, J. S. *Secular Justice in an Islamic State: Maẓālim under the Baḥrī Mamlūks, 662/1294–789/1387* (Istanbul, 1985).

——. "Maẓālim," *Encyclopaedia of Islam*, 2nd edition, Brill Online.

al-Nimr, Ihsan, *Ta'rikh Jabal Nablus wal-Balqa* (The History of Jabal Nablus and al-Balqa), Vols. I–IV (Nablus, 1961) [in Arabic].

Nubola, Cecilia, "Supplications between Politics and Justice: The Northern and Central Italian States in the Early Modern Age," in van Voss, Lex Heerma (ed.), *Petitions in Social History, International Review of Social History*, Vol. 46/Supplement 9 (2001), pp. 35–56.

von Oppenheim, Max Freiherr, *Die Beduinen: Die Beduinenstämme in Palästina, Transjordanien, Sinai, Hedjāz*. Vol. II (Hildesheim, 1983).

Özbek, Nadir, "Philanthropic Activity, Ottoman Patriotism, and the Hamidian Regime, 1876–1909," *International Journal of Middle Eastern Studies*, Vol. 37 (2005), pp. 59–81.

Pakalın, Mehmed Z., *Osmanlı Tarih Deyimleri ve Terimleri Sözlüğü* (Dictionary of Ottoman Historical Idioms and Terms), Vol. I (Istanbul, 1983) [in Turkish].

Pamuk, Şevket, *İstanbul ve Diğer Kentlerde 500 Yıllık Fiyatlar ve Ücretler 1469–1998* (Prices and Fees in Istanbul and Other Cities during a Period of 500 Years) (Ankara: 2000) [in Turkish].

Papastamatiou, Demetrios, "The Right of Appeal to State Intervention as a Means of Political Mobilisation of the *Reaya* in the Ottoman Provinces: Some Preliminary Remarks on the Eighteenth-Century Morea (Peloponnese)," *Political Initiatives "From the Bottom Up:" Halcyon Days in Crete*, pp. 165–90.

Papataxiarchis, Evthymois, "Reconfiguring the Ottoman Political Imagination: Petitioning and Print Culture in the Early Tanzimat," *Political Initiatives "From the Bottom Up:" Halcyon Days in Crete*, pp. 191–226.

Pappe, Ilan, *Aristocracy of the Land: The Husayni Family, Political Biography* (Jerusalem, 2002) [in Hebrew].

Porath, Yehoshua, *The Emergence of the Palestinian-Arab National Movement, 1918–1929* (London, 1974).

Powers, David, "On Judicial Review in Islamic Law," *Law & Society Review*, Vol. 26/2 (1992), pp. 315–41.

Quataert, Donald, "Rural Unrest in the Ottoman Empire, 1830–1914," *Peasants and Politics in the Modern Middle East*, pp. 38–49.

Rantisi, Ilyas, "Mawsim Rubin" (The Festival of Rubin), in *'Itr Madinat Yafa* (The Perfume of the City of Jaffa) (Nazareth, 1991), pp. 71–3 [in Arabic].

Reilly, James, "The Peasantry of Late Ottoman Palestine," *Journal of Palestine Studies*, Vol. 10/4 (1981), pp. 82–97.

Reimer, Michael, "The King–Crane Commission at the Juncture of Politics and Historiography," *Critique: Critical Middle Eastern Studies*, Vol. 15/2 (2006), pp. 129–50.

Reinkowski, Maurus, "Late Ottoman Rule over Palestine: Its Evaluation in Arab, Turkish and Israeli Histories, 1970–90," *Middle Eastern Studies*, Vol. 35/1 (1999), pp. 66–97.

——. "The State's Security and the Subjects' Prosperity: Notions of Order in Ottoman Bureaucratic Correspondence (19th century)," *Legitimizing the Order: The Ottoman Rhetoric of State Power*, pp. 195–212.

Rogan, Eugene, "Aşiret Mektebi: Abdülhamid IIs School for Tribes, 1892–1907," *International Journal of Middle East Studies*, Vol. 28 (1996), pp. 83–107.

——. "Instant Communication: The Impact of the Telegraph in Ottoman Syria," in Philipp, Thomas and Brigit Schaebler (eds.), *The Syrian Land: Processes of Integration and Fragmentation, Bilād al-Shām from the 18th to the 20th Century* (Stuttgart, 1998), pp. 113–28.

——. *Frontiers of State in the Late Ottoman Empire: Transjordan, 1850–1921* (Cambridge, 1999).

Rubin, Avi, "Legal Borrowing and its Impact on Ottoman Legal Culture in the Late Nineteenth Century," *Continuity and Change*, Vol. 22/2 (2007), pp. 279–303.

——. *Ottoman Nizamiye Courts: Law and Modernity* (New York, 2011).

——. "From Legal Representation to Advocacy: Attorneys and Clients in the Ottoman Nizamiye Courts," *International Journal of Middle Eastern Studies*, Vol. 44 (2012), pp. 111–27.

Safi, Khaled M., "Territorial Awareness in the 1834 Palestinian Revolt," in Heacock, Roger (ed.), *Temps et éspaces en Palestine* (Beirut, 2008), pp. 43–54.

Sa'id, Ibrahim Hasan, *Yafa: Min al-ghazw al-Nabolyonni ila hamlat Ibrahim Basha, 1799–1831* (Jaffa: From the Raid of Napoleon to the Campaign of Ibrahim Pasha) (Beirut, 2006) [in Arabic].

Salzmann, Ariel, "Citizens in Search of a State: The Limits of Political Participation in the Late Ottoman Empire," in Hanagan, Michael and Charles Tilly (eds.), *Extending Citizenship, Reconfiguring States* (Lanham, Maryland, 1999), pp. 37–66.

Schacht, Joseph, "The Schools of Law and Later Developments of Jurisprudence," in Khadduri, Majid and Herbert J. Liebesny, (eds.), *Law in the Middle East: Origin and Development of Islamic Law*, Vol. I (Washington, DC, 1955), pp. 57–84.

Schatkowski, Linda S., "Violence in Rural Syria in the 1880s and 1890s: State Centralization, Rural Integration, and the World Market," *Peasants and Politics in the Modern Middle East*, pp. 50–84.

Schneider, Irene, *The Petitioning System in Iran: State, Society, and Power Relations in the Late 19th Century* (Wiesbaden, 2006).

Schölch, Alexander, *Palestine in Transformation 1856–1882: Studies in Social, Economic and Political Development* (Washington, DC, 1993).

Segev, Tom, *One Palestine, Complete: Jews and Arabs under the British Mandate* (New York, 2001).

Shafir, Gershon, *Land, Labor and the Origins of the Israeli-Palestinian Conflict, 1882–1914* (Cambridge, 1989).

Shahvar, Soli, "Iron Poles, Wooden Poles: The Electric Telegraph and the Ottoman–Iranian Boundary Conflict, 1863–1865," *British Journal of Middle Eastern Studies*, Vol. 34/1 (2007), pp. 23–42.

Shapira, Anita, *Land and Power: The Zionist Resort to Force, 1881–1948* (New York, 1992).

Shaw, J.E., "Writing to the Prince: Supplications, Equity, and Absolutism in Sixteenth-Century Tuscany," *Past and Present*, Vol. 215 (2012), pp. 51–83.

Shaw, Stanford J. and Ezel Kural Shaw, *History of the Ottoman Empire and Modern Turkey: Reform, Revolution, and Republic – The Rise of Modern Turkey, 1808–1975*, Vol. II (New York, 1976).

Shim'oni, Ya'aqov, *'Arviye Eretz-Yisrael* (The Arabs of Eretz-Yisrael) (Tel-Aviv, 1947) [in Hebrew].

Singer, Amy, *Palestinian Peasants and Ottoman Officials: Rural Administration around Sixteenth-Century Jerusalem* (Cambridge, 1994).

Smelik, Klaas A.D., *Writings from Ancient Israel: A Handbook of Historical and Religious Sources*. Translated by G.I. Davis (Louisville, KY, 1991).

Smilansky, Moshe, *Rehovot: Shishim shenot hayeha* (Rehovot: Sixty Years since its Establishment) (Rehovot, 1949/1950) [in Hebrew].

Stein, Kenneth W., *The Land Question in Palestine, 1917–1939* (Chapel Hill and London, 1984).

Stern, S.M., "Petitions from the Ayyūbid Period," *Bulletin of the School of Oriental and African Studies University of London*, Vol. 27/1 (1964), pp. 1–32.

al-Tabba', 'Uthman, *Ithaf al-a'izza fi ta'rikh Ghazza* (Presenting the Notables in the History of Gaza), Vol. I–IV, edited by Abu-Hashim, 'Abdullatif (Gaza, 1999) [in Arabic].

Tamari, Salim, *Mountain against the Sea: Essays on Palestinian Society and Culture* (Berkeley, 2009).

di Tarrazi, Filib, *Ta'rikh al-sahafa al-'arabiyya* (The History of Arab Press), Vol. I (Beirut, 1913) [in Arabic].

Thalmann, Naftali, *The Character and Development of the Farm Economy in the Templer Colonies in Palestine, 1869–1939* (Unpublished Dissertation: Hebrew University of Jerusalem, 1991) [in Hebrew].

———. "Fritz Keller – A Pioneer of Modern Agriculture in Eretz-Israel: The Man and His Work," in Ben-Artzi, Yossi, Israel Bartal and Elchanan Reiner (eds.), *Studies in Geography and History in Honour of Yehoshua Ben-Arieh* (Jerusalem, 1999), pp. 333–51 [in Hebrew].

Tibawi, A.L., *A Modern History of Syria, including Lebanon and Palestine* (London, 1969).

Tidhar, David (ed.), *Encyclopedia of the Founders and Builders of Israel, Vol. III* (Tel-Aviv, 1949) [in Hebrew].

Tillier, Mathieu, "*Qāḍīs* and the Political Use of the *Maẓālim* Jurisdiction under the 'Abbāsids," in Lange, Christian and M. Fierro (eds.), *Public Violence in Islamic Societies: Power, Discipline, and the Construction of the Public Sphere, 7th-19th Centuries CE* (Edinburgh, 2009), pp. 42–66.

Toledano, Ehud R., *As if Silent and Absent: Bonds of Enslavement in the Islamic Middle East* (New Haven, 2007).

Tucker, Judith E., *In the House of the Law: Gender and Islamic Law in Ottoman Syria and Palestine* (Berkeley, 1998).

Tyan, Emile, "Judicial Organization," *Law in the Middle East: Origin and Development of Islamic Law*, pp. 236–78.

Ursinus, Michael, *Grievance Administration (Şikâyet) in an Ottoman Province: The Kaymakam of Rumelia's 'Record Book of Complaints' of 1781–1783* (London and New York, 2005).

Vilnay, Zeev, *Toldot ha-'aravim veha-muslemim be-Eretz-Yisra'el* (History of the Arabs and Muslims in Eretz-Israel), Vol. II (Tel-Aviv, 1932) [in Hebrew].

van Voss, Lex Heerma, "Introduction," *Petitions in Social History*, pp. 1–10.

Watenpaugh, Keith David, *Being Modern in the Middle East: Revolution, Nationalism, Colonialism, and the Arab Middle Class* (Princeton, 2006).

Waterbury, John, "Peasants Defy Categorization (As Well as Landlords and the State)," *Peasants and Politics in the Modern Middle East*, pp. 1–23.

Würgler, Andreas, "Voices from among the "Silent Masses": Humble Petitions and Social Conflicts in Early Modern Central Europe," *Petitions in Social History*, pp. 11–34.

Yazbak, Mahmoud, *Haifa in the Late Ottoman Period, 1864–1914: A Muslim Town in Transition* (Leiden, 1998).

——. "Templars as Proto-Zionists? The 'German Colony' in Late Ottoman Haifa," *Journal of Palestine Studies*, Vol. XXVIII/4 (Summer 1999), pp. 40–54.

——. "The Islamic *Waqf* in Yaffa and the Urban Space: From the Ottoman State to the State of Israel," *Makan*, Vol. 2 (2010), pp. 23–46.

Zandberg, Haim, *Land Title Settlement in Eretz-Israel and in the State of Israel* (Ph.D. Dissertation: Hebrew University of Jerusalem, 1999) [in Hebrew].

Zaret, David, "Petitions and the "Invention" of Public Opinion in the English Revolution, *American Journal of Sociology*, Vol. 101/6 (1996), pp. 1497–555.

Ze'evi, Dror, *An Ottoman Century: The District of Jerusalem in the 1600s* (Albany, 1996).

INDEX